MW00641529

Rethinking Slave Rebellion in Cuba

ENVISIONING CUBA

Louis A. Pérez Jr., *editor*

Envisioning Cuba publishes outstanding, innovative
works in Cuban studies, drawn from diverse subjects
and disciplines in the humanities and social sciences,
from the colonial period through the post–Cold War era.
Featuring innovative scholarship engaged with theoretical
approaches and interpretive frameworks informed by
social, cultural, and intellectual perspectives, the series
highlights the exploration of historical and cultural circumstances and conditions related to the development
of Cuban self-definition and national identity.

Rethinking Slave Rebellion in Cuba

LA ESCALERA *and the*
INSURGENCIES *of* 1841–1844

Aisha K. Finch

The University of North Carolina Press
Chapel Hill

*Published with the assistance of the Authors Fund
of the University of North Carolina Press.*

© 2015 The University of North Carolina Press
All rights reserved
Designed and set in Merope Text by Rebecca Evans
Manufactured in the United States of America

The paper in this book meets the guidelines for permanence
and durability of the Committee on Production Guidelines
for Book Longevity of the Council on Library Resources. The
University of North Carolina Press has been a member
of the Green Press Initiative since 2003.

Cover illustration: List of slaves missing after the rebellion on
March 27, 1843. Courtesy of the Archivo Nacional de Cuba.

Library of Congress Cataloging-in-Publication Data
Finch, Aisha K.
Rethinking slave rebellion in Cuba : La Escalera and the
insurgencies of 1841–1844 / Aisha K. Finch. — First edition.
pages cm. — (Envisioning Cuba)
Includes bibliographical references and index.
ISBN 978-1-4696-2234-7 (pbk : alk. paper)
ISBN 978-1-4696-2235-4 (ebook)
1. Cuba—History—Negro Conspiracy, 1844. 2. Slave
insurrections—Cuba—History—19th century. 3. Slavery—
Cuba—History—19th century. 4. Blacks—Cuba—Social
conditions—19th century. 5. Africans—Cuba—History—19th
century. 6. Cuba—Race relations—History—19th century.
I. Title. II. Title: La Escalera and the insurgencies of 1841–1844.
F1783.F55 2015   972.91'05—dc23   2014038127

This book was digitally printed.

For those who lived and died through 1844

Contents

Figures

Acknowledgments

This book represents a personal intellectual journey that has taken place over the course of many years, and there are many people who have helped to make it a reality. I want to acknowledge a cherished group of people who made my time in Cuba meaningful and memorable, including Jesús Moya Martínez, Reina Alejandrina Lén, Yesenia Selier, Caridad Monterrey, Ivonne Chapman, and Mikiko Thelwell. From this group, I want to single out Nehanda Isoke Abiodun, who has been a most beloved teacher, mentor, and friend. I also want to recognize Janette Viaña Pérez, who was a large part of the reason why I could do my research in Havana. She and her children, SolAngel and Enrique, opened their doors to me with extraordinary love and generosity, a gift for which I will be forever grateful. Finally, I want to thank Yaneissi Moliner many times over for taking me in as a close friend and a sister, as did her family.

I want to extend a special note of gratitude to the staff of the Archivo Nacional de Cuba, especially Julio López Valdés and Joel Fonseca Ramírez. I also want to thank long-time researcher Barbara Danzie for her incomparable warmth, collegiality, and generosity over the course of many years. I am most grateful to Henry Heredia and Elena Socarrás at the Centro de Investigación de la Cultural Cubana Juan Marinello for facilitating my entry to the National Archive. I am deeply indebted to the late Gloria García, who listened to each and every one of my questions and taught me more than I could have imagined. In Matanzas, I would like to thank the generous staff of the Archivo Histórico Provincial de Matanzas. I offer the warmest thanks to Isabel Hernández Camps, who welcomed me to Matanzas and gave so generously of her time and energy at the Castillo de San Severino.

This project was supported in part by funding from the President's Research Fellowship in the Humanities, University of California, as well as by the Ford Foundation, the UC Presidential Postdoctoral Fellowship, and the Institute of American Cultures Research; and the Ralph J. Bunche Center, the International Institute, the Council on Research, and the Hellman Fellowship at UCLA. I would like to express my deepest appreciation to these institutions for their funding and resources.

I owe a heartfelt thanks to Ada Ferrer, who has given me support, mentoring, and intellectual guidance since the very beginning. I continue to benefit immensely from her dedication and belief in my work. I am extremely grateful to Michael Gomez for his extensive mentorship and encouragement over the last few years. His thoughts, questions, and provocations have shaped my work since its earliest inception, and continue to do so. Sinclair Thomson, Barbara Krauthamer, and Walter Johnson were all extremely generous with their time, support, and feedback during the early stages of this project. Fannie Rushing has been an unwavering ally, co-conspirator, and friend over the last few years. She has planned with me, written with me, encouraged me, and mentored me. For all of this I cannot thank her enough. Joseph Dorsey has taught me as much, if not more, than any book I have read about Cuban history. I am enormously grateful to him for his mentorship and for sharing his encyclopedic knowledge with me. My exchanges with Melina Pappademos, Matthew Pettway, and Manuel Barica have been an invaluable and treasured part of this project. I also want to thank Gloria Wade Gayles and Dorothy Denniston, two of my earliest mentors, who believed in me and nurtured my intellect years before I entered graduate school.

I cannot begin to express how much I owe to Grace Hong. She has been my biggest supporter during my time at UCLA, and I simply have no figure for the amount of time she has invested in me. I want to thank her, more than words can convey, for challenging my thinking, supporting my intellectual growth, and offering her mentorship. Sarah Haley has been a phenomenal colleague and friend. I continue to be inspired by her remarkable intelligence, her visionary politics, and her depth of support. Stephanie Smallwood has been the most amazing mentor. Her caring and intellectual generosity are staggering, and I owe her an enormous debt of gratitude in finishing this book. Jennifer Morgan gave me such painstaking and thoughtful commentary as this project evolved, and I thank her for all the time she invested in my work.

Over the years, Jessica Johnson has sharpened my intellectual insight, deepened my political analysis, and sustained me with her forceful friendship and love. I cannot imagine my life, or this book, without her. Natasha Lightfoot has been a cherished fellow traveler for many years. So much of my thinking has been shaped by our interactions, and her intellectual generosity and encouragement continue to keep me afloat. Tamara Walker is a true gem. Much of this book developed and matured in conversations with her, and I continue to be enriched by her friendship.

I have been fortunate to have a wonderful group of colleagues and friends in LA. Jayna Brown has been an incredible friend and mentor whose generosity knows no bounds. Shana Redmond keeps me going with her incomparable wit, keen political eye, and her very presence. Scot Brown's advice, humor, and wisdom have been real gifts that have gotten me through many a rough period. Imani Johnson and Terrion Williamson have been my soul survivors since my first year in LA. Their friendship helped me to create a personal and intellectual home, and I am thankful that they always seem to get it. Lalaie Ameeriar has been a sparkling light over the past few years; her humor and perspective help keep me sane.

I especially want to thank a treasured group of friends who I have known for many years (and in some cases, across several continents), and who have carried me and sustained me for a decade or more. They include Leslie Abrams, Catherine John, Gina Davis, Oriana Bolden, Sarpoma Sefa-Boyake, and Gia Winsryg-Ulmer. I have been privileged and blessed to know Imani Tolliver and Janet Quezada; although I met these women only a few years ago, it feels as though I have known them for a lifetime. I also want to recognize a special group of comrades without whom I would never have made it through graduate school: Tanya Huelett, Edwina Ashie-Nikoi, Sherie Randolph, Brian Purnell, Peter Hudson, Mireille Miller-Young, Sherene Seikaly, and Emily Thuma. They continue to impress and inspire me.

I have had an outstanding group of mentors in African American Studies at UCLA, whose support and guidance have made all the difference in my experience as a faculty member. They include Brenda Stevenson, Richard Yarborough, and Robin Kelley. I am especially thankful to Cheryl Harris for the depth of her generosity, faith, and support over this past year. I have also been fortunate to have an inspiring and courageous group of colleagues in Gender Studies, including Mishuana Goeman, Beth Marchant, Purnima Mankekar, Michelle Erai, Sharon Traweek, Kate Norberg, and Sondra Hale, and a highly supportive mentor in Juliet Williams. I especially want to recognize the staff of the departments of Gender Studies and African American Studies who in no small way made this book possible. Van Do-Nuyen, Samantha Hogan, Richard Medrano, Jenna Miller Von-Ah, and Eboni Shaw, I thank you for all the things that are too numerous to name.

I can hardly begin to count all of the stimulating and supportive interlocutors I have been privileged to know in recent years. In addition to those mentioned above, they include Treva Lindsey, Uri McMillan, Tiffany

Willoughby-Herard, Arlene Keizer, Yogita Goyal, Jodi Kim, Erica Edwards, Nick Mitchell, Maylei Blackwell, Mignon Moore, Kara Keeling, Jessica Millward, and Sharla Fett, just to name a few. Thinking with them has taught me so much.

I am extremely grateful for the magnificent research assistance I have had in completing this book. For their thoughtful labor I would like to thank Maria Aguilar-Rocha, Loron Bartlett, Jessica Lee, Amrey Mathurin, and Nicole Ramsey. I am also most grateful to Geoffrey Jacques and Janet Quezada for their careful and thoughtful editing of this book, and to Sherri Barnes for her meticulous indexing. CZ Wilson provided me with much-needed office space, mentorship, and kind words during my fellowship year. His immense knowledge of UCLA never ceases to amaze me. Elaine Maisner at UNC Press has been a tremendous editor, whom I am grateful to have worked with. I also want to express my gratitude to the anonymous reviewers and to the staff of UNC Press, especially Mary Caviness, Allie Shay, and Ian Oakes.

I owe an everlasting thanks to Marlene Jaffe, who has been a beacon of light in my life. She has pushed me, taught me, and nurtured me; that I have made it to this point is due in no small part to her love and support. I also want to extend my deepest thanks to "Rainbow" Michael Lisinsky. He has absolutely been my rock and my inspiration, and has taught me more in these last four years than I ever thought possible. I also want to recognize the rest of my Van Nuys crew: David Jude Owens, Diane Robin, Brett Bogeaus, Marlene Levy, and Gary Zoron. I also owe a special thank you to the Monday night stalwarts, Cynthia Sophiea, Cari Daly, Clare Fox, Dallas Malloy, and Kate Long. You show me who I really am and why it all matters. I am so grateful for your presence in my life.

Finally and always, I am profoundly grateful to my parents, Ellen Nixon Finch and Charles Sumner Finch III; my six siblings, Tehani Finch, Thembi Jones, Rabiah Lewis, Kemit Finch, Ife Floyd, Peri Finch; and their beautiful families. Even when I doubted, you have always had an unshakable belief in my work. You have been my oldest teachers and guides, and you have brought me to this place in life as no one else could. You remain to this day a precious gift whose value knows no measure. Thank you.

Rethinking Slave Rebellion in Cuba

Introduction

The early 1840s ushered in a tumultuous decade on the island of Cuba. In 1843 slave insurgents in western Cuba mounted two resistance struggles that shook the rural plantation world to its core. Their efforts were part of a larger anticolonial momentum that had taken root in urban communities of color across the western region. As the year drew to a close, a series of events unfolded whose scope and impact few would have been able to predict. In late December, Cuban authorities began to uncover a widespread movement that encompassed the major urban centers, much of the western countryside, and allegedly some of the island's most prominent people of color. According to legend, this discovery was made possible in part by the revelations of an enslaved woman named Polonia. In order to eradicate this activity—and with it a number of closely related struggles against slavery and colonialism—the Cuban government unleashed a bloody reign of terror in 1844, holding parts of the island under quasi-martial law for over a year as confessions were extracted by the hundreds from accused people of color and a few white men. In some of the more infamous episodes of torture, accused witnesses were tied face down to a ladder and beaten. Hence the name "La Escalera" that eventually fixed itself to the trials and later, to the plot itself.

Merced Criolla, a woman enslaved in one of the sugar heartland's east-ernmost districts, was among those who lost her husband in the 1844 pros-ecutions. Merced was one of the first to testify about a rebel movement steadily evolving on her home estate of Encanto, "whose head was her hus-band, Dionicio Carabaly."[1] She went on to speak about clandestine meetings between her husband and a cohort of other organizers who were galvanized by the rebellions of 1843. In her statement, she revealed a world of subter-ranean political organizing that crossed lines of ethnicity, freedom, gender, and plantation borders.

For his part Dionisio Carabalí refused to testify, even after several in-terrogation attempts. This did not stop the prosecutors from concluding that he was one of "the principal heads and promoters of the attempted rebellion" and condemning him to death. In the spring of 1844 Dionisio was shot in the back by military authorities, his head subsequently mutilated. Dionisio was one of hundreds of black men in 1844 who died in this way, a highly masculinized form of public punishment designed to underscore the state's power to take black life.[2]

The story of Merced and Dionisio repeated itself again and again across the western rural landscape in the early months of 1844. Together they call attention to the central claim of this book: that rural slaves of African descent helped to organize and lead one of Cuba's most memorable resistance struggles. Their experiences illustrate that the movement of 1844 cannot be understood apart from the revolts of 1843, nor can they be separated from the political architecture of West and Central Africa. In short, the story of Dionisio and Merced directs attention to the least-known and presumably most marginal figures in a struggle that spanned the Atlantic world and stimulated much of Cuba's early anticolonial organizing.

One of the first things that someone is likely to learn about La Escalera is the devastating repression it unleashed in 1844. This narrative remains deeply entrenched in Cuban popular memory to this day and has become part of a larger historical memory of slavery and empire that spans the Atlantic world. The torture, executions, and banishments of 1844 have in fact come to constitute their own sort of pedagogy, both in Cuba and within the wider Atlantic world. To learn about La Escalera, then, is to learn intimately about the Spanish colonial state—its ideological power, its expansive reach, its capacity for pain. This knowledge mirrors intelligence that black people gathered throughout the Americas about white racial power—its endless capacity for humiliation, its recurring promise of violation, its chronic and yet unpredictable intrusions. These two strands of knowledge woven together—the lengths to which the colonial state would go to contain its threats and the endless possibilities for black degradation under slavery—might be said to reflect the enduring historical lessons of La Escalera. In other words, the legacy of state violence has profoundly shaped what we know about this conspiracy and how we know it.

Nevertheless, this pedagogy of state terror contains a variety of teachings for those who study its history. Some of these teachings have become crucial lessons about the brutality of chattel slavery and colonial rule. But some of the most important lessons of La Escalera have become muted, if not altogether lost. Prominent among them are the stories of rural black people who organized a strategic and widespread movement, developing

List of accused conspirators on Matanzas properties. Courtesy of the Archivo Nacional de Cuba.

political cultures and social networks as they went, and who became part of a larger mobilization to challenge slavery and colonialism. In other words, they knew those lessons but defied them anyway.

This book moves these stories to the forefront by exploring the visions of resistance that developed in rural black communities of western Cuba from 1841 to 1844. It calls attention to the major organizing collectives in that resistance movement and also to the individuals—the slave women and the nonelite men—who rarely took part in those collectives, and were indeed frequently hard to find in the archives. Positioning these slaves at the center of a larger black political culture opens up some useful analytics with which to reconsider—and engender—the production of knowledge about enslaved people's political struggles. Calling attention to the hidden labors of resistance often performed by women and less visible men, this study invites larger questions about how the 1844 movement was assembled, where and with whom the movement began, and how scholars can expand the terms of collective protest.

||||||| Historical Background of 1844

By the early 1840s Cuba was one of Spain's last but most important colonies. It had become the largest producer of sugar cane in the world and was by far the wealthiest colony in the Caribbean. But at the same time, however, Cuba found itself swimming in a fierce political whirlpool amid endless debates over slavery, abolition, and colonial rule. The island itself was becoming a slave-based sugar goliath at exactly the same moment that the transatlantic movement against slavery was reaching its peak. In the years leading up to 1844, the Spanish colonial government faced endless attacks from British abolitionists who led the global crusade against slavery. For these abolitionists, Cuba had become ground zero in a heated battle against the now-illegal slave trade. These years also coincided with a moment in which Cuban anticolonial dissidents were becoming more aggressive and more organized, and small groups of creole elites found surreptitious ways to express their displeasure with the Crown. Finally, Cuba's midcentury prosperity was beginning to attract the attention of U.S. slaveholding interests, who hoped to annex the island for the southern plantocracy. On the whole then, this was a period in which Spain was repeatedly forced to protect "la siempre fiel isla de Cuba."

In 1840 the fiery Scottish abolitionist David Turnbull was appointed to the British consulate in Havana. During his brief term in office he acted as a kind of one-man machine against the illegal slave trade. Turnbull is also believed to have stoked the nationalist sentiments of local white creoles during and after his time in office. With the openings created by the threats to Spanish imperial power in 1841 and 1842, a small group of dissident white men and men of color came together to consider overthrowing slavery and Spanish colonial rule. The archival evidence suggests that Turnbull promised military and financial backing for these efforts.

As early as 1841 local authorities had begun to receive word of a resistance movement taking shape against the Spanish metropole. On the heels of the two largest slave rebellions in recent years, Cuban officials gradually began to prosecute a movement that by January 1844 was already deeply entrenched. The repression that followed ensnared some of Cuba's best-known artists and intellectuals, both white and of color, casting a particularly wide net around prosperous blacks and mulattos. Among the most famous targets of the 1844 backlash were the mulatto poet Plácido and the white creole intellectuals Domingo del Monte y Aponte and José de la Luz y Caballero.

In the immediate aftermath and even in recent decades, historians came to believe that the Spanish colonial government created a black rebel movement in order to dismantle a burgeoning—and notably multiracial—anti-colonial struggle, targeting upwardly mobile free people of color. For years writers supporting this position maintained that there was no organized conspiracy, only a cynical strategy of containment by the colonial state, in which any actual resistance had been greatly exaggerated by the authorities.[3] These arguments reached a climax during the Cuban wars for independence, and the history of 1844 remains closely tied to a longer memory of Spanish colonial repression.

Historians who doubted the existence of a conspiracy were often justified in their skepticism of colonial accounts and justifications. The problem is that this skepticism has left very little room to discuss the actions and political visions of accused rebel conspirators. Moreover, very few authors have delved into the landscape of black political life in western Cuba *after* the repression of La Escalera in 1844 and *before* the opening of independence in 1868. This absence, combined with the nonconspiracy scholarship's insistence that a movement never took place, has helped to sustain the image of a repressive colonial apparatus that first embellished, then eradicated most visible forms of organized black dissidence in Cuba by 1844. As seen in the very title of this book, *Rethinking Slave Rebellion in Cuba* challenges this literature in a number of critical ways.

More recent historical accounts of La Escalera have shifted the debates to highlight extensive links between the Cuban events of 1844 and the larger international debates over the slave trade and colonial rule that regularly swept onto Cuba's shores. The most significant challenge to the claim of an unfounded conspiracy came from Robert Paquette's impressive monograph *Sugar Is Made with Blood: The Conspiracy of La Escalera and the Conflict between Empires over Slavery in Cuba* (1988).[4] In the last two decades, the Atlantic context that Paquette established in this book has become vital for a range of scholars seeking to understand the 1844 movement in new and more expansive ways.[5]

But the present book offers still a different center of gravity for the history of La Escalera. In the midst of one of the world's most thriving slave institutions, at a moment when global slavery was under siege by powerful forces—indeed when the strongest challenge to Cuban slavery seemed to come from the British government—black Cubans mounted a struggle that took center stage in these pressing political debates. *Rethinking Slave Rebellion in Cuba* places the political vision of rural black slaves at the center of a multidimensional movement with international ramifications for slavery and empire. Otherwise stated, this book seeks to excavate a longer narrative of black political struggle that has been obscured by the shadow of state terror.[6]

My goal in this book is to reframe the conversations around the 1844 movement to highlight the centrality of rural black Cubans to local resistance movements, regional organizing, and transatlantic events. The extensive judicial records from 1844 demonstrate that a far-reaching movement was indeed in the making and that this project became the work of hundreds of rural slaves across the countryside. The lives of these enslaved Africans—that is to say, their political subjectivities, social and community formations, and gendered identities—offer important new ways to understand the making of this and other slave movements.

In its broadest sense, *Rethinking Slave Rebellion in Cuba* seeks to understand what happened in rural black communities during the years leading up to the 1844 repression. The chapters that follow chart the emergence of a rural slave leadership as it fashioned insurgent collectives within and beyond—sometimes far beyond—the borders of its respective estates. In trespassing what was regularly expected of them, rural Cuban slaves created social networks and alternative geographies that pushed the literal boundaries of their estates, and sometimes the very logic of the plantation world itself. As they engaged in dangerous talk, subversive ideas, and rebellious plans, groups of slave men and women built the growing insurgent project, shaping its contours in radical ways. This book traces the outlines of a black political culture in the rural plantation world that produced an insurgent struggle, and transcended its limitations.

But the creation of a new kind of narrative for the 1844 movement also requires an alternative approach to understanding the way in which this and other slave insurgencies were organized and led. Perhaps most important, the records I examined have yet to yield a singular leader or a cohesive group that united the rebels of the rural countryside. The 1844 movement must therefore be understood through a series of smaller mobilizations at the level of the individual plantations. This book builds on the contributions of several historians whose work was part of a historiographic shift to expand slave rebellion histories beyond their elite or privileged organizers.[7] But it also represents a departure from much of the existing historiography, shifting attention away from the iconic and invariably male figures whose actions tend to dominate slave rebellion histories. As such, my work both relies on and expands these earlier bodies of scholarship by complicating the questions one might pose about slave agency, empowerment, and subjectivity. Partly by arguing that black slave women were critical to shaping and producing insurgent possibilities, this book questions the very actions that became most legible during moments of slave unrest, and those that are most consistently read as legitimate forms of resistance.

Such an approach insists that scores of nonelite slaves—both female and male—remain central to the narration of this movement. In particular, this approach requires close attention to the many accounts by women who claimed few if any ties to the rebel movement. Some of these women maintained that they knew little or nothing of a coming rebellion, others stayed far removed from rebel activities when insurgencies actually broke out. On the surface, these stories present a distinctively gendered disavowal of the insurgent project. A careful rereading of them, however, sheds light on a variety of investments that were both personal and political. Such a reading calls attention to the hidden labors of rebellion in their many incarnations and extends the boundaries of what we understand an insurgency to be.[8]

The traditional focus on highly aggressive forms of masculine identity has consistently elided women from the insurgent project and thus constitutes its own form of historical violence. In addition, the familiar emphasis on highly visible male leaders and violent militant acts has also rendered scores of *men* invisible during moments of insurgency. Placing women at the center of the narrative opens up new theoretical possibilities for the entire entity known as "the slave rebellion." The conceptual dexterity such a positioning requires can offer new ways to rethink the actions, words, and subjectivities of those people who were involved or not involved. And sometimes the latter can reveal just as much about the making of a rebel struggle.

While the resistance of slave women has largely come to light through the historical literature on day-to-day or nonviolent resistance, it is my hope that this book will continue troubling the distinctive categories through which we often understand slave struggle. As Stephanie Camp and Jennifer Morgan have shown in British and North American contexts, the stories of slave women tug insistently at the established borders of "violent" and "nonviolent" resistance. The slave women's testimonies examined here shed light on a range of activities—some of which would rarely be categorized as resistance at all—that were intimately linked to the making of an insurgent movement. Thus to the extent that I frame this moment as a spectacular staging of black belligerence and a "macro" story of political contestation, I also frame it as part of the mundane work of living in and surviving the plantation world. Such an approach can make those who tend to fall through the cracks of rebel histories more visible.

These rebels in the cracks, so to speak, invite broader consideration of how scores of Cuban slaves, some of whom received little more than passing notice about a rebel movement, encountered and understood the project of resistance. In so doing this book searches other kinds of landscapes, including the canvas of African Cuban ritual practice and sacred work, to narrate this story. Closely investigating the political and religious sensibilities of West and Central Africa points to some of the ways this movement became translated into a living reality for hundreds people and offers a compelling alternative archive of the possibilities of black freedom.[9] The central question of this book cannot be solely one of how the rural "theater" fashioned itself; it must also contend with the emergence of a black political consciousness in rural Cuba. It must show how the categories of gender and ethnicity informed these political cultures, and how the political architectures of African people shaped the emerging struggle.

||||||| A New Narrative of 1844 and Its Implications

Most historical accounts of what came to be known as the conspiracy of La Escalera locate its genesis in the major cities of Havana and Matanzas, where a prominent group of free men of color helped to coordinate the outlines of a widespread anticolonial movement. Though he never officially admitted his involvement, much of the evidence indicates that the free mulatto poet Plácido was critical to organizing an inner circle of associates who identified other allies of color across the island. While the commitment of white creole patriots and British abolitionists eventually dissipated, the circle of free people of color with whom Plácido associated continued to lay the groundwork for what would be remembered as Cuba's most brutally repressed challenge to slavery and colonial rule.

One of my central aims in this book is to widen the story of La Escalera beyond the urban sphere. Such an expansion calls attention to the scores of people, mostly black men, who crisscrossed the western regions from the fall of 1842 to the spring of 1844, taking news of an underground struggle with them as they went. By the fall of 1843, scores of rural black workers were stealing time away from their chopping and hauling, holding clandestine gatherings after dark and arranging meetings in town squares and taverns to discuss the impossible: taking the land for themselves, retaining the fruits of their labor, and overturning the existing structures of power. As these designs came under increasing scrutiny from colonial authorities, Cuba's military commission ushered in the year 1844 with unprecedented waves of bloodshed and terror. Its officers spanned the western department of Cuba, taking testimony after testimony from Cubans of African descent. Nevertheless, the movement continued to grow and expand for several months after authorities began their concerted efforts to stamp it out.

The political organizing of 1844 was intimately connected to the successive waves of organized slave resistance in the countryside that preceded it. Two of the most significant slave rebellions during this time were those that took place in March and November 1843. Black urban dissidents in Havana and Matanzas felt the impact of both uprisings, and most expressed clear links between these rural battles and their own plans for insurgency. Such linkages underscore an argument critical to many histories of Atlantic slavery—that slave institutions were central to maintaining colonial forms of governance—but they also demonstrate that organized slave resistance became critical to the *unraveling* of colonial systems of power, particularly in Cuba. For this reason, it is critical to view the slave rebellions of 1843 as part of a larger anticolonial movement uncovered in 1844.[10]

While an important body of work has pushed us to rethink the ways Cuban nationhood has been framed and understood, few scholars have explicitly examined the centrality of black historical actors in the project of nation-making.[11] Part of the importance of this book lies in its contention that a group of slave dissidents—largely Africans living on the farms and plantations of the western countryside—profoundly shaped one of Cuba's largest anticolonial endeavors *before* the formal opening of independence in 1868. It underscores the importance of situating the organized—and often autonomous—struggles of rural plantation slaves squarely within the best-known and most accepted narratives of Cuban anticolonialism. Such a story highlights how insurgents of color in mid-nineteenth century Cuba turned to but also bypassed liberal creole registers of citizenship in their quest for autonomy and personhood. These arguments suggest important ways to map the trajectory of anticolonial insurgency in Cuba and throughout Latin America.

The uncertainty about the existence of a slave rebel movement in 1844 necessarily brings any historian of La Escalera face to face with the predicament of the archive. It returns newer scholars to older questions of how to verify slave plots and conspiracies, and how to extract subaltern stories from hegemonic documents. In short, it is a predicament that continually forces historians to revisit Gayatri Chakravorty Spivak's famous question of whether or not the subaltern can speak.[12]

In recent decades, a rich body of literature has emerged to address these questions in a variety of fields. This body of scholarship has come to understand the colonial archive as a unique genre unto itself, one that relies on a powerful mythology of its own reason and coherence, and one that often produces the deepest and bloodiest of erasures.[13] Scholars of slavery and slave resistance have paid extensive attention to these kinds of dilemmas.[14] For years, they have illustrated that turning to these archives necessitates turning to a public transcript profoundly marked by bodily and discursive violence, and often to the writings of the very people responsible for that violence. Any study of a movement like 1844 must therefore contend not only with the sheer exigencies of the archive itself, but also with the very forms of knowledge that slave regimes rendered verifiable, documentable, and legible.[15] Perhaps nowhere is this more visible than in the archives of La Escalera.

So, as others have argued, the colonial archive was as much a fiction—a product of colonial imagination and desire—as it was a reality. I want to clarify, however, what I mean when I speak of the archive's imperial fictions. During moments of slave unrest like the one that took place in Cuba, the state often worked with the embedded apparatuses of racial violence to justify massive antiblack repression and widespread torture. Across western and central Cuba, authorities proceeded to frame a narrative of insurgency that was compulsively linear, deeply militarized, leadership-heavy, and threaded with violence. The documents these authorities created can thus be described as "fictitious" because of their deeply politicized nature, their violent forms of selectivity, and their protean assemblages of truth.

But to the extent that authorities were able to create these selective truths, they had to rely on the words, bodies, actions, performances, and epistemologies of enslaved black people. While the archive attempted (and in some ways succeeded) in creating its own narrative, it was only able to do so *because of* and *in relation to* the narratives being crafted by enslaved people. The reading practice I employ here questions an approach to the archive first *and* last as a diagnostic of colonial pathos, fear, and fantasy. In so doing, it necessarily asks what we foreclose by reading slave's testimonies as stories that consistently reproduce or enable the desires of the colonial state, or in this case as emerging primarily from a place of narrative complicity with colonial military designs. In exploring the movements of 1844, I ask what might be opened up if we hold an organized commitment to black sovereignty and survival alongside (and even within) an organized state-backed impulse to subdue and contain those same desires. The former arguably provides the very conditions of possibility for the latter, and therefore cannot be easily dismissed by it. In other words, while we must remain critical of the means by which we arrive at a narrative of black militancy, we must also acknowledge that slaves' critiques of white domination were very real and often found their way into state-produced documents in complicated ways.

Recent scholarship has argued that historians risk colluding with white slave regimes when the former use slave testimonies to highlight stories of resistance, particularly when they ignore or sideline those claiming not to have participated in rebellious plans.[16] The methodological approach that I employ here in no way dismisses the terror of the 1844 trials, but it does seek to disrupt the intellectual paralysis that such violence was meant to induce. I am suggesting that the very attempt to acknowledge the violence of the archive can sometimes produce other kinds of violence in the way we remember our histories. What are the implications, for example, of failing to explore complex black responses to colonial violence, even as we acknowledge the power of white hysteria? Do we reproduce the power of the state to define and document black life? Do we arrest the lines of inquiry into slaves' political actions—particularly the smaller actions or the gendered actions that might only become legible when we read the archive in certain ways?

I submit that it is possible to weave a path through the archive's epistemological violence, in part by reading state documents both as an index of colonial power and self-fashioning and also as texts with multiple authors. Such a path can be forged by reading practices that consider silences as texts unto themselves, often with gendered implications, by privileging utterances meant to be small and insignificant, by paying close attention to even one or two words—such as "slaves of *both sexes* invaded the *batey*"— and by combing alternative sites of consciousness, such as ritual and sacred practice to make enslaved people's political practices legible.

Conspiracies like that of La Escalera that ended not in a revolt but in a massive state repression highlight this claim in particularly important ways. In this case, the trope of a failed or a nonexistent rebellion disciplines the terrain in which we pose questions and offer analyses. Among other things, narrating the history of 1844 through a narrative of guilt or innocence, or through the overarching question of whether the conspiracy "happened," can miss not only the larger context of black oppositional cultures but also the wealth of information the trial records contain about the lives of Cuban slaves.

The stories that black Cubans chose to tell about themselves gesture to a range of methodological practices that allow us to think beyond the violence of the plantation regime, even as one is embedded in it. For example, when an enslaved Gangá man named Gonzalo was questioned about leaving his home property in March 1844, he denied doing so to attend secret meetings. But he did state that he left twice to visit a woman at La Victoria with whom he was in love.[17] Gonzalo's tale should not be seen as an easy story of triumph over plantation boundaries; he was to be whipped for his admission of nighttime truancy. Here lies the inextricable conundrum of these documents. The colonial interrogations produced torture and brutal pain for this Gangá man. Yet they also produced a story whose importance cannot be dismissed—about how slaves found ways to refuse the boundaries prescribed by their captivity and commodification, and to use their time, their bodies, and their desires in the manner they chose.

Gonzalo's story is also inseparable from the deeper context of organized resistance that was unfolding around him; that is, from the dozens of accounts from *other* slaves on his estate who did admit to subversive meetings, conversations, gatherings (including several who insisted that Gonzalo was present for them).[18] These stories *together* frame a wider set of oppositional politics that emerged during moments of collective resistance that can indicate a different way to narrate the possibilities of black freedom and redemption, autonomy and survival.

This book stands on the shoulders of several previous historians who successfully established the parameters for an insurrectionary movement in 1844. The most important recent scholarship on La Escalera has been written by the Cuban historians Gloria García Rodríguez and the prolific Manuel Barcia Paz.[19] The archival research conducted by Robert Paquette and Rodolfo Sarracino also demonstrates that a resistive movement, or more aptly a series of such movements, began to form in either 1841 or 1842.[20] These historians draw in part on a significant body of work that has alternately supported and criticized the idea of a black conspiracy, particularly by examining the life of the poet Plácido.[21]

But some of the most powerful and convincing support for the existence of a rebel movement comes from the testimonies of slave witnesses themselves. Military authorities took declarations across practically the entire western department of Cuba—from the city of Havana to its surrounding areas, into the city of Matanzas and its countryside, into what became Cárdenas in 1843 and its countryside, pushing as far as the region of Sagua La Grande into areas that are today the central Cuban regions of Villa Clara and Cienfuegos.[22] In these areas authorities visited hundreds of sugar plantations, coffee estates, smaller ranches and farms, prison forts, urban jails, hospitals, and other colonial detention centers, taking testimonies wherever they went. The trial record they compiled was amassed by a significant cohort, including district magistrates, military officials, and local authorities. During the early days of the conspiracy's discovery, a few overeager vigilante planters even extracted witness statements on their own, sometimes without the presiding officer. The earliest trials began in January 1844, the bulk of them unfolding from March to May 1844. Many, however, continued into the summer and fall of 1844, and even trickled into the summer of 1845.

The testimonies selected for this study represent a microcosm of the trial record as a whole. I chose them primarily because their interrogations center on rural slaves and were predominantly taken in the western plantation zones. It is clear, however, that the sugar economy of the nineteenth century eroded many of the boundaries between slaves and free people of color, and therefore to write about rural Cuba is to write about a rural black culture that developed across lines of legal freedom. As a group these records represent a cross-section of the spaces in which these slaves and free people worked, including sugar mills, coffee plantations, ranching farms, urban homes, artisan shops, and urban sectors. Finally, they represent most of the major districts across the western department, including Havana province, Matanzas, and Cárdenas, and they encompass a number of different trial locations within the major cities.

The presiding officers recorded witness declarations as third-person accounts that often took the form of summaries rather than verbatim statements and these accounts were read back to the witnesses for accuracy.[23] It is quite possible, however, that many officers used their own words and phrasing to record what they heard, some even inserting their own ideas wholesale. Moreover, these hearings differed from other colonial trial records in that they were compiled mostly by military officers rather than civil magistrates and were rarely taken in formal courtrooms. Finally, it has been well documented that some notorious judges coerced outlandish testimonies, and some even received prison sentences for their conduct.[24] Hence, to the extent that they represent enslaved people's responses, they also represent the mental universe of white military officers, and for this reason must be treated with the utmost care.[25]

In this manner, and under the orders of Captain General Leopoldo O'Donnell, Cuba's trenchant military commission extracted hundreds of testimonies from Cubans of color in 1844. The file Comisión Militar Ejecutiva y Permanente contains 169 sets of trial proceedings for the year 1844 alone—some of which are upward of 500 pages—many of which contain two or three different sections or *piezas*. Collectively this represents thousands of pages of testimony, and it is difficult to know how many statements were taken during the course of that year. Also perhaps for that reason, the trial record itself has only been looked at sporadically, and in small pieces since the time it was first created.[26] Even this study represents only a portion of the entire record, and while the conclusions herein speak only for the documents examined, it is my belief that these trends pervade throughout.

The synchronicity and overlap of these testimonies—submitted from dozens of different locations, over some eighteen months of questioning, by scores of different interrogators—is far too striking, compelling, and important to ignore. The question that plagues most scholars, however, is not so much whether common linkages can be made across space and time but whether or not witnesses told the *truth*. We may never know who was telling the truth and who was not. In recent decades, scholars across disciplinary boundaries have revealed the limits of searching for unassailable truths, arguing that such endeavors often carry their own myth-making projects rooted in Western or masculine positivism. But for the purposes of a project that uses witness accounts to reconstruct a historical moment, the question remains relevant about how accurately witnesses reported their conversations and sightings, comings and goings.

Black men and women questioned in 1844 knew they were on trial for crimes considered unforgivable, for which there could be little justification or repentance. As enslaved persons, they understood better than anyone how thin the line was separating them from imprisonment, whipping, torture, and execution. In fact by the time rural black Cubans testified, many had already been held in chains, stocks, and dingy plantation jails for periods lasting from a few days to several weeks and were awaiting the arrival of interrogators or the start of their second, third, and fourth examinations. It is also important to consider that enslaved black women may have been faced with gendered forms of punishment through sexual assaults and reprisals. Thus there can be little doubt that scores of witnesses constructed themselves as distant or uninvolved parties to protect themselves against torture that was often privatized, extralegal, and wholly sanctioned.[27]

Scores of witnesses renounced their earlier statements of innocence or ignorance when pushed, particularly when confronted with overwhelming evidence against them. Others, when confronted with their accusers or with testimonies that could not possibly make sense, simply refused to answer or stuck to their illogical stories. The reverse also happened, and some declarants retracted or changed their previous testimonies that implicated important leaders and strategies. Still others finally admitted to charges against them or accepted their charges from the very beginning.

In other words, slaves actively stretched the "facts" at their disposal to protect themselves and those they cared for as much as possible. Large numbers of slaves stretched the truth as far as the corporal protection it promised, and others simply stated—truthfully or untruthfully—that they did not know. But most slaves did not fall quite so easily into either category. The majority of those under interrogation did not fabricate tales that were unequivocally false; instead they told a *version* of the truth. Black people under interrogation cobbled together the pieces of information that seemed least incriminating, adroitly evaded certain questions, highlighted the responsibility of other people, deemphasized their own accountability, and told the stories they believed would be most advantageous to them.[28]

Those being accused were not infrequently the witnesses' godparents and friends, children and spouses. The number of times that people indicted their loved ones suggests that such witnesses felt compelled to produce carefully selected truths that drew from actual events in order to secure for them the least amount of pain and humiliation. And although little information has emerged about where slaves were held on most estates before and between questionings, it is quite possible that those who could worked together to craft mutually beneficial stories to tell the judges.[29] Finally, it is impossible to dismiss the fact that at least some slaves decided for whatever reasons to tell all or much of the truth.[30] Perhaps the most intriguing group was comprised of slaves who admitted to the charges against them. Members of this group usually held central leadership positions, and they were almost always men. Their significance should be carefully highlighted because their admissions rarely ever obtained for them a lesser sentence, usually quite the contrary.

In most cases only those deemed the most important leaders were taken to the city of Matanzas for imprisonment and further questioning. Once in Matanzas, the most heavily accused rebel conspirators were executed by firing squad, their bodies mutilated. The others were given prison sentences ranging from one to ten years. Those considered to be troublemakers but not as treacherous as the primary leaders were returned to their masters, with orders to be placed in the estate's most taxing and onerous labors, or to work in shackles anywhere from six months to ten years. The majority of the rural slaves taken to the urban areas were sent back with these kinds of punishments, in part because they represented precious investments to their owners, and in part because the jails simply could not hold them all. As it was, hundreds of men of color were sent overseas to be imprisoned.[31]

While we know what happened to those viewed as ringleaders, discerning what happened to the rest of those indicted proves more difficult. It was not uncommon for witnesses to accuse several fellow plantation residents, some of whom were formally interrogated but many of whom were not. Others were questioned and even admitted comparatively minor roles but were not sent to prison in Matanzas. For this in-between group, there was often no recorded documentation of the sentences they received, or how their sentences varied from those of others in similar situations. Usually they were handed over to plantation managers to be punished as the latter saw fit. In other words, once accused, it is not always clear that there was a direct correlation between giving the "right" answers and the kind of punishment meted out.[32]

Finally, though the reign of terror was considered necessary by colonial authorities, it also came at great cost to sugar production and to the proper functioning of the colonial state. The 1844 inquisition affected the harvests of slaveowners across the western region, and it tortured, imprisoned, or killed hundreds of badly needed workers. In short, it injected terror and immobilization into black and white communities across the island. It was not, therefore, an endeavor that could be carried out lightly.

While the testimonies can often be unwieldy and contradictory, reading them makes it very difficult to conclude that there was no movement to rise up in 1844. My research has yet to uncover a scholar who has examined the trial records and argued that the conspiracy was a figment of the Spanish imagination.[33] There can be no doubt that military officers exaggerated the numbers of people involved in the conspiracy, perhaps to a significant degree, and sometimes luridly embellished the stories of insurgents' plans. There is, however, every reason to believe that scores of slaves did intend to commit acts of insurrection if they believed many others would be doing the same thing at the same time, and if as claimed their efforts received powerful support from beyond the shores of Cuba. Most important, if even half or a quarter of those declaring their intention to take part in a rebel movement spoke truthfully, the movement they mentioned was indeed vast and far-flung, surpassing any anticolonial effort that had been mounted up to that time.

As a final note on racial terminology, I have chosen to employ the language used in the trial records to describe the racial identities of the historical actors. In these documents, when African-descended people are referred to as a collective, this is almost always done with the term *negros*. This term was intended to be disparagingly one-dimensional, a constant reminder to the African-descended of their lower social status, and it had the intended effect of flattening out a range of different cultural and ethnic experiences. In spite of this, I have chosen to use the term *black* as a way to signal the particular racial landscape in which slaves operated, one whose racial possibilities became narrower and narrower as the nineteenth century progressed. I use the term *African* when referring to people with "nation names," and thus presumably born on the continent, especially if I want to call attention to an African cultural specificity. I additionally employ the terms *African-descended* (or *afrodescendientes*) if I am trying to reference the cultural inheritance of people born in Africa as well as Cuba. Finally if

I am specifically referring to urbanites, or speaking of them together with country-dwellers, I sometimes use the terms *people of color* or *black and mulatto* in accordance with the way they appear in the documents.

|||||| Structure of the Book

Chapter 1 examines the social and political landscape of Cuba during the first half of the nineteenth century. During the years leading up to 1844, the sugar economy expanded exponentially in Cuba as the island swiftly filled the void left by the regional powerhouses. The alliances of 1844 emerged from this expanding economy and from the vortex of anti-Spanish dissent in a context of disintegrating social conditions for free people of color, liberal white creole desire for independence, British frustration with the illegal slave trade, and of course the murderous experiences of the plantation slave. During the early years of the nineteenth century, slaves were brought to Cuba in unprecedented numbers, which continued to soar well into the 1830s. This meant that thousands of men and women from vast stretches of West and Central Africa were being funneled into the farms and plantations of the western countryside. Thus by the time of the 1844 movement, the institution of slavery had been radically altered to reflect a labor-intensive economy and a sugar monoculture built on rigid racial hierarchies. Many of the slaves who literally built that monoculture would eventually play critical roles in the 1844 movement.

Chapter 2 canvasses the everyday locales in which men and women discussed and contemplated a rebel movement during the 1840s. It explores how work regimes and social networks became critical to the evolution and dissemination of insurgent ideas and designs. Throughout the plantation world, enslaved people created rival geographies and alternative itineraries in their work and leisure that facilitated an entrenched culture of black mobility and enabled rebel collectivities to emerge. Both the licit and illicit movement that fed these fissures, together with the community networks that reached into towns and cities, illustrate how slaves and free people found a range of opportunities to plan for a rebel movement.

Chapter 3 argues that the insurgent designs of 1844 grew out of a longer insurrectionary tradition in the rural plantation countryside. While slaves in rural Matanzas had unleashed destructive rebellions for close to two decades, the greatest concentration of these rebellions took place in the 1840s, culminating in the two slave insurrections of 1843. Chapter 2 tells the story of the Bemba and Triunvirato rebellions, which erupted in March and November 1843, respectively. It explores the possibilities that insurgent rupture both opened up and closed off for women and men in nonleadership positions. As the smoke cleared, literally and figuratively, authorities began to discover plans for an even more encompassing rebellion that was intended to erupt in 1844.

Chapter 4 takes a step back from these rural mobilizations to examine the organization unfolding in the urban centers of Matanzas, and to a lesser extent, Havana. During the early 1840s these urban centers became a crucible for scores of dissident men — rural and urban slaves, free men of color, and white creole patriots — hoping to organize against slavery and colonialism. The chapter explores the political dynamics that were radicalizing urban blacks and mulattos by the middle of the century, and the ways these ruptures brought together groups of privileged free men, a pair of British abolitionists, and a group of anticolonial white creoles who contemplated a rebellion against the Spanish regime.

Chapter 5 begins by exploring the gendered intersection of betrayal, infidelity, antiblack violence, and state terror in the historical memory of 1844. Alongside the trope of duplicity, the most pervasive theme of black women's involvement in this and other slave movements is their silence and invisibility. This chapter calls attention to the scores of rural black women who molded the 1844 resistance in visible and public ways, and to those who shaped the movement through means often obscured or unnoticed. The chapter focuses special attention on small groups of women who stand out in the insurgent organizing, some of whom were cited as rebel queens and others of whom were named as field lieutenants or captains. But I also turn to those women who negotiated complex relationships to the movement and to masculine-defined practices of freedom in ways that were less visible in the trial record, yet arguably map out new ways to think about movement participation.

While the historiography of La Escalera has long made Plácido, the renowned mulatto poet, synonymous with the leadership of the 1844 movement, chapter 6 highlights those enslaved men and women who rose to prominence as estate lieutenants and captains across the western rural landscape. It examines those who came to the forefront of the rebel leadership on these and other estates — particularly the black assistant overseers — and the ways their perceived status, mobility, and access helped to consolidate their positions of leadership. Yet even while this chapter works to create an alternative knowledge of 1844 leadership, it also pushes against the trope of "leadership" itself. Partly by exploring the women who made critical contributions on their home estates, I attempt to loosen the tradition of this iconic figure by examining slaves who were critical to local rebel planning, who helped shape this planning in unacknowledged ways, and who often fell on the periphery of these designs.

Chapter 7 explores the ways a range of African spiritual practices became the lynchpins in a sacred insurgent geography of 1844. This cultural architecture, particularly through amulets and rituals, proved useful to slave organizers as they encouraged awareness and support for the bourgeoning movement. This chapter considers how the cultural infrastructure of West and Central Africa—primarily its religious cosmologies and expressive cultures—provided a vehicle and a language for rural black people to access rebellious ideas and articulate a revolutionary agenda. In doing so, these practices became instrumental in connecting people to the idea of insurgency in the rural areas.

This study, then, will ask scholars to think more expansively about how slave insurgencies and other liberation struggles are brought to life. I would like to treat this movement not as a self-evident or foregone conclusion but rather as a political juncture that had to be fashioned, molded, and lived. Rather than assuming that by now we "know" what a slave rebellion looks like, I want to understand instead how such rebellions come into existence as real possibilities and living prospects.

Chapter One

Africans in Colonial Matanzas

On June 7, 1844, Eloisa Carabalí found herself in front of local military authorities being questioned about a most "criminal and horrifying conspiracy." Eloisa was recorded as being a woman of mature age, a Roman Apostolic Catholic, a member of the Carabalí nation, and a widow. Her Carabalí name suggests that she boarded a slave ship somewhere along the Biafran coast, perhaps at Old Calabar. By 1844 Eloisa was working as a field laborer on the Buena Suerte sugar mill "in the service of her owner," Miguel Cárdenas. From what we know of Buena Suerte, Eloisa lived and worked among people whose origins ranged from Igboland to Senegambia, scores of their descendants who were born in Cuba, and the free people she learned to identify as *negros*, *chinos*, or *mulatos*, according to the local racial taxonomy.

The story of how this woman from the Biafran coastal region became Eloisa Carabalí, worker of cane at Buena Suerte, tells the story of Cuba's emergence as a thriving sugar colony. By the time Eloisa was arrested in the spring of 1844, Cuba was undergoing massive changes—new growth, new technologies, new levels of slave labor—all of which were making the island increasingly central to the principal markets of the Atlantic world. The financing, construction, and first harvest of the Buena Suerte mill ultimately pulled Eloisa to the Biafran coast and placed her in the hold of a slave ship. Eloisa's journey across the Atlantic to a rugged and rather remote part of Matanzas was one of many that marked the seismic shifts in labor, land, and capital taking place in nineteenth-century Cuba. The life that she encountered there was but a smaller node in a much larger story of slavery and empire. The following chapter will explore the collision of Atlantic world forces that brought Eloisa and many other Africans to the island, and the political shifts within Cuba that entangled her in a "horrifying" conspiracy.

During the early years of the nineteenth century, a revolution was taking place in Cuba.[1] By the 1840s that revolution had matured, become smug, and settled in to enjoy the peak of its glory. Sugar had officially become king, and by midcentury it was producing dizzying heights of wealth. From this place on a saccharine throne, Cuba was hailed as the "bright jewel in the Spanish diadem," as visitors marveled at the prosperity that seemed to smile on Cuba without end.[2]

For years beginning in the late 1700s, Cuban creole planters had petitioned the Spanish government to remove restrictive tariffs and open up the slave trade.[3] Realizing this was the only way to compete with the region's major sugar leviathans, the Bourbon throne finally responded with a series of legislative reforms in the late 1780s and 1790s.[4] With a new tax structure in place, its ports opened up to new trading partners, and the unprecedented possibility of obtaining slaves from foreign merchants, Cuba's planter elite was poised to usher in a massive increase in production that would have far-reaching consequences.[5]

Alongside economic liberalization and the expansion of the slave trade, a series of other events paved the way for this metamorphosis to occur. In 1791 slave insurgents in Saint-Domingue launched a revolution that eventually created the state of Haiti—the second independent nation and first black republic in the Americas. In 1807 Britain outlawed the transatlantic slave trade and in 1834 it formally abolished slavery in all its territories. The fall of Saint-Domingue (now Haiti) and the demise of slavery in British colonies such as Jamaica and Barbados created a void in the region's powerhouses that Cuban planters rushed to fill. As the nineteenth century progressed, the triumphs of the Industrial Revolution and the mechanization of sugar production further stimulated the island's growing sugar industry. By midcentury that industry accounted for millions of dollars in revenue.

This yearly sugar crop was unapologetic in its demands—ever more land, hefty financial investments, and massive quantities of labor. More than anything else sugar needed bodies, and as many of them as possible. This demand brought hundreds of thousands of people from a vast stretch of West and Central Africa to the shores of Cuba. By 1844 the saying *Con sangre se hace azúcar*[6] was no figurative phrase; it had become an instruction manual for how black limbs, psychic memories, and entire empires were transformed into over 170,000 metric tons of sugar per year—numbers which overseers quoted with pride, and foreign travelers reported with awe.[7]

The 1841 census was a telling indicator of how important the institution of chattel slavery had become to Cuba's economic and political landscape. By 1841 the enslaved population of Cuba totaled 425,521.[8] As many historians have noted, this census marked the first time in the island's history that the population of color surpassed the white population. In many ways it functioned as a wake-up call for white elites, as the specter of Haiti's Revolution loomed in front of them for much of the nineteenth century.

Across the rural landscape of Matanzas, slaves constituted not only the majority of the population but also, in most districts, the *overwhelming* majority. Two of the districts that became sites for the region's most catastrophic slave rebellions recorded 75 percent and 76 percent of their populations as enslaved in 1841.[9] The impact in the rural districts of such massive numbers of slaves—most of whom had been born in Africa—cannot be underestimated. This steady shift during the early years of the nineteenth century has been described by some historians as the "Africanization scare." On the rural plantations it was easy for white people to think of themselves as surrounded by a sea of blacks everywhere they looked.[10]

During the years bookending Britain's abolition of the slave trade—from 1801 to 1810—54,167 Africans were forcibly brought to Cuba. That number had increased by nearly 40,000 since 1781, when the number of imports set a new record. During the 1820s the number of slaves nearly tripled, to 136,381. In the decade leading up to 1840, the number increased further, to 186,179.[11] All told, between 1801 and 1850 Cuba received approximately 547,000 slaves, more than any other port, nation, or colony in the nineteenth-century Americas, save Brazil.[12]

The 1807 prohibition of the slave trade marked a turning point in Cuba's North Atlantic integration.[13] The aftermath of the ban effectively removed Britain, France, and the United States from the slave trade and created a vacuum that allowed Cuba and Brazil unprecedented access to merchants along the African coast. By the 1830s the entire slave trade had essentially shifted its energy south of the equator, and the implications of this new access for Cuba were profound.[14] As historians Laird Bergad, Fe Iglesias García, and María del Carmen Barcia have shown, the price of slaves remained largely stable until the early 1850s, and this meant that African labor remained abundant and affordable for Cuban planters for decades after the trade was banned by other nations.[15]

The men and women who were taken to Cuba represented a huge swath of West and Central Africa, stretching from the Upper Guinea coast down to present-day Nigeria; further down the coast to the region of Angola; and even around the Cape of Good Hope to Mozambique.[16] From 1806 to 1845, the largest African ethnic groups in Cuba were the Congos, the Carabalís, the Gangás, and the Lucumís. These groups were taken respectively from West-Central Africa, the Bight of Biafra, Sierra Leone, and the Bight of Benin. While scholars have differed on which of these groups dominated numerically during the period in question, the most recent estimates indicate that the largest numbers vacillated between the Congos and the Carabalís—a fact that often surprises students of Cuban history because of the strong cultural influence of the Lucumís. It is also critical to bear in mind, however, that these regions *fluctuated* in the number of slaves they sent to Cuba over the course of the century.[17] And while collectively smaller in number, four other ethnic groups also constituted a critical presence on the rural plantations: the Mandingas, the Ararás, the Minas, and the Macúas. In the records of the rebellions, the names of the *naciones* involved reveal participation from many of these disparate origins, hinting at the way the crucible of Atlantic slavery forged new alliances among diverse people against the common enemy of slavery and its masters.

Some of the most recent insights about these demographic statistics are attributable to the historians Manuel Barcia Paz and Oscar Grandío Moráguez, and to the researchers of the Trans-Atlantic Slave Trade Database.[18] The development of this database has critically enhanced, if not revolutionized, the study of the slave trade in Cuba and throughout the Atlantic world and a growing body of literature has emerged to address both its merits and its methodological problems.[19] Among other things, this database underscores the difficulties of assessing the largest ethnic groups in Cuba and elsewhere. With figures like these, it is extremely difficult to tally the number of people coming from each ethnic group with absolute precision.[20] What can be said with confidence is that the African cultures that grew up in rural Cuba represented a vast amalgamation of ethnic and cultural groupings from West and Central Africa.

Those Africans destined for sale in the Spanish and Portuguese colonies were generally assigned an ethnic "nation name" thought to correspond to their port of embarkation. Monikers such as *Lucumí* or *Gangá* denoted an enslaved person's presumed African ethnicity and were known as their *casta* or *nación* names. The pitfalls of interpreting enslaved people's ethnic identities through these *nombres de nación* are well known to scholars of the African Diaspora, and several historians have highlighted the problems inherent in these ethnic ascriptions and cautioned against interpreting them literally.[21] For each ethnic designation a broad range of linguistic systems, cultural practices, and political traditions were folded facilely into such names as "Congo" or "Mandinga."[22] Moreover, the region where a slave was initially captured did not necessarily correspond to the place where he or she was forced onto a slaver, and the place where the ship embarked could easily be quite far from home.[23] Researchers have overwhelmingly shown that these nation names should be understood primarily as geographic identifiers; that is, as indications of where on the African coast the captives embarked, rather than precise indicators of ethnic, linguistic, or cultural backgrounds.

In nineteenth-century Cuba the largest number of slaves arrived from West-Central Africa, partly because this area was more difficult for the British antislavery squadrons to police after 1807.[24] The region that historians have designated "West-Central Africa" encompasses a longer stretch of coastline than any other slaving area and therefore includes an overwhelming number of ethnolinguistic groups and political entities. West-Central Africa is generally understood to begin at Cape Lopez in Gabon and extend through the present-day Congo and down to the southernmost tip of Angola. Because of the historical significance of the latter two areas, many have referred to the entire region as "Kongo-Angola." In previous centuries, the Kingdom of Kongo had dominated economic and political affairs, but by the eighteenth century the kingdom had disintegrated, leaving no strong, centralized polity during the height of the Cuban slave trade. This meant that the West-Central African trade was carried out primarily by mercenary forces that targeted individual people and villages.[25] Scholars generally concur that Kikongo speakers, or those who understood Kikongo, constituted the majority of captives sent to Cuba. While Kikongo essentially functioned as a regional lingua franca, and therefore says little about the specific ethnic groups involved, the peoples who became collectively known as the Bakongo figured prominently in the slave trade.[26]

The Bight of Biafra produced some of the largest numbers of slaves in the entire transatlantic trade, particularly to Cuba. As a whole, the Bight of Biafra covers nearly 370 miles of the western coast, extending from the Nun branch of the Niger River to Cape Lopez in Gabon. While most Biafran captives were taken from the Niger and Cross River Deltas, the region also encompasses large portions of contemporary Nigeria and Cameroon, Equatorial Guinea and Gabon, and several of the islands off the coast.[27] Slaves from this region came to be known as the "Carabalís" because they were largely sent through the ports of New Calabar (also known as "Elem Kalabar"), Old Calabar, and Bonny. But *Carabalí* was also a sweeping term that encompassed a variety of ethnic and linguistic groups from the Biafran hinterland. The best-documented of these groups were the Igbos, the Ibibios, and to a slightly lesser extent the Efiks.[28]

The Bight of Benin also sent thousands of slaves during the nineteenth century, particularly during the 1840s.[29] The Bight of Benin extends for about 400 miles from the Cape St. Paul in Ghana to the Nun River outlet in Nigeria. The "Lucumís," as they became known in Cuba, were the main group taken from this region. The vast majority of them came from Yoruba territory through the ports of Ouidah and especially Lagos.[30] Until the close of the eighteenth century, the Oyo Empire was the political center of Yorubaland and the most powerful state in the region. Its collapse—beginning in the late 1790s, but greatly accelerated by the Fulani-Hausa jihadic invasion of 1835—pushed thousands of political prisoners and refugees into the Atlantic trade.[31] The term *Lucumí* therefore encompasses Yoruba speakers who identified strongly with metropolitan Oyo; Yoruba speakers from the outer towns and "tributary states" of the empire; refugees, migrants, and slaves who learned the Yoruba language and customs; and scores of others caught in the Lagos market, such as the Hausas and Fulanis, who were actually professed enemies of the Yorubas. Hence the "Lucumís" in Cuba included Yorubas, Ijeshas, Ketus, Ijebus, Fulanis, Hausas, Nupes, Ewe-Fons/Ajas, and others sent from the Benin ports.[32]

The upper part of the Bight of Benin has been less studied in the Cuban trade, but at least two ethnic groups are intimately linked to this region, the Minas and the Ararás. The precise provenance of the Minas is hard to pinpoint, but Gwendolyn Midlo Hall argues that the Minas in the Americas were comprised mainly of Gbe-speaking groups including the Ewes, Fons, Ajas, and Gen Minas (or just Gens).[33] These captives would have begun the Middle Passage somewhere along the coastal stretch between the Slave Coast and the Gold Coast, an area that cumulatively encompasses modern-day Togo, Benin, and parts of Ghana and Nigeria. While earlier generations of scholars believed the Minas to have originated in the region of the Asante Empire, the number of slaves arriving from the Gold Coast was *extremely* low after 1806, and many of their numbers were probably included in the estimates of those coming from either the Bight of Benin or the Windward Coast.[34]

Geographically speaking, the Ararás shared a great deal of overlap with the Minas. More research is needed to understand their cultural background, but the most accepted definitions of the Ararás cohere in their shared origins in the Kingdom of Dahomey. The Ararás also identified primarily with the Gbe language cluster and most of them were speakers of Aja, Fon, Ewe, or Popo, with geographic roots in what is today Benin and Togo.[35] Especially during the eighteenth century, Dahomey was one of the most powerful polities in the region, and its imperial ascent was closely tied to controlling the slave trade. Though the Aja-Fon/Ewe-Fon captives were fewer in number, it is clear that they were still being taken to the coastal markets in the nineteenth century. Most Araráss would have embarked from ports such as Ouidah, Porto Novo, Badagry, and Popo. The ethnic overlap with the Minas suggests that some captives from the Dahomey region could have easily been labeled "Minas."

Despite the centrality of British antislavery operations in Sierra Leone, scholars such as Joseph Dorsey have shown that Cuban slavers continued to target the area known as the Upper Guinea coast well into the 1840s.[36] "The Upper Guinea coast" usually refers to the area encompassed by the modern nation-states of Sierra Leone, Liberia, Guinea-Conakry, Guinea-Bissau, Senegal, and Gambia. Yet an influential generation of historians that included Walter Rodney and Boubacar Barry has persuasively argued for the cultural continuity, economic integration, and political linkages that joined these areas. By the early nineteenth century, ports such as Gorée and Freetown had all but stopped exporting significant numbers of slaves, but thousands were still being taken to embarkation points further south. Those coming from the Senegambia region would have encompassed the Wolofs, Mandingas, Peuls, Tukolors, Sereers, Joolas, Soninkes, and other ethnicities.[37]

Those who became known as the "Gangás" in Cuba were taken primarily from the interior of Sierra Leone, western Liberia, and Portuguese Guinea (Guinea-Bissau).[38] As Dorsey and others have shown, most of the Gangás left from a concentrated area of southern Sierra Leone where the British had little or no maritime presence. Captives for the Sierra Leonean trade were funneled mainly through various ports spread along the regional coast, but especially through the ports of Gallinas (or Galhinas), Río Pongo, and Sherbro.[39] Recent linguistic evidence indicates that the Gangás largely came from the Mende or Mel ethnolinguistic groups in the interior of Sierra Leone, which in and of itself encompassed a number of different languages. The registers of liberated Sierra Leoneans captured from 1824 to 1841 indicate that Mende speakers were the largest ethnic group among them, followed closely by speakers of Kissi/Kono, Mandingo, Susu, Temne, Fula, and others.

Those who became known as the "Mandingas" were also sent to Cuba through Sierra Leone and Gambia. The Mandingas (or Mandinkas) included a range of people from the northern part of the Upper Guinea coast, and they also formed part of the Mande ethnolinguistic group. In the late eighteenth and early nineteenth centuries, Mandinga communities stretched across much of the West African littoral, from Senegambia down to Sierra

Leone and Liberia.[40] But Philip Misevich has argued that the only thing the Cuban Mandingas had in common was their shared departure from the slave port of Rio Pongo.[41] Many who identified as Mandingas were sent to the same ports as the Gangás, so they would have *either* been labeled as "Mandinga" or "Gangá" once in Cuba. Islam had a strong presence in Senegambia, and it is almost certain that a portion of these captives were Muslims. While the Mandingas and others who converted to Islam undoubtedly brought their faith with them through the Middle Passage, more research is needed to find documentation of this in Cuba.[42]

Though they emerged quite infrequently in the archival documents, the number of slaves landing in Cuba from southeast Africa was in some cases quite staggering. From 1790 to 1840, those from Africa's eastern coast constituted approximately 10 percent of the overall trade to Cuba, significantly more than regions like Senegambia.[43] The Macúas, as they were known in Cuba, were taken from the lower regions of southeastern Africa and overwhelmingly from the ports of Mozambique. Most were drawn from two main ethnolinguistic groups in the interior of Mozambique, the Makuas and, after 1810, the Yaos.[44] The number of Mozambique-embarked slaves became particularly noticeable in Cuba from 1835 to 1841. This is important to remember because the Macúas are rarely discussed as a significant ethnic group in Cuba, little has been written about them, and they surfaced quite infrequently in the trial records. Nevertheless, their numbers were clearly significant.

The overwhelming majority of those captives bound for the Americas were kidnapped during their daily routines, snatched up as their homes and villages were being raided, and most especially captured during war.[45] In particular, the internecine cycles of warfare that erupted in and around the Bight of Benin from the 1790s to the 1840s sent untold numbers of people to the coastal forts. While the geopolitical forces that produced these wars looked vastly different across wide stretches of west and central Africa, it is nevertheless possible to identify some common themes. By the start of the nineteenth century, the major polities of West and Central Africa had become critical to and integrated within the wider Atlantic economy, and their efforts to expand were central to the thriving traffic in human commodities.[46] The dissolution of the Oyo Empire, the separation of the Dahomean Kingdom from Oyo, and the spread of several powerful jihadist movements were among the campaigns that swept up thousands of prisoners and funneled them toward the Atlantic.

The impact of these conflicts cannot be underestimated. The imperial collapse of Oyo in particular facilitated the rise of a professional military class that vastly accelerated the trade in slaves. This class included roaming mercenaries, unattached soldiers, and armed outlaws who formed part of a larger predatory force that sought slaves for their own profit. Moreover, these cycles of political violence significantly increased the availability and use of arms and helped fuel a massive militarization in and beyond the Oyo region. These cycles of warfare also forced thousands of people to flee their homes and created many vulnerable migrant populations.

While more research is needed on the subject, the historiography of the slave trade suggests that many of the slaves coming from Senegambia, Sierra Leone, Igboland, and West-Central Africa were more likely to be enslaved by kidnapping or raids—which of course rose exponentially with the trade's profitability and reach.[47] But whether through state-sponsored warfare or slave-trading expeditions, these assaults disrupted long-standing institutions of security and statecraft, rendering both individuals and entire communities infinitely more vulnerable to capture.

Slaves had been traded for centuries across this entire region, but by the nineteenth century the implications of captivity and enslavement had long been transformed. The victims of warfare and raids could now be converted into saleable commodities as never before in the continent's history. The unparalleled openings created by the Atlantic market in previous centuries, together with the completeness with which millions of people were severed from lineage, kin, and personhood, fundamentally altered the meaning of bondage across the Atlantic world and put millions of people into motion through what is now called the Middle Passage.[48]

ⅠⅠⅠⅠⅠⅠ The Middle Passage: The Drowned, the Disremembered, the Unimaginable

> *Where are your monuments, your battles, martyrs?*
> *Where is your tribal memory? Sirs,*
> *in that gray vault. The sea. The sea*
> *has locked them up. The sea is History.*
>
> —Derek Walcott

By the time they arrived in Cuba, there was no telling how long it had been since captive Africans had seen their homes, families, or places from whence they were taken. Most would have spent anywhere from several weeks to several months in the forts and dungeons of the coastal towns, usually in shackles and subsisting on scanty rations or practically starving. As Stephanie Smallwood eloquently demonstrates, their time there was marked by the ebb and flow of new captives arriving on coffles, as well as the passing of other slaves who died, fled, or boarded the ships that would take them away forever.[49]

Inevitably, nearly all slaves would face that departure as they walked physically or figuratively through the door of no return. And indeed, while Africans from up and down the coast were no stranger to maritime travel, this was an Atlantic that few of them had ever encountered. While the time that slave ships spent on the coast waiting to gather cargo was shorter than it had been in the eighteenth century, it was still not uncommon for captives to remain in the holds for weeks at a time while the captains sailed to collect more people.[50] During the nineteenth century, journeys from Lagos, Gallinas, and Ambriz to secretive points along the Cuban coast averaged a little over a month. For enslaved Africans this meant hundreds of hours in the ship's hold with little to pass the time, let alone assuage their trauma and psychic distress.[51]

During those months African men and women below were literally walled in by the darkness and closeness of the slave hold, surrounded on all sides by death and sickness. In the 1830s and 1840s, nearly 18 percent of the passengers would have died before their ships reached Cuba.[52] Whereas, by the 1830s, slave ships heading across the Atlantic were getting smaller and smaller, the number of people packed into the holds was getting larger and larger. A typical ship during this time would have carried somewhere between 350 and 400 slaves, with the deck space allotted to each slave totaling about four feet. Most of the Cuba-bound ships held more male than female captives, but the number of women also noticeably increased as the nineteenth century wore on.[53]

In ships invariably packed to the brim with people, the sickly, the traumatized, and the dead became a perpetual part of one's sensorium and psyche.[54] For those who survived a crossing of this kind, it is safe to presume that its memory would install itself in places both reachable and unreachable, with no posttraumatic care or psychological attention waiting for them on the other side. Some may have even questioned whether their crossing of the *kalunga*, as the watery line between the living and the dead is known in traditional Bakongo cosmology, was taking them out of the realm of the living altogether.[55]

Much remains unknown about what actually happened down in the slave holds — how those spaces changed people, and what kinds of relationships were forged there. What kinds of knowledge were assembled, what new dialects developed? What kind of contraband was snuck onboard, as in the story of the *otans*—the sacred stones of Ocha/Lucumí practice—that are said to have come to Cuba in the bowels of a slave ship?[56] The significant number of Atlantic crossings that recorded some kind of slave rebellion suggests that a range of resistant strategies were conceived and enacted in the slave holds. That new and recently arrived Africans figured so prominently in rebellions of the period indicates that the political consciousness that manifested itself on the plantations of Cuba was forged in part here, in this watery passage.[57]

Some of the most important expressions of resistance took the form of care, attention, and human interaction. As Omise'eke Natasha Tinsley eloquently points out in her framing of the Black Atlantic as a queer Atlantic, this entailed "connecting in ways that commodified flesh was never supposed to, loving your own kind when your kind was supposed to cease to exist, forging interpersonal connections that counteract imperial desires for Africans' living deaths."[58] Such an analysis helps explain why the *carabela* bond, the connection forged between people who survived the Middle Passage, became so pivotal to Africans' understanding of family.[59] By the 1830s and 1840s, most slaves who landed in Cuba were disembarked in secret, along one of the many harbors and shoals that dotted the coastline. These carabela mates had survived the passage together and would acknowledge that bond whenever next they encountered each other; this also would have an impact during later rebellions.

The farms and plantations of rural Cuban presented the African captives with a newly taxing and disorienting set of circumstances. Though some joined the small groups of slaves who maintained the local farms and pastures, most would become part of the huge plantation workforce that tended the expanding number of fields. Among other things, the new arrivals would have to learn how to plant cane, cut coffee berries, pick tobacco, operate machinery, learn bits of Spanish, and adjust to back-breaking work. Like the Atlantic crossing and the coastal barracks before it, the plantations brought them in contact with countless new people, including Cuban-born blacks and Africans from Senegambia to Kongo-Angola.[60]

For the duration of their time in Cuba all of these individuals would share labor, living space, punishment, and leisure. On the other side of the Atlantic the newly arrived had been freeborn peasants, trained warriors, domestic slaves, political prisoners, lineage priests, long-distance traders, agriculturalists, midwives, metallurgists, monarchs, or praise poets. Now if these identities were to be experienced at all, they were to be filtered through the lens of chattel slavery. In this strange system that made one collective out of the highborn and the lowborn, out of bitter warring enemies, and out of nations spread over thousands of miles, anyone with distinctly African features was now a "black person" and a slave.

||||||| "Life is Cheap, and Sugar, Sir . . . Is Gold."[61]

The farms and plantations of western-central Cuba were undergoing a period of tremendous growth during the first half of the nineteenth century, particularly those that cultivated sugar. The heart of Cuban sugar production lay in the western regions of the island from the province of Havana through the belt of Matanzas, into what would become Cárdenas, and beyond into Cienfuegos and Trinidad. Many of the island's most prosperous mills were situated in the province of Matanzas, a region often regarded as the sugar heartland of colonial Cuba. In the years leading up to the 1844 movement, Matanzas was being converted from a rugged frontier zone to a thriving sugar empire, and the hundreds of forced *exilios* from Igboland to Angola brought this empire to life.[62]

During the early 1800s the sugar frontier had begun to push south and east from Havana in an unprecedented way, making its way slowly to Matanzas. As Havana-based investors began to search for new markets, they frantically cleared land for new mills. This happened first in the areas surrounding the city of Matanzas and the bay, and then further east and south. In these regions huge tracts of forest and untamed land fell to ax and plow, and acres of new earth were cultivated in districts that would later become central in 1844. It was in these newer regions–some so far east that they were later reorganized into a separate province called Cárdenas—that the establishment of sugar and coffee plantations was usually the greatest.

By the late 1830s and early 1840s, planters from the turn-of-the century would have hardly recognized the countryside of Matanzas. The frenzied buildup that marked the first half of the nineteenth century had radically altered the landscape and the slave institution itself. By 1841, the districts east and south of the bay boasted the highest number of sugar and coffee estates and the largest populations of slaves. Perhaps not surprisingly, they also became some of the most important centers of slave insurgent activity in the early 1840s.[63] In 1839 Matanzas had 145 sugar mills. By 1842 the total number of mills had reached between 340 and 393. In three years, Matanzas planters—or, more accurately, their slaves—had built some 200 new sugar mills.[64] Between 1841 and 1845 Cuba exported approximately 170,000 metric tons of sugar, nearly triple the amount of previous decades.[65] By the year of the Escalera trials, Cuba accounted for 22.24 percent of global cane sugar production, more than any single producer in the world.[66] Thus one traveler in the 1850s appropriately noted that "in this country, it is nothing but the raising and making of sugar."[67]

Among the most important catalysts for this change in western Cuba was the advent of the railroad. The opening of the first railroad in November 1837 revolutionized the transportation of plantation products to port cities. Stretching from Havana to Bejucal (in Havana province), and the following year to Güines, the railroad allowed planters to cultivate much more acreage at faster rates, and to move their goods with greater speed. Many of the region's most prosperous planters became backers and shareholders in the railroad, and through the Junta de Fomento (Society for Progress) they extended the line for miles to the east, often as close to their estates as possible.

The railway lines that spider-webbed Cuba's western landscape were among the earliest in the world. As such, the African laborers who built these railroads were indispensable to a new kind of modernity that was emerging in Latin America and elsewhere. Their labor facilitated a massive transformation in shipping that revolutionized the production (and consumption) of plantation commodities, the development of circuits of capital linking Cuba to ports and bankers throughout the Atlantic world, and the expansion of the countryside that would eventually make the island "the sugarbowl of the world."[68]

As the sugar estates began to overtake the rural terrain, many slaves on smaller farms (sitios) and ranching pastures (potreros) were slowly absorbed into ingenio (sugar mill) life. Many more were slowly pulled into the world of sugar as the coffee estates closed, and experiments in coffee-growing were gradually abandoned for the more lucrative crop. As the 1840s drew to a close some 40,000 black laborers were relocated to sugar estates from the coffee sector.[69] By 1841, 71 percent of the slave population of Sabanilla lived on sugar mills, as did 52 percent of those in Yumurí. By 1844 those percentages had increased even more.

It would be a mistake, however, to think that the coffee plantations ceased to have importance on this part of the island. While historians have debated the decline of coffee, in the early 1840s the island was still exporting about 15,000 metric tons of coffee.[70] Moreover, many of those who were caught up in the 1844 insurgencies were enslaved not only on *cafetales*, or coffee plantations, but also on *potreros* and in urban homes. Nevertheless, it is vital to appreciate the hold that sugar had taken over the Matanzas economy by the mid-nineteenth century, and over the lives of those who would become involved in the movements of 1843–44.

While sugar production was reorganizing the terrain of the island over-all, the plantations themselves were reorganizing large tracts of land to ensure maximum exploitation and profit. As a space, a form of logic and a mode of production, the plantation was inherently a carceral regime, one designed to contain and discipline black workers through various forms of violence. This prisonlike system was so pervasive as to seem ordinary, yet it was absolutely central to the plantation's geography and functioning. For example, in the morning it was common for the overseers and their assistants to line up the *dotación* (workforce) in an orderly fashion, or place them in broad semicircles to determine who was present and who was absent. The *barracones*, buildings with small, cell-like rooms that could be locked at night, came to dominate the western landscape and provided another powerful example of this carcerality at work.

But the potential and the triumph of the sugar mill were ultimately measured by their acreage of sugar cane. In these rows of cane, the *hacendados* spatially marked out their hopes for profit and their prospects for wealth, and indeed the very future of capital. Across the western countryside enslaved men and women spent their days working this cane, cultivating these fields. Their chopping, loading and planting delineated the most apparent and unavoidable of these carceral features, what Derek Walcott has called a "green prison": the lush but violent panorama of the fields. This feeling of carcerality was accentuated by the promise of pain that followed in the form of overseers and their assistants (the mayorales and contramayorales) bearing whips. The cane rows represented a history of fortunes built and lost, bodies purchased on credit, dispersed people, and exhausted limbs.

As Piya Chatterjee tells us, "cultivation is . . . an ontological act." Its labors thus constitute a "fleshy cartography" that can map out important contours of enslaved people's daily experience.[71] Whether compelled to pick coffee beans, wash dirty shirts, chop hedges, boil sugar, repair fences, make tiles, or cook over hot fires, slaves' work was exhausting, numbingly constant, and sometimes bloody. The former slave, maroon, and Cuban independence fighter Esteban Montejo simply recalled it like this: "Working in the fields was like living in hell."[72]

Before the harvest months ended, the sun would drum down a heat frequently described as "unbearable." The summer months opened with powerful thunderstorms and pouring rains. The soundscape of the field merged the innocuous with the menacing: slaves' private conversations and work songs, the parading hoofs of overseers' horses, the elevated voices of black drivers, the slow creaking of wagons, the slashing whips that countered slowness or insolence.[73] On any given estate the work hours were marked by exhaustion, soreness, detachment, and boredom, and undoubtedly pride, attentiveness, and amusement as well—an intricate structure of feeling known only to the slaves themselves. But very little could stand in the way when the *zafra* (harvest) arrived, least of all heat, sweat, and exhaustion.

The zafra lasted six or seven months out of the year, generally beginning in December or January, sometimes as early as November. The reaping continued until May or June—"when the rains broke"—at which time pulling the canes, let alone the carts, up to the mill became impossible. But harvest labors tended to conclude slowly as the last of the cane stalks were cut, the final sugar stems ground, the last juices boiled and purged. The coming of *tiempo muerto* (dead time), as the months between the harvests were known, brought with it more than the passing of sugar stalks, juices, and profit. The arrival of the rains often brought literal death, as slaves died from dysentery and other diseases, their bodies spent from the demands of sugar.[74]

When the canes were ripe, black cane cutters spent much of the day slicing or pulling the long leaves from the cane stalks, then, usually in one machete swing, hacking the canes to the ground. Felling the huge sugar stalks—"thick as a stout walking cane" and nearly six feet tall—with one machete swipe required unusual strength, concentration, and resolve, making a mockery of the category of "unskilled work."[75] These cutting gangs were comprised of both men and women and worked at an accelerated pace. The life span of sugar cane was very short, and the cane had to be processed quickly to prevent its juice from spoiling. Therefore every hour was "precious to the master." Other workers—usually women and younger teenagers gathered the cane onto carts and wagons, spread it out in the central *batey* (the area where the main sugar processing was concentrated), transferred it to the grinders, and hauled away the *bagazo* (cane trash) once it had been pressed of its juice.[76]

During this season, a select crew of men exchanged the heat and exertion of the fields for those of the boiling and purging houses (*casas de purga*). The famed activity of the boiling house was a world that most plantation workers, and certainly most women, never experienced as laborers. Inside, men labored over large fires, oversaw the boiling and evaporation of sugar juices, filled the cane-troughs, and packed the drying molds and crates. Amid the clatter of engines and machines and the calls for more fire and cane stalks, they produced "white Havana" sugar, molasses, and rum.[77] Sugar masters, increasingly Irish or American, oversaw and managed the process. But as with the railroads, these boiling house slaves were effectively the implementers of the new sugar technology that was starting to spread by the 1830s.[78]

During the harvest season, the men who worked in the fields were required to relieve those working in the *casa de purga*. After an entire day in the fields then, some were required to keep watch over the boiling sugar long into the night.[79] Although the 1842 slave codes limited the official harvest day to sixteen hours, most plantation managers ignored this limit, and during the zafra workdays often lasted twenty to twenty-two hours.[80] Many slaves spent entire zafras sleeping four or five hours a night, laboring each day under a sedimented exhaustion that packed new layers of tiredness onto that of previous nights.

The slaves who labored on coffee estates had to endure parallel regimes of labor. Their work was just as deeply taxing, although it has often been portrayed otherwise by visitors of the period and later historians. As William Van Norman has shown, the coffee harvest usually took place in either late winter or early spring, but the picking necessarily stretched over several months. In other words, unlike sugar, the process could feel continuous because of the way coffee berries bloomed. The picking of coffee berry was an extremely delicate process; they had to be plucked gently and carefully, which could involve gathering them one berry at a time. Then the beans had to be washed and dried, separated from their husks, and packed into bags to be prepared for the market. In a manner not unlike the rotating shifts of sugar harvest workers, the labor of coffee workers could easily extend far into the night. The British abolitionist Richard Madden wrote that "even on the coffee estates . . . at certain times of the year it is a common practice, during the bright, moonlight nights, to work the slaves at field-work for four or five hours by the 'Clara de la luna,' as it is called."[81] At other times of the year *cafetal* slaves were compelled to cut away the undergrowth of wood, sow and care for the coffee seeds, and transfer the young plants to neat squares.[82]

Free black men were employed on the estates for different spells in stonemasonry, carpentry, or tilework, but it was not uncommon for enslaved men to hold these positions or assist in these labors. Their work repairing buildings, tending cattle, or soling shoes gave them a level of prestige unavailable to other workers. Save the handful of women who worked in domestic capacities, the vast majority of adult women labored in tasks that were largely unspectacular. As a group they frequently labored alongside enslaved men, but they also differed from the men in that they were rarely selected for specialized work or trades. Women rarely sat up higher than others like the drivers of oxcarts, nor were they commissioned to walk around and mete out orders like the black overseers, and they were almost never entrusted with special tasks for which they alone were responsible, such as those of the *candelero* (fire stoker) or *maquinista* (engineer). The prestige that accrued to these kinds of jobs was an acutely masculine one.

Those women who were not employed in the fields were distinguished by their domestic or curative labors. While men certainly worked in domestic capacities, women were particularly likely to nurse those who came to the sickhouse, cook or clean for estate owners or white employees, or watch over slave children whose parents were in the fields. But domestic and skilled workers constituted a small and privileged minority of the overall labor force. Dotaciones of any note often numbered upward of 200, and most of those people were forced to work in the field with little opportunity to escape its brutalities. After the harvest, rural slaves labored in a variety of other tasks such as planting new cane, hoeing and chopping in and beyond the fields, and repairing buildings and paths.

At the close of the eighteenth century, spokesmen for the planter class like Francisco Arango y Parreño stressed the importance of modernizing Cuba's sugar mills. Arango and several fellow hacendados set out to gather knowledge from sugar colonies such as Barbados and Jamaica, and other planters soon began to try out these newly imported techniques, equipment, and savoir faire.[83] During the early decades of the nineteenth century, these planters began to substitute the sugar-crushing *trapiches*—until then powered by oxen or water—with impressive steam engines. They consolidated the number of cooking fires, installed horizontal rollers and "French-style" kettle trains, substituted cane stalks for wood, and switched the drying process to new "Jamaican" ovens. By midcentury this industrial shift had dramatically begun to increase the output, efficiency, and production capacity of the island's mills.[84]

These innovations yielded impressive results. Whereas in 1838 an average estate of 161 slaves might have produced 243 tons of sugar, by 1849 such an estate could use only 150 slaves to produce 400 tons. This meant that each slave went from producing approximately one ton of sugar to producing close to four.[85] The boiling houses of Matanzas yielded higher ratios of processed sugar per cane than ever before, and they considerably increased both output and efficiency. As with the railroads, these new innovations placed African slaves at the center of newly emerging scripts of modernization, written in the language of industrial technology.

Yet in that strange irony of capitalist alchemies, these technological advances often *increased* rather than decreased the amount of labor that slaves had to perform. As Rebecca Scott has classically argued, not only did the daily work of enslaved people change little over the course of the nineteenth century, but in many cases, their work actually expanded or became more difficult. Improved milling capacities could only be effective when combined with an efficient and productive workforce. Although new techniques increased the amount of sugar that could be extracted and the amount of acreage that could be planted, the mills still had to rely on human hands to cut and process all that cane. At midcentury, the only real way to expand production was to plant and harvest more acres in cane—and to cut and process faster. Without such labor, the heady technological innovations of the 1830s and 1840s could translate into little that was tangible, except heavy investments.[86]

For all slaves, and especially those working in the fields, this cycle of work, overwork, and punishment took a heavy toll. The Cuban historian Manuel Moreno Fraginals has placed the average mortality rate on the ingenios between 1835 and 1841 at 63 percent, and argued that many estates counted the bulk of their populations between the ages of fifteen and fifty-five.[87] Outside observers frequently concluded that typical ingenio slaves only lived through their twenties or thirties.[88] The value of black life could be summed up in a simple question that Alexander von Humboldt claimed he "heard discussed with the greatest coolness": Was it more profitable to get all you could out of your slaves in a few years, or to replace them slowly and space out the purchases? The conclusion that it made more economic sense to buy new slaves was pervasive throughout the Caribbean, and it was especially visible in Cuba.[89] Thus from the coastal forts to the slave ships to the plantation fields, this balance sheet of flesh-versus-profit was a constant for enslaved Africans.

This mode of industrialized agriculture that required so much work from African laborers needed only a handful of white workers to fulfill the managerial and administrative functions. In fact, to say that white people were few in number on the ingenios and cafetales was a serious understatement. By the 1840s it was not uncommon to find five to seven white workers on estates of 200 or 300 slaves, especially on the large sugar mills. In the frequent absence of the estate proprietor himself (or herself), a tiny handful of white managerial staff came to symbolize much of the insidious brutality of enslavement and its skewed racial geography. The most notorious member of this group was the *mayoral*, the estate foreman or overseer. An *administrador* supervised and oversaw the estate's entire population, white and black, and a *mayordomo* acted as a bookkeeper or accountant. Other supervisors included the *maestro de azúcar* (boiling-house supervisor), the *maquinista* (engineer), and the *boyero* (cattle supervisor). Usually these were all white men, and the sugar master and engineer were increasingly foreign technocrats from the United States or Britain, though occasionally these positions were filled by free men of color or even elite slaves.

It was almost unheard of for a woman, certainly a white woman, to hold any of the above positions. The wives and children of these employees did sometimes live on the estates, but it is not clear how common that was.[90] In fact little has been written about the white female culture of the Cuban plantation, and much remains unexplored about the ways white women of various classes helped to perpetuate and underwrite its violence.[91] For most rural slaves, the control and discipline of the plantation was deeply linked to men and masculine power, and the white racial power of the countryside was strongly legitimated by patriarchal authority. At the apex of this power structure sat the hacendados, or plantation owners, often depicted as urban-dwellers who visited their estates on occasion. The records, however, suggest that many *dueños* were a more present force, and could enact various forms of discipline and terror just like the other plantation staff.[92]

The exploitation of African bodies and energies was underwritten by violent forms of control. After his visit to a series of rural plantations in the 1830s Madden concluded, "so terrible were [the atrocities of Spanish slavery] . . . that at first I could hardly believe the evidence of my senses."[93] He and others, particularly travelers from North America, often perceived in Cuba the brutality and racial discipline they somehow failed to see in the fields of the U.S. South, the homes and taverns of the North, and the free-labor plantations of the British West Indies. But in spite of this myopia, they also bore witness to a particularly violent form of control in the Cuban countryside that fascinated and troubled foreign visitors.

Much of the bodily terror that rural Cuban slaves experienced has to be interpreted from archival documents that use deceptively simple verbs like *castigar* or *maltratar*, or from descriptions such as "muy malo." These words belie a system of violence that was clearly as central to the logic of sugar and coffee harvesting as the crops themselves. Indeed, it was integral to the very way the plantation constituted itself, and it is doubtful that the plantation could have existed without it. Whether growing coffee, tobacco, or sugar, Cuban plantations elaborated similar apparatuses of disciplinary control that were common throughout the Caribbean but were also specific to the Spanish-speaking colonies. This litany of discipline included the use of stocks, jails, irons, shackles, bloodhounds, and whippings.[94]

Whippings were by far the most frequent and widespread tool of this regime, used even on expectant mothers.[95] Slaves throughout Matanzas understood what it meant to be whipped—the public humiliation, the horrific pain. It happened in the fields as an everyday motivation to work; it happened in the boiling houses to keep people awake; it happened in more ceremonial routines to make an example of rule breakers, runaways, and rebels. In those moments, the pain and psychological trauma of the person being whipped became collective. Slaves usually knew the people being whipped, cared for them afterward, were there when the offending acts took place, and had done the same things themselves in the past.

Other ever-present reminders of the plantation's disciplinary regime were bloodhounds so vicious they "could drag you out of the woods in their jaws," and makeshift jails, for which just about any space could be requisitioned.[96] Outside witnesses described men and women being kept in holes beneath the overseers' cabins, iron collars placed about slaves' necks, heads forced through stocks, and prisoners left in the damp and cold.[97] As Fredrika Bremer poignantly concluded in later years, "This is the history of the sugar-cane before it comes into your coffee-cup."[98] Enslaved people in Cuba challenged these systems of brutality in a number of ways, however. Some of them were able to exploit the Spanish legal system that provided a formal channel for slaves to redress their grievances.[99] Many more of them resorted to other forms of resistance.

The gendered violence of rape and sexual assault was also deeply ingrained in the plantation culture, although these acts were often much less legible to those in power as serious transgressions. This violence, too, must often be inferred from other texts and testimonies, such as one account of an estate owner who "had been obliged to dismiss his mayoral, on account of his conduct to the women, which was producing the worst results."[100] These stories highlight the callous devaluation of enslaved women's bodies that was central to black captivity and ignominy, and the extent to which sexual assault on slave women was normalized. Like other black Atlantic women, female slaves in Cuba were presumed intrinsically available for the plantation's white male workforce. But sporadic accounts from the period along with the substantially higher numbers of men on most estates, many of them without partners, suggest that black women also had to be vigilant about sexual violation from black men.

In the aftermath of the slave trade ban, slaveholders began to purchase African women in ever-increasing numbers, hoping to ensure the regime's health and longevity.[101] Right up through the 1840s, however, plantations struggled to maintain the desired number of women. Especially on the sugar mills, it was not unusual for men to outnumber women two to one, although the demographics were significantly more balanced on coffee plantations.[102] Greater scholarly attention must be paid to the pervasive possibility of sexual violence that met black women in the slave cabins and barracks as well as in white men's beds. In tracking the lives of enslaved women from Africa to Cuba, there is no way to know how many times women were raped during times of war or domestic servitude, en route to coastal destinations, in the coastal barracks, on slave ships, and of course on the farms, plantations, and homes of the island. This recurrent infliction of sexual harm—like whippings, shackles, and plantation cells—offers a different way to map the slave's corporeal displacement to and within Cuba, and underscores the importance of reconciling this bodily ledger with the profits of sale.

While the bloody conditions of plantation existence were impetus enough for enslaved men and women to rebel, free people who lived and worked in the rural areas were also highly motivated to participate in the 1844 movement. Most *libres* in the countryside were not born free but had managed to purchase their freedom as adults. One traveler opined that "in no part of the world, where slavery exists, is manumission so frequent as in the island of Cuba; for Spanish legislation . . . favors in an extraordinary degree the attainment of freedom."[103] While the path to *coartación*—literally "cutting the ties" by purchasing one's freedom in installments—was littered with hardships and difficulties, it was nevertheless true that by the mid-nineteenth century Cuba had the largest free black population in the Americas. In 1827 this population was counted at 106,484. By 1841 the number had reached 152,838—increasing by close to 50,000 people in less than twenty years.[104]

The free black population in Cuba has long been assumed to be synonymous with an *urban* black population, that is to say with people either born in the cities or who had migrated there. Yet the consistency with which free black people surface in the records of rural life paints a very different picture. The existing scholarship has shown that the cities were home to the largest free black populations, but it is also clear that a considerable number of free people chose to remain in the countryside once they had paid their final installments. Scores of newly freed blacks built homes and worked land plots right on the outskirts of their former plantations.[105]

On small farms and estates across western Cuba, slave women and men saved whatever money they could get by selling pigs and chickens, garden-plot vegetables, and their own handiwork, with the hope of joining the legally free. Yet upon paying the last installment on their freedom contract and formally receiving their manumission papers, these individuals left behind more than hellish memories of the fields. Frequently their departure also required them to leave behind spouses, children, godparents, and other kin.[106] For all these reasons, some newly freed blacks chose to remain in the rural districts where they had lived the rest of their Cuban lives, often putting down roots in the vicinity of their former plantations.

The other crushing reality that newly free people faced was the question of where to work and how to maintain a livelihood. Some free people chose to tend small plots of land or sought artisan and trade jobs in the nearest towns. But many of the newly freed ended up working on their old estates. Free black men in particular were often employed seasonally on the estates, often clearing land or working as carpenters or tile makers. The documents examined in this study have yet to identify free black women who returned to work on the plantations. Many free women tended their land and their homes, but others sought work in local towns as washerwomen, cooks, and so forth.[107]

All free people however, were pulled into some of the same cycles of work, exploitation, and discrimination that defined the lives of enslaved people. For example, free black men were often harassed by local overseers, and one traveler noticed "the vexations they receive from the *capitanes de partido* [judges of the district], and *cabos de ronda* [foremen of the night patrols], who plunder them to the utmost extent by pretexts and infamous exactions."[108] The overlapping spheres of work and play, discipline and discrimination, family and cultural practices connected free and enslaved people in many ways, particularly in and around the plantations. Although the status of *libre* versus *esclavo* was hardly a trivial distinction for black rural dwellers in the nineteenth century, the worlds that slaves and free people inhabited were often very much the same.

While the lives of urban free people are often depicted as being distinctly different from those of rural black people, their experiences also were closely connected to them in a variety of ways. The people who made up the black populations of Matanzas, Havana, and other major cities spanned the social spectrum in race, ethnicity, occupation, and cultural identification. Few descriptions of the urban landscape were complete without them. As one crossed the bridges of Matanzas and headed down its narrow streets, one might see men of color driving carriages over rickety streets, black women buying vegetables for their employers, or young mulatto servants trailing their señoras to church services.

By 1841 free people accounted for one fourth of Cuba's population, and this ever-increasing number of people who were black but not enslaved was not lost on white Cubans, who began to legislate away the citizenship rights of free black people.[109] The massive expansion of racial slavery during those years ensnared all people of color, enslaved or not.[110] Landholders in the countryside, for example, were not allowed to hire black laborers unless the latter produced free papers or a legal permit signed by local authorities. Stories like those of Cristóbal Agramonte—compelled to deliver appropriate paperwork to the local *comisario* when he returned from rural Macuriges—or José Francisco Matamoros, who had to get a license to return for his daughter's baptism, can be found throughout the testimonies.[111] The experience of José Subiza, arrested after being taken for a slave, was also not uncommon.[112] These measures provided a constant reminder, especially to black urban men, that the discipline of slavery was often inescapable. Indeed it was sometimes only a permit away.

Yet even in the face of this antiblack thought and practice, many groups of urban free people found ways to survive and prosper. Scores of these men and women made their living doing manual labor and performing odd jobs. Black men worked along the docks and wharves, rolled tobacco and cigars, sold small trade items, and traversed the countryside to cut trees, construct buildings, and make tiles. Free women of color cooked meals, sewed and laundered clothes, sold foodstuffs in the street, ran inns and taverns, took care of white children, made soap and candles, and assisted their husbands and fathers with their businesses.[113]

The free men who enjoyed the greatest material comfort and social prestige usually worked in managerial tasks or artisan trades—as dock foremen, tailors, carpenters, shoemakers, masons, barbers/blood-letters, and so forth. Or they worked in more traditional middle-class professions as dentists, teachers, and musicians. Women of color with a certain skill and social rank were more likely to become midwives, preschool teachers, or perhaps shop owners. By the time of La Escalera, free black people had become so intimately associated with this kind of labor that it was difficult to find white people—creole, peninsular, or otherwise—to maintain the artisan trades. To have one's shoes soled, saddle repaired, shirt tailored, or child delivered, one was usually forced to seek out a person of color.[114] Scores of men in this artisanal class also joined black and mulatto military battalions, which offered unparalleled paths to social ascent for black men.[115]

As in slave societies throughout the Atlantic, a person's skin color and cultural legibility in Cuba often influenced her or his ability to obtain everything from jobs, to gifts, to compliments—sometimes with gendered consequences. Urbanites of color keenly understood that the distinction between *moreno* (black) and *pardo* (mulatto) was no legal fiction. These classifications, and the color gradations marked by such categories as *chino* or *trigueno*, merged with a careful calculus of race that proliferated throughout the Spanish-speaking world.[116] By contrast, the racial logic of the countryside was heavily driven by the overriding distinction between free and enslaved, and it was generally flattened out in dichotomous terms of "whiteness" and "blackness." The category of *mulato* most certainly existed in the rural areas, but it was common for mulattos to be subsumed under the category of "black," *especially* if they were slaves. The stakes of these distinctions undoubtedly became higher in the urban areas and among free people, yet no one formula defined the free "colored" bourgeoisie in Cuba.[117] Race, education, occupation, family background, wealth, cultural affinity, and geography all helped to determine one's social circles and access.[118]

The most privileged of this elite black and mulatto class managed to attain wealth and property that even many white Cubans could only dream about. Many in this upper stratum of free blacks rode in fine carriages, owned stately homes, dressed in sumptuous clothing, and sometimes owned small groups of African slaves. In the Havana of the 1840s, one could have one's suit tailored by Francisco Uribe, hear an orchestra conducted by Claudio Brindis de Salas, read poetry written by Plácido, or have one's teeth cleaned by Andrés Dodge. These men were among those who most chafed at the racial discipline of their world, who could most easily sense the higher echelons of society just beyond their reach, and who became some of the most central conspirators in the urban movement to topple the Spanish government in 1844.

Studies of black urban women are only slowly emerging. Luz Mena has shown that free and enslaved women of color were a pervasive presence in the urban landscape, especially in Havana.[119] Like their counterparts elsewhere in Latin America, black, mulatta, and African women became a constant presence in the island's courts and legal offices. As more and more women purchased their liberty, obtained freedom for their children, or were born legally free, the Spanish legal system became a part of their daily arsenal. During the mid-nineteenth century, these free women merged with urban slaves, pardo and moreno battalions, market women and dockworkers, artisans and escaped slaves to create a heterogeneous and fluid black community ripe for insurrection.

The 1844 movement, built and sustained by this heterogeneous group of African descendants, jolted the already unstable political landscape of colonial Cuba and the Spanish Empire itself. Particularly in the urban sectors, many movement participants had watched as most of Latin America gained its independence. They had become involved in political movements that leveled trenchant critiques at the Spanish regime. And it was clear to them that the dismantling of black citizenship was intricately tied to their status as a colony.

In 1824 the Spanish Empire looked vastly different than it had at the turn of the century. The battle of Ayacucho in December had ended over two decades of revolutionary struggle in South and Central America, and two years later the last strongholds of royalist resistance were defeated in southern Chile. By 1826 every former Spanish colony on the mainland had declared its independence, from New Spain to Río de la Plata. During all of this upheaval Cuba remained loyal to Spain, largely because white creoles believed that any independence struggle would incite the rapidly growing slave population to press for its own freedom. Memories of Saint-Domingue tied independence to racial anarchy, destruction of property, and threats to white life. Thus to paraphrase one historian, Cuba's fear of its black population outweighed the dismay with its colonial status.[120]

The Spanish Crown rewarded Cuba by granting several long-desired concessions to its creole elites. By the 1820s however, Spain was reeling from the Napoleonic wars that had depleted its treasury, from its own internal battles over the new liberal constitution of 1812, from the loss of nearly all of its overseas empire, and from a new wave of independence conspiracies and slave revolts in Cuba and Puerto Rico. After being deposed by liberal forces for three years, the newly reinstalled King Ferdinand began to reconsolidate royal power in Spain by suppressing the 1812 constitution, jailing and executing hundreds of its supporters, and centralizing Spain's hold on its remaining colonial possessions: Puerto Rico, the Philippines, and Cuba.

In the aftermath of the mainland independence wars scores of Spanish soldiers, government ministers, priests, and merchants began to pour into Cuba and Puerto Rico. Their arrival introduced more tension between Spaniards (*peninsulares*) and Creoles than ever before. And with some 20,000 troops taking up posts across Cuba, the island became more heavily militarized than at any point in its history.[121] In line with the repressive mood back in Spain, the Cuban governor, Dionisio Vives (generally referred to as the captain general), began a systematic campaign to eradicate any vestiges of liberal thinking and anticolonial activity in Cuba. In 1825 Vives was accordingly granted *facultades omnímodas* (absolute powers) over the island.[122]

More than any other event during this period, the appointment of Miguel Tacón to the position of captain general (1834–1838) galvanized the nationalist sentiments of the liberal creole community. While previous governors had made some effort to appease the island's elite planter class, Tacón made no such efforts. His commitment to absolute monarchy prejudiced him against all Cubans, and he deemed their interests inherently opposed to those of the Crown. Tacón's administration marked the first time that upper-class white creoles lost their favored place in the colonial order, and the lenience they had enjoyed in previous decades evaporated almost overnight.[123]

Tacón implemented a widespread culture of policing and surveillance to consolidate his rule.[124] Tightening the control over the island that had begun under Vives, the new captain general condemned, deported, or banished many in his own administration. In the wake of several independence movements in the 1820s, he prohibited public meetings of any kind, confiscated liberal books and printed materials, and vigorously censored the press. Elite clubs such as the Sociedades Filarmónicas and the Sociedad Económica de los Amigos del País that had been central to Havana's intellectual culture were now viewed with suspicion and mistrust. The slightest discussion of reform was treated as treason, and it became a crime to even say the word independence or anything antagonistic to slavery in public.[125]

One of the most inflammatory measures of Tacón's rule was the 1837 legislation that eliminated all representation of Cuban, Puerto Rican, and Filipino colonists from the Spanish seat of government, the Cortes. Colonial seats in the Cortes had only been won in 1810 under the new constitution, and men like José Antonio Saco and Domingo del Monte, who became synonymous with early nationalist thought, were outraged at this dismissal.[126] The longtime Cuban resident Richard Madden concluded that the act's passage "produced a feeling of hatred against the mother country that never before existed in Cuba," driving anticolonial sentiment and action in the coming decades.[127]

Cubans of color arguably had even more reason to feel embittered toward the colonial regime during the 1830s and 1840s. Thousands of them were of course regularly subjected to the horrors of legal servitude. Yet for most enslaved people, particularly in the rural areas, their immediate torment came at the hands of white people of various nationalities, especially Cuban creoles. Rural black people also condemned colonial rule, of course, but their condemnation of colonialism was filtered first and foremost through a condemnation of slavery. They sought an end to the white power structure—be it creole or peninsular.

But people of color in the urban areas—particularly those of a certain class—could more readily point to a colonial system that directly denigrated them as black subjects. During the 1830s and 1840s, free people of color in Matanzas and Havana were targeted with unprecedented levels of abuse and violence. Police officers and urban officials, many of whom came from the flood of newly displaced Spanish military men, harassed people of color with petty fines and charges, demands to produce work permits, coercions to renew travel licenses, and sharp restrictions on socializing. A wide range of daily activities could easily bring any person of color under colonial scrutiny, and a significant portion of black urban life was rendered unlawful, immoral, and legally punishable during that period.

Much of the heightened militarization of Tacón's administration was concentrated in urban areas with large black communities, such as the Havana neighborhoods of Jesús María and Guadalupe, where Tacón intensified infantry patrols and increased the size of the police force. The Sundays and holidays when black people often danced and drummed became increasingly subdued as the colonial state sought to establish "tranquility" in its public domains. As state surveillance began to invade the most intimate aspects of black people's lives, this period produced heightened alienation and anger in urban black communities. Although their lived experiences were often vastly different, Cubans of all colors could cite some sort of grievance against the colonial government. Beginning in the late eighteenth century, these collective feelings of injustice gave rise to political mobilizations against the Spanish Crown, some of which were multiracial in scope. In 1812 a series of insurgent movements collectively known as the Aponte Rebellion erupted across the island. The Aponte Rebellion, which condemned slavery and colonialism and took inspiration from the Haitian Revolution, stands as one of the most important political struggles of the nineteenth century.[128]

This current of anticolonial energy became even more concentrated during the 1820s as independence movements raged in Mexico and Central and South America, and as a new constitutional period came to life on the Iberian Peninsula. Some of the best-known independence plots emerged from Cuba's masonic lodges and secret societies, including the Soles y Rayos de Bolívar conspiracy in 1823 and the Gran Legión del Águila Negra conspiracy in 1829, both of which were harshly repressed. Other plots against the Spanish continued to surface well into the 1830s and 1840s, some of which were mobilized by people of color.[129] The latter included a demonstration organized by rural Lucumí rebels at the outer walls of Havana in 1835, a massive protest of black soldiers and harbor workers in 1839, and a strike staged by Lucumí slaves who were building Domingo Aldama's Havana palace in 1841. The responses to these protests were swift and brutal.[130] These movements made urban black Cubans highly conscious of their political situation and helped them develop a vocal critique of the institutions that denigrated their lives.[131]

Alongside this growing political awareness in the cities, colonial authorities also had to contend with frequent and destructive insurgencies mounted by rural slaves. By early 1844 provincial authorities like the governor of Matanzas were acutely aware of how often they had to dispatch military troops, arm and reinforce district captains, and calm white residents. From the 1820s to the 1840s colonial military officials from Güines to Bayamo were summoned to quell no fewer than twenty-seven confrontations with rebel slaves, revolts that became increasingly concentrated in the west-central districts of the island. A few of these uprisings mobilized hundreds of people, including the Guamacaro rebellion of 1825, the Bemba rebellion of March 1843, and the Triunvirato rebellion of November 1843.[132] Each resulted in extensive damage to estates, injury or death to several white employees, and harsh repercussions for the island's slave population.

In response to the 1825 rebellion, colonial authorities developed a repressive apparatus that would have lasting effects on Cuban blacks for years to come. The expanded military presence under Vives and Tacón increased the frequency of *rondas* (patrols) that circulated in the rural districts and the number of vigilante slave hunters who tracked down runaways. In addition, the government created Cuba's infamous Comisión Militar Ejecutiva y Permanente and between 1825 and 1844 issued two sets of slave codes. These measures both responded to and created an intensive wave of slave rebellion that continued into the 1840s, especially as new Africans continued to arrive and swell the ranks of recalcitrant slaves. Many of the threats to Cuba's security and prosperity that the commission was established to protect came from *afrodescendientes*.[133]

Alongside the anticolonial and racial friction that continued to erupt across the island, the colonial government also faced another form of powerful opposition in the form of the British-led abolitionist movement. In 1807 Britain outlawed the slave trade, touching off a heated ideological war with the remaining slave societies of the Americas. Cuba was among the primary targets.[134] In the decades that followed British statesmen and abolitionists struggled to reign in Cuba's thriving slave trade and the incredible wealth it was producing. In 1817 and again in 1835, Britain signed anti–slave trade treaties with Spain, but for years these treaties remained essentially legal fictions.[135]

By the mid-nineteenth century, it had become common practice for illegal slavers to land on the Cuban coast with 150 to 1,000 or more slaves.[136] British squadrons pursued these illegal slavers and set up mixed commissions in Havana, Kingston, and Freetown to prosecute them.[137] Yet as late as a decade after La Escalera, Maturin Ballou could still write of Cuba: "She is solemnly pledged by treaty stipulations, to make unceasing war against it, and yet she tacitly connives at its continuance, and all the world knows that slaves are monthly, almost weekly, landed in Cuba."[138]

Increasingly faced with new victories for the antislavery interests, the Spanish colonial state in Cuba adopted a singular prerogative: "Employ all measures to frustrate the plans of the abolitionists, [and] adopt the necessary measures to secure the tranquility of the island."[139] The surviving documents convey one important message: antislavery ideologies were omnipresent, and they had to be guarded against at all costs. This included everything from scrutinizing English-language newspapers to monitoring visiting British nationals.[140]

Antislavery crusading in Cuba reached its zenith with the appointment of David Turnbull to the newly combined position of British consul and superintendent of liberated Africans in August 1840.[141] Turnbull effectively acted as a one-man crusader for the abolitionist cause, and his appointment was greeted with pure alarm by wealthy planters and colonial officials. His campaigns to assist *emancipados* (Africans taken from apprehended slave ships), his inquires on behalf of free people from the British Caribbean resold in Cuba, and his unannounced visits to estates suspected of owning illegal slaves enraged Cuba's planter elite.[142]

Early in Turnbull's appointment ministers in London and Madrid were "informed of the grave situation created by Turnbull," and the latter even asked for an audience with the British foreign secretary—that he might "take measures to substitute [Turnbull] for a less controversial figure"—but to no avail. Urgent pleas to remove Turnbull from office continued throughout the superintendent's tenure in Havana.[143] The naming of David Turnbull to the British consulate marked the highest stage of what had become a highly charged ideological war on both sides of the Atlantic.[144]

The recurrent challenges to Cuba's slave regime and the increasing dissatisfaction with colonial rule set the stage for a series of critical conversations to unfold. Against this backdrop the 1844 movement began to take shape in living rooms, cane fields, slave barracks, general stores, and taverns across the western department. In these spaces the plans for a comprehensive rebel movement began to emerge, which created unlikely coalitions and strange bedfellows. Slave organizers radicalized by previous waves of rural rebellion found in the 1840s an explosive conjunction: a relentless British abolitionist movement, a rapidly spreading anticolonial sentiment, and an increasingly politicized sector of urban free people. Across the western countryside black residents began to use their mobility and networks to organize a revolutionary struggle.

Chapter Two

Rural Slave Networks and
Insurgent Geographies

It is not that History is obliterated by this sunrise.
It is there in Antillean geography, in the vegetation itself.

|||||||| Derek Walcott

By the 1840s the conversion of the sugar heartland of Matanzas from
a rugged and sparsely settled frontier to a lucrative plantation zone had
produced a ruthless labor regimen marked by elaborate systems of discipline,
surveillance, and control. Yet, in the midst of all this brutality, enslaved
men and women found ways to shape their worlds, and contemplated
means to unmake them. Those slaves questioned in 1844 consistently (if
inadvertently) revealed that many of them found ways to slip through the
cracks of the plantation world, or to create cracks where there were none.
Plastering over these cracks required continual effort from planters, local
managers, and colonial employees throughout Cuba.

As Stephanie Camp has shown for the U.S. South, slaveholders tended to
express their power in deeply spatial terms, through "a spatial impulse" to
control terrain and regulate movement.[1] Throughout the Caribbean slaveholders and managers attempted to restrict the worlds of enslaved people
in similar ways, and by the mid-nineteenth century, Cuban plantations were
profoundly organized around this logic of containment. At the center of
slaveholders' effort to contain black movement in Cuba was the need to
establish fixed boundaries that presented themselves as immutable and sovereign. This then was a question not only of black restraint but intimately
about the "where" of that control. More importantly, it was about the ability to delineate what was possible for slaves to experience and know. Thus
the plantation was invariably more than just a physical space. It was also a
psychic space intended to travel with the enslaved—demarcating the bor-

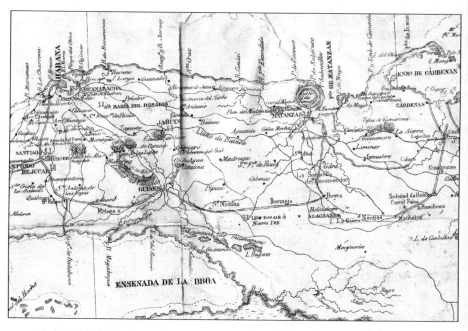

Map of the regions of Havana, Matanzas, and Cárdenas. Courtesy of the Archivo Nacional de Cuba.

ders and possibilities of the known world — beyond which they were not to travel, experience, or imagine.

But the documents of the period demonstrate that enslaved people used their "Antillean geography" to push open and envisage new modes of existence. As Camp observes, the use of plantation space was highly contested; planters sought to exert spatial and temporal control over black bodies, yet those same black bodies pushed back and created their own routes, itineraries, internal maps, and places of refuge. Camp accordingly describes the "rival geographies" that enslaved people, and enslaved women in particular, carved out across the U.S. South.[2] The social and physical landscapes of Cuba and the U.S. South were of course different, and the spatial fantasies that slaves and slaveholders nourished in these two locales were necessarily different. Nevertheless, Camp's framework offers a valuable model to explore the methods and routes through which black Cubans transgressed their enslavement. As such, this chapter looks closely at the rival geographies that Cuban slaves created within and beyond the boundaries of the plantation.

When scholars like Katherine McKittrick speak of black geographies, they speak of the terrain afforded by landscapes of earth, flesh, memory, and imagination but also—most poignantly—of the "terrain of political struggle." For McKittrick, understanding the geographies that map out black life, from the slave ship to the plantation grounds, enables a deeper understanding of where and how these struggles emerge and where the urgency for this struggle resides. The Martinican literary critic Edouard Glissant similarly believed that for Afro-Caribbean people, the landscape offered a particularly precious way to know something about Caribbean consciousness. In claiming that "the landscape is our monument, its meanings can only be traced on the underside," Glissant contended that the landscape offered a way to access what is barely perceptible in black subjectivity.[3]

Following this line of thought—if the rural landscape represents one of the few evidences or historical memories of lives lived on the underside, moving through its sites and stories may very well yield something telling about how black Cubans imagined and structured their resistance. Simply stated, this chapter will be concerned with slave mobility and networks, the spaces this mobility traversed and created, and the ways in which these contributed to the emergence of a rural movement. Mapping out some of the public and the liminal spaces where enslaved black Cubans reclaimed their bodies, time, and relationships will enable us to understand how black Cubans continually created their own rival geographies.[4]

In the 1840s, however, this rival geography became an *insurgent* geography. In following the paths that African and Cuban-born slaves took through the rural plantation world of 1843 and 1844—through cane fields and boiling houses, across neighboring plantations to dances and rituals, through thickly wooded hinterlands and rural roads, and out to general stores and into town squares—one can also piece together an insurgent movement that grew up in the western Cuban provinces during the early 1840s. Through their personal mobility, their circuits of labor, their social networks, their wayward acts, and their ritual practices, rural black residents established familiarity among themselves and created a larger culture of black transgression. It was through this habitual movement and this skein of relationships that the 1844 movement came to life.

||||||| Rural Black Mobility and Networks

Of all the pieces of black life confined and controlled under slave systems across the Americas, black mobility was one of the most important but difficult for slaveowners to police. Throughout 1843 and 1844, black people in Cuba moved around in ways seen and sanctioned, unseen and illicit. Both ways proved instrumental to the rise and propagation of a rebellious movement in 1844. It is to these sanctioned forms of mobility that this chapter will now turn, as the insatiable needs of sugar required a select group of black people to be mobile, and sometimes highly so. Such mobility in turn enabled select groups of male slaves in particular to reconfigure the spatial and social limits of the traditional estates, to nurture the growth of an organic rural leadership, and to facilitate the spread of revolutionary ideas within their districts.

Because black laborers made up the vast majority of the plantation work-force, some of the outside plantation business was inevitably conducted by people of color. In some ways, nothing could have been more normal than to see black men (and on rarer occasions, women) moving about the Matanzas countryside performing tasks for their owners or running requested errands for other white bosses. While the luxury of mobility was mainly afforded to a small group of privileged males, these men did not have to be unusually cunning to find their way off the estates or unduly stretch the limits of their assigned jobs. The needs of the sugar regime were voracious and the health of that regime often required the very mobility that estate managers and overseers sought to prevent. Slaves with privilege on the plantations hence found opportunities for contact with laborers on other estates, in rural towns, and in the city of Matanzas. Cuba's slave institution in many ways sowed the proverbial seeds of its own demise, unwittingly laying the contours for a larger movement to unfold. This phenomenon manifested itself in similar but distinctive ways throughout Latin America and the U.S. South.[5]

Particularly for those who held positions like wagon driver, coachman, muleteer, or foreman, mobility was often inherent to their work. While the earliest railroads had been laid in the late 1830s, it would be years before they were extensive enough to link most of the countryside with the major cities and towns. With the exception of a few planters whose political in-fluence could direct the railroads near their own estates, most slaveowners relied on a small group of wagon drivers and muleteers to haul finished products to warehouses and rail stations. Some of these wagon drivers were free black men, and a few were even white, but by 1844 the majority of them were black slave men from the plantations.[6]

While the deplorable state of Cuban roads made his work incredibly arduous, for a slave cart driver, the freedom to leave the plantation peri-odically and spend time alone or with a few other drivers was precious.

These drivers took the sugar to warehouses, docks, and wharves and carried supplies to nearby plantations. In the process, they learned the geography for miles around and met people throughout their districts. And as they traveled between plantations or on the byways of Matanzas, news, written messages, and even packages sometimes circulated with their cargo.

Scores of men accused of playing prominent roles in the 1844 movement held these kinds of positions, and more than a few spoke of rebellious plans that emerged during the course of this work. In late February of 1844, for example, José Carabalí—an accused rebel organizer on the Las Nieves sugar plantation—reported a conversation between himself and Tomás Lucumí, in which Tomás asked José "if he wanted to fight against the whites." Four days later, José met up with a Mina slave named Andrés from another property who normally drove a sugar-laden cart to the Bemba railroad station. Andrés allegedly used this opportunity to inform José that "the blacks of his estate had decided to wage a war with the whites."[7] Slaves like Felipe Carabalí spoke of a black wagon driver "who always passed by the main road and spoke to him[,] . . . saying that he and his companions were going to rise up."[8] For these men movement was woven into the fabric of their work and they were apparently able to shave off small slivers of sugar's time to use for their own purposes.[9]

Coachmen had similar opportunities to puncture the discipline that rural estates tried to impose, and they helped to fuel the growth of a rural movement. This story of José Trinidad, a muleteer and coachman for a local sugar proprietor highlights this fact particularly well. About thirty years of age, José Trinidad was described as tall and thin and "well-dressed," with a scar on the right side of his face. As a coachman, José worked in much closer proximity to his master than most other slaves on the mill. In addition to driving, he could easily be required to wait on his master while the latter conducted business, to lift ladies over puddles, even to carry grown men if the carriage could not move.[10]

During his travels, José was said to have patronized Havana's underground economy and obtained a flask of gunpowder. During his return trips to the countryside, José had occasion to stop with his owner at the Soledad de Jáuregui estate. During these Soledad trips, José was described as "always" going by the cabin of Mamerto Arará, one of the two main organizers there. One witness claimed that in Mamerto's cabin the Havana gunpowder reached its destination. Other examples of coachmen's transgressions can be found throughout the testimony.[11]

In addition to cart drivers and coachmen, male personal domestic servants also had occasion to be mobile, particularly if they were required to travel with their owners. It was common for white planters and their families to travel with one or more of their domestic servants, particularly when they journeyed back to the country for holiday balls and festivities. The male proprietors frequently took trips between their country estates and the major cities to attend to business matters, and stories of "Ramón who is with his owner in Havana," or "José Criollo who is traveling to the countryside with his master," were commonplace. Such travels were much rarer for female slaves, though there is reason to believe that some did take place.[12] In the Rancho Veloz region, for example, the manservant Ciriaco Criollo frequently traveled with his owner to the Ingenio Santa Rita, where the two usually spent the night. According one witness, Ciriaco spoke to several slaves there about a coming insurrection.[13]

Workers like wagon drivers and muleteers straddled the world of those with privilege and those without, but domestics and coachmen in many ways occupied a different world from the rest of the plantation laborers. Among those who moved most frequently among the many worlds of the plantation were the black assistant overseers or the contramayorales. Like other privileged slaves, these assistant foremen were able to etch out moments of independence for themselves, inserting moments of reprieve into their enslavement that few others could. For contramayorales, movement between rural properties was also a critical part of their geography of labor.

Rancho Veloz was one of the far eastern districts, in what is today Villa Clara, and was probably still very underdeveloped in the 1840s. Two contra-mayorales there, Julián Mandinga and Perico Criollo, were described as "the ones who took care of the trips off the estate, running errands to different places."[14] Hilario, an overseer in the same district, was sent to obtain lime for the boiling house. All three men were either accused of acting as the primary rebel organizers on their plantations or of becoming involved in seditious conversations while on their errands. Other assistant foremen also were frequently asked to carry messages, obtain supplies, or conduct minor business on behalf of the plantation administrators or overseers, and some were accused of using these opportunities to discuss the coming rebellion.[15]

In this way butlers accompanying their owners, coachmen driving their owners, overseers on occasional errands, and wagon drivers making deliveries had unique access to the open spaces of Matanzas, and the greatest ability to navigate the province's terrain with a small measure of freedom. This mobility was also a highly gendered form of movement. Women rarely held these kinds of positions, and they were rarely recorded as moving about for work purposes. Because men held these privileged positions, men by and large left the estates for work. This fact would have critical implications for who made up the local estate vanguard of the coming rebellion. While many—though as we will see not all—women were more likely to be tied to home spaces, slave men with elite positions found ways to expand their personal geographies by moving around in ways both seen and unseen. Thus men with power on the estates traversed new terrain—literally and figuratively—in the business that took them off the estates and in the work that took them to other plantations.

This ability to travel to other plantations, local towns, and as far as Matanzas and Havana offered unparalleled opportunities for some male slaves to expand their own horizons and meet a wide spectrum of people of color and whites of varying nationalities, some of whom became caught up in powerful political currents. When they stepped off the estates, these men merged with a larger stream of rural black workers who traveled the roads and towns of Matanzas, making contacts and connections as they went. This mobility also propelled them into something of a liminal space between slavery and freedom, what Douglas Egerton has called the "twilight world."[16]

While these men were the primary beneficiaries of their positions, the fact of movement did spill beyond the upper echelons of the slave community as scores of black laborers found other ways to be mobile. For those who could not justify leaving the plantation grounds for any other purpose, the opportunities for sanctioned mobility were largely channeled into one day of the week, Sunday. Sundays were usually the days that plantation dances and drummings were held, and these celebrations became focal points of plantation activity. For field laborers in particular these hours were among the few not claimed by their superintendents, though the little time available to women was often taken up by domestic chores or children. Those not dancing used their Sundays to cook, tend their *conucos* (garden plots), or rest, but again those who cooked and tended were often women. Still other slaves would sneak away for flirtation and sexual entertainment.[17]

Sunday was also one of the few times, if not the *only* time, that free black neighbors and slaves from adjoining estates met little or no resistance when they came to visit. This day also provided opportunities, otherwise forbidden, for trips to nearby plantations or into the closest town. In 1843 and 1844 a number of men who took an interest in the coming insurrection but were unlikely to be mobile during the week found opportunities to attend to personal errands *and* conduct more political business on Sunday.[18] A slave named Julio Criollo testified, for example, that he "left one Saturday unbe-knownst to his overseer [*á escondidas de su mayoral*]" to go to a local general store and when he came out, "he ran into [a free black man who] told him that they were ready for the uprising."[19]

One particularly intriguing case of this mobility is that of Miguel Lucumí, who would reportedly "go to the general stores every Sunday." Miguel's mobility was tellingly framed in terms of a weak work ethic; one of his fellow slaves testified that "since they bought him, [Miguel] has been a poor worker, because he was always sick or trying to roam about [*siempre quería andar paseando ó estava enfermo*]." Sometimes Miguel was rumored to get as far as Matanzas.[20] During his sojourns between Sabanilla and Matan-zas, Miguel reportedly spoke to several "outside blacks" and returned to tell others about these conversations.[21] Other couriers and field lieutenants also traveled about on Sundays, using that day to circulate the latest information about the coming revolt.

Thus in Macuriges Andrés Mina drove sugar into the town of Bemba, and further west Simón Criollo drove cargo into the town of Jarúco. Other rural black men were said to have made it even farther. Miguel Lucumí patronized the general stores of Sabanilla and was rumored to have got-ten as far as Matanzas, and the coachman José Trinidad reportedly bought gunpowder while in Havana. All of these slave men—later named as rebel organizers—either were cited as, or admitted to, meeting people, making purchases, and obtaining information in the course of these sojourns. The 1844 testimonies are filled with stories of individuals such as these who moved back and forth between the rural regions and the towns and cities of Matanzas. Scattered as they are, they might initially seem inconsequen-tial. Lined up next to one another, however, they call attention to a steady stream of laboring men who crisscrossed the region, scores of whom would eventually carry in their persons the blueprint for a massive rebellion. Both sanctioned errands and illicit trips frequently brought country-dwellers—slave and free—into these towns.

In other instances free black urban residents traveled out to the rural plantations, sometimes for long spells. In a sort of reverse migration, these free men from the urban centers often came to the countryside in search of work, which was usually plentiful during these years of growth and ex-pansion. For example in March 1844, a free African named Jacinto Lucumí testified to authorities about his involvement in the local movement. Jacinto stated that "about three and a half months ago, he believes it was a Sunday, he ran into [a free black man named] Campuzano on his way to buy things at the Beronda general store." Though Catalino Campuzano lived in the city of Matanzas, he earned money digging wells in the rural districts. This work took him out to the Rancho Veloz district, where he met the Lucumí carpenter Jacinto.[22] Campuzano would later testify that he had learned about "a conspiracy of blacks against whites" from two African organizers in Matanzas.[23]

Other free black men were charged with even more direct involvement in the events of that year. Toward the end of 1843 two black city-dwellers, Catalino Criollo and Margarito Quintana, joined a work gang heading south from Matanzas to the district of Yumurí. The two were contracted as masons to build the sugar-purging house on the property of Francisco Calderón; likely a very new mill if no such building yet existed. The following year several of Calderón's slaves reported that Margarito and Catalino had become deeply embroiled in the political organizing on the estate as principal organizers.

Margarito and Catalino were described as having maintained close contact with a small group of Gangá men, particularly the contramayoral Cleto, later cited as the primary leader at Calderón.[22] When hostilities broke out, Margarito and Catalino were to bring rifles and bayonets to Calderón and take the recruits to Matanzas, "where they had many people gathered."[24] Stories of this kind proliferate throughout the testimony. They draw critical attention to the scores of slave men with mobility and free men seeking work who traversed the countryside and regularly exchanged information, news, and gossip. Between the fall of 1842 and the winter of 1844, these interactions effectively placed the rebellious inclinations of the countryside in dialogue with the currents of radicalism then emanating from cities like Matanzas. As we will see in chapter 4, some of the 1844 movement's best-known organizers formed part of this group of mobile free men who linked the urban and rural regions.

These were some of the ways—the legitimate and accepted ways—that black people punctured holes in the boundaries of their world during the daylight hours. A whole other world of activity seemed to open up once night fell. In the years leading up to 1844, scores of slaves were on the move after dark. The 1844 testimonies are filled with references to slaves who traveled at night to other estates, nearby woods or fields, and local taverns. While the daylight mobility was limited to those with permission, nighttime mobility was open to anyone who dared. Even slaves not intimately involved in planning a revolt were more willing to risk bold or seditious activities once night fell.[25]

In addition to stealing away to see loved ones, more than a few men and women used the protection of the night to attend clandestine gatherings and discuss an impending rebellion in the late months of 1843 and early 1844. Those questioned about a growing movement would later report their daytime encounters as chance encounters that interrupted their routines as they passed by the tile-making house, stood outside the boiling house, or headed to a nearby store for supplies. By contrast they invariably recounted the nighttime assemblies as more purposeful, more focused, and more secretive, frequently involving leaders or central organizers.

During the early months of 1844, dozens upon dozens of these meetings were taking place throughout the Matanzas countryside. In fact, it would not be an exaggeration to state that after the sun went down, the fissures of the Matanzas plantation system were literally pried open—sometimes wide open—as clandestine gatherings sprung up in locations across the province to acquaint workers with the growing movement. Rather than obscuring enslaved people's activities from view, these nighttime hours actually shed important *light* on a series of formal meetings. Such gatherings highlight the ways in which individual transgressions became collective as slaves in groups of five, ten, twenty, or thirty gathered to discuss a growing movement.

As the time for a projected rebellion drew near, one such congregation took place in late March 1844, in the eastern district of Ceja de Pablo. A week before Easter, Dionisio Criollo summoned workers on the Buena Suerte estate. Dionisio was a man of about twenty-five who worked as a coachman and domestic servant for Miguel Cárdenas. Dionisio, who was described as the most important leader at Buena Suerte, was known to travel back and forth to the nearby town of Coralillo to be trained as a carpenter. There he obtained information about an emerging resistance movement whose objective was, as he stated, "to cause the complete downfall of the whites, and to make the people of color masters of the Island." Early one morning Dionisio reportedly spread the word among the Buena Suerte workers to join him in a secret gathering. The incident was reported as follows:

> Eight days more or less before Holy Week, as the slaves were getting
> up in the morning with the ringing of the first bell [Ave María], and
> as all were preparing to make their way to their tasks. . . . Dionisio
> Criollo told them that on that same night he wanted to speak to
> them together, to which they agreed, [and with that] Dionisio left
> for the carpentry of Don Miguel Casaña, where he was learning the

carpenter's trade . . . Indeed that night, Dionisio gathered everyone together around the hour of ten [o'clock] after all the white workers had gone to bed. At his invitation, all the slaves left their cabins, with the exception of Elias, Gabriel, and Estanislao, who were in the boiling house, and the women Mónica Lucumí, Juana, Trinidad, and Crispina Criollas, who were sleeping in another part [of the ingenio] and could not come. . . . The occasion of this [meeting] was when Dionisio addressed some twenty slaves, among them men and women who made up the majority of the workforce of Buena Suerte, and discussed the planned uprising with all of them, a plan which earned their general approval; afterward he told them to be prepared for the Thursday of Holy Week, when it appeared the movement was scheduled to break out. Immediately thereafter, the contramayoral Candelario Criollo offered them these words: "Gentlemen, you already see what Dionisio is saying [is true]." They all agreed, and everyone withdrew to their cabins.[26]

During the sugar harvest season, nocturnal activities at Buena Suerte and other sugar mills were concentrated primarily around the open, plaza-like area known as the *batey*. For five or six months out of the year men like Elias, Gabriel, and Estanislao, members of the rotating sugarhouse gangs, remained hard at work practically until sunrise. It is also important to note that the testimonies describe four women—Mónica, Juana, Trinidad, and Crispina—as being unable to attend. It would be intriguing to know what kept them from participating. Were they working in the infirmary? Were they attending to the family of Miguel Cárdenas, or perhaps their own? Were they being forced to satisfy the sexual appetites of white overseers or managers? The answers to such questions would flesh out our understanding of how a rebellion took shape at Buena Suerte.

Dionisio apparently used the meeting to share with a critical mass of workers that a rebellion was looming. It seems that Dionisio's report was met with excitement, for "as soon as Dionisio spread this news, they accepted it with pleasure, and prepared themselves for when Dionisio would notify them to take part in the uprising." With the Easter attack date in sight, the people of Buena Suerte were ready.[27]

Farther back to the west in the settlement of Guanábana, a series of meetings was taking place on the coffee estate known as Buena Esperanza, belonging to the retired lieutenant Pedro Domech. For a number of reasons the Buena Esperanza meetings stand out as some of the most important political gatherings in the course of the 1843–44 resistance. A few reports of these gatherings claim that they attracted emissaries from miles around. Rotating attendees, whose numbers may have exceeded forty people, made their way to Buena Esperanza at night after the bell had rung for silence. These included slave men and women from three neighboring plantations—owned by Juan Bautista Caffini, Thomas Owens "the Englishman," and Francisco Ruell—as well as a small cohort of free black men and women from Matanzas.

On some nights the company allegedly met near the wood or coal shelters; at other times they gathered near the garden plots or coffee patches; still other times they met in the woods and clearings bordering the Domech property. Though the larger composition of the group changed with almost every meeting, a core group of individuals were consistently named as attending. These included eighteen men and three women from the estates above, two men with different owners near Matanzas, and four free black people from Matanzas. Some nineteen other free people were variously reported as attending one or two meetings, including an almost unheard of appearance by two free black women, and even one white man.[28]

It is important to note that those who attended these meetings escaped not just in ones or twos but in fives, sixes, and sevens as they came to the grounds of Buena Esperanza. Moreover, these gatherings beckoned to free people from the city of Matanzas, who would have had to travel almost thirty miles to reach the rural settlement of Guanábana. Such congregations therefore represent more than a small breach of protocol, custom, and legal decree.[29] Most of the cited attendees came from coffee plantations where security measures may have been less strict. But for such high numbers to consistently desert their estates these measures would have had to be *very* lax, or else those doing the guarding would themselves have had to be among the attendees. We will examine the high probability of this fact, and its significance for the planned rebellion, in greater detail presently.

In this way, black Cubans were able to constitute "twilight space" between freedom and enslavement by evading the prescribed restriction of mobility. Likewise, they took advantage of already existing spaces of liminality in the *linderos*, those uncultivated areas of forest between the orderly plantations. In his famous lithograph *Los ingenios*, Justo Cantero described the landscape of the Ácana sugar mill—the same mill that became a focal point of rebellion in 1843—nearly a decade after the rebellion's occurrence.[30] In a text accompanying the lithograph, Cantero described the success of the Ácana estate in terms of its twenty-five planted *caballerías* and twenty-three more that gave way to a potrero and wooded areas.[31] The distance between those hundreds of planted acres of planter glory and the uncultivated wood just beyond the plantation represented what Clyde Woods and Katherine McKittrick have called "the tension between that which is mapped and that which is unknown." So too did the distance between the world of the fields and the world of the slave cabins, between the labor of the fields—with its heat, exhaustion, and blood—and black people's visions of something better, and the very distance between death and survival, constitute the tension between what is "mapped" and what is "unknown."[32] Precisely this space between what was knowable and unreachable produced the black political culture that exploded so volatilely in 1843 and 1844.

In Cuba, domination was very much a spatial project embedded in the organization of the plantation itself, the access to its land, and the physicality of transforming that land into capital and profit. The boundaries between most properties were rather loosely defined, marked primarily by the places where straight rows of cane and coffee berries began to give way to *la manigua* and *el monte*—the woodlands, the hills, the wild. These unclaimed spaces formed something of a no-man's-land in the midst of a heavily regimented plantation world. Contrasting starkly with the neat hierarchies of sugar and coffee rows, these wild areas intervened in the plantation's sense of order and rigidity and became part of an alternative landscape for people seeking out temporary reprieve. La manigua and el monte thus represented the literal and figurative linderos—boundaries or borderlands—between carefully demarcated sugar realms and (e)states.

In this way the linderos offer an ideal framework in which to consider the historical terrain of the "unmapped" or the "unapparent."[33] From Matanzas to Barbados, forests were traditionally havens for enslaved people, and particularly potent places for slave men to reclaim their masculinity through activities like hunting. Moreover, wooded areas were often considered sacred spaces in Congolese and other West and Central African cosmologies. As such, plantation residents sought refuge there to perform sacred rituals, leave behind the suffocating barracoons, and snatch moments of privacy and freedom.[34]

On the Nueva Esperanza sugar mill, the rebel slave leader Román Macúa gathered together interested parties "at night after the white workers had gone to bed, in a place situated between the woods and the cane fields . . . and would exhort them not to be faint of heart about the uprising."[35] On the Montalvo property, Dimas Criollo was described as sending messages to José Santos Criollo from a neighboring estate to meet him at the linderos of their respective plantations to discuss an insurrection. The leader Patricio Gangá stated that three organizers from the nearby Nieves estate "would come every night to the path [*guardarralla*] at the estate border to have meetings." Similar meetings took place along the edges of insurgent properties before the March 1843 rebellion.[36] The unmapped land of wooded hills points to the means of survival that kept African people going far from home and hints at the political alternatives they created. In Cuba of 1843–44, these areas proved ideal for organizing resistance across plantation boundaries. It was in some ways fitting that these liminal spaces were appropriated to formulate plans at the edges of hope, reality, and possibility. The manigua thus became central to the insurgent geography that took shape in 1844.

Women like Caeytana from Nueva Esperanza and Juliana from Montalvo were also cited as attending some of these border gatherings. The stories of Caeytana and Juliana suggest that the movement that took place after nightfall opened up opportunities for women to leave their prescribed locales and take part in rebellious conversations. Women usually emerged in the testimony with greater frequency when these nighttime encounters were described. As such, the nocturnal hours make visible a gendered mobility that would otherwise be elided from the record. While the daytime was a temporal experience that often felt fixed and hedged in for enslaved people, especially women, the borders of the nighttime were more porous and fluid. Its boundaries tapered off in more subtle, staggered, and uncertain fashion and therefore could be more easily transgressed. This fact gestures to the strong possibility that "insurgent time" was also a gendered temporality.

Taverns in particular represented an oasis of vice within easy reach of most sugar and coffee plantations. In many places, it was customary for black male workers—slave and free—to patronize the taverns on weekends and on holidays, many slipping out illegally after dark. Taverns were notoriously a place for slave men to sell things that they or their women had grown, made, or stolen, but they were also places where black slaves and free men and lower-class white men could go to drink rum, play cards, and place bets. In contrast to the natural environment, then, these enclosed taverns were very much spaces for men, dominated by (working-class) masculine sociability, and generally considered by elites to be a dangerous influence on the slaves.

For those slave men who reached them, the taverns provided a way to escape the rigors of their work and create community with other working-class men. In the mid-1840s, this space produced much conversation about a coming insurrection. Indeed, many would later testify that critical plans were made for an insurgent movement in and around the country taverns with details decided about weapons, local leaders, and mobile ambassadors. This flight to the taverns enabled slave men to develop and maintain critical networks as a rebel movement mushroomed across the western countryside in the 1840s.

The pervasive nature of black slave mobility through the day and night strongly suggests that in Cuba as throughout the Atlantic world, freedom as such did not begin (or end) with the moment of manumission, or in this case with violent rebellion. On the contrary, these practices of movement illustrate how enslaved people repurposed and reoriented plantation space for their own objectives. They consistently mapped their own meanings of existence onto a violent rural landscape, thereby creating small spaces of freedom within their enslavement.[37]

The lindero was not the only liminal space in the plantation. The plantations themselves were highly permeable spaces that black Cubans traversed with regularity. At the same time, the slave quarters themselves, even the notorious barracoons, could provide enough concealment to protect conspiring slaves. Within these dwellings, slaves lived in such close proximity to one another that information could not help but circulate, sometimes inadvertently. As such, some of the most significant gatherings for 1844 took place inside the dwellings of elite slave men, and white authorities were panicked by the inadequacy of their efforts at containment.

As in most slave societies, the slave quarters on Cuba's larger estates were sequestered a respectable distance away from where white employees slept; even this fact of geography relegated enslaved people to the margins of plantation life. Thus to reach the area where the slaves lived, one had to walk a little ways from the central batey. Though a short walk, it inevitably took one across invisible borderlands and into a world noticeably different from the cane fields, boiling houses, and masters' homes. Physical distance translated into social distance as those born in Africa and those born in Cuba rested, cooked meals, braided hair, played with children, argued, had sex, and stole away into the night. And since movement and sound permeated at all hours of the night, it is difficult to believe that the rest of the plantation was completely tranquil. Taken as a whole, the evidence demonstrates that the nighttime hours constituted a point of acute vulnerability for whatever institutions had been established for policing and surveillance.

While occasionally semipublic gatherings convened upward of thirty people, it was the smaller, more private meetings between estate leaders that most frequently pricked the mantle of control in the countryside.

Throughout the early months of 1844 dozens and dozens of witnesses spoke of outside organizers coming to meet with the resident captains on their estates.[38] These meetings almost invariably took place in the homes of rebel leaders, usually those of the African foremen. Because these privileged slaves often had separate cabins, sometimes situated a bit away from the others, their homes became the focal points for insurgent planning and revolutionary discussions.

Yet the received wisdom of the plantation world mandated that private domains and personal space were either stifled or nonexistent for most black people; true privacy and separation were luxuries afforded mainly to whites. Within the slave quarters cabins stood little more than four or five feet apart, and within the larger slave barracks, rooms were situated right next to one other. The barracoons helped streamline the ever-evolving technology of black confinement during the nineteenth century, and they met a variety of needs. In addition to preventing nighttime roaming and conspiratorial plotting, their spatial logic was organized to encourage sexual intimacy between those who exhibited proper marital relations and to prevent intimacy between those who did not.[39]

Slave men *and* women were thus forced to delineate new intimate cartographies—for the purposes of courtship and coupling, enacting sacred rituals, and in this case planning a mutiny. Also for this reason, those who were not key rebel organizers could still report who was coming and going. This was particularly the case in the barracoons, where all of the individual quarters opened up to a common patio. On the Ingenio La Victoria, for example, two Congo boys claimed they were aware that slaves and free people came to talk to rebel leaders at night toward the back of the barracoons.[40] As such, while black workers slept like logs, tended conucos, or nursed children, nocturnal movement—licit and illicit—became so common as to be inevitable, and it was impossible for residents who lived literally on top of one another not to notice its occurrence.

Though the nighttime hours provided cover, enabling more women to be on the move, women's domestic and familial responsibilities often compelled many of them to remain closer to home than did men. Surviving accounts suggest that the domestic labor of adult women positioned some of them in the more public and accessible spaces of the barracks, as they washed clothes on the patios, cooked evening meals, or swept and cleaned floors. Indeed, their maintaining of homes and families invites the question of what forms of *immobility* were required in order for other forms of mobility to take place? But since people commonly drifted into the open and shared areas like the central patios, it is unlikely that other residents of the barracks would have been oblivious to what was taking place there. Ironically, this spatial order seems to have allowed some women who may otherwise have remained on the margins of rebel knowledge circuits to become acutely aware of plans being laid for a rebellion.[41]

The above examples suggest that either the safety precautions taken on most plantations were more lax than authorities assumed or the relationship between those being watched and those doing the watching was much more malleable than has previously been appreciated. As early as 1828, the American reverend Abiel Abbot stressed the importance of "securing the [slave] tenants from nocturnal rambles, and from temptations to desert," but by the 1840s, such "nocturnal rambles" were still rampant.[42]

Many white plantation residents never really knew when "a negro may have attempted to steal out, or some strange negro may be trying to steal in, or some prowling white, or free black, has been reconnoitering."[43] For all the presumption that slaves were secured during the evening hours, we have little evidence of how this was accomplished, or who was doing the securing. Though ideally poor white men would be hired for this task, by the 1840s there were simply not enough white workers residing on the plantations to maintain the necessary vigilance. The task of watching over the enslaved population thus generally fell to other black people, particularly the foremen and other trusted appointees.[44]

On the one hand, there is little to suggest that loyalty to fellow slaves led these guards to leniency or permissiveness. On the other hand, it is clear that black overseers across Cuba consistently allowed people to enter from outside—whether they were slaves from other plantations, runaways in search of food and supplies, or free blacks from nearby villages—defying explicit orders to the contrary. The frequency of these outside visits, and the number of slaves traveling to other plantations at night, confirm either that the guards were cursory in their surveillance, turning a blind eye to certain individuals, or that they used the nighttime hours to conduct their own business.[45]

Many of the black drivers had their own cabins, and they were often the main ones holding meetings with outside emissaries or slipping off themselves to meetings on other estates. In districts across Matanzas, this literal and figurative "leaving the gate open" allowed a variety of transgressions to take place, and permitted a steady hemorrhage of black men and women who used the nighttime for their own purposes. Indeed, it was at night that many slaves found ways to make the boundaries of their world permeable.

The white rural community was never oblivious to these cracks and fissures, and most viewed them as an ongoing menace in their midst. Many white rural residents would have agreed, for instance, with the sentiment voiced by one traveler that "the thieving and violence of Negroes from other plantations, their visits by night against law . . . are all to be watched and prevented or punished."[46]

The dilemma of slaves slipping onto local plantations and sometimes wreaking havoc is perhaps best captured in the stories surrounding José Dolores. During the early 1840s Dolores, a former slave likely from the region of Limonar, became the most visible leader of a group of *cimarrones* (maroons) that included both men and women. This collective became notorious for their attacks on local plantations and for their reputed connection to insurgent activities in the region from 1843 to 1844. Throughout 1843, particularly from the summer into the late fall, furious communiqués about Dolores went back and forth between government officials in Guamacaro, Limonar, and other nearby districts. Members of Dolores's *cuadrillo* were famous for entering local plantations, usually after dark, stealing farm animals and food, and trading with or attacking black residents who could supply them with needed resources.[47]

Alarmed by the consistency, range, and organization of the raids carried out by Dolores and his followers, local authorities issued repeated directives to "exterminate them," but they did so in vain.[48] Portions of the historical record suggest that Dolores may have developed connections to rebel slave organizers on plantations across the western district and attempted to help realize the movements planned for 1843 and 1844. The historian Juan Sánchez, for example, has argued that Dolores was not only aware of the rebellion of 1843 but that in its aftermath he also tried to coordinate an assault on the jail where a number of the prosecuted rebels were being held in order to free them.[49] Manuel Barcia has uncovered testimony from January 1844 that indicts Dolores in the wider uprising that was supposed to take place that year.[50]

One missive from late in 1843 stated frankly how humiliating it was for the colonial state to expend such energy on Dolores's capture with no result. In November 1843 the governor of Matanzas wrote to the military captain of Guamacaro saying, "Out of respect for the public good and the credit of the government, I hope that you will occupy yourself in this matter without rest." The governor went on to convey his displeasure about "this handful of contemptible people [*miserables*] who go around the countryside of this district and its immediate surroundings at their pleasure, robbing and disturbing peaceful residents . . . [because] a well-thought out plan for capturing them has not occurred to any of the captains in this district." Attempts to capture Dolores and others connected to him continued to frustrate government officials into 1844.[51]

As the nineteenth century wore on, planters began to experiment with elaborate measures to streamline the task of policing slaves. The greatest achievement in this process was the development of the slave barracoons, which became notorious for their claustrophobic rooms, unhygienic living conditions, and poor lighting and ventilation. In short, they were inescapably evocative of incarceration. For those properties that had yet to construct barracoons, the primary means used to thwart "nocturnal rambles" was to secure the estate at night and post a watchman to monitor the slave quarters. On the estates where barracoons existed, slaves were to be securely restrained and locked in for the evening.

To emphasize the importance of these measures, Article 25 of the 1842 slave codes officially mandated the construction of barracoons on all the major estates. Issued in November 1842, the *Bando de gobernación y policía de la isla de Cuba* was formally promulgated in January 1843. Barracoon construction was painfully slow, however. In May 1843, two months after the destructive Bemba rebellion, a local slaveholder named Benito García y Santos penned an urgent letter. He argued that the lack of security in the slave quarters "should be considered the principal cause of the uprisings and other crimes" of the period, and he urged the captain general to examine the matter further. Macuriges was one of the newer rural districts to the east of Matanzas Bay, but it already had some forty ingenios by the time of the March rebellion. García y Santos was horrified that only five of these properties had complied with orders and established slave barracks. Carlos Gheri, the district captain of Macuriges, took personal charge of the matter and conducted a detailed investigation. In early June, Gheri responded with the following assessment:

> Most excellent señor:
>   I believe that the dangers we have seen come from the lack of secure barracks for the slaves to live in . . . and their corruption and depravity emanates from this source. In this district, as well as in other areas, which are those that I can speak of with certainty, there are very few estates that have them — these do not number more than five — including those that are being constructed at this moment. On the other estates, the slaves sleep in frail wood or mud cabins, most

of them with straw roofs, others with tile. . . . On the sugar mill where there may be as many as 300 slaves, one will not find more than seven white employees . . . during the grinding period; as well as during the dead season [the white employees] are reduced to four, and from one season to the next the only people in charge are the estate manager (where there is one), the overseer, and the cattle tender, who are supposed to watch over the slaves when the work is concluded; but it is impossible for three white employees to spend the whole night awake when they have to work the next day; and if it is possible to do so on one or two nights, this kind of caution cannot be a daily routine, as is truly necessary.[52]

By July 1843, Captain General Gerónimo Valdés had sent out a communiqué to all of the district captains in the immediate western jurisdictions stressing the importance of the barracoon regulation and emphasizing "that the measure should have prompt and immediate application." But some owners were hesitant to comply, wary about the barracoons' effect on Matanzas slaves. They had serious misgivings about the wisdom of congregating hundreds of enslaved people together who had been forced to labor all day and who all shared common grievances against the white power structure. The Marqués de Campo Flórida, for example, argued that instead of preventing rebellions, the new regulations might actually encourage them, "reminding [the slaves] daily at the sound of the bolt . . . of their deprivations." Other owners balked at the cost of constructing the barracks and the time and labor this would take away from plantation work.[53]

The idea of living in these barracks was of course intolerable to many slaves, particularly since many of them had been forced to endure similar kinds of structures in their journey across the Atlantic. For this reason, the slow and steady multiplication of the barracoons sometimes met with stiff resistance from the people who were to be enclosed in them.[54] By January 1844 only sixteen estates in the Sabanilla region were listed as having constructed the barracks. This was far more than the Macuriges summer count, but it still represented less than half the mills in the district.[55]

Even when estate managers were successful in instituting the barracoons, however, the barracks often failed to prevent slaves from slipping out. During the 1844 trials it became clear to colonial officials how serious the problem was. The evidence indicates that up to that point, such nighttime travels were almost viewed as necessary safety valves, relatively harmless as long as all workers returned by the following morning.[56] For the three, four, or five white men who sought to live and keep order among 100, 200, or even 300 black people, tacitly allowing these brief escapes must have frequently seemed the best option. By the spring of 1843 however, this continual seepage could no longer be viewed as a local problem to be addressed individually by each estate. It had to be seen instead as a broader social crisis that was "placing the lives, properties, and general security of the region in danger."[57]

Clearly black men and women had pried these gaps open far enough to shape a growing insurgency, and to link the various contagions emerging around the province. Authorities could no longer tolerate such breaches. As the 1844 trials began, prosecutors developed nagging and persistent questions about which persons enslaved witnesses had spoken to on different estates and which "outside blacks" they had seen on their home grounds. These questions reflected an acute awareness and a deep concern with the movement of enslaved people beyond their circumscribed places.

It would not be a stretch to state that the bloody purge of 1844 found powerful white people throughout Cuba profoundly introspective about the state of their colony and the slaves who maintained it. The need to contain black laborers within proscribed spaces was a long-standing and central preoccupation for slaveholders in Cuba, and it resonated with planter concerns across the Atlantic world. From South Carolina to Salvador da Bahia, planter elites designed elaborate systems of policing and containment to deter and punish slave mobility, particularly after hours. In short, this obsession with the influence of "outsiders" on the part of slaveholders was a widespread phenomenon, and it helped shape the interrogation strategies of prosecuting authorities in a variety of locales.

During the course of the 1844 trials, Cuban authorities kept asking themselves how such consistent communication between slaves could have taken place in their very midst in spite of "the distances that separated" them. Throughout 1844 and after, bureaucrats attempted to determine precisely how a revolt of such proportions could have been attempted, and they endeavored to put into place a series of measures to prevent its recurrence.

In July 1844 after the momentum of the trials had begun to slow, a local district captain identified another salient problem: the fact that some slaves in the rural areas were apparently allowed to obtain work for themselves. He railed against this state of affairs.

> Slaves go . . . working throughout the countryside for themselves, as
> if they were free, and outside of the sovereign authority, with only the

papers of their owners. These owners are not interested in anything else except . . . that [their slaves] bring them the weekly or monthly payments, and that the government officials take up the responsibility of Vigilance. This is an incontestable truth . . . it turns out that [the slaves] do not work as they are supposed to, and those who give them work do not consider themselves responsible if [the slaves] commit any wrongs. As, for example, the most common; which is [for slaves] to go around at night from farm to farm, or go into town taking the loose animals and mistreating them[,] . . . mocking the vigilance of their owners . . . and that of the militia. The most damaging result is [the slaves'] interaction with white people, who view them as free men, for they come to be considered as such where people do not know them.

To do away with these misfortunes, it would be highly advisable to prohibit any slave from leaving with [only] a paper from his owner to look for work in the countryside; instead his actual owner should arrange for the work and negotiate with the person who needs it, obliging this owner to answer for the conduct of the slave.[58]

The image created in this memo is one of black slaves effortlessly strolling about the countryside "as if they were free," in the process making a mockery of slaveowners, militia, and all existing prohibitions against black mobility. For whites looking back on how a conspiracy could have emerged, the possibilities for slaves—particularly male slaves—to "roam" must have been amplified in their minds. There can be no doubt that by the summer of 1844, the opportunities for slaves to move about, obtain work, and enter other plantations had begun luridly multiplying in the minds of white citizens. I have not come across documents, however, that explicitly outline instances of rural slaves' being able to look for their own work, although the high number of slaves found working on other properties suggests that such a practice was possible.

One can surmise then, that while slaveowners and local authorities desired as much vigilance as possible in policing the activities of their slaves, their ability to exercise it was limited. Instead, a sizeable number of black men and women were able to use the opportunities that their daily existence provided them to travel the length of their own ingenios, move around the countryside, and even venture into the towns and cities of Matanzas.

Given the permeability of the slave quarters and the plantation itself, it is not surprising that there was considerable interaction between the free and the enslaved. Some of the individuals most frequently cited as meeting organizers on the estates—the "outside blacks" whose presence was a constant irritant to slaveowners—were free black people, overwhelmingly men. Because many former slaves chose to live in the vicinity of their former plantations, their homes became part of the daily landscape for people still enslaved on the plantations nearby. Indeed local free people, especially those only recently freed, were a familiar and consistent presence on rural estates throughout Matanzas.[59] Sometimes in the course of everyday work, but particularly after nightfall and on Sundays, more than a few of the men who had attained nominal freedom filtered back to the plantations to buy and sell wares, socialize with friends and loved ones, and verify plans for a coming rebellion. The historical documents indicate that black plantation residents frequently made their way to the homes of the legally free. Indeed, both spatially and conceptually, it is often difficult to identify a clear and definitive line marking where the plantations ended and the former slaves' homesteads began. On the surface, this movement also seemed to be highly gendered. There are very few accounts of enslaved women leaving the plantations to spend time in free people's homes, and even fewer of legally free women receiving these guests. Nevertheless, it is clear that the nocturnal hours allowed slave women to travel the length of the plantation and beyond, and since more than a few women took advantage of these opportunities it seems reasonable to suggest that at least some of the traffic to and from free people's homes involved women. This might have been the case especially during childbirth or other critical moments that concerned women particularly.

There are definite indications that legally free women went back to the plantations to visit relatives or perhaps to attend social events, especially if their children were still there. But these women do not appear to have visited or conducted business on the estates with anywhere near the consistency that free men did. While free women's absence from the trial records makes the latter a poor source to assess their mobility, other documents suggest that free women chose to interact with the plantations substantially less than their male counterparts. There is every indication then that the "outside blacks" who so aggravated rural slaveholders were overwhelmingly male. And as such, the continual attempts to fortify the plantation against this intrusion might effectively be read as a heavily masculinized attempt at border security and protection—that is, as an effort to defend the estates from unfamiliar black men.

Scores of other free black men who became a part of the insurrectionary momentum lived on the outskirts of sugar and coffee estates and smaller farms, and they used their acquaintances and friendships with those still living on the estates to cement rebellious ties.[60] Silvestre Criollo, for example, was among those free men who made his home on or near the grounds of a prominent sugar mill in Sabanilla. Local slaves were known to go to his home, and Silvestre was reported as entering the cabins of several rebel leaders.[61] Others, like the free black couple Baltasar Veytra and his wife, María, were similarly accused of holding secret meetings "frequented by both free black people and slaves alike, who enter and leave constantly." Baltasar, who was a Lucumí, lived on the fringes of the San Antonio mill and admitted to knowing several of the slaves on another nearby estate "for having been his acquaintances [compañeros]," though he insisted that he had no real friendships with any of them.[62]

In the early months of 1844, the free black man Florencio Brito allegedly visited several properties in the regions of Yumurí and Sabanilla. As with Silvestre Criollo, some of Brito's most extensive interactions with plantation organizers took place at the Soledad de Jáuregui sugar mill. Florencio was one of the many conduits that connected Soledad with the rest of Sabanilla, and he allegedly fed the growing plans for rebellion on the Soledad de Jáuregui estate. The cabins of rebel organizers that local free black men like Brito visited became the political centers of the sugar mills. So steady was the stream of visitors that one might think these conferences with "outside blacks," and free men at that, were authorized. It would seem that, for all intents and purposes, as far as the authorities keeping watch over nocturnal slave movements were concerned, they were.[63] Brito was eventually executed for these actions.[64]

The fluidity with which slaves and free black people circulated onto nearby sugar and coffee estates illustrates the extent to which such plantations were unable to fully demarcate the boundaries of the world in which enslaved people moved, particularly at night. One feature of the plantation world that helped to facilitate this contact was the close proximity of the estates, which in the testimonies seem at times to flow into one another.[65]

The importance of this closeness cannot be underestimated. Such proximity created opportunities to tug away at the boundary lines of individual farms and ingenios even as slave codes, whips, and threats endeavored to make them real. The flourishing Macuriges estate of La Victoria, for example, was surrounded on all sides by sugar mills, coffee plantations, and ranch farms. The border that Victoria shared with San Nestor enabled slaves on both plantations to develop acquaintanceships with one another. This is evidenced by the amorous relationship that Gonzalo Gangá, from San Nestor, developed with Marina Congo, from La Victoria. Another man from San Nestor, Ignacio Congo, confirmed that he knew several slaves from La Victoria who had each been implicated in the rebellion there.[66]

Other slaves stated even more explicitly that they had met individuals known to be involved in planning an uprising as a result of the closeness of their respective plantations. Diego Criollo of the Arosteguí plantation testified that he knew most of the slaves accused as rebel organizers from the Ingenio Soledad de Jáuregui. The reason he gave was "because the two mills [were] next to each other, and they used to see each other frequently, and these are the friendly relations he has with them."[67]

It was also not uncommon for slaves to be solicited to work on other estates and fill whatever gaps existed, especially during the harvest season. The sugar plantation harvest had a gluttonous demand for labor, and the need for workers almost always exceeded the available supply. No clear pattern has emerged, however, to indicate what kinds of estates were more prone to release their workers, which slaves managers were more likely to relinquish, what kinds of work these laborers were sent to do, and whether or not money changed hands. Sometimes the enslaved workers came from large estates that could be perceived as having a surplus of labor, other times they came from smaller estates that could be perceived as having a dearth of tasks to accomplish. Sometimes slaves were employed to cut trees and clear land, other times to cut cane or work in tiles.

During the three-year period (between 1839 and 1842) in which some 200 mills were built throughout the Matanzas region, intensive labor of all sorts would have been needed to get the mills fully operational, including razing dozens of acres, erecting buildings, installing machinery, and planting fields. While the practice of hiring (or lending) out slaves is well-documented for the urban areas, its rural dimensions remain obscure. From the evidence examined here, three firm conclusions can be drawn: that work crews from the sending estates were usually small in number, that sugar properties were the overwhelming recipients of this labor, and that men were invariably sent rather than women. While women most certainly chopped in the fields, they did not by and large speak of going to *other* plantations to do fieldwork, or of meeting other people while they chopped cane. Those who referred to such experiences were primarily men speaking of other men. It is possible that women were sent to work on other plantations, but there is little indication that this was the case.

One thing that *is* clear from the accounts is that the work required to keep the sugar mills running brought enslaved people together from plantations throughout the immediate, and sometimes not so immediate, vicinity. By the 1850s the estate where the 1844 conspiracy was presumably first discovered, Santísima Trinidad, had more than 1,000 slaves, but only a portion of them actually worked on the property; "the rest were employed on the outside."[68] In this way a substantial number of individuals were thrown into acquaintanceship, friendship, or more tenuous bonds by the grueling work that was the lifeblood of the plantations. The endless labors of sugar drew black laborers together from around the districts of Matanzas.

A spate of examples from the Macuriges district illustrates how the labor of black men was frequently requested to fill holes in the work regimen. Rafael Criollo, who lived on the Victoria estate, admitted that he had come to know two self-proclaimed leaders from the nearby Nieves Ingenio during his time working in the boiling house there. Antonio Carabalí, on the Achury mill, met the rebel leader Antonio María while felling trees at Encanto.[69] Domingo Criollo, José Gangá, and Narcisco Criollo, who all lived on nearby coffee plantations, claimed to know the conspirator Santiago Gangá from their time working at the sugar mill.[70] León Mozambique reportedly met the leader Félix Gangá (from Victoria) when the latter came to the Apersteguía estate to pull up plantains. Eduardo and Domingo Criollo were brought in from the Recurso coffee estate to cut cane at Encanto.[71] Stories of this kind proliferated throughout the district and the province.

One story from further west in Sabanilla calls attention to how black laborers were drawn into a rebel movement through their work across plantations. Such was the case on the Dos Felices sugar mill in Alacranes—better known as the Mesa property—and the mill adjoining it, the Ingenio Dichoso. Located almost thirty kilometers south of the bay, Alacranes was one of the newer developing regions whose estates needed continual clearing of weeds, grasses, and brambles. During the fall of 1843, with the harvest looming near, additional hands were requested to fill the work gaps on the Mesa estate. A small work gang, which included Calisto Carabalí and Perico Gangá, made their way over from Dichoso. On the way to the Mesa property the two men came across Casimiro Lucumí. Both men claimed to be aware that Casimiro was the main rebel organizer on the Mesa property, and that the local leaders had named Perico as captain. For Perico and Calisto, then, their work on the neighboring plantation brought them in contact not only with men from this new estate but also with the rebellion.[72] From Havana province to Rancho Veloz stories abound of enslaved men who worked on other properties in their districts, expanded their networks and contacts, and swelled their political consciousness of a growing resistance movement.[73]

Many who performed more specialized tasks or seasonal labors on the major estates were free black men who came to the plantation world seeking employment and pay, however minimal. Sometimes free laborers would negotiate a contract with estate owners and plantation managers, but at other times they were hired out as gangs. From these collective labors a broad spectrum of relationships took root between those who were free and those who were tied to the estates. At the very least, many enslaved and free blacks across Matanzas recognized one another's faces and knew each other's names. Several men enslaved on the Escorial sugar mill, for example, spoke of knowing a free man who worked there named Belén Ramírez. Ramírez stated that he knew of all of the slaves in question, and that he was in fact friends with a few of them. Other free laborers like Pío Romero, who himself "had been free for a very short time," became acquainted with enslaved workers on several Matanzas estates in the 1840s.[74] In some cases, these free men stayed for months or even years at a time, fostering strong ties with the others who worked there. This was the case with Ramírez, who at the time of his interrogation had been working at Escorial for six years.[75]

Men like Belén Ramírez and Pío Romero formed part of a mobile laboring class of black men who moved from one plantation to the next, picking up whatever work was available and leaving in their wake a trail of acquaintanceships with enslaved residents. Pío, for example, was a former slave on the same property as a Carabalí man named Jacundo. After he became free, Pío reportedly advised Jacundo and others to join "the fray" and to "get ready for the war, which would take place during Holy Week."[76] The consistent presence of free black men on the plantation grounds laid a foundation for more than casual acquaintanceships with enslaved workers. The labor that ensnared hundreds of black workers created a shared experience and forged a common identity that transcended legal freedom. Because some of the violence of slavery extended to all those who were black, the lines of legal freedom were already blurred, and workers who had obtained their freedom had often been slaves but a short time ago. Whether from the commonality of these shared and overlapping universes, or for more strategic and tactical purposes, scores of rebellious conversations crossed lines of freedom on estates throughout the province. Thus the importance of this interstate labor exchange to the emergence (or maintenance) of a network of male rebel slaves cannot be underestimated.

Belén Ramírez provides a perfect example of free men's centrality to subversive organizing taking place on the estates. Then about thirty years old, Ramírez had come to Cuba from Santo Domingo as a child, already free.[77] In the late 1830s he began working on estates in the Sabanilla district like Escorial, and developed relationships with men there like Antonio Congo and Andrés Criollo. Sometime in either 1843 or 1844, Antonio and Andrés reportedly took on the positions at Escorial of first and second captain, respectively, and began carefully laying plans for a rebellion there. Though Andrés and Antonio were the primary captains on the estate, Ramírez was widely accused of fomenting insurrection at Escorial, as well as on other estates in that area of Sabanilla.

|||||||| Conclusion

It is clear that Cuban slaveholders in the mid-nineteenth century created a landscape and a labor regimen that was deeply animated by various forms of violence. Yet even as slaveowners maintained elaborate systems of surveillance and punishment, black Cubans consistently found ways to loosen the mantle of control. Even as it daily asked the impossible of black workers, the world of slavery in Matanzas also unwittingly laid the contours for a larger insurgent movement to unfold. This chapter has shed light on the ways enslaved people's rival geographies made black oppositional cultures visible. In thinking about the Cuban plantation-scape as a series of interwoven black geographies, one can more closely consider the literal and figurative "terrain of political struggle."[78] Together, these explorations help flesh out how enslaved people fashioned insurgent collectives across the rural landscape in 1843 and 1844. During the early months of 1843, these collectives would raise a rebellion that would effectively usher in the 1844 movement in the rural areas.

Chapter Three

The 1843 Rebellions in Matanzas

Caminante, no hay puentes, se hace puentes al andar.
(Traveler, there are no bridges; you make them as you walk.)

|||||||| Gloria Anzaldúa

The dramatic shifts occasioned by sugar's coming of age in the nineteenth century spawned a labor-intensive and violent regime that rural black laborers nevertheless found multiple ways to navigate. Across the plantation sugar belt, enslaved people routinely molded their work regimes, confronted the oppression they faced, and evaded consistent efforts to police them. As they created their own rival geographies through the plantation world, these slaves received and began to consider the pieces of insurgent news circulating through the countryside.

The older generations of slaves had lived through remarkable transformations in the Atlantic world, including the birth of the Haitian state, the independence of much of Latin America, and the abolition of slavery in the British territories. Even those who had only been in Cuba for a few years had learned about the British condemnation of the slave trade, and some had gleaned that urban residents of various backgrounds were displeased with colonial rule.

By the early 1840s a powerful convergence of factors had created an explosive set of conditions in the rural plantation zones. First, slaves were being increasingly moved to sugar plantations, where the growing technological advances naturalized a culture of bodily dishonor and mental desecration. Second, the ever-increasing number of slave captives arriving in Cuba from across West and Central Africa came with protracted exposure to warfare and often had extensive military training. Third, local black networks were filtering news of political dissent that stretched from Havana to London about independence movements, anticolonial plots, and antislavery struggles. This explosive combination produced a powerful string of slave rebellions in the 1830s and 1840s. Among the most significant of them were the March 1843 Bemba rebellion and the November 1843 Triunvirato rebellion.

The 1843 rebellions were hardly a new phenomenon. These insurgencies were in many ways a continuation — if an amped-up continuation — of the kinds of activities that had been taking place in the countryside for years. Between the Aponte trials of 1812 and the Escalera trials in 1844 colonial officials on the island recorded no fewer than twenty slave rebellions, conflicts, and protest movements. Indeed, more slave rebellions erupted in Cuba during these three decades than at any other point in the island's history. Most took place in the west-central districts from Havana to Cárdenas from 1825 to 1844.[1] As a result slaves in this region, and indeed throughout the island, retained a long memory of collective protest that was constantly replenished by newly arriving Africans. That these two rebellions were not singular occurrences, but rather part of a recurrent and consistent pattern of struggle in the plantation zone, suggests a dynamic web of cognitive, political, and material structures linking a broad span of opposition in the nineteenth century — a phenomenon I refer to elsewhere as "the repeating rebellion."[2]

The Bemba and Triunvirato movements of 1843 were nevertheless distinctive in this rebel tapestry for what they represented and unleashed. These uprisings created a powerful incentive for rural slaves, and the ensuing state terror helped to birth new insurgent clusters. Urban organizers understood that these revolts embodied the political energy of the plantation countryside and carefully assessed the impact of their eruption on the wider movement. Historians have uncovered few concrete linkages between these rural uprisings and the urban opposition. However, their simultaneous eruption at a moment of heightened anxiety about abolitionist designs, separatist movements, and black revolution powerfully shaped the way black and white Cubans understood them. These two rebellions were therefore critical to a larger surge of black political activity in Cuba during this moment, and no story of 1844 would be complete without them.

The archival narration of these two events also draws attention to the state's most wanted targets, and this focus had critical implications for who became most visible during the trials and sentencing. Women were only questioned in small handfuls, and their movements and activities were rarely reported in the trial testimonies. While enslaved women were central to both the March and November rebellions — and indeed the latter was directed in part by two women — their stories were often explicitly elided in the historical record or implicitly erased by the political register in which "rebellions" are typically understood. The attendant regime of visibility that emerges from the ungendered, yet masculinized, slave collective likewise obscures a range of other actions usually considered to be peripheral to slave insurgencies but that were in fact quite central to them. A gendered analysis of the 1843 rebellions thus makes other forms of nonaggressive protest legible—such as opportunities for mass escape or finding loved ones rather than following insurgents—not as the "secondary" or hidden rebellions but rather as part of a larger "fabric of refusal" necessarily woven into these moments by a range of oppositional acts. The rebellion that was discovered on March 26, 1843, though not in time to prevent its occurrence on March 27, affords several opportunities to understand how legitimate resistance becomes configured during these episodes.[3]

I spend time with the details of how these rebellions unfolded in order to illuminate the range and complexity of actors, positions, and practices that collectively constituted these struggles. Any insurgency is always a collection of situated acts whose sum is greater than its parts. With this in mind, I endeavor to frame the rebellions of 1843 as knotty questions that had to answer themselves as they went, and as entities composed of many different fragments. The extended narrative that follows allows closer attention to the choices, decisions, conflicts, and desires that went into producing this moment of black political consciousness.[4]

|||||| The Bemba Rebellion, March 1843

Ingenio La Trinidad, Macuriges District

SUNDAY, MARCH 26, 1843, 1:00 P.M.

It was the height of the grinding season. On a Sunday in late March, the sugar mill known as Trinidad must have looked like any other in the district of Macuriges—preoccupied with moving cane, unmoved by piety, or dignity. That particular Sunday was to be unusual, however, and would remain lodged in memories across eastern Matanzas for months and years to come. That day Mateo Lucumí and Vicente Criollo informed their owner, Rafael Aguilar, that his slaves were about to rise up en masse.[5] Duly alarmed, Aguilar contacted the district captain, who alerted the neighboring landowners and began interrogations. But these gestures were already too late.

Ingenio La Alcancía, District of Cimarrones

SUNDAY, MARCH 26, 1843, 5:00 P.M.

In the next district over lay the sugar estate of Alcancía. On that same afternoon of March 26, the estate manager José Cano received word of a coming rebellion and urged his white workforce to maintain the utmost vigilance.[6] As an extra precaution, he made some inquiries of Camilo, his manservant of thirty-one years, "because of the confidence that he had in [Camilo's] loyalty and fidelity." Camilo "assured him that he did not know anything."[7]

MARCH 27, 1843, 5:30 A.M.

My lieutenant has informed me that the
Ingenio La Alcancía has risen up.

—Apolinar de la Gala, prosecuting judge

The men working the night shift heard it first. Long after they should have been asleep, men like Germán Lucumí were feeding the grinder, others like Anacleto Lucumí were stoking the fires, and still others were attending the boiling vats and troughs. In the midst of this nocturnal ritual they heard shouts. Someone had set fire to the *bagaceras*, where the cane trash was stored.[8] The fire brought every person on the grounds of Alcancía, and more people from miles around. A fire meant the loss of precious cane. It meant imminent danger and disorder. It meant heat and smoke and ashes. Most of all it unleashed fear, uncertainty, and an unnatural daylight into a scene that had only moments ago appeared an ordered labor regime.

Marcelino Carabalí, one of the black foremen, later said he tried to get all available hands to extinguish the fire. But they met with sharp resistance from the Lucumís, who in most accounts were the primary organizers of rebellion. Apparently the boiling house men "came to throw water and put out the fire, but the Lucumís, armed with their machetes, objected and said, that anyone who went to put out the fire they would cut off their heads, with their machetes."[9]

The most loathed targets at Alcancía were the black overseers. In plain view of other slaves, rebels assassinated one *contramayoral* named Domingo Congo, another named Jacinto Brican, and still another named José María Congo. They also killed a white American machine operator named Mr. Edward. Overseer Marcelino Carabalí was warned that "he should flee because the Lucumís were mutinous [*alborotados*] and had already killed his companions."[10] The group of insurgents, many of whom remain unidentified, sounded their drums which apparently summoned more rebels from the neighboring plantations. They were headed for the white overseer next.[11]

Sometime around two o'clock in the morning, the rebels went in search of José Cano. They shouted to Cano's manservant, "Tata Camilo, open the door," and told him to entice Cano out with word of the fire. When Cano did not emerge, they began to attack the windows and doors but stopped short of breaking into his home. Cano emerged only after their departure and, "having seen that in that area there was no one, for everyone had withdrawn to the cane trash houses, he resolved to go out, armed with his saber, to find out . . . what was happening." He discovered that "the slaves, or a large number of slaves, had risen up in a tumult, and that they were not working to put out the fire; and the cries that he heard of 'Fire!' and 'Kill the whites!' convinced him there was no doubt that this was a real uprising which he could not contain and . . . he decided to retreat and hide himself, in order not to fall into the hands of that savage horde." After some white employees found Cano hiding in a woodshed they set to work putting out the fire, "which they managed to do with great difficulty because of the few people that were around."[12] The rebels burned the cane trash holdings, the carpentry, and part of the cane fields, and they stole some forty raw hides, which they used as shields.

As night fell on March 26, Rafael Aguilar kept a close watch on his property of Trinidad. On the alert for any signs of rebellion, he and a group of white employees vigilantly made their rounds, but "nothing notable occurred that night on his Ingenio." The night passed without incident. But the Aguilar slaves had not been mistaken; Alcancía rebels were indeed on the move. Early the following morning they reached Trinidad. When he realized this Aguilar locked himself, his wife, his children, and two domestic servants inside the estate house, "believing that there was not enough time to retreat, and this being the only way to save themselves."

The rebels attacked the doors and windows of the *casa de vivienda*, Aguilar's estate home. They entered the main parlor, breaking furniture, taking clothes, money, and watches. In the confusion, Aguilar realized two things: first, the house servants had "left them" and, second, there were no other whites around. But for reasons unknown, the rebels inflicted no further harm to Aguilar or his family. After leaving the casa de vivienda, they set fire to the slave cabins and continued on to the next ingenio.[13]

Like those of Alcancía and Trinidad, the proprietors of Nieves received word early that local slaves were planning a rebellion. They complied with the captain's orders to be vigilant and kept watch over the slaves. Nothing transpired during the night, but by morning they learned that slaves from Alcancía and other estates were headed their way. The rebels arrived at Nieves in much the same way as they had at the other estates, burning the sugar-manufacturing buildings and the boiling house and spreading fire to the cane fields. After this "they divided into several platoons, attacked the big house and the lodgings of the [white] workers, breaking the padlocks or smashing the doors, and taking anything there they could find." The slaves at Nieves seemed to have little intention of defending the plantation. The *mayordomo* later testified that when the army arrived, "the slaves of this estate, on whom they were counting for the planned resistance, dispersed to go to their cabins to get everything they had, leaving only himself and the four white workers, who, convinced they could not resist the growing number of rebels, decided to withdraw on foot."[14]

Similar scenes replayed themselves across the districts of Macuriges and Cimarrones. On the coffee plantation known as Moscón, the rebels burned the slave cabins and the infirmary, one of the cooking areas, and several pigpens.[15] The estate manager at the Aurora mill gathered the entire black workforce in one of the sugar grinding houses and held them there for almost four hours. The rebels came to Aurora and set fire to the cane fields, burning fifteen *cañaverales* (cane patches).[16] The owner of the San Francisco potrero returned to his property to find some eighty slaves waging battle against a significantly outnumbered but armed group of white men.[17]

|||||||| The Bemba Railroad Connection

"The railroad to Bemba is well worthy the attention of the stranger, and a ride on it will afford him a fine view of the neighboring country." With these words, John Wurdemann boarded a Cárdenas-bound train in the spring of 1843 and disembarked at its terminus of Soledad de Bemba. Perhaps the last thing the South Carolina physician expected to find on his arrival was a town deeply shaken by the recent suppression of a massive slave insurrection, "one of the most extensive that had occurred on the island." Among those who had the most reason to be shaken was the wealthy sugar planter Joaquín Peñalver, the Alcancía estate owner who would soon be appointed president of the young Cárdenas Railroad.[18]

The Cárdenas line would eventually reach from Cárdenas port into the town of Bemba, but in 1843 this line was still under construction.[19] Local slave leaders had planned to rise up with slave men working for the Cárdenas Railroad Company. It seems they moved back and forth between their barracks and nearby potreros like San Francisco and were easily recognizable.[20] The railroad rebels were reportedly armed with machetes, leather bags, swords, two rifles, an explosive or artillery cap, another spark gun, and two barrels of gunpowder.[21] At San Francisco, they killed the estate manager and took his machete. Though the other workers on the railroad had been imprisoned, the rebels managed to get them out and most of them joined the insurrection.[22]

This insurrection would later be dubbed the Bemba uprising. At its height, the total number of rebels reportedly swelled to nearly 500. The district captains of Cimarrones and Macuriges eventually raised the alarm to local infantry and cavalry units. A fierce battle ensued, spilling over into the following day and the next. In the end 132 rebels died, and scores of others sought refuge in the hills and forests of Bemba.[23] Three weeks after the uprising, the official tallies reported 33 who had failed to escape during the uprising, 29 who presented themselves for questioning, 3 who were apprehended, 5 who were wounded, and 123 who were missing.[24]

|||||||| Infrared Insurgencies

None of the statistics collected by plantation owners and colonial authorities from that night captured a most significant story buried in the testimonies of estate managers and overseers. On the Alcancía estate where the rebellion first erupted, José Cano had proclaimed that the large number of black slaves who "had risen up" were doing little to help extinguish the fires that had been lit on the plantation grounds. Putting out the fires, he added, was particularly arduous for himself and his white coworkers, "because of the few people that were around." A few estates over, Rafael Aguilar similarly stated that the domestic slaves had "left them," meaning they had deserted the slaveowner, his family, and his home. Vicente Alvero, a bookkeeper on the neighboring Nieves property, reported that the slaves there, "on whom they were counting for the planned resistance [to the uprising], dispersed to . . . their cabins to get everything they had, leaving only himself and the four white workers."[25] One after the other, white authorities recounted their frustration, exasperation, and resentment that at this crucial moment when their world was under attack scores of black people who had not openly rebelled had nonetheless fled their estates or gone into hiding.

What these statements lay bare is that a parallel insurgency was spilling forth that night alongside the one that militias sought to put down. As plantation managers and authorities recounted the disappearance of black people—who should have been extinguishing burning buildings and tending to wounded foremen—they unwittingly shed light on the dozens upon dozens of slaves who fled local farms and plantations that night. While the authorities recorded that 123 slaves were still missing the following day, the accounts of white plantation staff suggest that an even more significant number of slaves may have fled the estates when the rebels attacked. These testimonies reveal that the burning of sugarhouses and ransacking of foremen's cabins was in many ways only the most visible part of the March rebellion.

The actions of Cayetano Abreu, the administrador on the Aurora mill, highlight the attempts of white managers to forestall the deeper implications of the March rebellion. As soon as Abreu learned the rebels were approaching, he gathered the slaves of the estate—presumably as many as he could find—and held them in the sugar-grinding house until the rebels had passed on. During the insurrections that erupted some distance to the west several months later, other managers would take similar precautions. But Abreu's counterparts on neighboring plantations either were unable to replicate this kind of quarantine or were more disposed to first attend to their own survival. As such, black residents on mills like Alcancía and Nieves took their leave (or abstained from helping), apparently in such substantial numbers that employees like Vicente Alvero felt as though he and a handful of embattled whites were the only ones left to defend the mill.

Abreu's actions call renewed attention to slaveholders' continual efforts to fix black people's movements in geographic, temporal, and bodily spaces as violent as they were limited. Such desires were amplified to the point of hysteria with the eruption of collective slave resistance, as men like Abreu sought to incarcerate entire plantation workforces. On nights like that of March 26, however, this "spatial impulse" that helped organize white supremacist control of the countryside was momentarily thrown into a tailspin.[26] While Abreu was able to secure most of his slaves, on other properties the unexpected ruptures opened up by the March attacks enabled significant black flight and mobility. These estate departures are thrown into even sharper relief when viewed against the backdrop of the massive evacuation of railroad slaves that took place later that day. Thus part of our understanding of what comprised the March insurgency should be informed not only by the direct actions of a group of slave militants and their supporters but also by the devastating fissures the rebellion opened up.

These crevices are additionally captured in José Cano's observation that "a large number of the slaves rose up tumultuously and were not doing anything to put out the fire." What is intriguing about Cano's statement is its feeling of being overwhelmed by the sheer number of slaves who had converged on the scene—slaves who only hours before had presumably been asleep or working at nighttime tasks. Only hours ago Cano had been "convinced of the state of order" of the mill, and now it was in anarchy and tumult. Indeed, the spatial and disciplinary norms of the estate had been breached to such an extent that apparently "the cries that [Cano] was hearing of 'Fire!' and 'Kill the whites!' convinced him there was no doubt that this was a real uprising that he could not contain."[27] Even more intriguing, Cano's narrative makes it difficult to get a sense of exactly what the Alcancía slaves were doing at this moment beyond the fact that they had risen up "tumultuously." Yet it is fairly easy to identify what they were *not* doing— that is, putting out the fire. Likewise, at Nieves, the bookkeeper or steward emphasized that the slaves he encountered "dispersed to . . . their cabins," again highlighting what they were *not* doing, which was assisting the white employees in securing the plantation.

The accounts of these managers thus underscore another critical reality: the actions of a relatively small group of slave militants essentially allowed many *other* slaves a variety of opportunities for noncooperation and noncompliance with racial norms, if only out of self-interest. This kind of racial disorder enabled a radically dissident black subjectivity to come to the surface, if not newly into existence. This subjectivity was roomy enough to allow for a range of actions, from those that were benignly uncooperative to blatantly aggressive. Thus the March rebellion produced a wider set of feelings, perceptions, and experiences that unwound the threads of white planter control, if only temporarily. It facilitated an unsettling of white racial power that allowed and encouraged disruptive behavior, even for those who had little to do with the immediate insurgent activities.

Though local plantation authorities in Cimarrones and Macuriges worked hard to put the pieces back together, smaller movements of slave unrest continued to emerge throughout the spring and summer. Some seven months later another broad rebellion erupted in the district of Sabanilla, about twenty miles west of Bemba. This time the epicenter of insurgent planning was a sugar estate known as Triunvirato, owned by Julián

Alfonso, whose family—similar to the Peñalvers—constituted something of a sugar dynasty in the region. Little did the Alfonsos know that five sugar plantations belonging to members of their extended family would be attacked during the fall of 1843.

llllll The Triunvirato Rebellion, November 1843

Sunday, November 5, 1843

8:00 P.M.

It began in November much as it had in March. That evening, groups of black workers were scattered across the Triunvirato sugar mill finishing their regular Sunday chores. While they were being directed toward their nightly food rations, slaves like Zacarías Carabalí later claimed they heard a voice behind them say, "Get back" and "all of a sudden [they] saw the people in turmoil running from one side to the other."[28]

Carlota Lucumí was one of the people who would become particularly important to the insurgent movement that night. In fact, Carlota would become the most famous of all the Triunvirato martyrs. Her memory was revived in later slave historiographies and by the postrevolutionary Cuban state in the 1970s. In spite of this historical attention, however, little was recorded about what she did on her home grounds. What is known is that Carlota traveled with the rebel group at night as it went from plantation to plantation. She and another Lucumí woman, Fermina, became particularly known for the attacks they launched on the neighboring estate. While at Triunvirato, it is likely that Carlota supported and helped to carry out a series of attacks that erupted in rapid succession.

According to most accounts three men of the Lucumí nation—Eduardo, Santiago, and Bonifacio (consistently identified as "the one carrying the machete"), as well as a Gangá named Manuel led a group of slave men and women.[29] Galvanized by this alarming series of events, the administrador Domingo Madan, the estate doctor, and the doctor's brother retrieved weapons from the house and headed out to where the group of Africans was advancing. They saw several Lucumí men carrying the wounded white foreman. The latter, bathed in blood, exclaimed to the administrador, "Don Domingo, they have killed me[!]"[30]

Overwhelmed and outnumbered, the white men tried to "contain any lawlessness" and "find a way to pacify the slaves."[31] The whites however, "convinced that they could not contain the now apparent insurrection of the slaves, returned to the house, took their horses, and left to alert the authorities."[32] According to several accounts, a collective of mostly Lucumí men organized the larger, swelling crowd of slaves. In addition to Manuel Gangá and Bonifacio, Eduardo, and Santiago Lucumí, the group also included three other Lucumí men: Nicolás, Cristóbal, and Secundino. The rebels eventually moved on to the neighboring estate of Ácana."

Late that Sunday evening, after most of the Ácana slaves had retired to their quarters, a number of black slave women were gathered in the plantation infirmary. There these women heard the din of the Triunvirato rebels, many of whom sounded triumphant. Though some distance away, the women gathered at the infirmary door could see that people were on the run and that the overseer's home was in flames. One of these women, a young creole named Juliana, stated that she saw the rebels bringing piles of cane trash to the foreman's house and setting them on fire. Not long after this one of her companions, another young woman named Camila Criolla, advised Juliana "to hide herself in the plantain grove, so as not to see what the rebels were doing."[33]

Catalina Gangá had a similar experience. At half past nine, her owners — including the estate doctor for whom she cooked and washed — had already retired for bed. Catalina later recalled that she went out to the porch to have a drink of water and as she did so turned her attention toward the batey. There she "saw everything inundated with slaves of both sexes, the males armed with short machetes and leather shields." Catalina "presaged evil things from that strange invasion and went immediately to warn her masters so that they could leave."[34]

In addition to their machetes and leather shields, the rebels were armed with other blades, sharp sticks, and self-fashioned lances. Far fewer carried firearms, and two members of the group beat war drums. One witness stated that the Triunvirato rebels marked their entrance with "great uproar [alvoroto]," and the insurgents began "pushing open the doors of all their rooms, ordering [the Ácana slaves] to get up and join them." When they asked what was going on, the Ácana workers were told, "We are going to wage war and kill the whites[;] we have already killed the foreman of our mill."

Reports differ on how Ácana's 270 black workers responded. The above witness Adriano Gangá stated that most of the Ácana slaves, "realizing the evil the rebels were attempting [to commit], answered that they would not take part in their objective and began to disperse themselves among the cane patches and other parts of the estate."[35] Other reports, however, stated that about half of those on the estate came out of their cabins to join the uprising. It is clear that more than a few did so.[36]

Among the Ácana slaves who responded to the rebels almost immediately was a group of seventeen who had been locked in a makeshift cell for attempting to run away. One of them—allegedly Adán Lucumí—began yelling to the rebels "in a language that [the testifying witness] could not understand" and asking the insurgents to help.[37] The rebels immediately forced open the room with machetes, took everyone out to the batey, and removed their shackles. One witness insisted that they only took the manacles off the prisoners who would follow them.

A woman named Fermina Lucumí emerged most consistently as a leading figure in the Ácana events. She had a history of rebelliousness and had only been released from a plantation cell three days before.[38] According to several accounts, Fermina directed a group of rebels to the overseer's home, "showing them the doors of the white people's rooms so they might attack them."[39] In these reports, Fermina ordered other slaves to carry out the goals of the insurgency to their fullest. Fermina herself denied these accusations, so it is difficult to know exactly how much of the Ácana retribution she was actually responsible for. As I discuss in chapter 5, however, Fermina's history of incarceration and the multiple witness accounts of her actions strongly indicate that she was one of the leading organizers.

The Ácana overseer, Juan Miguel Pérez, claimed that he and the other white residents "did not have time to take any precautions" and locked themselves inside the overseer's house. Although their group included eight people, "not all of them were armed, and they could not resist the multitude that was bearing down on them [se les venía encima] armed with machetes and other offensive instruments . . . and rocks they were throwing."

The mutinous slaves now included scores of slaves from Triunvirato, and a number of other Ácana residents who had joined them.[40] The white group trapped in the overseer's home instructed Gonzalo Lucumí, the slave who was with them, to ask the rebels "what they wanted with the whites, and [to ask them] not to kill them." The overseer said the rebels' only response was "to insult them and threaten them with death." Although one of the organizers stated "what they wanted was the machetes of the whites and that they would not kill them," these measured negotiations were apparently overridden. Gonzalo was apparently told, "Hey, you are the whites' stool pigeon [alcahuete] . . . so we will kill you, too."[41]

Eventually a few of the leading male insurgents got inside the home, where the mayordomo and other whites were hiding. Bonifacio was said to have "swooped down on [*se abalanzó*] the white man with much vigor, [taken] the machete from him, [and] killed him immediately thereafter with machete blows." He then handed the machete to Santiago. The two of them cut down most of the other whites in the house, including three women, a small child, and another white man.[42] As the other white men tried to escape the house, Fermina shouted to other rebels and herself took off in pursuit of them. According to these accounts, she continued to direct other slaves to free the incarcerated prisoners and to seize the foreman who was responsible for their brutal punishments.[43] Meanwhile Carlota Lucumí carried out her own vendettas, as she and two other slave men caught the overseer's daughter. Carlota was said to have inflicted the gravest wounds, urging her male comrades to continue the attack until the young woman was dead, and boasting about the deed afterward.[44]

Eventually the group continued on to the Ingenio La Concepción, where they arrived "without obstacle." Though they entered through the main slave quarter path, they encountered none of the plantation's 260 slaves, save a man named Julio Gangá. Unbeknown to them, most of the workers at Concepción had been locked inside the boiling house by the administrador. Aside from Julio, the only other slaves they found were eight women outside the purging house, who subsequently joined them. They said the white employees "had mounted horses and left the estate."[45] The rebel contingent lit the cane trash houses afire and tried to force open the purging house where the others were imprisoned, but to no avail.[46]

By the time they reached the grounds of San Miguel the group included at least 100 slaves. Following a similar trajectory, they broke into the homes of the white staff; they broke furniture; took clothing and gold necklaces; destroyed mahogany cupboards, clothing chests, and engineering tools; they seized linens, a steal cutlass, and twenty-nine pesos and six reales.[47] When they searched for the white occupants, they found only one "who fled on horseback."

The motley group made its way into the next district and entered the Ingenio San Lorenzo where the script was very much the same. They burned and attacked the cane trash house and other buildings, attacked the mayoral's home, and appropriated equipment, money, pistols, and a knife.[48] Upon hearing that most of the slaves had fled to the cane fields, "the rebels called to them so they would stop running and not hide." But few of the San Lorenzo slaves joined their ranks, and the rebels moved on.

It was about two or three o'clock in the morning when the insurgents arrived at the San Rafael sugar mill. On all of the previous estates, the group—

frequently described as "a large number of rebellious slaves"—was able to take apart the small white plantation authority and those close to them. A few they had killed, others they injured; most had fled on foot or horseback to distant parts of the estate, to neighboring farms, or into town. But at San Rafael the rebels encountered stiff resistance and all of the power that the rural authorities had been able to muster in the last few hours. When they got there, the rebels set fire to the sugarhouse and were informed that the white residents had left. Again they seem to have had little success with most of the San Rafael slaves, who "responded that they were going to take clothing to their cabins" and come back, but it appears that very few of them actually returned. Manuel said the group stopped in the batey to rest and gather "those who were falling further back in the march."[49]

In that position he said "they were attacked from several points by the cavalry troops and some local country people, and this sparked [se armó] a complete dispersal of all the black rebels." The San Rafael manager recalled that some of the slave rebels carried drums, beating them "according to the custom in the African nations, and others carried leather strips to defend themselves from the blows of the cavalry." He vividly described how slaves got underneath the horses and fought with machetes, "those who did not find themselves armed with this type of tool" threw other instruments at their attackers. Though it is likely that the local militia had more firepower, the troops "fought with the rebels for about an hour and a half, more or less." When the tumult finally subsided, the list of casualties was sobering. Some fifty people had been killed, including Bonifacio. Sixty-seven slaves were taken prisoner, several of whom were severely wounded.[50]

||||||| The Ruptures of Triunvirato

In the days that followed, estate managers and plantation owners around Sabanilla noticed that scores of their slaves were missing, just as their counterparts had back in March. The administrador of the Concepción sugar mill was one of those who had locked most of the estate slaves in the purging house. In spite of this, he responded that at least six slaves were "missing from this estate" the following day.[51] As we saw in chapter 2, slaves generally found numerous ways in their subversive mobility and social networks to experience various levels of freedom. But moments like the night of November 5 also allowed for the kind of massive undermining (and in some cases complete dissolution) of plantation control that usually only manifested during episodes of organized rebellion. In a world run by the logic and legalities of chattel slavery, even a momentary suspension of its legitimacy and mundane practice was nothing short of phenomenal. With this suspension, slave rebels deliberately circumvented the nineteenth century's liberal narratives about emancipation, which privileged *coartación*, metropolitan abolition, and manumission as the normative and sanctioned modes of freedom and autonomy. The methods of this rebellion did not accord with anything that liberal whites or state officials had in mind.

Yet is not clear how many of these departed slaves joined the rebels. In fact, much of the evidence suggests that for all those who joined the rebel ranks, just as many probably headed to their own destinations. Recall that when asked to join the rebels, some of the slaves at San Rafael supposedly responded "that they were going to take clothing from their cabins and did not come back."[52] Inocencio Carabalí, who had been imprisoned in the Ácana plantation jail, stated that he and his companion fled to the woods and used a machete to break the chain that held them. He claimed that afterward they separated but he returned to the mill the next morning. Most of those incarcerated with Inocencio seem to have followed the rebels, but the revolutionaries also lost a good number of them in the woods.[53] When a slave named Macario Lucumí was asked whether or not he went with the rebels on the evening of the rebellion, he responded that his primary objective was to look for his wife, and in doing so, "he followed the bulk of the rebels to the furthest reaches of this estate. . . . Not finding her, he happened at that moment to link up with the slave Basilio of his nation [and] they retreated together and headed toward the estate potrero hiding themselves in the guava patch where they spent the night, until the morning when they were caught by two white men who led them to the San Rafael mill."[54]

The departure of Macario and others for their own paths indicates the complex ways that black Matanceros came to understand this and other oppositional struggles. For some, it meant continuing with the rebel army onto other plantations and continuing to attack properties across the district. For others, their immediate vision of liberty seemed to include no such objectives but entailed more the selection of their own routes, and possibly the desire to create other kinds of communities with those who had already escaped plantation life. Again, the divergent courses that people pursued also took on heavily gendered implications for a group of women at Ácana. We will review their stories presently. The people making such departures may have been motivated by fear for their safety as the insurgency unfolded, or by concern that remaining on the plantation would expose them to further harm by black insurgents or white authorities. For others, the sudden reversal occasioned by the incineration of familiar buildings and land, and the debilitation of white (and sometimes black) chains of command on the estate—bosses and overseers locking themselves in homes, fleeing for their safety, nursing bleeding wounds, or falling dead by slaves' hands—presented an extraordinary opportunity.

The decisions of black residents in that moment must have indeed ensued from fear, confusion, and instincts to protect themselves as much as from joy, elation, defiance, or a desire for revenge. It also must have been abundantly clear to everyone on the grounds near Triunvirato that the normal prohibitions against slaves' departure and escape had been dismantled. As such, scores of slaves left sugar mills like Triunvirato and Ácana that night just as they had in March; some took refuge in the woods, others escaped to the hills. Others did not go very far, but rather hid among the acres of cane fields, the guava trees or plantain groves, sometimes for two or three days.[55]

Many of those slaves who departed eventually returned to the plantations, some turning themselves over to local authorities. Confronted with the problems that all runaways eventually faced, slaves who escaped would have had to locate food, shelter, and a source of protection. During the early days of November especially, the countryside south of the bay was besieged by an unusually high number of white patrols and militiamen, whose presence made permanent escape much more perilous. Finally, those who had children in tow, elderly relatives, or sick companions to worry about might not have gotten very far, if they were able to leave the plantation at all.

Adán Gangá, for example, stated that he did not follow the rebels but rather hid himself in a cane patch for three days, eating nothing but cane the whole time. He reported that he did not come out for fear of white vengeance, but heard from others passing by that the mayoral had been killed. The start of the repression was a familiar reason that people gave for taking their time coming back to the estates. Inocencio stated that he heard or saw "that soldiers were going around killing black people." Many were rounded up by the mayoral, his son, and other white men helping with the effort; others reported turning themselves in, but it is likely they heard or saw the patrols of whites and decided not to take their chances. Some were immediately put to work putting out the fires.[56] Nevertheless, it still took several days for the slaves who had scattered to return to the plantations. As of November 6, the Concepción manager claimed that if the missing

Lista de los esclavos de ambos sexos, pertenecientes a la Dotación de esta [finca]... que [suministra], antes del acontecimiento ocurrido en ella en la madrugada... veinte y siete de Marzo p[róximo] p[asa]do con expresión de los que faltan en la actualidad... sea porque murieron en la refriega ó porque están prófugos, así como los [prendidos?]... [muertos?] ó fallecidos de aquella fecha á la presente.

Enum	Son	Nombres	Nación	Faltas	Enum	Son	Nombres	Nación	Faltas
1	1	Juan Día	Carabalí		40	37	Rafael	Criollo	
2	2	Miguel	Congo	Presentado	41	38	Guillermo	P.	
3	3	Bonifacio	Carabalí		42	39	Jose M.ª	Mina	
4	4	Eugenio	Ganga		43	40	Esteban	P.	
5	5	Sebastián	P.		44		Crispín	Lucumí	Ninguna
6	6	Bernardo	id.		45	41	German	P.	Prófugo
7	7	Lino	P.		46		Eutero	P.	Noremia
8	8	Jose M.ª	P.		47		Simón	P.	id.
9	9	Waldo	Carabalí		48	42	Diego	P.	
10	10	Marcial	P.		49		Alejo	P.	Suicida
11	11	Andres	P.		50	43	S.to Cristóbal	P.	
12	12	Severo	Congo	Presentado	51	44	Teodoro	P.	
13	13	Eusebio	P.		52	45	Cecilio	P.	
14	14	Besugo	P.		53	46	Benigno	P.	
15	15	Nicasio	Ganga	Presentado	54	47	Matías	P.	
16	16	Marcelino	Bricamo	Presentado	55	48	Leandro	P.	
17	17	Luciano	P.		56	49	Abraham	P.	
18	18	Canuto	Congo	Presentado	57		Pepin	P.	Ninguna
19	19	Valentín	Lucumí		58		Felix	P.	Suicida
20	20	Benito	P.	Presentado	59	50	Apolonio	P.	
21	21	Gonzalo	Congo		60	51	Servio	P.	
22	22	Maximo	Ganga		61	52	Blanco	P.	Apuntó
23	23	Julián	P.		62	53	Ifigil	P.	
24	24	Camilo	Lucumí		63	54	Geronimo	Congo	
25	25	Carlos	Macua		64		Francisco	Lucumí	Noremia
26	26	Marcelino	Congo		65	55	Cristobal	P.	Apuntó
27	27	Julián	Griza		66	56	Eligio	P.	
28		Jose M.ª	Congo	Asesinado	67	57	Jacinto	P.	
29	28	Gregorio	P.		68	58	Nicolás	P.	
30	29	Alejandro	P.		69	59	Amaro	P.	
31		Domingo	P.	Asesinado	70	60	Santiago	P.	
32	30	Ciriaco	Ganga		71	61	Silvestre	P.	
33	31	Domingo	id.	Presentado	72	62	Telesfero	P.	
34	32	Gabriel	P.	Presentado	73	63	Martin	P.	Prófugo
35	33	Francisco	Mondingo		74	64	Nestor	P.	Prófugo
36	34	Simón	Congo		75	65	Casimiro	P.	
37		Jacinto	Bricamo	Asesinado	76	66	Melitón	P.	
38	35	Damian	P.no		77	67	Raymundo	P.	
39	36	Patricio	Grza		78	68	Leon	P.	

List of slaves missing after the rebellion on March 27, 1843. Courtesy of the Archivo Nacional de Cuba.

slaves did not appear in adequate time, he would notify the local examining magistrate.[57]

But some slaves never returned. At least the organizers like Cristóbal, Santiago, Eduardo, and others like Eugenio, Nazario, Vidal, and Damián apparently did not, since the following March they were still listed as "fugitive" (prófugo). It is likely that searches for fugitive slaves continued for weeks afterward, and that some were eventually captured. Others may have committed suicide. But it is also sensible to conclude that those who never returned continued to live as runaways, or joined mobile or settled palenque communities in the mountains, caves, and forests of Matanzas. The unfulfilled death sentences and prison sentences represented by these missing slaves trouble the idea that no slaves were freed as a result of the November rebellion or those that preceded it.

IIIIIIII The Rebels

The question of where the slaves went when they dispersed, and the divergent courses they pursued, opens an especially propitious window to examine the sweeping category of "the slave rebels" that was consistently invoked by colonial authorities and others. In November as in March, the attacks on people and property were physically carried out by a handful of individuals, yet nearly every report of those two nights spoke in terms of sizeable numbers of "rebels." Rebels—plural, extremely plural—who set fire to buildings, rebels who marched on neighboring estates, rebels who were "in a tumult"; if the trial record can be read as a text, these sublevados became a character unto themselves who moved and acted as though of one body. The continual mention of "un gran número de negros" of course served many purposes, and underlines the manner in which a disobedient collective—particularly a disobedient black collective—would have expanded and multiplied in any narrative produced for prosecuting military authorities.

More to the point, part of what people were invoking when they spoke of a "mass of rebel slaves" was a larger feeling of racial bedlam; a deeply unnerving sense that the existing plantation order, the self-sustaining racial reason of the countryside, had gone grievously awry. Yet the repeated invocation of "the rebels" also draws attention to an unspecified number of people who attached themselves or became attached to the revolutionary cohort in a number of different ways: including scores of slaves who traveled to five different estates that night, threw more cane trash to heighten the fires, indicated when targeted individuals came into view, failed to warn white workers of the danger they were in, vocally supported the destruction happening around them, or otherwise encouraged the reversals happening before their eyes.

The all-encompassing term *the rebels*, however, would have also included at various moments those who came out to the batey or down to the fields to find out what was happening, those who lingered in the vicinity out of fascination or horror, those doing their evening chores who also happened to be in the area, and those who were in fact not fanning the flames at all but rather looking for loved ones or making plans to escape. Under the appellation of "the rebels," any slave's proximity to mutinous activities was effectively coded as dissidence and even assault, even for those doing little or nothing to disrupt the plantation world.

This undifferentiated reference to "the rebels" performs two equally important but radically divergent functions. First, it invites us to see an *array* of activities and inclinations that are rarely viewed as central to "the" rebel narrative but that are often critical to the rebellion's maturation, such as the domestic slaves who abandoned Rafael Aguilar and his family in March 1843. Such actions seldom become legible in later histories in the same way that bloodshed or other expressions of violence become part of "the rebellion." They typically have deeply gendered implications, as I discuss further in chapter 5. In other words, they tend to make women much less visible in the historical record.

Nonviolent actions such as these are often considered peripheral to more important events. But the sudden proliferation of people who openly disobeyed orders, placed their own self-interest or protection above that of their owners, failed to align with certain standard expectations, spilled out from their cabins and otherwise failed to remain "in place," or simply failed to act in compliance with the established plantation codes—these actions in their *collectivity* are what constituted the rebellion. This wide span of noncompliant behaviors was vital to creating the "conditions of possibility" for any slave insurgency, particularly ones that lasted as long as those in November and March. Without the "slave collective"—including all of the slaves who may have never touched a white person or broken down a door—there would have been no slave rebellion.

A term like *the rebels* therefore obscures as much as it illuminates, flattening out a wide range of responses to relationships with the events of that evening. Here it is useful to return to the March rebellion and the example of the Alcancía manger José Cano, who observed a large number of slaves "not working to put out the fire." Cano would have been unable to distinguish between those who were happy to let the cane trash house burn, and those who were setting it on fire under the Lucumís' direction. Recall, for example, the testimony given by the *candelero* Anacleto, who related that boiling house men "showed up to throw water and put out the fire, but the Lucumís, armed with their machetes, objected, and said that anyone who went to put out the fire, they would cut off their heads with their machetes."[58] Thus in the retelling of the rebellions, a range of actions were collapsed into one broad description, eliding the different reactions of the enslaved.

While the insurgency opened up critical opportunities for those who supported the retaliation, it also compelled thorny questions for those who were uncertain of what to do, for those who disliked bloodshed or carnage, for those who preferred to follow their own paths, for those who feared for their friends and loved ones, for those with emotional ties to the targets of the rebellion, and for those who disapproved of rebel violence even while they understood it. In short, the short-lived rebellion brought to the surface a range of critical questions about how black freedom should best be understood and enacted.

This dissemblance can be seen particularly well in the testimonies of those who set off on their own paths as the rebel group left the estates, and it is especially visible in the accounts of slave women spread out over two estates. Several of these women testified that they were bodily threatened and forced to follow the rebels. Recall that several women from Ácana had gathered at the infirmary earlier in the night. Catalina Gangá stated that a portion of the rebels "came to where the black women were and, threatening them with death, made them leave the Ingenio toward the direction of Concepción." On the San Miguel sugar mill, María del Rosario Lucumí similarly reported "that she came to the Batey out of curiosity to see [what was happening] and at that moment was threatened by some of the rebels who approached her, who told her that if she did not accompany them they would give it to her [*le darían*] with machetes that they were carrying in their hands." María del Rosario continued that in view of "such threats," she believed that "she had no choice but to follow the rebels."[59]

When asked why she did not hide herself in the cane fields, María responded that "she tried many times to fall back, but that when she tried to put this in practice, she always ran into several of those who were [walking] further back, and they forced her to follow them anew."[60] For this reason, she followed the rebels as far as San Rafael. Pilar Carabalí, also enslaved at San Miguel, similarly testified that she was forced at machete-point to follow the rebels. She stated that "a black man was following close behind her, and therefore she could not hide herself in order to return to this estate."[61]

Several of these women later reported that they took pains to hide themselves, often in groups. For example, Filomena Gangá reported that she was "scandalized and uncomfortable" at Fermina's conduct at Ácana and withdrew to hide in the plantain grove with other women, where she remained until the following morning. Camila Criolla similarly voiced her disdain for the attack on the mayoral's home and went to hide among the plantain trees. Other slave women like Catalina, Matea, Martina, and Magdalena told authorities that they felt compelled to follow the rebels part of the way, in some cases as far as Concepción, but then several of them broke off from the rebel march as they reached the outskirts of Ácana, hiding themselves among the cane patches.[62] Juliana Criolla reported that once she and her husband got to Concepción he went on ahead, and she continued with other women to the infirmary. When asked why she separated from her husband, she said "the child she was carrying in her arms was making things very difficult."[63]

These accounts suggest that part of what it meant to wage an insurgency in November was rooted in masculine forms of discipline, whereby the direction, course, and actions of the night were directed largely (though not solely) by militant African men. Such militancy appears to have been deeply tied to aggressive displays of masculinity and various forms of coercion bordering on violence. There is every reason to believe that these women emphasized their unwillingness to abandon the estate in the hope of reducing punishment by the authorities, but the consistency of such reports on more than one property suggests that there was some accuracy to this picture. It is disturbing to contemplate this picture: of women corralled and threatened into joining a male-dominated insurgency.

There are, however, points that complicate this portrait. First, several male witnesses also proclaimed their revulsion at what was happening, and it is difficult to believe that they too would not have been forced to follow the insurgents. Moreover, the phrasing and timing of the women's responses suggest that they may have turned to the white masculinist logic of presiding authorities; that is, relying on a self-presentation (one might even say a performance) of docile womanhood that would have theoretically rendered their participation in a violent—read male—insurgency dubious. It is particularly telling that aside from Fermina and Carlota, the women who became most visible in the 1843 trial record were those who took great pains to distance themselves from the insurgency. Each one of the handful of women interrogated insisted that she had had no connection to the rebel activities. But an alternative reading of the trial records shows that these statements did not represent the full scope of female responses to the insurgency.

On the contrary, the trial record is interspersed with a range of stories that disrupt the narrative of November 5 as an exclusively or overwhelmingly masculine enterprise. For example, when Catalina Gangá spoke about seeing the rebels invade her estate, she said "she saw everything inundated with slaves of both sexes," and we know that at least two women from Triunvirato were shot in the battle at San Rafael.[64] Of the forty-two people taken prisoner by the cavalry troops, thirteen of them were women.[65] The *mayoral* of the San Miguel mill later reported that only two slave men had fled the estate or left with the rebels, but that eleven slave women had done so.[66] Other reports indicated women who either joined the rebels or escaped from the plantations during the rebellion.[67]

Ironically, the women who joined the rebels, escaped, or were captured are much more difficult to find in the trial record. An interesting form of textual erasure is at work here in which the women who condemned the revolt were given (or more appropriately, forced) into vocality, and those who potentially did just the opposite emerged only as numbers and occasional names—several of them were likely imprisoned. Moreover, one is left with the image of the belligerent-black-man-as-bloodthirsty-rebel, only deepening the justification of the colonial state to punish precisely that man.

In the days that followed November 5, colonial officials began to piece together the events of that night. The authorities were particularly interested in decapitating the movement and brutally dismantling any and all leadership and rebel cells. Eighteen of the nineteen slaves deemed to be the most dangerous and critical to the insurgency were sent to the Cárcel Pública in Matanzas, where they remained for several months. Bonifacio died at San Rafael. The Lucumí slaves Cristóbal, Santiago, and Eduardo from Triunvirato all managed to escape and as of the final sentencing had not been found. The remaining eight of the Triunvirato and Ácana leaders were sentenced to death. These included Manuel Gangá (whose extensive confession did not exonerate him), Fermina Lucumí, Adán Lucumí, Narciso Lucumí, Zoilo Lucumí, Cirilo Lucumí, Agustín Carabalí, and Nicolás Gangá.

Two of the eight leaders were slated to be executed on the grounds of Triunvirato, two more each on Ácana, Concepción, and San Miguel. Military officials ordered their bodies burned. In addition to the entire slave population of each mill, ten black representatives "from each of the contiguous estates" were required to watch.[68] Inocencio Carabalí was sentenced to ten years in prison and 100 lashes with the whip. Dimas Gangá, Martín Mina, and several fugitive slaves were sentenced in absentia to fifty lashes and six years of "correction" under ball and chain (*con ramal y grillete*), to be "employed in the harshest labors of the estate." Two more slaves were sentenced to twenty-five lashes; sixty-nine slaves captured in the aftermath were sentenced to ten lashes.[69]

|||||||| Connecting the Fibers of Unrest: 1843 into 1844

The news of these two insurgencies traveled quickly. Although organized slave resistance was hardly unusual in the Matanzas countryside, the rebellions of March and November were significant for those already committed to a new movement. The reign of terror enacted after these two revolts foreshadowed the nightmare to come in the following year. For many, the counterinsurgency must have had its desired effect, sowing fear and terror into the hearts of hundreds of slaves across Matanzas who heard the news, saw the carnage, or knew those tortured or killed. Dozens of those who joined the fray had dispersed to the forests and mountains of the still developing regions, but many others had been shot down or captured. During both repressions enslaved people were summoned from miles around to watch inhuman acts perpetuated on human bodies. Both times the suspected leaders were whipped anywhere from 10 to 100 times, beatings which must have left little skin on the rebels' flayed backs. The severed heads of other leaders remained posted on spikes outside the estates until such time as they were deemed ready to remove. Still other troublemakers were compelled to continue the brutal labors of sugar under the weight of ball and chain for months afterward.

By the following year, slaves in the area were again being questioned about a black rebel movement. It is difficult to know whether some of the same people who joined the March and November insurgencies in 1843 became involved in the insurgent movement of 1844. What can be said with greater certainty is that a few of those who reported becoming closely connected to this new movement were either living on the same estates that rebelled in 1843 or in the areas close to where those slaves had taken up arms.

The archival evidence also makes it difficult to insist that people living on the same estates felt compelled to join new waves of organizing because they were politicized by the dissent of 1843. At the same time, however, it hardly seems possible that those living in or around Bemba or Sabanilla could have failed to be affected by what transpired during those days. Few black people in eastern Matanzas or further west in November would have remained impartial about the fact that over 300 bondpeople from neighboring estates had taken up arms. Those who challenged or failed to join them were often treated as traitors and may have been targets for violence or coercion. It also seems likely that some of those who opposed the way in which the violence unfolded became more sympathetic as the repression set in, as local militias slaughtered dozens upon dozens of blacks and jailed even more, as friends and relatives were subject to humiliating interrogations, and as they were all forced to watch human bodies beaten and burned. Such moments left little room for neutrality.

Finally, it is difficult to pinpoint when news first started to spread about a rebel movement in 1844, but it is clear that these two revolts became especially important signposts in several of the testimonies. While other rebellions, some of them sizeable, ensued in the months between March and November, these two episodes emerged with the greatest frequency when 1844 witnesses spoke of important occurrences from the previous year. While most reports of organizing for 1844 began to circulate later in the year, few accounts reveal extensive discussion of an 1844 plan in the rural regions before the March revolt at Bemba.

For some, Bemba seems to have functioned as a critical rupture that opened up possibilities for entertaining more subversive talk. By April of that year, buildings burned and ransacked had to be repaired, and cane patches scorched and charred had to be replanted. For some the aftermath of these events meant acclimating to new foremen, for others mourning their dead or acknowledging their own survival, and for still others moving about with telling reminders of retribution on their backs and ankles. Again, though black plantation residents must have attached a variety of meanings to those memories, the awareness of what had transpired had to have been inescapable.

Toward the end of the year, a small group of slaves from Nieves, Trinidad, and Alcancía began to circulate plans for an even larger insurrection in the coming year. These individuals—mostly African men but also a few African and Cuban women—began to connect with others from nearby plantations, especially those of Encanto, Achury, and Victoria. Together, this cluster of mills became the epicenter for a new movement in the eastern part of the region.

"Since the previous year, with the happenings of Bemba, there was born in the slaves of this sugar mill the desire to rise up." In March 1844 these words poignantly bespoke the catalyzing energy that the Bemba insurgency unleashed for certain slaves.[70] They were recorded from Merced Criolla, the Encanto slave whose husband was eventually killed, a woman others tried to install as a rebel queen the following year. Alongside Merced's account, the Encanto mill produced other provocative testimonies about the coming movement. In the weeks and months following the March revolt, a small group of African men at Encanto took the reins to organize and direct the new (or renewed) insurgent activities. A Gangá tile maker named Patricio rose to become the most significant or at least the most oft-cited captain of the Encanto rebels.

Patricio and others were reported to have had frequent contact with the nearby Nieves mill, where the main organizers included Tomás, a Lucumí foreman; Manuel, a Mina cart driver; and José, a Carabalí former overseer. For months after the March defeat—indeed long into the winter of 1844— the cabins of these and other men became sites to map out the next steps, and to lay some of the architecture for the new movement. The cabin of Tomás Lucumí, frequently portrayed as the head organizer at Nieves, was one such site. More than one of the meetings in Tomás's home included among its attendees emissaries from still another local property, Trinidad.

Here it is important to return momentarily to the Trinidad sugar mill back in late March, to the moment when Rafael Aguilar first learned that armed resistance was brewing on his estate. The day before the March revolt exploded, at least two men came to Rafael Aguilar with the news that trouble was on the horizon. One of them was Mateo Lucumí. Not much is known about young Mateo. The archival records indicate that he was of the Lucumí nation and close to twenty-five years old, and he was listed simply as a member of Trinidad's workforce. The Sunday morning before the March rebellion, he and three other men reportedly made their way across Trinidad's border, to a farm near Alcancía. Among those who accompanied Mateo was another young Lucumí in his twenties named Dionisio. Though they later denied it, Mateo, Dionisio, and others allegedly tried to entice several slaves to join the insurrection on this Sunday visit. One of the men they tried to recruit threatened to report the conspirators to their owner. Possibly in the hopes of preempting such an action—but ultimately for reasons known only to them — Mateo and a few others decided the following week to inform their owner that a rebellion was afoot.[71] As retribution for this betrayal, the cabins of each of these individuals were destroyed when the insurrection broke out the following day. As Dionisio saw it, "The rebels burned the cabins of [himself] and his companions out of revenge."[72]

Given the seemingly traitorous actions of Mateo and Dionisio Lucumí the previous March, it is strange that almost exactly a year later — when Tomás Lucumí spoke about the meetings taking place in his cabin — that Tomás would cite two individuals by those exact same names coming to the nocturnal gatherings from Aguilar's Trinidad. It is difficult to determine whether these were the same two men who reported to Aguilar in March 1843, but the coincidence is too striking to ignore.

According to several witnesses, Dionisio and Mateo came to Tomás's cabin with a small contingent from Trinidad that included Dionisio's wife, Dolores, and another man named Federico, all Lucumís.[73] Still another meeting in Tomás's cabin convened an even more interesting group that included a free black man named Antonio González and a local Gangá muleteer. Still another meeting reportedly found a Joaquín Gangá from Alcancía among the participants.[74] Tomás would eventually travel from Nieves to Trinidad for similar purposes, and he joined a gathering held in Mateo's cabin (again, it is unclear whether this was the same Mateo from the March denouncement). The assembly that met at Trinidad included Mateo; Mateo's wife, Catalina; Federico; and Federico's wife, whose name I have not found. The reported attendance of Catalina, Dionisio's wife (Dolores), and Federico's unnamed wife implies that it was not uncommon for women to be present for these early conversations about an 1844 movement. That these women all came with their male partners, men who themselves were named as central leaders, suggests that as a group women who were involved with male organizers knew about some of the emerging plans and maintained an investment in their overall outcome. This is a phenomenon I will discuss in greater detail in chapter 5.

Thus it was that representatives from Trinidad, Alcancía, and Nieves eventually resurfaced in juntas that pondered the next phase of what increasingly began to appear as a continuous movement. The recurrence of these three plantations in the trial record suggests that in spite of — if not because of — all that had happened on these estates in recent memory, a few individuals began to mobilize for another more substantial insurrection, one that they hoped this time would not fail.

Bit by bit, the numbers of what might be called the new Bemba movement grew, as men like Patricio and Tomás made contact with other high-ranking slave men and women from other surrounding plantations like Achury and Victoria. Most of the 1844 plantations whose leaders intended to link up were located next to one another, and organizers traversed the boundaries of their respective properties fairly often and with relative ease.[75] The plan was carefully laid. On March 7 or 8, 1844, the leaders at Encanto were to set fire to the countryside, thereby indicating that the rebellion had begun in Macuriges. Neighboring properties would follow suit, meet up on the grounds of Encanto, and the army would continue toward Bemba following the railroad to Cárdenas. Such a route further evokes the idea of unfinished business from the previous year. On March 1, 1844, a fire broke out unexpectedly at Encanto, and military officials began to question the slaves there.

Additional testimonies about items found on the grounds of these estates strengthen the connective strands between the Bemba rebellion of 1843 and the subsequent movement of 1844. In their testimonies, Tomás Lucumí and José Carabalí stated that they came across two pistols in the fields of Nieves not long after the March offensive, as well as a flag in the cane patches alongside the railroad, "where it appeared that the rebels of . . . Bemba left it the previous year." Tomás stated that "he kept it among the same canes and [later] took it to Encanto."[76] The guns and the flag formed part of a broader military gear that would have come in handy had the 1844 conspiracy morphed into an insurrection.

One of the most provocative stories highlighting the connection between the events of 1843 and those of 1844 concerns a group of free black men living near the rebellious estates from March. All of these men knew one another, lived in relative proximity, and maintained relationships with several important slave leaders. During the March insurrection of 1843 and the movement of 1844 Jacinto Roque, Cristóbal Linares, José Subiza, Mariano Fuentes, and Antonio González were among the more frequently cited conspirators, and their names surfaced more than once during the trials of both years.[77] Each of these men worked as a seasonal laborers on the local plantations (that is, in the districts of Cimarrones and Macuriges) and each one had been a slave himself anywhere from three to ten years before. Most of them had also been born in Africa. To varying degrees, Jacinto, Cristóbal, José, Mariano, and Antonio were each thought to have planned secretly with slave men on estates nearby for a spring insurrection in 1843. If this is any indication, the places these men allegedly visited were indeed attacked on March 27.[78] A year later, during the 1844 trials, all of these men were implicated in another rebellion that was discovered in the same region.

Enough stories have emerged about this group of free black men to render their reappearance in the 1844 trial record more than coincidental. For example, Jacinto Roque was accused of being one of the "principal promoters" of the local insurgent movement in 1843. Though not much evidence has emerged to sustain that characterization, it is very possible that he was involved in its unfolding, as he was cited (more than once) as holding meetings with slaves from the Primavera sugar mill and another nearby estate. Of particular importance, however, is the charge that Jacinto was a spiritual adept, accused of selling "witchcraft items" to the slaves with whom he met. The authorities argued that with the aim [intento] of inciting the Primavera slaves to rise up, Jacinto Roque, "who they gave the title of padre, sold the others dolls or witchcraft items, persuading them that the possessor of these would be free of the weapons of the whites, who they could later kill without risk." Roque was charged with other offenses related to insurgent spiritual work, including holding a seditious meeting in his house to practice "witchcraft" and "going out to all the estates of this district and that of Cimarrones to sell the cited witchcraft, which might perhaps be found in his [Roque's] possession."[79]

Others like Mariano Fuentes Congo and José Subiza were also described as traveling to the Nieves estate to recruit slave participants for the movement, attempting to sell them protective spiritual amulets.[80] Such stories clearly point to the existence of a lively subterranean commerce in spiritual protection among people of African descent in Matanzas, a trade I discuss further in chapter 7. For the moment, however, it will suffice to underscore that each of these men was thought to have fomented not only portions of the insurrection that erupted in March 1843 but also segments of the rebellion that was to erupt in March 1844.[81]

But perhaps no story is as provocative and as illustrative as that of Antonio López (or González), a former slave of the Carabalí nation. Antonio had been a slave on Peñalver's Alcancía estate — one of the first estates to rise up that March — but he had gained his liberty sometime in 1841. Because of his previous residence at Alcancía, Antonio knew the Lucumí slaves who received news of the March rebellion not long before it broke out.[82] In addition to Alcancía, Antonio either worked at or spent time on La Luisa, another insurgent property from 1843. It is not clear if Antonio had any direct involvement in the 1843 insurrections, but he was thought to have helped organize people on the Nieves estate for the 1844 uprising.[83] These kinds of stories strongly suggest that free men like Jacinto, José, Antonio, and Mariano once again began circulating to rural plantations a few months after the March 1843 rebellion was put down—talking to slaves, feeling out their interest, and offering to sell them protective amulets. For rebel leaders free and enslaved, then, it is plausible to conclude that the Bemba rebellion that authorities thought they had put down was only the beginning—or, in truth, the middle—of a larger insurgent movement. Rather than marking the end of one insurgency, Bemba's conclusion was in fact the start of a new one.

|||||||| The Triunvirato and Oviedo Connections

The spring months of 1843 gave way to summer. The arduous grinding season came to an end, heavy rains and heat settled in, and black workers slowly began to recover from yet another harvest. Many would be forced to bury friends or family members whose bodies had succumbed to the arduous labors, or to the effects of dysentery. The work turned to planting new seeds, mending fences and buildings, and cleaning sugar machinery. And throughout these months, almost unbelievably, a few black plantation residents continued to receive news of another rebellion.

Throughout the summer and into the early fall of 1843, this news made its way beyond the boundaries of Macuriges, traveling further east to the Sierra Morena districts of Ceja de Pablo and Rancho Veloz, back west toward Sabanilla and Alacranes, and up toward the bay area of Yumurí. When questioned a year later, more than a few local organizers stated that from June to August, they heard from the lips of itinerant leaders, primarily free black men, about an underground movement that was gathering steam.[84]

Smaller uprisings continued to break out during the spring and summer months. On the ingenios Santa Rosa and Majagua, slaves lit fires and staged an open protest in May. On June 2, 1843, Fermina Lucumí and her fellow captain Eduardo organized a rebellion of over fifty slaves on the soon-to-be-infamous estates of Ácana and Concepción. As the rebellion frayed, Fermina was captured along with fifteen others from Ácana, laid down on the floor face down (bocabajo), and beaten. Her feet were then placed in shackles that she was forced to wear for months afterward.[85] During that same month of June close to 300 slaves joined an insurrection on the Flor de Cuba sugar estate. In July the Arratía sugar plantation saw an uprising of about forty slaves, mostly from the Lucumí nation. Though these districts were sometimes miles from one another, the contagion of violent protest was spreading.[86]

By the fall of 1843 plans were literally being made right and left, from Havana all the way to Cárdenas. As September and October passed, more and more would-be leaders and recruits began to hear through the black grapevine that a larger insurrection was afoot. During the first few days of November, a series of critical events took place in rapid succession. On November 2, the new captain general, Leopoldo O'Donnell—who would soon preside over a reign of terror—set foot on the shores of Cuba. On November 3, five months after the June rebellion, the shackles were finally removed from Fermina's ankles. On November 5, the Triunvirato insurrection erupted.

As explosive as the rebellions of 1843 were, there is a strange silence around their genesis. People like Fermina and Bonifacio took a leading role in fanning the flames of insurgency on their respective plantations, but little is known about their planning and preparation, and even less about how they were tied to the urban organizing. There is some scant evidence to suggest that slaves involved in organizing these revolts had direct contact with urban agitators in planning for a larger insurrection.[87] But the rebellions of 1843 are better understood for what they ultimately catalyzed.

While on Sunday trips with his owner, Jorge Gangá testified that he would talk to another slave named Perico Criollo. Perico "would tell him that the slaves on the Ingenio El Triunvirato had risen up, along with those from other farms, and had killed the whites. What were those slaves on the Ingenio La Rosa [Jorge's estate] doing? Why, they must be numbskulls, good-for-nothings. The mulattoes and the freedmen were going to get involved in fighting the whites, and they would become the landowners." Jorge claimed to have been similarly prodded by one of the contramayorales who pointedly asked, "What were they waiting for? Didn't they know about the slaves fighting over on the Ingenio Alcancía?"[88]

Other slaves who knew about or had themselves experienced these rebellions were even more mobilized when they received word of a larger movement with more support. The November Triunvirato rebellion became a particularly important reference point for urban organizers who were taking the temperature of the movement in the fall of 1843. During his interrogation in 1844 the free man Vicente Borrero indicted José Parreño, a carpenter and officer in the firefighting corps, as one of the conspirators. Vicente stated that when he asked José to return a carpenter's bench to him,

José purportedly responded that he could not do so right now, "that . . . his frequent travels to Matanzas and Guanabacoa [and] the critical circumstances [created by] the slave uprisings in the first location did not give him time for anything, and that after everything calmed down he would return the bench to him."[89] While it is unclear whether Vicente was telling the truth, it *is* clear that the 1843 rebellions made a strong impression on urban organizers, and the repression had a devastating impact on them. In other words, the discourse, around Triunvirato especially, indicates that urban organizers viewed rural black laborers as integral to a larger struggle.

Of all the free black agitators who traveled back and forth to the cities, José María Mondejar was the most ubiquitous in the testimonies I examined. Mondejar would eventually testify that he was recruited by Plácido, the renowned mulatto poet and accused leader of the urban mobilizations of 1844. Mondejar stated that in their first meeting, during the same month of the November rebellion, Plácido spoke to him about the tragedy of Triunvirato. In his recounting Plácido remarked of the insurgency being planned for 1844, "they were not going to make a drunken mess [*borracheras*] of things like the [uprising] of Triunvirato." He said the arrival of the troops had signaled the Triunvirato insurgents' downfall: "they dropped like flies because being few, [the rebels] could not defend themselves."[90]

The defeat at Triunvirato had a profound effect on Mondejar and others to whom he was closely connected. Rebel cohorts across the region seem to have been forced to regroup after this setback. Mondejar took the news about Triunvirato with him to other places he went, spreading the word as far as Havana. During one trip to the capital, Mondejar visited the home of José María García, a free black conspirator who made his living in rural Cárdenas. According to García, "When Mondejar arrived at his house in Havana, he gave him the news that the Triunvirato rebellion had taken place, saying that as he was leaving [Matanzas], the troops were starting to make their rounds of Sabanilla, and then . . . [García said to Mondejar] that there was no need to be careful anymore, since the government had sent troops to suppress that movement."[91]

In one of his many late fall trips through the Sabanilla countryside, Mondejar visited the Santísima Trinidad plantation. One of the primary leaders there, Marcos Gangá, stated that after the events of Triunvirato, "half of the people were discouraged." In spite of these gruesome events, Mondejar came to encourage Marcos and other lieutenants, "saying he had at the ready all the other slaves from outside." Marcos reported that in spite of the fears pervading the ingenio, a group of men on the estate still wanted to arm themselves for battle. Others also testified that Mondejar had either spoken to them in the weeks following the Triunvirato revolt, or that Mondejar somehow alluded to its occurrence.[92]

The next chapter explores this world of urban rebel organizing that arose in the early 1840s, a world that became increasingly linked to mobilizations in the countryside around the time of the Triunvirato revolt. Both the rebellions that erupted in 1843 and the insurgent designs of 1844 emerged from a longer tradition of radical slave resistance and anticolonial organizing that expanded across the western countryside, linking disparate groups of people in unexpected ways. The movement that would envelop the western part of the island during the early 1840s was fed by a number of powerful streams that would converge explosively in 1844.

Chapter Four

To Raise a Rebellion in Matanzas
THE URBAN CONNECTION, 1841–1843

In March 1844 Patricio Mandinga and Blas Lucumí, two slaves of a British sugar proprietor, were indicted as rebel captains in their district of rural Matanzas. Both men testified that they had traveled to the city of Matanzas at various points, and these sojourns brought them in contact with black organizers there.[1] Although the particulars of such an account can be difficult to verify, it is clear that Patricio, Blas, and several other accused activists on nearby plantations—miles and in many ways worlds away from the city of Matanzas—had reason to know the names of some of the most highly sought-after urban leaders of the 1844 movement.

The insurgent organizing in Cuba's plantation countryside during the 1840s emerged from the distinctive social and political networks that shaped western Cuba's black political landscape. This organizing was also heavily informed by a series of political struggles unfolding across the island including growing anticolonial sentiment, international abolitionist activity, and urban free people's struggles for full citizenship. While the question of precisely when the 1844 conspiracy began is one of La Escalera's most intriguing mysteries, an equally riveting but unexplored line of inquiry is how these urban mobilizations overlapped and intersected with those in the rural areas. In closely examining the linkages between these diverse mobilizations, this chapter will shed light not only on the ways that rural Africans were defining their own resistance but also on how urban organizers were influenced by, and responding to, rural black political struggles.

||||||| Linking the Urban-Rural Centers

Several of the best-known leaders of 1844 testified that by the close of 1843, a core group of rebel "agents" had been carefully identified and charged with advancing the insurgency.[2] Most of these testimonies are conflicting and sporadic, however, and it is difficult to get an accurate picture of who the official ambassadors were. More obvious are the many *unofficial* ambassadors who circulated news about the movement across Cuba's western and central districts. By 1843 hundreds of black people crisscrossed the region with news, rumors, and information about a coming rebellion. Some of them came in contact with lieutenants formally appointed for this task, but many of them did not. Nevertheless, this intelligence was authentic enough for small groups of slaves to begin making plans with others on nearby estates. For all intents and purposes, the message about the 1844 movement—in all of its unwieldy permutations—was moved through the countryside by these unofficial interlocutors: free men who worked on the estates, as well as slave men with mobility and specialized jobs. In their hands the insurgent movement slowly came to life.

The stories of several free women of color suggest that another current was running alongside this rebel stream. In general, urban women of color did not traverse the countryside with anywhere near the same frequency as their male counterparts. Nevertheless, they were mobile, especially within the cities. Particularly if they had children on the estates, free women's movement could take them out of town to the surrounding farms and plantations.

By 1844, one such free woman, Trancito Robaina Mandinga, had been living in the Matanzas neighborhood of Versalles for close to five years. Several years before, she had been a slave of Pedro Domech on the Buena Esperanza coffee plantation, fifteen or twenty miles from the city. By 1844 Buena Esperanza emerged as one of the most active centers of political agitation in the region, and Trancito was named more than once as a significant figure in this local movement. In March of that year, Domech testified that he had discovered an elaborate plot "to assassinate [him] and rise up against all the whites, those of the countryside joining with those of Matanzas."[3] Other witnesses continued to name the streams of visitors who came to Buena Esperanza on Sundays and after nightfall to discuss an insurgent movement of considerable breadth. Several of them reported that a handful of free people from Matanzas had come to the meetings, including Trancito Robaina.

Other slaves from the nearby properties of Juan Bautista Caffini, Francisco Ruell, and Thomas Owens ("the Englishman") also came to these gatherings. And though she now lived in Matanzas, Trancito evidently maintained a close relationship with Blas Lucumí and Patricio Mandinga, who both belonged to Owens. Patricio and Blas were apprentices in Owens's shoemaking enterprise and they often came to Trancito's house on their trips to Matanzas.[4] Trancito made her home across from the *cabildo* Mandinga Moforo and most of the time she seems to have lived with her husband, a Sebastián Peres of the Mandinga nation. As with Mandingas, Sebastian and Trancito were very likely taken from the port of Río Pongo in present-day Guinea and may have been part of the Mande-speaking communities that stretched from Senegambia and Sierra Leone. While Sebastián was in fact a slave who belonged to Julián Sicar, he was allowed to work "por su cuenta"—that is for himself—like others in the urban sector, in exchange for returning most of the profits to his owner.[5]

Sebastián, Trancito, Patricio, and Blas had a complicated relationship. Trancito was Blas's godmother. Blas was the only Lucumí of the group, but he may have actually come from regions further north of Greater Oyo which would have allowed him a closer identification with the Mandingas. The themes of religious ritual and healing were recurring motifs in the relationships among these four Africans.[6] According to Sebastián, Blas and Patricio once brought herbs and "other little things that they usually call witchcraft" to take care of Trancito, but though Sebastián saw them, he allegedly "did not believe in that nor had he used such things."[7] However, at least five witnesses described Sebastián as a medicinal priest (*brujo*), who provided Patricio and Blas with protective amulets. The amulets became critical to the mobilization on the Domech estate.

Trancito and Sebastián were cited by several witnesses as taking part in the assemblies held on Domech's property, traveling out of the city of Matanzas to the plantation where Trancito once lived. In these gatherings Blas and Patricio came from the nearby Owens estate to sell a few of their amulets, perform a series of sacred rituals, and eventually outline a plan to "rise up like those in Matanzas." If Sebastián was indeed the source of the amulets above, this would have rendered him much more foundational to the plans at Buena Esperanza than the authorities realized. However, these officials ultimately concluded that he and Trancito were critical enough to the impending plans to warrant serious punishment. Sebastián was sentenced to "ten years of the harshest labor with [iron] collar and [foot] shackles" on his home property. Trancito received one of the harsher sentences of the trials, "four years of imprisonment in Africa with the prohibition to return to this Island or Puerto Rico." But before the authorities could prosecute her, Trancito fled the city. As of June 1844 her name was still listed under the heading of "prófugo."[8]

Trancito's story brings several important points into focus. She was among the many African Cubans who purchased their freedom, moved to the nearby towns and hamlets to establish new lives, but returned to their old properties for a number of reasons. Most of those who returned for extended periods of time were free urban men in search of work. But scores of free women like Trancito also made brief visits from the cities, not to find work but to visit their children and loved ones. In both cases, when free urbanites returned to their old properties, they were often described as joining conversations about an imminent uprising. Thus for women like Trancito, the affective register—that is to say, the familial relationships she retained in the plantation world—was deeply imbricated with the insurgent one. This suggests an intriguing gendered axis for rebel participation that I explore further in the next chapter.

Trancito and her husband, Sebastián, also constituted an important social anchor for Blas and Patricio during their sojourns in Matanzas. Their stories underscore the critical role that African-born people and their cultural referents and traditions played in the 1844 movement. The bonds of friendship, god-parentage, and spiritual exchange they shared also shed light on the kinds of relationships that set these four in motion, literally and figuratively. As a collective, their relationship helps to map out the colliding geographies—spatial, personal, and linguistic—that defined an interconnected black world in the years leading up to 1844.

In Matanzas Blas and Patricio came in contact with a larger network of political agitators, namely, the urban coachmen who constituted one of the city's most important rebel columns. In the course of clandestine conversations and meetings, the two men obtained precise information about plans for attack, names of other conspirators, and locations of potential arms. By the time troops arrived to question the Owens leaders in early March, Patricio and Blas could legitimately be called a part of this rebel community. Their story was replicated throughout the towns of western Cuba as rural slaves interfaced with a broad spectrum of city-dwellers, including dock workers, market vendors, coopers, masons, cart drivers, and others who had some level of commitment to the insurgency.

As we saw in the previous chapter, the struggle that Blas and Patricio joined had roots stretching back to at least the previous decade and grew from several dissident political strands that collided in the late 1830s and early 1840s. This unintended collision of recurrent slave rebellions, urban black opposition, and white creole dissatisfaction tied together a set of political fuses that in hindsight only seem to have needed the right match.

That match came in the form of David Turnbull, the antislavery activist appointed British consul in 1841.

|||||||| The Birth of an Urban Conspiracy

David Turnbull's unwavering abolitionist stance made him the object of disgust and antipathy for most of Cuba's wealthy elite. Nevertheless, while in office he managed to cultivate a small group of allies among a more "enlightened" group of slaveholders.[9] Most of them were white men of means, raised on the island, and disturbed by the conservative direction of the colonial government. Many had also been students of the well-known priest and philosopher Félix Varela at the University of Havana, and these "young reformers" imbibed much of his progressivism and his critique of absolutism.[10]

The literary patron Domingo del Monte y Aponte was arguably the most influential of these young liberal reformers, and his influence on the creole writers of the day cannot be underestimated. The list of attendees at del Monte's literary salons reads like a roll call of the most celebrated authors of the time, including José de la Luz y Caballero, José Jacinto Milanés, Anselmo Suárez y Romero, Félix Tanco, and Cirilo Villaverde, among others.[11] These gatherings became the focal point for articulating a Cuban national identity and an emerging creole intellectual culture. But they were also exclusively masculine circles closed to the contemporary female writers of the day, namely, María de las Mercedes Santa Cruz y Montalvo, whose work was important to this early genre of literature.[12]

These circles were traumatized by the reign of Miguel Tacón, who had thwarted their dream of a Cuban Academy of Literature, terminated their beloved *Revista Bimestre Cubana*, and choked their public literary voice. The final blow came in 1837, when the newly restored Spanish monarchy— to which Tacón answered—expelled del Monte, Luz y Caballero, and the slightly older José Antonio Saco from the Spanish Cortes, effectively stripping the colonies of parliamentary representation. Saco, one of the white creoles' most respected leaders and a close friend of del Monte, had been living primarily in exile since 1834 for his political critiques.[13] For many of these writers, the del Monte circle became a place of refuge, and the work they produced marked a defining moment in Cuban nationalism.

By the time David Turnbull arrived in Cuba the liberal creoles were intellectually scarred, politically embittered, and eager for autonomy and change. Turnbull was aware of their resentment and was knee-deep in his own troubles with the Spanish government. His dogmatic activism quickly incurred the wrath of a conservative planter elite and a colonial government uninterested in repressing the slave trade. This was a regime that frustrated any real attempts at political reform, mocked all efforts to end the slave trade, and marginalized anyone who opposed its mandates. Both Turnbull and the liberal white creoles shared a deep frustration with the Spanish Crown, and this mutual antagonism planted the seeds for a relationship to emerge between men like David Turnbull and Domingo del Monte.

The British consul's arrival thus marked the opening of a fortuitous window for Cubans seeking radical change in the structures of colonial rule. It was time to see how far that window could open.[14] Much of what historians know about this nascent movement comes from the confession of Turnbull's chief aide and closest confidant, Francis Ross Cocking. Two years after the trials of La Escalera, Cocking penned an elaborate account of a plan to topple Spanish colonialism and slavery, some of which may have been embellished for his own gain.[15] In 1841, a series of meetings took place that concretized these desires into a plan for creole independence backed by the British. Although the precise details of this early plot remain unclear, the evidence indicates that a group of Cuban dissidents began to forge active plans with the two British civil servants.

In October of that year one of the white creoles, Pedro José Morilla, drafted the closest thing that exists to a "separatist manifesto" of the movement—a petition to the British Anti-slavery Society. In response, Turnbull assured the dissidents that "the powerful and influential abolitionist societies of England . . . offered to the natives of this Island whatever resources of money, arms, boats, and men that might be needed to acquire their independence from Spain, provided they would proceed at the same time to emancipate the slaves."[16] However, Turnbull was acting much more on his own initiative than on behalf of the British government. Aside from Cocking, there is little indication that British authorities ever intended to pursue such a rash endeavor, and this lack of support would soon become evident.

During the same time that they were nurturing separatist designs with the white liberals, Turnbull and Cocking also developed relationships with a small group of black Cubans who themselves had strident critiques of slavery and the colonial government. During the course of that year two distinctive groups emerged from this budding movement—a "colored committee" and a "white committee"—for which Cocking claimed to be the primary go-between.[17] Much less is known about the black and mulatto associates, but most of them were likely legally free, urban-based men. The conspirators of color argued firmly from the beginning that eradicating slavery had to be a central part of the insurgent platform. But the elimination of slavery was hardly a foregone conclusion among the white dissidents.

Their disquiet on the subject underscores the limits of white liberal thinking in Cuba during this time. The "liberal" part of the liberal creole sentiment stemmed from their clear opposition to repressive monarchy and censorship, their desire for economic liberalization, and their opposition to the slave trade. However, the moral terrain in which they traveled was much less certain. As a group, the reformist creoles disapproved of slavery and viewed it as an outmoded form of labor that should be replaced by free (white) labor.[18] Many of them agreed with the planter José Luis Alfonso that slavery was morally indefensible and abolition was therefore a commendable goal but that it should unfold "gradually, with prudence and discretion."[19] They thought immediate emancipation would result in social chaos and economic ruin. As a result, most reformers favored a more gradual course that involved ending the slave trade, increasing white immigration, and slowly abolishing slavery.[20] For the moment, the white creoles saw slavery as "an inherited evil" that represented "the best of all available alternatives."

But the transatlantic slave trade was a different matter. Del Monte and others were heavily influenced by writers like José Antonio Saco who believed the continuation of the slave trade threatened the future and security of Cuba. In the hundreds of slave ships that docked clandestinely around the island they saw the precarious future of the white race and the cultural deterioration of their world. As del Monte tellingly wrote in 1843, "The slave traders in Havana, vulgar and dirty people [*gente soez y ruin*], who have no God other than money, have branded me an abolitionist for some time, because I, like Señor Luz and Señor Saco, and all of those enlightened [*y todo el que piensa*] on the Island of Cuba do not want to see it transformed into a republic of africans [*sic*], but a nation of civilized whites. . . . I have written against the trade, and I have, furthermore, done everything that could have done to end it."[21] White creoles like del Monte also knew their reliance on the slave trade was inextricable from their reliance on the colonial government. The connection between slavery and empire had become something of a white creole truism by the 1840s—the more black people who flooded the island, the greater the need for Spain's repressive apparatus. This then, was one of many inconsistencies in their value system.

While the hacendados in particular had little desire to free thousands of black slaves, Spain labeled anyone who disputed the slave trade an "abolitionist." This makes the term particularly slippery in Cuba during this period, as it encompassed a broad range of individuals with differing critiques of slavery. The best-known representatives of the abolitionist movement were British consular representatives like Richard Madden and David Turnbull, and the historiography has generally presumed that abolition did not begin in Spain until the 1860s. But a fledgling abolitionist culture did in fact exist in cities like Barcelona during the 1840s and effectively laid the foundation for the emergence of the Spanish Abolitionist Society in 1865.[22] Even more important for the events of 1844, there was also a small but vocal core of whites—largely born on the island—who vehemently criticized slavery in Cuba. Much of the creole abolitionist energy of the nineteenth century came from writers as such as Félix Tanco and Cirilo Villaverde whose antislavery novels helped to define a new canon of Cuban literature. Both were part of del Monte's salons and reflected the wide spectrum of participants who all opposed Spanish tyranny but harbored different levels of antislavery sentiment. Turnbull's list of "liberal white" contacts was drawn from this diverse group.

The white men at the core of Turnbull and Cocking's plans derived from three main groups: those men most slighted—whose careers, finances and reputations had been most hurt—by the hardening of Spanish rule in the 1830s; the more idealistic and committed of the antislavery thinkers; and the veterans of earlier independence movements in Cuba. Domingo del Monte, who later claimed Turnbull "wanted to make me the leader of his revolutionary plans," was at the very least one of Turnbull's contacts.[23] The official members of Turnbull and Cocking's "white committee," however, have never come to light. Aside from del Monte, the most likely candidates were men like José de la Luz y Caballero and Pedro Morilla who either appeared on Turnbull's list of contacts or participated in the del Monte salons. Other possible participants included the "liberal" planters José Luis Alfonso, José del Castillo, and Juan Montalvo y Castillo. But in the end, a precise list of early white conspirators must remain speculative.

The anonymous white creole committee finally reconciled enough to agree that all free men should be enlisted to fight against Spain, and any who abstained would be denounced as traitors. Slaves who fought for independence would be allowed to bear arms and would be manumitted, with their owners duly compensated, once the battle was won. Abolition would come gradually and painlessly, and slave reprisals against their masters would not be tolerated. Britain would be granted "omnipotent influence" in

Cuba. Discussions also ensued among the white conspirators about sending all African libres back across the Atlantic, removing the children of slaves born after 1842, and encouraging the arrival of white immigrants.[24]

The committee of black and mulatto conspirators evidently had vastly different ideas. From the beginning slave liberation was a key part of their agenda, and they wholeheartedly embraced the idea of separating from a regime that forced them to live as second-class citizens. As such, they immediately set to work galvanizing people of color across the island.[25] As with the original "white committee," no names of members were provided for the black and mulatto group. It is therefore unclear who formed a part of this circle, when they established themselves, and under what circumstances. Yet if an original central committee existed, it must have included, or at the very least worked with, Plácido, the celebrated Cuban poet.[26]

Plácido, the most famous martyr of 1844, was without a doubt, one of the most active connectors between urban and rural worlds. Born in Havana as Gabriel de la Concepción Valdés, Plácido was raised as an orphan and spent much of his youth on the brink of poverty.[27] He might have continued on that way, no different from any other young man of color struggling to make ends meet in Havana, had it not been for his ability to write poetry. Plácido's skill eventually caught the eye of del Monte, who introduced the poet to his literary salons. In this setting, Plácido met and befriended some of the most distinguished intellectuals in western Cuba and became a favored guest of creole literary circles.[28]

Over a century later, Plácido remains a storied, if mysterious figure. His poetry is marked by a noticeable penchant for subtlety, hint, and allusion — a propensity for "saying without saying," as one critic has observed, making it difficult to determine his political leanings or his racial allegiances.[29] For instance, his verses continually eulogized the Spanish Crown, while at the same time espousing social and political liberation. Although he only occasionally strayed into the realm of the incendiary, Plácido was consistent in his invocations of political autonomy, and these allusions did not escape the notice of the colonial authorities. In April 1843, with rumors already circulating about a British-backed insurgency, government officials arrested Plácido in the town of Trinidad, and kept him imprisoned for six months.[30] The question of Plácido's political commitment is matched by an equally burning curiosity about his racial allegiances. Plácido himself was multiracial, and the world of nineteenth-century Havana would have provided him frequent reminders that his light skin set him apart from other blacks. Moreover, as an eminent writer, Plácido moved in a world of wealthy elites and cultured intellectuals, circles that were either impenetrably white or only integrated by a few mulattos like himself.[31]

Yet it does not appear that Plácido ever lost sight of several powerful facts. He was a person of color, of illegitimate birth and humble origin, and constantly lived on the edge of poverty. These facts erected definitive borders between himself and his elite white friends, sometimes traversable, but not always. Plácido's circles in Havana, Matanzas, and other cities included both whites and people of color. But recent scholarship has argued that Plácido was much more deeply politicized than critics have previously thought. Matthew Pettway, for example, has convincingly argued that Plácido used satire and wit to deconstruct racial hierarchies, subvert aesthetic rules, and construct an African-based racial identity through his representation of the *curro*, a gritty urban street figure. For Pettway, Plácido's rejection of aspirational whiteness imperiled the poet's light-skin privilege and posed a challenge to the system of white supremacy.[32] It is also worth noting that the two great loves of Plácido's life were black women. In November 1842 Plácido wed María Giles Romana Morales, and for this *saltatrás* ("marrying down") he was derided by some of his contemporaries.[33] In short, the poet was clearly invested in a number of different communities by the 1840s, one of the most important of which was of color.

By the late 1830s Plácido was more-or-less openly supporting the cause of Cuban independence from Spain, a sentiment reflected in both his personal associations and his writings. From Havana to Villa Clara, Plácido was developing a broad network of contacts who either were sympathetic to the cause of liberation or had adopted a defiant separatist stance.[34] Plácido's testimonies about his involvement in the 1844 movement are fascinating documents. He states that a movement existed, in fact giving lengthy and elaborate accounts of its genesis. He never admits to being the central leader of this movement, however, instead describing a number of incidents in which he was pulled into a political conspiracy, against his will. In Plácido's accounts, his actions were not premeditated but innocuous and innocent.[35] Yet his confession contains some surprising statements about having been identified as a potential organizer. He stated, for example, that Turnbull knew about his "sharpness, talent and ability" and wanted to recruit him, as the poet's "natural gifts" would be of great benefit to the cause. It is very likely that Turnbull did contact Plácido, but Plácido does not state this explicitly.[36]

While the exact nature of his involvement has not come fully to light, it is telling that thirty-two witnesses accused him "of being the president of the principal gatherings, recruiter, instigator, and one of the first agents of the conspiracy." The trial record gives a very strong indication that he knew about the movement, retained a strong commitment to its principles, and exercised a central leadership role.[37] But Plácido's involvement with the events of 1844 would enter a new phase when he met Luis Jigot.

Luis Jigot, also referred to as "Jigó" or "Gigaut," was one of the most elusive and controversial figures of the 1844 conspiracy. Not much is known about his personal life. Originally from Santo Domingo (the former Saint-Domingue), Jigot worked as a carpenter in Havana, where he became part of the capital's free black artisan class. As the grisly trials of 1844 unfolded, Jigot was never found by the military police, and it is likely that he left the island altogether. Nevertheless, he was charged with one of the highest crimes against her majesty's government and a death sentence was pronounced against him in absentia. This has led some scholars to question whether Jigot ever actually existed, but the interactions reported throughout the trials indicate that he was very real. And nearly all of those questioned about Jigot agreed on one point: that he acted as an agent or contact for David Turnbull, though the precise origins of this relationship are unclear.

While in Havana Jigot befriended a group of men belonging to a free and elite enclave of color. Along with Plácido, this group included Andrés José Dodge, a London-educated dentist; Santiago Pimienta, a Matanzas estate owner; José Miguel Ramón, a violinist and orchestra conductor; Antonio Bernoqui, a carpenter; and Jorge López, a painter and lieutenant of a *pardo* battalion. All of these men became prime suspects in the 1844 conspiracy a few years later. They were nearly all free-born, urban-based, literate, highly educated, skilled, and employed in enviable occupations. While their intimate associates included a diverse group, they seem to have associated mostly with other free pardos and morenos and not, by and large, with slaves or African-born people.

During the late 1820s and early 1830s this group, like other Cubans, was becoming politicized by the rise of a draconian colonial state. For as far back as they could remember, one captain general after another had responded to slave unrest with shocking brutality, and to support for constitutionalism or independence with harsh penalties. Colonial officials had steadily eroded or eliminated any "rights" that free people of color had. The group that Jigot encountered was highly attuned to the shifts of power in the colony and within Spain itself, having been connected to politically minded circles for a decade or more.

An 1831 meeting hosted by a free black man named Bernardo Sevillán highlights the vulnerability of these groups to government surveillance during this period. The twenty or so people of color gathered there were described as toasting the South American liberator Simón Bolívar and the Mexican general Anastasio Bustamante. The authorities also found among them incendiary books on constitutionalism, the Mexican revolution, freedom in Switzerland, and the *Diccionario o nuevo vocabulario filosófico democrático*, but the group's members protested that they were merely trying to organize a theater production.[38]

Two of the participants in these meetings were Antonio Bernoqui and Jorge López, the latter of whom owned most of the books mentioned above. López and Bernardo Sevillán were condemned to six months of work on public projects.[39] A twenty-six-year-old when he was charged for antigovernment sedition, Jorge López was nearly forty by the time the mobilizations for La Escalera began. He had spent six months imprisoned in the Castillo de San Severino for his incendiary literature, a sentence only commuted because of his service in the pardo battalion. This and other stories demonstrate that many of the free urban conspirators had been politically engaged and active for decades before La Escalera and contextualize their decision to become involved in this new movement. Whatever the circumstances of the intervening years, López was either more than ready or had been sufficiently convinced to join the new movement for 1844 by the time he met Luis Jigot.

According to most reports, Jigot made a month-long trip to Matanzas in 1841. During that time, the group of men mentioned above gathered to discuss the imminent possibility of a rebellion against the metropole. Several of these gatherings took place in the home of Desideria Pimienta, a light-skinned mulatta, mother to Santiago Pimienta, and mother-in-law to Andrés Dodge. Jigot was also said to have dined at the home of Jorge López. The López dinner would later be recounted as a key moment in the germination of the 1844 conspiracy.[40] Accounts differ as to who the actual attendees were, but most reports included López himself, Santiago Pimienta, Plácido, and Antonio Bernoqui.

Desideria's dinners provide an important way to rethink the making of the urban movement. In particular, these gatherings help to disrupt the implicit characterization of these meetings as masculine spaces and invite a gendered reading of the places and times where women become visible in this struggle. While most of the reported meeting spaces were clearly dominated by men, other kinds of political gatherings, such as the meetings at Bernardo Sevillán's house, certainly included women. It is in these meeting spaces that we can find some of the less visible work that women performed as movement builders.

Desideria herself played a minor role in the rebel organizing. She was not brought up on any formal charges and she was rarely mentioned in the trial records. Her story, however, indicates that she *was* in fact part of the movement in ways that have heretofore been invisible.

While Luis Jigot was in Matanzas, Andres Dodge brought him to Desideria's house to dine at least once. Desideria described a gathering that included "herself, her daughter, her other child Santiago Pimienta and her aforementioned nephew Andres Dodge," who were all present at the table with Jigot. This dinner does not seem to have been an isolated affair, however. On the contrary, Desideria's home was a regular meeting place for an elite group of free men of color. A number of men who eventually became well-known conspirators—including Luis Jigot, Plácido, Jorge Lopez, Tómas Vargas, José Miguel Ramon, Pedro Nuñez, Manuel Quiñones, and others—frequently came to Desideria's house to visit her son. Desideria owned an estate in rural Matanzas, and because of her frequent trips there, she said she knew nothing about their conversations, much less about a plan to "alter the tranquility of the Island."[41]

Jorge López's sister, Andrea Sotolongo, had a similar narrative. Although she normally lived in Havana, Andrea lived with Jorge for a time while she was separated from her husband. When asked about who normally came to visit her brother, Andrea said she could not remember exactly, "because his relationships in the pardo class [were] very extensive," but "those who came with the most frequency were Plácido the Poet, Santiago Pimienta, Antonio Verroquí [Bernoqui], [and] José Miguel Roman," whom she described as his closest friends. When the authorities pressed her for more information about their conversations, she said she knew nothing about their interactions, because "even though she was living in the house, most of the time she was outside cooking in private houses."[42]

Desideria and Andrea's stories draw attention to a common theme that defined the testimonies of women in 1844. Both of their statements are conspicuous for their repeated disavowals, yet these same disavowals are compromised by other factors. Andrea, and especially Desideria, reported their knowledge of men who stopped by their homes, conversed with their male relatives, and made plans with them. Their experience of being physically in the home but not involved in its political activities—being "in" but not "of" its political sphere, so to speak—was a highly gendered narrative that surfaced repeatedly in women's testimonies that year. Desideria was an educated woman, a landowner, and evidently a respected member of the community. She described Jigot's repeated visits to her home, an important dinner for which she was present, and the free men in her acquaintance who were later brought up on charges of conspiracy. In this context, it is difficult to believe that she was unaware of what was going on, or oblivious to the fact that her home had become a major political center.

Not enough details have emerged to speculate further about what Desideria knew or how deeply she was involved. The trope of "awareness," however, arguably shifts the conversation in a more fruitful direction because it offers a framework in which to consider Desideria as a politicized figure—regardless of how much she knew. The undeniable fact of Desideria's presence, awareness, and mindfulness changes the invisible boundaries of political planning and action for the urban movement. It allows us to think of Desideria and to a slightly lesser extent Andrea as figures who understood the political stakes of the moment, very possibly took part in its shaping, and recognized the implications of these comings and goings. This awareness or cognizance, which both women framed as more of a mindless presence, enables us to place women like Desideria and Andrea within the struggles of 1844. It helps us to imagine their political subjectivity and invites us to reassess who was a part of the movement.

This is particularly important when we consider the question of homeownership. Luz Mena has shown that most Havana homeowners of color in the mid-1840s were women, and the evidence suggests a very similar pattern in Matanzas.[43] The many testimonies that speak of gathering in the home of this or that free person therefore create a different kind of picture of the urban organizing, suggesting that much of the movement's formulation took place in female-owned properties. This fact illustrates what feminist scholars have long argued, that the household is inherently a site of political struggle, subjectivity, and negotiation. Situating mothers, wives, daughters, and female partners within the physical space of these meetings necessarily changes the site of "the meetings" themselves. It suggests the need to include within its contours places like the kitchen, a highly feminized space that would introduce a different domestic geography of political work. Ultimately the stories of Desideria Pimienta, López's wife, and of his sister Andrea, call attention to these hidden spaces of political struggle and the experiences of urban women of color in 1844.

One of the most important accounts of Jigot's visit to Matanzas comes to us from Jorge López himself, though the gendered implications of this meeting are more muted in his telling. Lopez later stated that "in the middle of the year [eighteen] forty-one, whose day and month he cannot recall, a pardo of the carpenter trade named Luis Jigó came to this City from Havana and told him that he was attempting to write a petition to the English Government to carry out the emancipation of the blacks, according to the [terms of the] Treaty of the year [eighteen] twenty; that there were agents scattered throughout the whole island to gather people of color they could count on for the enterprise, in which he stated there had also been several whites involved, [and] that they had appointed him to Matanzas and its Jurisdiction for this purpose, and . . . they were counting on him to seduce and incite people."[44]

Of all of the attendees, Antonio Bernoqui gave the most detailed account of what transpired at that meeting. Bernoqui's report must be read with caution since his lengthy confession was critical to acquitting him, whereas his other comrades were sentenced to death. Several aspects of his story, however, were corroborated by other witnesses. Bernoqui testified, for instance, that Jigot informed them of his "close relations" with David Turnbull, the latter of whom had charged him to come to Matanzas "and inform the friends he might have there that the English Government desirous as always . . . to prohibit slavery, wanted to carry out the treaty of emancipation at all costs."[45] According to Bernoqui, Jigot went on to speak of a plan that required great fidelity and commitment. Jigot impressed upon the attendees the importance of their participation, conveying his certainty "that the English Government would reward the services that each one might lend[,] and that with this same aim other emissaries ordered by said consul had left for different points on the Island." The attendees expressed their willingness, on the condition that the whites "would give liberty to all the blacks who were considered part of the pardo class with more privileges than they enjoyed today." They finally agreed that "each one should talk to the people he knew and these last should communicate with others, so in this way everyone could . . . be ready for when they were notified [of the outbreak]."[46]

One of the most intriguing points about Bernoqui's account is the acutely ambiguous nature of "the plan" that Jigot articulated. There is mention of an antislavery agenda, but the insurgency's immediate objectives and the broader political vision are left unclear. Although the above narratives represent the testimony of only two men, the unconditional liberation of enslaved people seemed implied at best, and this implicitness is striking. Its absence, particularly in the midst of a narrative hinging on the nobility and altruism of the English government, in itself constitutes a loud presence. In the end, it is not entirely clear what these nameless, faceless British supporters wanted.

The tangible gains this group sought to extract from the collaboration are much clearer. Those gathered at López's home that evening were artists, intellectuals, and craftsmen; they would have been counted among Matanzas's best and brightest had they been white. Instead, many of them were barred from prestigious professions, refused adequate schooling for their children, and denied entry into public venues. Intent on expanding the boundaries of Cuban citizenship, they wanted to see an immediate end to the strictures that circumscribed their lives and made them second-class citizens.

Plácido, who famously refused to confess any direct role throughout the trials, nevertheless admitted to being present at López's house. When asked about the evening at López's house, Plácido admitted that he had been there, but he clarified that because he was frequently absent from the table, he could not speak to the conversation at hand. When the judges prodded further, Plácido explained that this was not a dinner for a prestigious person, and therefore "there was no need to maintain such etiquette, much less when there was no one to serve them at the table."[47] However, if Plácido was indeed present in the house, it is unlikely that he would have been missing at such a crucial moment.

|||||||| The Long Reach of the 1844 Movement

Though Plácido never confessed to taking a role in the 1844 movement, he implicated others who did, some of whom were powerful white creoles. Among the whites suspected of involvement in the 1840s, Domingo del Monte shows up most consistently in the archival evidence. In many ways it would only make sense for del Monte to be involved in, or at least recruited for, such a movement. He was, after all, perhaps the best-known and most influential man in Havana's intellectual and political circles, and he had a relationship with both David Turnbull and Francis Ross Cocking. Originally from Venezuela but reared in Cuba, del Monte had long been critical of Spain's colonial regime, and he vocally supported a number of liberal reforms.

Perhaps the most damning evidence against del Monte came from Plácido himself, though this testimony came after Plácido knew he had been condemned, and scholars have speculated that the poet was frustrated with del Monte for his preferential treatment of Juan Francisco Manzano. Plácido stated that del Monte met with him one afternoon in Havana in late 1841 or early 1842 and commissioned him to write "a composition in praise of the English Government, for its humanity in the part that it took in the liberation of the enslaved populace."[48] Plácido continued that del Monte spoke to him about Turnbull, "to inform him of plans that might suit him, and that he [Plácido] might want to have an interview with the English Consul, an individual who was a very good friend and an ardent defender of all the slaves, who all people of color should view as a liberator and protector, and as such join with his ideas and execute his orders as a representative of the powerful British Nation."[49] Plácido said he was reluctant to participate, "knowing that del Monte's aim was to involve him, or rather, use him as an instrument . . . [in the antigovernment] conspiracy." It is difficult to know which portions of Plácido's testimony are true, but it is likely that del Monte was a strong proponent of the original project and perhaps even a member of the planning committee.[50] In the summer of 1842, David Turnbull was expelled from office and replaced by the more temperate Joseph Crawford.[51] Left as Turnbull's sole representative on the island, Francis Ross Cocking stated that he continued to implement the conspiratorial plans. That summer Cocking acted as something of an ambassador for the nascent movement, traveling around the island and even as far as Jamaica. But by the time Cocking returned to Havana in September, he had all but lost the support of the white conspirators. Turnbull had been expelled from Cuba and forbidden to return, black dissidents seemed to be getting more and more militant, and many of the white separatists were developing interests in other avenues for political autonomy.

Particularly in the early 1840s, U.S. statesmen like Alexander Hill Everett began traveling back and forth to Cuba and waging a quiet campaign to court powerful white creoles with promises of support for independence. Unlike the impending collaborations with the British, this independence need not come at the cost of sacrificing their slaves. Quite the contrary; the only requirement the United States had was for Cuba to become a southern slaveholding state. Though the annexationist movement had been developing for several decades, it picked up unusual momentum during the years leading up to 1844.[52]

Such a decline in white interest is perfectly captured by the dwindling enthusiasm of Domingo del Monte, who had developed a lasting friendship with Alexander Hill Everett. Not only was the independence-without-emancipation option attractive to del Monte, but the intellectual had become gravely concerned about the events recently set into motion. In November 1842, del Monte wrote an anxious letter to Everett. In it he explained that "the English abolitionist societies" had begun "to clandestinely solicit the immediate and total destruction of the Island." He continued, "All of her is today scattered with her agents, who offer independence to the Creoles, provided that they join with men of color to declare the general emancipation of the slaves of the island, and ultimately convert this beautiful land . . . into a black-military-republic, under the immediate protection of the British." Del Monte reiterated the importance of Everett's discretion several times: "What I require from you is the utmost secrecy with respect to the name and circumstances of the person who made this revelation to you, I consider it of utmost importance for our respective countries, [and] I have believed it my duty not to conceal this from you, even though I fear, as I write these words, for the loss of my life."[53]

Everett took the precaution of sending del Monte's warnings to Daniel Webster, the U.S. secretary of state. This action only further propelled America's growing mission to "protect" the island from encroaching forces. By January 1844 Leopoldo O'Donnell was not the only one on a mission; the U.S. minister in Madrid had received similar instructions to get to the bottom of all British maneuverings in Cuba. Successive U.S. presidents, from Martin Van Buren to John Tyler, seeing the island as a natural place to extend U.S. empire, kept an eye on Cuba's internal affairs and remained wary of Britain's growing interest.[54] From Cocking's solicitation of the famed Venezuelan general Santiago Mariño to the anxious reconnaissance missions of U.S. officials, this movement was taking center stage in a series of wider negotiations over slavery, empire, and nation-building in the Atlantic world.[55]

Del Monte's early interest in and later defection from the anticolonial project of the 1840s exemplified the trajectory followed by other white creole supporters. The evidence indicates that del Monte was involved in early machinations against the Spanish Crown, but a violent insurgency led largely by black slaves was surely not what he had in mind. By the close of 1842 most of the white creoles had distanced themselves from the most radical strands of the movement, and most appear to have channeled their resistive energies in a different direction altogether.

In stark contrast to the white creole liberals, however, the black and mulatto abolitionists became the most galvanized and coordinated during the autumn months of 1842. Within days of receiving the faulty news from Cocking about support from the British abolitionist societies, they reportedly sent out emissaries across the island.[56] Their boldest gesture came at the end of the year when they drafted a petition to the London-based Society for the Extinction of the Slave Trade and for the Civilization of Africa.[57] In Cocking's words, the dissidents of color remained "ready to risk their lives and all they possess[ed] in an attempt to gain for themselves and their still more degraded brethren, that Liberty . . . which as men they deserve to enjoy."[58]

With fading white support, Cocking claimed that he tried desperately to convince "the coloured committee" to stand down, to persuade them that forging ahead now would be foolhardy. But the people of color "had Agents traveling all over the Island, [and] had raised a spirit of revolt which it was not easy to prevent from breaking out." To all appearances they would not be deterred, a dampening of white loyalties notwithstanding. It is possible that news of an insurgency had spread too far and resonated too deep to turn back at that point; in any event the black and mulatto committee made plans to forge ahead.[59]

By late 1843 and early 1844 streams of mobile black laborers were steadily taking into and out of Matanzas whatever news they had acquired about the movement. The insurgent mobilizing had spread outward from the city for miles into the countryside, some claimed as far as Cienfuegos and Villa Clara. Those inclined to share information frequently met at the crossroads of small towns, finding one another at general stores, artisan shops, and on the streets. While towns like Sabanilla and Guanábana located just outside Matanzas were among the best situated locations for this dialogue, it was not long before word reached farther south and east of the bay. Among the most important of these smaller towns was Alacranes, situated about thirty-five kilometers south of the provincial capital.

More than a few accounts indicate that the local Alacranes planning found its epicenter in the home of Altagracia Villa. Altagracia was a free African woman taken from the Bight of Benin who had at one time belonged to José María Gálvez, owner of the Dos Mercedes sugar mill. Altagracia had done quite well for herself since gaining her freedom and leaving the estate; she now owned a home in Alacranes and at least three slaves of her own.[60] Her husband, José Marta, had also been a slave at Dos Mercedes, and Altagracia maintained contact with others from the old ingenio. These included eight men later named as the "principal seductors" in a bourgeoning local insurgency. In February 1844 a group of mostly self-appointed inquisitors arrived at Dos Mercedes and extracted several statements from this group. José Roque, also formerly of Dos Mercedes; another slave named Domingo

Gangá; and eventually a woman named Rosa Lucumí produced extensive testimonies that implicated a wide swath of people.[61] Altagracia was among those arrested.

The story of Altagracia's involvement began on the Ingenio Dos Mercedes in the early 1840s. In the years leading up to 1844, a number of free black men converged to work on the Gálvez mill as carpenters, masons, and land clearers. Among them were José Marta Gálvez, José María Mondejar, and Mondejar's son-in-law José Ynés. Rosa Lucumí later testified that these three men and at least five others regularly came to the grounds of Dos Mercedes, where they spoke to José Roque (then still a slave), herself, and another companion about an uprising against the whites—a point "on which they frequently insisted when they were working on this estate."

These conversations began in 1841 or 1842, but at that time nothing substantial came of them. By the end of 1843, however, the moment was much riper and the conversations about a rebellion began again. Mondejar began collecting money from the small circle to buy machetes, gunpowder, rifles, and poisons. He told them that "all the free men had been united together [estaban juntados] for two years already."[62] Altagracia's husband was named as one of the more avid participants in this effort, and he "would always come here to talk about the war, inviting them for that effect."[63] José Marta was later charged with other offenses in connection to the rebellion.[64]

Roque indicated that a similar set of discussions had taken place in Altagracia's home with several free men based in Alacranes and a few itinerant slaves. In a series of statements Roque told authorities that "in his trips to Alacranes, he used to visit various [houses] of the free black people there, but the place where he would stop the most . . . was in the home of Altagracia." Roque described a group of about nine or ten black men who convened in Altagracia's house, all either free or highly independent. They included Félix Gálvez and his brother Lucas; Ramón Gangá from the Ingenio Las Cañas; Félix (sometimes written "Feliz") Mandinga from the Villa estate; Esteban García, "the half-French free carpenter"; Mateo Quiala, the free chino "married to a slave of Doña Fula La Mar"; and Julián Criollo, "from the Vuelta Abajo." Those who lived in Altagracia's house were also gathered there—including José Marta Gálvez, their slave Antonio Lucumí (who "looks Mina"), and the country laborer Antonio Gangá. Together they "would gather to talk about the uprising and about inciting the slaves."[65]

Roque later testified that during one of these meetings, Antonio Lucumí (or Mina) "put a knife on his chest, drawing together [cercando] all the others and making them swear on the cross." They told Roque "that [the uprising] was not to be spoken of until the day of the deed[,] that if he did . . . they would kill him even if it was in his own cabin."[66]

It is difficult to know what actually took place at Altagracia's house, since Roque was the only one who spoke about it. Most of the others denied any knowledge of these gatherings, and many insisted that they had not seen Roque in years. Altagracia herself denied any involvement, and Roque concluded ambiguously that "he does not know if she has knowledge of this."[67] In spite of these negations, however, Roque's testimony deserves serious consideration. The military authorities brought him face to face with many of the people he accused, and Roque gave explicit details about how, when, and where they had interacted. He stated, for example, that Esteban García arrived at Altagracia's house at four o'clock, just before they ate; he picked Félix Gálvez out of a lineup; he reminded Antonio José Rodríguez how the latter arrived on a mule; he recalled that Nicolás Torres took him across the street to see his pregnant wife; and he asked Julián if it was not true that he had come to his mother's house on a mule, and after arriving at Altagracia's invited Roque to eat, after which time they went to the patio to talk.[68]

Whether admitting or denying their involvement, these questions and answers consistently returned to Altagracia's home. Several of those who denied the charges admitted that they had gone to Altagracia's home for other reasons. Félix Gálvez, for example, stated that he had "been in her house a few times buying foodstuffs [viandas]"; Esteban García claimed he was invited to her home "for this year's Día de Reyes"; and Roque's mother Concha claimed she would often see Antonio Gangá "when she goes to Altagracia's house." Still another of the accused testified that there had been a meeting at Altagracia's house but that the only issues raised were "asuntos indiferentes" (unimportant matters).[69]

It is clear though that Altagracia knew each of the men above, and for the most part they all knew each other. The strands of their entwined story reveal an intricate network of friendship, acquaintanceship, and extended kin that began on the Gálvez mill (if not before) and followed many of them into the town of Alacranes. The community they were a part of included those who had been slaves at Dos Mercedes, those free men who had worked at Dos Mercedes, slaves on other properties near Dos Mercedes, and those whose relatives were still on Dos Mercedes. Altagracia's home became something of a nucleus for this collective, a place where people dropped by when they were in town, where neighbors stopped in to visit, and where friends came to social gatherings.

Roque's testimony alone is inconclusive, but when placed alongside other sources a clearer picture emerges that hints at the importance of the meetings in Altagracia's house. Seven people, for example, testified about Roque's attempts to recruit them.[70] Once again Altagracia's home became a social center in many of these stories, and against the political backdrop of the moment it is likely that one or more of these gatherings turned to rebellious talk. As with Desideria Pimienta, it is not clear how involved Altagracia was in these meetings. The evidence suggests that she probably played a vital role but that the men who constituted her extended family were trying to protect her. Yet even if she did not, these conversations still unfolded in the safe space that Altagracia provided.

Women's homes were consistently portrayed as places of safekeeping, refuge, and asylum during the movement. For example, the free black woman Estefanía Goicochea testified, "It is that true two months ago now Francisco Abrantes entered her house, where Francisco Alba (a) Canita de Rosa was found, to whom he delivered a package of some volume." The package in question contained twenty-five lances or spears, and Francisco Alba allegedly stated, "You already know what this is and who it's for." Abrantes, whose name came up in more than a few testimonies, was a successful barber in Matanzas. Estefanía's testimony suggests that Abrantes knew her and felt comfortable in her home. While it is unclear whether he came to her house for the purpose she described, it is highly likely that he had gone on other occasions. Her story emphasizes the importance of women's homes as points of contact and exchange, both before and during the 1844 planning.[71]

Estefanía Goicochea was unique because she gave testimony about facilitating the exchange of weapons. Most free women vigorously denied the charges they faced and generally claimed no knowledge of a conspiracy. Their silence cannot completely hide the crucial contributions that black women made to the project of urban rebellion, such as opening up their homes and providing safe or inviting meeting spaces, actions often overlooked in discussions of political or revolutionary movements. Thus the domestic and affective labor that many women performed inside and outside the home was arguably one of the rebellion's most important hidden components, and one that has gone largely unremarked.

The stories of Trancito, Desideria, Altagracia, Estefanía, and other free women thus require a close examination of the underlying conditions that made insurgent organizing possible. They also require close attention to the ways in which movements like that of 1844 were both enhanced and enabled by women's property, domestic labor, and social facilitations.

It is likely that *some* kind of gathering with a political tenor took place in Altagracia Villa's home, but whether it did or did not occur should not fundamentally change our understanding of Altagracia's political subjectivity. Homes like hers became centers of activity across western Cuba, and while in the end Altagracia was not deemed a prime conspirator, the relationships she nurtured and the possibilities that her home represented create a different way to think about how the insurrection was fomented. In a manner similar to Desideria, "Altagracia's house" offered critical space and critical labor for the movement to unfold.

|||||||| The Spread of the 1844 Movement

Of all those who moved around the countryside from 1841 to 1844, José María Mondejar was one of the most significant. In the records reviewed for this study, Mondejar was cited with more frequency than anyone else in the rural testimonies. From the archival descriptions, Mondejar was probably in his fifties or sixties by the time the movement gained momentum. He spent time in the city of Matanzas, but he often worked cutting wood and clearing land on properties south of the bay. Little other biographical information has surfaced about him, except that he had knowledge of ancestral rituals and spiritual practices and frequently tried to sell amulets to slaves on the rural estates.

José María Mondejar was one of a group of free black men who were unique in their ability to move in and out of different circles. Mondejar seems to have had almost as many connections in the elite black homes of the city as he did on the plantations, a trait that would have made him an ideal field lieutenant. Of particular importance was Mondejar's claim to have maintained a friendship with Plácido's father-in-law. This relationship seems to have facilitated Mondejar's initial contact with the rebel movement.

Mondejar later testified that in November 1843 he visited Plácido's in-laws and came in contact with the poet. He testified that Plácido hoped to entrust him with an important mission in the countryside. Eventually Plácido called Mondejar into a room where a number of free black and mulatto men were gathered. Mondejar continued to narrate how he had learned that a movement was afoot: "Gabriel [Plácido] told him that he had called him in, not so that anything bad would happen to him, but rather to tell him of a plan that was shared among all who were present, and assuming that [one of their white confidantes] had already spoken to him, he could explain to him the secret, and having confidence in him, he proposed that he [Mondejar] go to the district of [Ceiba] Mocha and the other areas of the countryside, advising all of the blacks to prepare themselves to rise up against the whites."

Mondejar stated that he was skeptical about their prospects for victory. Plácido apparently brushed his fears aside, assuring him that powerful people—read, whites—were going to furnish them with arms and munitions. Mondejar found it difficult to believe that black insurgents could claim sovereignty over Cuba, but Plácido "asked him if he had not heard anyone talk about the Island of Santo Domingo, [and having responded yes . . . Plácido told him] how over there everyone was black, that they were the ones who governed, and when any white person went, they had to follow their orders. That here, nothing less would take place . . . that the English wanted this Island because it was very rich . . . and in this way he should carry out the proceedings with which they charged him with resolution and without fear."

At this point, Mondejar said, one of the others "gave him two or three claps on the shoulder, telling him to take heart and not to be a coward," and with this Mondejar "resolved to prepare the blacks [for the insurrection]."[72] Now that he was a part of the insurgency, Mondejar would have to change his behavior and exercise extreme caution in his movements, words, and itineraries. He was urged to seek out valiant men, in particular, free men who might be *"hombres de pecho."* In doing so, he would have to maintain the delicate balance of actively enlisting worthwhile men while maintaining the utmost secrecy; he was forbidden to tell even his children about what he was doing. In the ensuing months, Mondejar continued to give Plácido updates about the progress in the rural districts.[73] It is difficult to know how much of this actually transpired, but there is every reason to believe that Plácido and Mondejar knew each other well and engaged in frequent conversations.

As the Matanzas movement spread, so too did the clandestine meetings in communities of color. The way people interpreted the rebellious plans and how they were recruited comes through in the various testimonies after the fact. Among the men who entered the movement at this early stage was Marcos Ruiz, the primary architect of a plan to recruit scores of Matanzas coach drivers. The coachmen's ability to cross the city and the time available to them as they waited would have been invaluable assets, and this mobile infrastructure was indeed incorporated into the growing movement.

Although Ruiz himself was free, most of his fellow coach drivers—many of them friends and acquaintances also drawn to the rebellion—were enslaved.[74] Many urban slaves responded to the rebel momentum as the chain of recruitment spiraled outward to include well-positioned men like Gregorio la Ceí, coachman to the governor of Matanzas.[75] Along with men situated closer to the powerbrokers like Gregorio la Ceí, this network included other people like Pedro Núñez who would count among 1844's most prolific and respected urban organizers, and who suffered the death penalty for it.[76]

Of particular interest from this group is the enslaved coachmen Antonio Abad, who along with Pedro Núñez was considered a critical organizer, recruiting a series of other coachmen. Approximately thirty years of age and likely taken from the region of Yorubaland, Abad was one of those Lucumís fortunate enough to fall into a privileged, urban position in the house of José Baró. Abad's owner was not just any Matanzas resident. Baró was one of the city's wealthiest men and a well-known merchant who opened firms as far away as New York. As with Gregorio la Ceí, Abad's proximity to such a man must have seemed quite fortuitous for a budding movement.

The importance of men like Marcos Ruiz, Antonio Abad, and Pedro Núñez cannot be underestimated. The gatherings in the homes of Núñez and Ruiz were described as a hub for the different spokes of organizing that radiated outward across the city from 1841 to 1843. As men like Bartolo Quintero "enlist[ed] themselves for the conspiracy," others apparently followed suit, inviting men they knew into the two homes and into the movement.[77] These meetings simultaneously brought together some of the best-known free urban conspirators, including José Erice, Jorge López, Manuel Quiñones, José de la O'García, and Antonio Abad.[78]

In calling for people to gather in their homes and seeking out promising combatants, these men embodied a critical link on the insurgent chain. As these pieces were put into place, free and enslaved black men became bound to the insurrection by word and deed. These meetings were often framed as intensely masculine spaces defined by an ethos of spirited militancy and intense discipline. Testimony after testimony described prospective insurgents taking a sacred oath, pledging their fidelity and allegiance to the growing movement.

One such meeting reportedly took place in Marcos Ruiz's home in December 1843. In this account, Plácido administered the oaths to all the attending parties, with each man pledging to gather people for the insurrectionary cause and annihilate his master and white enemies when the time came. One of the coachman stated that "he received the oath from

Plácido the poet, who called the attendees one by one, and asking them to make the sign of the cross with the right hand, they swore [to do as described above]; this being concluded, they withdrew, Plácido charging them to gather together as little as possible so as not to become [suspicious]."[79] Above all, they were to "maintain discretion in order not to be discovered, and . . . he who failed to do so would be assassinated." Others similarly reported they were forced to pledge oaths of allegiance on pain of death. For example, one free black carpenter testified that, in a different setting, he was similarly obliged "to make the sign of the cross, and by the sun that gives us light, kissing the earth two times and promising to die or vanquish before revealing the secret."[80] In these and other ways the mere act of joining the movement was framed in deeply militaristic terms, and witnesses often reported being presented with two choices: pledge their loyalty or die; emerge victorious or perish.

One of the best-known organizers of the urban movement, and an important contributor to the London-bound petition for the Anti-slavery Society, was Juan Rodríguez, more commonly known as Miguel Flores. A free Havana-based entrepreneur, he was alternately described as a saddler and a furniture maker.[81] In the summer of 1843 he emerged as a critical leader in the Matanzas organizing. Sometime between May and July of that year, Flores made a trip to Matanzas reminiscent of Jigot's trip two years before and met with some of the same people Jigot encountered.[82]

Several historians have shown that Flores's contact with David Turnbull and Francis Ross Cocking reached back to the early months of 1842.[83] In these encounters, Flores emphasized to Turnbull that the impending revolution would need to be armed. He even addressed a letter to Queen Victoria requesting munitions that Turnbull was to deliver. The ousted British consul was to oversee a provision of arms by March 1843 that never actually materialized, but the closeness of this timetable to the Bemba eruption cannot be ignored. It suggests that organizers in the rural regions knew about Turnbull's promised cache and that the March conflagration resulted either because local leaders believed arms to be en route, or because they simply grew tired of waiting.[84]

By March 1843 word of a movement had spread to the farthest reaches of Cuba's western provinces. From Havana to Cienfuegos rebel contingents had begun to lay foundations, seek recruits, and solidify plans. The evidence indicates that urban organizers were particularly impatient and edgy, ready to move at a moment's notice. Flores, who seems to have acted as a spokesperson for the black urban rebels, decided once again to seek out British support via the new consul, Joseph Crawford. Crawford had been hearing rumors about an anticolonial undercurrent that was spanning the island for months now. He reacted to Flores's request with pure alarm and was shaken to hear that these plans were in fact true. In a letter to his superior, the British diplomat wrote, "I could only respond that I did not know how Mr. Turnbull could have given them such hopes. . . . I could not say what that person was doing or with whom, but I thought that they had been misled." In successive meetings with Flores, Crawford emphasized that yes, the British were interested in bringing emancipation to Cuba but no, they had never intended to do so through open warfare. He pleaded with Flores to abandon the "madness" of these designs. But Flores was evidently difficult to dissuade. He informed Crawford that rebels across the island would hear nothing of stopping their mobilizations and indeed felt "that if they were all sacrificed, it would be preferable to their present state of existence."[85]

With or without Crawford's support, the insurgency was moving ahead. Some free people and slave organizers still believed that selected agents were working to procure weapons, supplies, monetary assistance, and moral and political support from the British territories. Others reported concrete details about the form this assistance would take, including names and points of disembarkation, actual conversations, and the like. While many witnesses likely felt it strategic to testify about British support, there is ample reason to believe that news of British assistance had made its way through the black insurrectionary grapevine. These kinds of reports helped to create a powerful discourse of "English assistance"—a litany that began to circulate with greater frequency as the 1840s progressed. As the news wove its way around the city of Matanzas and out to the plantations, the insurgents became more and more confident that the English were coming.

David Turnbull's unusual activities around the island, especially the plantation visits he made to identify unlawfully enslaved Africans, undeniably contributed to this belief.[86] Vicente Pipa Criollo was among those slaves living in rural Havana who would later report tidings of English support. Vicente testified that he had been told "the English were coming to help them for the war, and [would] bring them weapons and munitions."[87] Similar news circulated to other properties and around the urban centers. The slave organizer José Lucumí testified that "all the blacks were supposed to rise up like those of Matanzas . . . because the English were coming with ships to wage war on the whites of this land."[88] One free black man reported being told that "the English were going to give freedom to the slaves and money to the free people, but he does not know what manner of government," and the urban silversmith Ramón Medrano testified that "the English were trying to liberate those of color in this Country, offering all the necessary resources for the endeavor, and protecting them so that they could achieve their objective."[89]

Those rebel leaders who had close connections to the free organizers in Matanzas were most responsible for validating the idea of British aid, which ranged in the retelling from vague moral support to an elaborate military intervention. It seems that the much-discussed Mondejar was more responsible for disseminating news of a British intervention than anyone else. Mondejar and others also spread reports that assistance would be forthcoming from the state of Haiti, united tenuously until that year by a Haitian monarchy. The idea that England and Haiti had pledged their commitment emerged in testimonies such as the following, claiming that "Englishmen were supposed to disembark at various points along the coast with blacks from Santo Domingo to fight with the whites and give liberty to all the slaves."[90] Again, witnesses may have referred to anticipated British and Haitian support because they had actual information or because they wanted to lay the blame for the insurgency on outside agitators.

The question that exasperated the military commission for over a year was never answered, and has continued to intrigue scholars ever since: Was David Turnbull working to provoke an insurrection of African slaves and an anticolonial uprising of free blacks and mulattos? In other words, were the expectations of British support relayed in the testimonies based on actual facts?

Several free black men in Havana and Matanzas stated that they believed this to be true. The free black carpenter Félix Ponce claimed that "the principal instigator of this conspiracy was an Englishman who was [the former] Consul in Havana, whom he deduced had been insulted and wanted to avenge himself with a profit for the people of color."[91] Other witnesses gave similar reports, stating that "the English Consul Turnbull was the principal organ of the plot, offering the people of color his protection." Even in the Matanzas countryside, the rebel leader Marcos Criollo stated that "he had heard of an Englishman named Turnbull who was offering them protection and went around inciting people."[92]

These accounts and others—such as those of Francis Ross Cocking and Plácido—portray a David Turnbull poised to play a major role in insurrectionary events. Turnbull himself vehemently denied these allegations. Given his ultimate mission of establishing free capitalist labor and peaceful emancipation throughout the Caribbean, it is unlikely that he envisioned or *organized* the conspiracy of 1844 as we know it. However, all of the evidence indicates that he knew about and helped to articulate a plot against the Spanish, acted as a point person for disgruntled creole factions, and encouraged slavery opponents of various hues. This was in the early stages, when the white creoles were still onboard, and emancipation was to be enacted slowly and peacefully. Turnbull also very likely became lukewarm about the project once he saw the radical turn the organizing had taken; once it became clear that the multiracial independence movement had changed into a black liberation movement.

Through individuals like those mentioned above, several important pieces of information were circulated as word of a massive black insurgency and the names of key insurgent leaders in the city of Matanzas were emerging in unexpected places. For example Melchor Robaina, a central organizer on the Buena Esperanza estate, reportedly heard his fellow organizers saying that "the Mulatto Plácido" was involved, and a Joaquín Gangá similarly testified about "a pardo named Plácido." Several other plantation residents invoked the names of well-known urban conspirators in Matanzas, including those of the coachmen Marcos Ruiz, Bruno Huerta, and Antonio Abad and others like Santiago Pimienta, Manuel Quiñones, José Erice, Pedro Núñez, and Tomás Vargas.[93]

It is certainly possible that some of these witnesses strategically produced the names that they had heard after they had been imprisoned in the jails of Matanzas. But it is also the case that many of them were never sent off the plantations. These men had reason to know the names of urban men who were, in many senses, worlds away and yet deeply interconnected with them. This connection is highlighted, for example, by the experience of the free bricklayer Jacobo Fernández, who testified that he had worked for a "Tomás Oeén" in the recent past, which must have been the same Thomas Owens who owned Blas and Patricio (whose story opened this chapter).[94] The men these slaves spoke of lived in bustling cities and had acquired skilled professions. Many of them were light-skinned. The rural rebels who heard about these individuals back in Guanábana were almost all born in West or West-Central Africa, lived on country plantations miles from Matanzas, and labored under coercive regimes that allowed them a fraction of the freedom urbanites enjoyed. Yet by 1844 they, and the men they heard about, had become entwined in the same movement. In short, their political aims—and thus their social identities—had come into closer proximity, and this would have a lasting effect on the way these disparate groups saw one another.

Such overlap also highlights the intriguing, and perhaps uneasy, coexistence of several different insurgent visions by 1843. In recounting their meeting with Luis Gigot, Jorge López, Antonio Bernoqui, Plácido, and Santiago Pimienta all spoke of an imperial contest between Britain and Spain, a more equitable and dignified existence for people of color, and greater involvement in the Cuban polity. One version of this meeting placed particular emphasis on the privileges they felt were due to them as free people and as pardos. When enslaved people in the countryside like Merced Criolla and Marcos Gangá spoke about the insurrection they knew of, they spoke of eliminating all the white people and taking possession of the island. Other witnesses expressed a range of ideas that fell in between these two poles.[95] Clearly the plans of 1844 represented multiple, and even contradictory ideas about freedom. Each of these visions seemed to other organizers quite radical, or too moderate, or "outright frightening," to use Bernoqui's words, depending on individual perspectives of class, color, and gender. The thread that held them together was liberation of some kind for all people of African descent.

Though their political visions diverged, the hub of the insurgent wheel somehow held together a wide swath of African-descended men and women, however tenuously. Over the course of a year or more, official and unofficial emissaries made contact with people in the countryside, and rural black people similarly sought out rebel networks in the towns and cities. The lynchpins of this plan were mass mobilization and metropolitan help from outside. Insurgencies continued to erupt in the countryside into the fall of 1843, but rebels in both locales were determined that the insurgency of 1844 would not be another failed rebellion. None of them were prepared, however, for what would take place as 1843 drew to a close.

Chapter Five

And the Women Also Knew
THE GENDERED TERRAIN OF INSURGENCY

As December 1843 drew to a close, an enslaved woman in the Sabanilla district named Polonia Gangá shocked her master with the information that his prized sugar property was about to be engulfed in open rebellion. The Santísima Trinidad estate was located only a few miles from the site of the November insurgency that had just been put down the previous month, and word of a new insurgent plan in his own backyard was sobering news to Esteban Santa Cruz de Oviedo, a wealthy and prominent owner of three plantations. Clearly, the epidemic of black revolt had not been cleansed from Sabanilla. Such a revelation could not be ignored.[1]

Polonia's infamous confession has since passed into legend as the event that sparked the unraveling of a mammoth insurgent movement in western Cuba. This discovery prompted investigations in the part of Sabanilla where Santa Cruz de Oviedo's plantation was located, and subsequently fanned outward through the province of Matanzas. By the dawn of 1844 Matanzas residents were already on edge from a spate of restrictions and regulations, as well as from the increased military presence that had invaded the region. Throughout 1843 these precautions had been launched by the former governor, Gerónimo Valdés, as successive rebellions erupted and rumors of a British-led conspiracy continued to circulate. But the inquisition that began in 1844 reached far wider and deeper than anything Valdés had undertaken. An inquiry that might have been executed over the course of a few days, or even a few weeks, stretched out for months.

The questioning expanded into a longer, bloodier, and more comprehensive inquisition than anyone would have imagined. The more strands the military authorities unwound, the more information they uncovered. Instead of leading the authorities to a definitive endpoint with a clear group of culprits and an identifiable leader, the questioning kept growing more convoluted and more extensive. A general hysteria rippled to the furthest reaches of the Matanzas and Cárdenas provinces, and back west toward Havana. The investigation did not come to an official end until a year and a half after Polonia's revelation. Many historical accounts of the conspiracy of La Escalera begin their chronology with Polonia's disclosure, and in so doing locate it at the heart of the long and bloody inquisition.

Polonia's revelation thus constitutes its own creation story, if one of a peculiar kind. Hers is a story that imposes its own ending at the precise moment that it announces its beginning. At the same moment, the massive slave movements of 1844 are thrust into naked visibility, and unraveled in sanguineous horror. Polonia consequently stands figuratively at both the movement's genesis and its undoing. Her actions consecrate this movement in Cuban history at the same time that they usher in saturnalias of destruction. But commencing the story of 1844 at the moment of Polonia's declaration also necessarily equates a woman's betrayal with the unleashing of a black bloodbath and effectively disappears a much longer trajectory of black political struggle in rural Cuba.

The *resistance* part of the slave rebellion, however, has traditionally been cast as a male enterprise. Traditional narratives of slave insurgency implicitly recount not only the collective passage from passivity to defiance, but also the passage from "slavehood to manhood."[2] In other words, to engage in armed insurrection is to give birth to a radical new masculine subject, and a particularly aggressive one at that. Together the highly visible male icon and the masculinized rank-in-file become pivotal to the slave rebellion's conceptual existence and therefore part of the collective inheritance of slave rebellion histories.[3] For this reason, it is important to appreciate how deeply masculinity and male embodiment have structured the way in which we think about black opposition, even as we recognize that masculinity (and aggression and violence) were hardly limited to the male body.

Until recently, Polonia was practically the only woman that readers of La Escalera would encounter—Polonia, who they quickly learned was a traitor. This story of female treachery is a familiar one that persists throughout the history of slave movements in the Americas. Although women were hardly the only ones who acted as "informants" to white authorities during times of unrest, men who revealed rebel plots were often implicitly feminized through their role as domestic servants, or indeed through the very act of treachery. As such, the trope of feminized betrayal is often a central feature in the story of black rebellion.[4] Barbara Bush has shown that enslaved women who maintained sexual ties to white men were often viewed as having a greater propensity for passivity, accommodation, and betrayal when collective resistance loomed on the horizon.[5] Such responses account little for the fact that these relationships often materialized through devastating moments of coercion and violence for slave women. Yet in the Cuba of 1843, some of the horror of Polonia's duplicity seems to be rooted as much in her position as Santa Cruz de Oviedo's mistress—and thus in the perpetual transgression of her sexual life—as in her decision to expose the plot in gestation. The most powerful narratives of slave insurgency, then, are often accompanied by stories of female betrayal or disloyalty.

The story of Polonia Gangá is but one of many in the rural opposition of the 1840s. Contrary to what the historiography would suggest, slave women took part in, helped to organize, and became leaders in the rebel movements of 1843 and 1844. Finding records of that participation however, can often be characterized with little irony as "searching for the invisible woman."[6] This chapter will focus on the women who became involved in the 1843 and 1844 movements in a variety of different ways.

Refashioning these and other narratives of collective insurgency should do more than highlight the fact that slave rebellion histories have traditionally placed men at their center. It should privilege the fact that women *shared* and helped *organize* larger critiques of white brutality. Enslaved women were an integral part of communities, kinship groups, and social collectives on the plantations. It should therefore not be surprising that the rebel movements of 1843 and 1844 found scores of women collaborating with their male counterparts, aligning with them politically, and sometimes directing them in a shared project of struggle. During insurgencies like those that erupted in 1843, a few women came to the forefront as visible leaders and organizers whom all rebels respected and followed. While their understanding of what it meant to engage in revolutionary action could and did diverge from that of their male companions, it also dovetailed with them in many instances. After all, when violent rebellions erupted, women's lives were also at stake. The question of rebellion was therefore also a question of their safety, their homes, and their families.

Moreover, what might happen to our picture of rebellion if scholars saw rape, sexual assault, pregnancy, birth control, and so forth as pivotal to the organization, form, and outcome of slave insurgencies? The gendered forms of violence that the plantation world meted out arguably provided just as much a motivation to revolt as whippings and overwork, particularly because sexual forms of punishment against women often became tools to discipline and humiliate entire slave communities.[7] The scholarship on slave women from the last four decades has rightly pointed out the dangers and limitations of casting everyday or unorganized resistance as categorically different from collective, organized protest.[8]

Such an analysis refuses to bifurcate the racial and gendered sensibilities of black slave women, arguing that the often complex and contradictory ways they encountered and sustained rebel struggles are just as critical to revising existing historiographic accounts as the ways in which they were excluded from them. In short, highlighting the privilege that has been accorded to men in slave resistance histories should not obscure the fact that organized rebellion was very much a collective enterprise.

|||||||| Women Slave Rebels and the Archives

In the aftermath of rebel movements across the Americas, as militias sought to round up conspirators and insurgents, female witnesses were usually brought in to testify in far fewer numbers than their male counterparts, and men were always presumed to outnumber women in moments of combat. When enslaved women were questioned, they frequently said very little, and if they did provide information it was rarely about their own involvement. This dearth of women's testimony in the public record has become a defining feature in the history of slave rebellions throughout the Americas.

While a rich and vibrant literature now exists on the gendered terrain of day-to-day resistance, pregnant silences remain about women and gender discourses in the history of slave rebellions.[9] Thus, while sensational in its scope—the female slave concubine who hands her brethren over to her master—Polonia's story is but a dramatic embodiment of a deeper impulse that gnaws at the edges of many slave resistance narratives, haunting them, if only subliminally: that of female incompatibility with the project of collective insurgency. In ways often unnoticed, this repetition of women's constant denial—denial that they were involved, denial that they had any information, denial that there was even a movement afoot—reflects an uncomfortable likeness to Polonia: on a textual level they collectively add up to a movement betrayed.

During moments of rebellion and rebel planning, the actions of slave women, like those of their male counterparts who made up the proverbial "rank-and-file," did not always line up with the actions of those who assumed positions of command. At times in fact, they diverged radically from these leading individuals, of whose behavior and decisions some women issued scathing critiques. But those women who supported, encouraged, or directed rebel groups are usually much more difficult to locate in the archival records. The pervasive tendency was for women under interrogation to critique or disavow revolutionary struggle, for men to say little about what women may have done, and for female participants to be listed as mere names or numbers. Such reticence must be understood as the protective mechanism that it was, rather than as equating the female subject with inherent critique of the insurgent project. This chapter consequently explores a range of responses that women exhibited to the movements of 1843 and 1844.

The ensuing narration focuses on two groups of women who highlight seemingly divergent aspects of rebel women's experiences during those two years. It begins with an exploration of Fermina and Carlota Lucumí, two women who took leading roles in the rebellion that erupted in November 1843. This rebellion was unusual in Cuban history—and in New World slave history—precisely because two African women emerged as leading figures. Their stories are vital because they compel a different kind of reading of slave insurgency. While Carlota and Fermina both acted in aggressive and combative ways, they nevertheless destabilize the presumed juncture between slave insurrection and male bodies, and they unravel the tightly enmeshed tropes of leadership, organization, and masculinity. Their heightened visibility in the trial record allows for a closer investigation of which people became particularly visible during moments of insurgent rupture and why. Indeed, the stories of these two women highlight the extent to which insurrection as a practice encompassed (or tried to encompass) all slaves across lines of gender, class, and ethnicity—even as these factors shaped the ways people responded to the insurgent call, agreed with its form or necessity, or were included in its ranks.

At the same time, excavating the stories of women who hovered along the margins of the 1844 movement—claiming, for example, that they knew little about a brewing rebellion or had only happened to overhear others making subversive plans—will reveal the intriguing and compelling paths by which many, and perhaps most, enslaved women (and men) came to the movement. A careful reading of these narratives indicates how such women existed near, moved into, and became connected with insurgent spaces across western Cuba. The involvement of these women, both less and more visible, invites deeper consideration of how to extend the boundaries of how we imagine insurgencies and social movements to be created and lived.

|||||||| Gendering the 1843 Rebellions, Finding the
"Invisible Woman"

After Polonia, perhaps the best known women of the 1843–44 struggles are
the two African-born women of the Lucumí nation, Fermina and Carlota.
Several contemporary accounts have characterized these two women
as principal organizers of the November movement, and much of the
documentary evidence supports this claim, at least for Fermina.[10] What is
clear from the records is that both Carlota and Fermina stood accused of
some of the most dramatic acts of the insurgency, and that both women died
as a result of this conflict. Carlota was found dead the morning following the
rebellion on one of the properties where slave combatants had battled local
troops and militias. During the trials that followed, Fermina was arrested,
interrogated, and kept imprisoned for several months. She was one of
eight accused ringleaders—alongside seven other men—to be executed
by a firing squad, her body subsequently burned. To witness this violent
spectacle of state power, all the other slaves of the mill were ordered to be
present, in addition to "ten slaves from each of the neighboring estates."[11]

Little is known about Fermina, a woman presumably taken from the
Bight of Benin, who was sentenced to death at twenty-four years old. Hilary Beckles and Barbara Bush have persuasively argued that the African
cultural background of enslaved women, especially their ideas about femininity, gender, and warfare, must be privileged when writing about women
and slave resistance.[12] In the case of Fermina, there can be no doubt that her
formative years on the African continent, her horrific experiences with the
slave coffle and coastal barracks, and her hellish journey across the Atlantic
shaped her interpretation of and response to her new life in Cuba—albeit
in ways that have yet to surface in the archives.

What the records clearly indicate is that she labored in the fields on the
Ácana sugar plantation and expressed her opposition to brutal working conditions on several occasions.[13] During the summer of 1843 Fermina escaped
from Ácana with a group of other slaves, and the historian José Luciano
Franco maintains that she and a fellow captain organized a smaller rebellion that June.[14] In short, by November of that year Fermina had acquired
a reputation as a troublemaker. For these transgressions she was whipped
and placed in iron shackles for five months. On November 5, 1843, several
days after the shackles were removed, a massive uprising erupted.

In the aftermath of the November uprising, several enslaved women gave damning testimony about Fermina's conduct that night. Filomena Gangá was asked about several suspected insurgents but stated that "she only remembers having seen the black woman Fermina among the rebels." When prompted for more information, Filomena reported that "Fermina joined the rebels to show them where the estate foreman and other families of the estate lived. . . . [Filomena] saw her leading some of them, showing them the doors of the rooms where the whites usually slept."[15] Catalina Gangá similarly reported having seen Fermina and another frequently accused male leader "clearly and distinctly." Catalina "saw with her own eyes" that Fermina was "involved in the whole uproar." While the overseer's house was on fire, Catalina said, Fermina showed some of the other rebels where the white plantation residents slept "so they might attack them."[16] Catalina also reported seeing Ácana's white employees flee to a nearby plantain grove. Catalina said she heard Fermina and another male rebel shouting to other insurgents, "telling them 'the whites are escaping . . .' and [starting] to run in pursuit of the fugitives."[17]

Camila Criolla, a fieldworker on the same estate, gave a similar account, testifying that Fermina "was shouting to the Triunvirato slaves[,] telling them that the whites were escaping that way; that right away [the witness] observed that Fermina was approaching the plantain grove directing several slaves and telling them 'Grab that fat white man and hit him with your machete [*dale de machetazos*], for he is the one who puts [us in] shackles.'" Camila subsequently clarified that she understood "the fat white man" to be the estate overseer.[18] Another fieldworker named Martina provided more indictments of Fermina, saying that "with great shouts she requested a large hammer [*mandarria*] to take off the shackles of the prisoners who were locked up on this estate."[19]

For her part, Carlota Lucumí was enslaved on the nearby Triunvirato estate where the rebellion first broke out. It is likely that she worked in the fields, but the background information about her is very scant. Carlota was best remembered for having attacked the overseer's daughter at Ácana, and for sharing this feat with several other slaves. A fieldworker named Matea Gangá stated "that a black woman from Triunvirato, who she . . . heard is named Carlota, was boasting that she had attacked with a machete [*había dado con el machete*] a white daughter of the overseer who is named Doña María de Regla." Magdalena Lucumí similarly testified that Carlota "was talking about having attacked the child María de Regla, daughter of the mayoral[,] with a machete."[20] As a result of these and other testimonies, the presiding officer demanded to know if there was a slave named Carlota of the Lucumí nation currently among this plantation work gang. Eventually he received the response that her body had been found the morning after the uprising.[21]

When authorities finally questioned María de Regla herself, the young woman gave a detailed account of the attack she sustained. The overseer's daughter stated that when the rebellion broke out she fled in the direction of the plantain grove, "where she realized she was being pursued by two black men and a black woman; unfortunately she fell on the ground as a result of having been attacked; in which position the black woman, who was carrying a pruning machete [*machete de calabozo*] in her hand, inflicted three wounds." María de Regla ended by adding that "when she was wounded, the black woman shouted to the two other black men that they should strike her harder [*que le dieran mas duro*] because she was still living, and . . . the black men responded that this was not necessary because she was already dead."[22]

It should be presumed that all of the above portrayals were carefully crafted by those being interrogated and strategically mobilized to highlight innocence or guilt where necessary. Nevertheless, it is helpful to read these testimonies as a textual archive of black female insurgency. For example, it is fascinating to note that Carlota and Fermina were both accused of acts that even most men only witnessed or supported. The accounts of Fermina chasing the overseer and shouting "grab that fat white man and hit him with your machete," together with that of Carlota's insistence that her comrades hit the overseer's daughter "harder" this time, present us with an image of two women who were as brazen as they were callous, a decidedly manly image of women who boldly pursued the most violent goals of the revolution. That these two were singled out as dangerous instigators is inseparable from their archival (and modern) portrayal as exhibiting a compromised form of femininity. The actions and bodies of these two women thus become an intriguing metonym through which to read individual eruptions of black rage and the collective desires of black militancy.[23] Carlota became so enshrined in popular memory that Cuba launched its 1975 attack in support of the Angolan liberation movement under the title "Operation Carlota."[24]

These and other stories can therefore present us with useful ways to think about the portrayals of black women during moments of slave rebellion. For while many women took part in the 1843 revolts—including several who joined the rebel ranks, ran away, and engaged in other insurgent activities—Carlota and Fermina were the only two condemned as primary agitators, the former killed in battle and the latter executed by firing squad. They were the ones who carried out assaults to body and property, becoming linked to the most violent transgressions of the revolt. Their stories illustrate how certain activities became coded as extravagant performances of masculine subjectivity during slave unrest. They call attention to a recurring truth in this and other slave revolts: that certain *actions*—as much if not more than certain *people*—became masculinized during moments of rebellion.

But Fermina denied the allegations against her. When questioned about what she had been doing the night of the uprising, she stated that "she was sleeping in her cabin" and maintained that when she heard the commotion she fled and hid in a cane patch. She insisted that those who testified against her must have done so "to place themselves in a good position [*buen lugar*] and leave her [in a bad one]," and that her accusers undoubtedly received some kind of compensation.[25]

It is difficult to know how much of Fermina's statement is accurate, certainly it should not be dismissed out of hand as false. It is indeed curious that all of the accusations recorded against Fermina came from other women, two of whom worked in domestic capacities, and another of whom took great pains to emphasize her horror at the night's events.[26] As such, there may be some truth to Fermina's belief that these women were accusing her for their own benefit. The question of Fermina's involvement, however, must also be examined alongside her previous history of rebelliousness; given her encounters with white plantation violence, the accounts of her actions that night seem very believable.

But while women brought in for questioning may have had ulterior motives for accusing Fermina and Carlota, it is also possible that the activities of these two were particularly noticeable to other *women*. This is not to say that such activities would have gone unnoticed by men, but it is worth considering why male witnesses were less inclined to report the details of what female participants did that night, or if they thought that only the actions of men were of interest to their interrogators. For example, several men who were called to testify described heading for the overseer's house and looking for cane trash to set the house on fire, but it was Filomena and Catalina who testified that once the house was burning Fermina "went with some of blacks toward the patio of the house, showing them the doors of the white people's rooms so they might attack them." Similarly, the two male witnesses who talked about the attack on the overseer's daughter testified mainly to their own role in saving the young woman from further harm.

Male witnesses also tended to respond to questions about who made up the leadership ranks by narrating confrontations between enslaved black men and the white men who oversaw them. But Carlota clashed with the white plantation apparatus by assaulting the overseer's daughter, María de Regla Pérez. The assault might also be read as an attack on the privileges that whiteness and femininity conferred on the Pérez women—for despite the comparatively lower-class status of the overseer's family, these would have been privileges that most black women could only dream of.

A number of different factors could account for why Fermina and Carlota are largely absent in the testimonies of slave men. For example, it is possible that male witnesses were trying to protect Fermina—who at the time of the interrogation was still alive—and intentionally left her out of their testimonies. This explanation would be more plausible, however, if more of them had named Carlota, who was already dead and did not need this protection. It must therefore be considered that when male insurgents were asked to testify, the actions of other men stood out to them particularly well, or that they presumed male slaves were of greatest interest to their interrogators. In other words, certain people became particularly visible (and memorable) to them during moments of insurgency. The recurrence of Fermina and Carlota in the testimonies of other women thus invites broader reconsideration of where one might locate the center of gravity in the midst of insurgent turmoil, of what the specific grievances of enslaved people might be during moments of collective unrest, and what might constitute significant acts of resistance during such uprisings.

|||||||| Trial Records and the Production of
Gendered Historical Memory

To better understand the emergence and disappearance of certain female figures in the 1844 trial records, it is important to see these records as part of a colonial knowledge project that sought to discipline and punish in particular ways. The questions that military authorities posed were inspired by events that did in fact take place, and the responses they recorded were most certainly drawn from enslaved people's statements. But their questions were also formulated to examine the most visible, dramatic, and violent episodes of a complex movement. Military officials framed their questions in terms of who killed, who set fire to buildings, who wielded machetes, who released people from shackles, who assaulted white employees, who led rebels to nearby plantations, and how the witnesses positioned themselves with respect to these events. Such questions indicate that the colonial authorities were clearly interested in prosecuting an easily identifiable set of agitators and punishing those who had exposed the fragility of white control.

The interrogators' patriarchal common sense equated slave rebellion with violence and combat and with actions that were plainly visible to—or, more to the point, directed at—militias and plantation authorities. This logic consistently called attention to black men, and consistently presumed that certain black men should be questioned and punished. But it also occasionally threw into sharp relief the black women who enacted similar threats to white bodies and property. In this way the colonial archive consumed women like Fermina and Carlota through narratives of masculinity that made their insurrections much more visible than others, thereby rendering Fermina (and probably Carlota had she lived) dangerous enough to be executed before a plantation public.

This reading of black insurgent impulses also legitimated a kindred logic that demanded spectacularly violent punishments of rebel slave men, and of those women the state deemed equally threatening. While it is clear that women were hardly spared from public discipline and that men were often terrorized behind closed doors, these same records suggest that the colonial state was particularly invested in forms of public punishment that could be attached to aggressive resistance and certain forms of masculinity. There seems then to have been a clear link in the colonial mind between black "masculine" misbehavior and public punishability—a link that made Fermina the only woman to receive a formal sentence in the two major revolts that erupted in 1843.

Whether shouting to other slaves to "grab that fat white man" or slashing the overseer's daughter, Fermina and Carlota Lucumí were viewed as immediately threatening to the custodians of the plantation world. And indeed they were. But their actions also became *more* relevant to prosecuting authorities than did those of women who escaped the plantations amid the chaos and confusion, for example, or fled to look for their kin and loved ones, or sought to protect themselves from further violence.[27] As such, the power of the colonial state should not be the first and last barometer of how these accounts are read, and the people and activities the state *failed* to ask about or prosecute must also be taken into careful consideration. The stories of women who were careful to underscore their minimal involvement invite further deconstruction of the idea that few women took part in these rebellions, and offer a compelling window into the broader ways one might understand the making of a rebellion.

‖‖‖‖‖ Insurgent Women at the Margins

The stories of Fermina, Carlota, and other women agitators expand and complicate the existing narratives of the November insurgency, adding nuance to the ways rebel leadership and movement organization are traditionally understood. While the presence of these two women is critical to understanding slave rebel struggles, there are also distinct limitations to the idea that recounting the stories of the few women who attacked people or burned sugar buildings is the best—or the only—way to make women visible during moments of revolt. Broadly encompassing terms like *the rebels* and *the leaders* both illuminate and obscure a range of actions, particularly those enacted by nonorganizer women, that nevertheless helped to propel insurgent planning and activity.

Little attention has been paid, for example, to people like Petrona Lucumí, whose husband was a central organizer on the Montalvo sugar mill in 1844, and who was reportedly named as a rebel queen, but who said comparatively little during her interrogation.[28] It is unclear exactly how much Petrona knew about the rebellion at Montalvo, but like Desideria Pimienta in the previous chapter, it is unlikely that she was unaware of a movement taking shape. That she retained some awareness of what was happening becomes all the more plausible when viewed against the testimonies that women were aware of those who left the estates to attend secret meetings and make rebel plans.[29] Petrona's potential failure to notify the estate overseer—for whom she worked as a personal cook—about any intelligence she may have obtained would have constituted an intervention as significant to the formation of a rebel movement as the conversations that ensued among her husband and others. In other words, the position of scores of women, and indeed men, as keepers of secrets and maintainers of discretion belies the fact that they had no connection to the conspiracies unfolding on their estate. Such an analysis highlights the ways in which the emotional and psychic labor of women (and also non-elite men) who may have been less active in the movement helped to create a set of vitally enabling conditions for it to unfold.

As 1844 began and the insurgency gathered momentum, scores of other women were cited as attending local meetings. A few of them were clearly central to molding the coming uprising, but the participation of most female attendees is much more difficult to assess. Consider, for example, one witness who spoke about Rita, a woman said to have attended a rebel meeting with her husband. In his words, "the free black man Joaquín Carabalí, and his wife Rita" were among those who used to come to his sugar mill to speak with a local slave captain.[30] This passing reference to Rita Carabalí might easily be missed, as might the implication of her presence at this gathering with members of the local organizing cohort. But if indeed Rita was involved, she gave no testimony to this effect, and no additional information explains the matter further.

Like Petrona and Rita, the majority of women questioned or mentioned in 1843 and 1844 were neither highly visible organizers nor public figures, and the activities they reported suggested little or nothing that "looked" like resistance. Together their accounts suggest that women's participation in the 1844 movement was an unusual occurrence. I believe, however, that it is possible to situate these enslaved women within the insurgent momentum of 1844. To do so requires a set of reading practices that explores what is left out of—or rendered marginal within—the archives as much as what they highlight and privilege. On the one hand, it is critical to recognize that portions—perhaps large portions—of women's invisibility were constructed to protect enslaved people from torture. On the other hand, the documents here reveal much that is worth exploring about these apparent silences.

Taking notice of women like Rita Carabalí, for example, suggests a critically important way to revise the existing narratives about organized slave resistance in Cuba and elsewhere. Such a reading invites the use of analytics that privilege utterances meant to be small and insignificant, and insists on closer examination of the shortest and least consequential portions of witness statements. This approach also requires an ability to identify nameless numbers and statistics as exemplary tools of racial capital that consistently disappeared bodies and stories—in this case, those of women.[31] Rather than limiting the analysis to women like Fermina and Carlota who provided exceptions to a masculine narrative of revolt, we could learn much by considering those women who seemed to evince little involvement, and who constructed their actions as oblique and circuitous signposts on the way to more "important" rebel activities. The case of Eusebia Criolla illustrates this point well.

On the surface, Eusebia Criolla's entry into the insurgent activities of 1844 was a singularly unspectacular event. One afternoon on Eusebia's home estate of Recurso, a small group of men including Pedro and Bienvenido Gangá were reportedly discussing provocative news: slaves on the nearby Echeverría mill were planning to organize a revolt, and they hoped that Pedro and Bienvenido would enlist other men to the cause. Slowly and cautiously the plans went forward, as Pedro maintained contact with a group of male organizers in the district.[32]

Almost a year later, Eusebia would relate how she chanced to overhear this conversation that, in hindsight, had seemed to spark the genesis of a movement at Recurso. When questioned, she gave the following testimony: "approximately one year ago in her master's home, she overheard her companion Pedro[;] that he was telling those of his class Antonio and Bienbenido in their language that on the sugar mill Purisima Concepcion de Echeverria,[33] they were attempting to rise up against the whites, assuring that she knows absolutely nothing more than what she has declared."[34]

To all appearances, this conversation marked the beginning and the end of her connection to a broader rebel movement. But Eusebia's account contains several features that are worth examining closer. Her observation that Pedro spoke to his comrades in "their own language" highlights the important ways that continental Africans created community in rural Cuba through familiar languages—in this case those from greater Sierra Leone—and suggests that these ties figured prominently in forging a rebel movement. Even more interesting is the heightened brevity of Eusebia's statement, and the insistence that "she knows absolutely nothing more than what she has declared." Finally, the verb *oír*, used here in preterit *oyó*, appears repeatedly in the testimonies of 1844. Given the context, I have translated it as "overheard," but the term carries significant ambiguity, as it can also mean "heard."

Eusebia's story, with its suggestive narrative of "overhearing," offers a unique way to trace and engender the circuitry of knowledge during the 1844 organizing, providing a compelling lens into the making of the rebel movement as a whole. Other women who surfaced in the transcripts of 1844 did so in a similar manner—neither as detached individuals who shunned rebellion nor as highly visible organizers with mobility and prestige but rather within a conceptual terrain that was much less precise and much more difficult to name. Across the rural landscape as insurrection brewed in those years, enslaved and free women listened to, overheard, and eavesdropped on conversations and passed on rumors. Within the terrifying realm of colonial interrogations, these experiences were often framed as chancing to stumble on insurgent news. While these patterns were particularly prominent in the testimonies of women, they occurred in those of men as well. Exploring the gendered dimensions of scant slave testimonies thus sheds critical light on one of the more common ways that *most* Cuban slaves—male and female—entered into the public transcript of 1844.

Testimony of Pedro Gangá (*left*) and Eusebia Criolla, Comisión Militar Ejecutiva y Permanente. Courtesy of the Archivo Nacional de Cuba.

The actions of people like Eusebia frustrate our understanding of what it meant to be a "rebel" or an "insurgent" during those days as much as they elucidate it. They trouble many existing analytical categories for organized resistance, and they leave in their wake much slipperiness and instability. Yet while at first appearing to obstruct investigation into the gendered world of slave insurgency, these gaps and confounding moments can actually be productive in what they reveal. Examining stories of this kind—from both female and male slaves—helps to paint a complex picture of what it meant for scores of enslaved people to be a "part" of an underground rebel movement, when the most visible role they played was presumably marginal.

Like Pedro Gangá, who later corroborated Eusebia's story, male rebel leaders across the rural landscape consistently reported that women on their estates learned of a coming rebellion by hearing it from other people. After providing authorities with a long list of men who had been complicit in rebel activities, for example, the rebel organizer Ramón Criollo added,

"The black women of the plantation force [*dotación*] had also known of the plot through hearing the conversations of the men."[35] Similar declarations to this effect were made by other leading male organizers.[36]

That women discovered the insurgent movement by "hearing [or overhearing] the conversations of the men" became a frequent refrain in the testimonies that authorities took from male and female witnesses alike. But when enslaved women were questioned directly, they wrapped much of the subversive knowledge they possessed in a sanitizing language of noticing, hearing, and observing. For example, in May 1844 a woman named Cecilia Criolla stated that "about four months ago she began to notice conversations among the slaves of this work gang that indicated they were plotting . . . a conspiracy to destroy and do away with the whites. . . . From what she has perceived, all the slaves of the work gang, with the exception of very few, were accomplices in and ready for the plot," but the organizers "did not discuss" their plans with the slave women. Cecilia's statement concluded that "she was very careful to listen stealthily [*ocultamente*] to their secret conversations"; as a result she had heard "from the very mouth of the organizers Alejandrino, Crisostomo, and José Belen all that she has expressed."[37]

In a district further south a woman named Teresa Mina reported "that she heard [them say] that the blacks were going to kill the whites." Her statement went on to specify the "them" as two key organizers, but she quickly concluded "that she has nothing else to record on the subject."[38] Near Guanábana, a creole woman named Antonia recounted that while she was bent over in the coffee plants she overheard a group of male organizers discussing who would captain the local movement.[39] On several other estates across these eastern districts leading male witnesses said that women, and sometimes significant numbers of women, were directly or indirectly "in the know."[40]

The suggestion weaving together these stories is that these women learned about the coming rebellion by osmosis or unconscious assimilation. These statements portray the women in question as passive and unaligned, making a truism of the slaveholding logic that black women pacify black men. Indeed a surface reading of these testimonies would suggest that these female witnesses became the accidental, and perhaps unwilling, recipients of revolution.

Yet a more careful examination of the act of listening in on subversive conversations sheds more complicated light on women's involvement in insurgent programs, highlighting delicate positionalities for the women in question. If in fact some women did nothing more than listen to conversations that took place, it is also true that this act of hearing could be at once passive and active—requiring one to take no action at all, at the same time that it could require the hearer to process, store, and evaluate information. Cecilia's testimony, if true, provides an intriguing example: in order to obtain the very information that she seemingly wanted no part of, she had to go out of her way to obtain it by eavesdropping. The second portion of Antonia's testimony—which relates how she was confronted by the two organizers she overheard when she emerged from the coffee bushes—suggests that the act of hearing, rendered passive and inadvertent in many testimonies, in actuality committed these women to insurgent struggles in ways that perhaps not even they would have imagined.[41] Given the full-scale battle that was planned, culpability became, in large part, a question of who knew. And in this moment of state terror, the mere act of possessing knowledge was, in and of itself, criminal. Perhaps most important, people who "knew" were given the dubious privilege of safeguarding rebel information, and the dangerous ability to pass it on. In short, hearing of rebel plans or knowing of their existence not only criminalized the hearer but also ensnared that person in a larger web of insurgent designs.

But perhaps even more to the point, these stories rarely seem to have been consumed in a vacuum. This will become clear in the story of women like Merced Criolla, who insisted that she rejected a special title of rebel queen but revealed a wealth of knowledge about insurgent planning.[42] Other slave women sought to tread a fine line with the authorities, yet their detachment from the rebellion seems called into question by the level of knowledge they possessed. Many women, while strategically seeking to absent or distance themselves from revolutionary activities, at the same time highlighted their location within it.

So even as women like Merced sought to exonerate themselves or frame their testimonies in terms of the interrogators' desired narratives, they called attention in their stories to a range of possibilities for connection to and understanding of an underground movement. Thus the claim that groups of women overheard or knew of seditious plans suggests a critical means by which scores of women developed complicated relationships to the 1844 movement. Indeed, this particularly gendered routing of insurgent knowledge highlights the ambiguous and tentative relationship that most women, and indeed most black Cubans, had with a movement that had yet to erupt.

|||||||| Crowned Queen of the Rebellion

As 1843 ended and 1844 began, scattered groups of women across the rural landscape became active in rebel organizing clusters, sometimes deeply so. One of the more significant, if less common, ways that women became involved in local insurgent plans in 1844 was by receiving the designation of "queen" on their estates during the course of the organizing, usually alongside a rebel "king." This periodic installation of royal figures on resistant estates was therefore a recurrent, if as yet little understood, part of the insurgent slave cultures that unfolded not only in Cuba but across the Americas.[43] As Elizabeth Kiddy has written, "Wherever Africans and their descendants suffered enslavement, the election of kings and queens went with them."[44]

But one of the most important questions begging to be asked is, Why have a queen or a king at all? Only a handful of witnesses in the western region stated that royal titles had even been given, and usually kings and queens were part of a longer list of organizers that included officers like captains and lieutenants. Those who carried the title of king were usually also named as local rebel captains and typically described as carrying out the same duties. But if the two positions were synonymous, there would have been as many kings as captains—which there were not—and the queens were rarely cited as captains at all. This suggests that something about the royal nature of the title was particularly compelling for slave insurgents, and that the modality of royal authority offered something to them that other lexicons could not.

Most notably, the category of kingship and queenship provided black plantation residents with the very things that Cuban enslavement had dispossessed them of: lineage, history, distinction, and stature. Moreover, the installation of royal figures on the plantations conveyed a corresponding political authority that was at once tangible and ethereal. Royal titles therefore contained possibilities that few other idioms of governance could capture, namely, public performances of power, ritualized forms of authority, and forms of community legitimacy that were much less available in military titles like *captain* or *lieutenant*. In short, they extended to slave insurgents something of the vibrant political cultures some of them had known in Africa. It is possible that such titles were intended to usher in the leadership structures of the postrevolutionary state, but the crowning of queens and kings seems to have bespoken an idea of power that drew from a higher authority.

The language of kingship and queenship would have reflected some of the most familiar, potent, and distinguished lexicons of sovereignty at the disposal of many slave insurgents. In the mid-nineteenth-century world of (still) precolonial Africa and colonial Cuba, these royal monikers would have circulated as a powerful form of currency on both sides of the Atlantic. In all probability the stature accorded to royal sovereigns across West and Central Africa resonated strongly with people born in these regions, and thus with the people searching for appropriate terms for rebel positions and hierarchies in 1844.

From Oyo to Greater Senegambia, from Dahomey to Kongo-Angola, royal figures occupied a central place in the social fabric of larger empires and smaller states. The women in the reigning king's household, particularly his sister or his mother, often played significant roles in matters of community and state. The appointment of a queenly figure alongside newly crowned kings in 1844 may have therefore mirrored a number of analogous traditions in Africa. The contours of these positions shed greater light on the worldview that likely influenced the understanding of a *reyna* among African dissidents in Cuba.

Though comparatively few slaves in Cuba were taken from the Gold Coast by this time, the most iconic and well-known queenly figure in West African historiography is undoubtedly the Asantehemaa, the accompanying female sovereign in the Asante Empire. The Asantehemaa's title has generally been translated as "queen mother," but she was more often than not the king's sister. The Asantehemaa did not, it should be emphasized, hold the same status as the Asantehene (the male monarch). But she did stand behind him when he was seated on the stool, a position that indicated her relative prestige and power. The Asantehemaa also attended meetings of the royal council, was frequently required to take charge of political affairs in the Asantehene's absence, and often took pains to develop a political career in her own right.[45]

A similar figure existed in the kingdom of Dahomey, where the male sovereign was attended and assisted by a woman diplomat, known as the Kpojito. Like the Asantehemaa, the Kpojito supported the king in official matters of state, and in many ways she became his extension. The Kpojito also frequently exercised a great deal of spiritual influence, even, in one instance, altering the pantheon of Dahomean deities.[46] Royal women in the court of Oyo enjoyed a similarly privileged status. The symbolic mother of the Aláfin, or the Yoruba king, had a particularly prestigious relationship to the king. On a few occasions, these women became aláfins themselves.[47] So while the vast majority of distinguished state titles were reserved for men, a few select women either moved very close to the centers of power or became the centers of power themselves.

In all likelihood, those who were taken from the empires, provinces, and autonomous communities of West and Central Africa retained such impressions of what it meant to be a "queen," even if they saw little of the inside workings of these offices. Thus, in one form or another, it is likely that these political rites followed enslaved people across the Atlantic and informed the idea of queenship that emerged on the plantations of Matanzas. But there is also strong reason to believe that these meanings merged with and took new inspiration from the ideas of royal sovereignty that dominated Western Europe and colonial Cuba. In fact, the most visible and best-known royal figures in African-descended communities at that time tended to mirror the sartorial and ceremonial practices of Spanish royalty. These offices of African kingship and queenship were most formally preserved in the space of the urban *cabildos*.

In colonial Cuba, the cabildos erected by free people of color and slaves were patterned after the Spanish *cofradías* (religious brotherhoods or fraternities) that established themselves under the patronage of a selected Catholic saint. Largely organized along the lines of ethnicity or nación, these cabildos allowed members of different African *naciones* to meet regularly, hold dances, collect funds, and help members purchase their freedom.[48] Most cabildos elected a king, a queen, and other presiding officers, who became known to the public during lavish dances and ornate street processionals associated with saints' feast days. This indulgence in centuries-old Catholic traditions combined with an equally old colonial myopia that feared black ritual life or perceived in it only "performance" and "play." There was entertainment and amusement to be had in African Cubans' donning of titles for the sake of parody and impossible fantasy. But pretense at grandeur was one thing; royal figures who had a hand in conspiring against the colonial regime was quite another.[49]

It was with great dismay then, that military tribunal officers discovered a series of regal titles that had been bestowed on slaves in the rural regions of Cuba—titles that emanated not from innocuous cabildo celebrations but from conversations and gatherings to mount a massive rebellion. One after another, witnesses responded that these royal titles were given not for plantation dances or cabildo events but for a much more explicit purpose. Many responded, as did one rebel leader, "that they did not have [these royal titles] before they planned to rise up, they were given with the sole objective of the conspiracy."[50] Moreover, the testimonies reveal that such coronations were concentrated not in urban centers or among free populations but rather among enslaved people in the countryside.

Enslaved witnesses spoke of men being named king with relative frequency, but it was rarer for them to mention women who were crowned queen. Queenly figures nonetheless emerged on several estates during the 1844 organizing, and it is possible that dual coronations were more prevalent than witnesses were wont to acknowledge. One of the places where witnesses spoke most freely about rebel queens was the Encanto estate that opened this book. There, two royal figures were allegedly to be installed for the rebellion: "Dionisio as the King and . . . Merced the Queen."[51]

During her time at Encanto, Merced worked as a nurse in the plantation infirmary and served the owner's family when present. She stated that the Encanto rebels tried to bestow her with the title of "queen" in part because of her relationship to one of Encanto's most important organizers. According to her statement, "Her husband wanted her to be named Queen[,] . . . and having opposed this measure, they decided to put in her place the black woman Teresa, wife of Antonio María Gangá."[52] Merced repeated this more than once, that her husband sought to have her enthroned as queen but she "was always opposed to it." She continued that Patricio and Santiago said she should be queen because she was Dionisio's wife, although she did not agree.[53] If Merced's testimony is to be believed, when she refused the title the position fell to Teresa Mina, wife of another rebel leader. Like Merced, Teresa was presumably chosen as queen because of her marriage to a prominent man. But rather than testifying that she contested her queenly role with the rebels, Teresa simply denied having a royal title.[54]

In the neighboring district of Yumurí, similar stories unfolded. Luciana Carabalí and Petrona Lucumí, two African women enslaved on adjacent farms, were named queens. Their husbands, both major organizers in the district, were respectively chosen as kings. Both men were also reportedly instrumental in the selection of their wives as queens. Luciana and Petrona both claimed ignorance of having been crowned *reyna* and denied any knowledge of the planned uprising.[55] Here a recurrent motif emerges in which women were allegedly chosen as queens because of their husbands' kingly status, yet these women remained "always opposed" to the idea, or even ignorant of the honor bestowed on them. If Petrona and Luciana were involved in the conspiracy, their stories accord with the many justifications for female reticence explored above. As with other female testimonies, it is intriguing that such denials contrast starkly to the attitude of male kings, who not infrequently admitted their titles.

The evidence generally indicates that to become a black king in 1844 meant to become a military captain. When slave witnesses spoke about kings, they usually referred to individuals who organized secret meetings, alerted potential recruits, and made tactical plans. In other words, slave men named as kings were generally also named as local rebel leaders, but by and large the queens were not. It is much less clear what it meant to be crowned as a queen for the coming rebellion. The wide variance in the queens' testimonies makes it even more difficult to draw conclusions about how their responsibilities were interpreted during this moment. And though it is certainly possible that ceremonial practices took place,[56] the surviving accounts of royal figures in 1844 make no mention of propitiation of ancestors and deities, formal state observances, or any other practices that resonated with the office of queen in various parts of Africa or Europe. It is tempting to conclude that crowning a queen was a largely symbolic act, possibly seen as a necessary heteronormative corollary to the installation of a king.

A closer investigation of these plantation queens, however, reveals that several of them were deeply involved in organizational plans and communication networks. Some were even described as pivotal to the execution of insurgent designs. What seems clear is that many of these queens had access to valuable information. In some cases, an interesting tension arose. For example, even as Luciana Carabalí claimed to know nothing about being reyna or anything else about the uprising, she provided vital information about leaders and rebel positions. As such, being a queen was one example of the complicated positionalities that women, particularly those with clear ties to male organizers, maintained within the tightly knit circuits of rebel planning. Examining their stories reveals the diverse and often critical labors that women performed as the rebellion took shape on a local level, and it highlights their role in defining rebel strategies and ideologies. Perhaps the most telling example of a queen's knowledge of insurgent planning is that of Merced Criolla.

Merced's testimony suggests that her position in the sickhouse provided ample opportunity to learn about the most important plans being laid at Encanto. As perhaps the most authoritative figure in the plantation infirmary, she was well positioned to hear any discussions that took place there.

Such an opportunity presented itself when a group of leaders came to the infirmary one night looking for her husband. In early March 1844 Merced recounted that "the previous week, the black men Fortunato, Pablo, Roque, and Clemente were in the infirmary one night conversing with her husband, and they stated to him that the uprising would take place at the end of the grinding period, to which her husband Dionisio objected because it was quite a long time away, advising them to execute the plan as soon as possible."[57] Out of all the Encanto slaves, Merced was the only one who mentioned this critical discussion about the timing of the insurgency in their region of Macuriges.

Although she did not place herself in this discussion, it is possible that her comments were either volunteered or solicited. In her testimony, Merced mentioned at least five other surrounding estates that were involved, and she claimed to have known who the couriers would be between plantations, how long the organizers had been planning a rebellion, the basic objectives for the insurgency, which persons came from nearby estates to meet with Encanto leaders at night, and the agreed-upon signal for insurgents to rise up. Whether because of her privileged role as a nurse and a domestic servant, her leadership position as a potential queen, or the interactions with her husband and fellow organizers, it is clear that Merced carried critical knowledge about insurgent designs. In all likelihood, she was not alone. Other queens who negated or deemphasized their role in the rebel planning may have actually retained intimate knowledge of rebel plans in gestation through their husbands, if not through other channels. In one organizer's opinion, such was the case with the tight-lipped Teresa Mina, who "also knows about the plan, because her husband Antonio María was one of the principal [leaders]."[58]

So although some queens said little about their involvement, others like Merced revealed a wealth of knowledge of local insurgent planning. In a few cases, witnesses even spoke about such women with no mention of a corresponding king. While their ties to male leaders were significant—and may have played a role in their being remembered as queens—the examples of the following women contradict the assumption that women became queens simply because their husbands were major organizers. In fact, the following women appear to have been crowned "queen" precisely because of their planned roles in the local insurgency.

Among the most intriguing examples of such a woman is Simona Criolla, who lived on the Macutivo sugar estate in the southern part of Sabanilla. Simona was a creole and a mulatta, an unusual combination for queens of this rebellion. She was personally recruited by one of the most notorious and respected leaders in the region, José María Mondejar. On the estate where Simona lived, Mondejar was shaping his military strategy around an attack on the owner, José Govin. Simona testified that during the months Mondejar had been working on her property, "he spoke to her expressing the plan in all its scope." Simona also spoke about the plan with Mondejar's son and two other free black men, who confirmed "that there was going to be a general uprising, in which the free people would get together with the slaves [to overthrow the whites]."

Simona's testimony suggests that there was often a direct correlation between what one could offer to the insurgency and the conferring of titles. Simona said she spoke with Mondejar and several other men, who "offered to make her Queen [as long as she] opened the door of the Master's house the night of the uprising, to kill their owner, his wife, and the children, in the process, taking possession of the [available] weapons."[59] Another witness agreed, "Mondejar himself was going to kill Don José Gobin [Govin] through the involvement of the mulatta Simona . . . [who was to] open the door for him."[60] Other men who would soon become a part of the rebel cohort were alerted to the crucial role that Simona was to play. During one evening conversation with Simona and two others Mondejar allegedly told those assembled "not to worry . . . everything would go well for them as long as they carried out well what Simona had [planned with] them."[61]

In light of these accounts, it hardly seems excessive to state that the success of the Macutivo rebellion hinged largely on Simona's actions. The evidence suggests that Simona was working in the owner's home, and her access to Govin and his family was seen as invaluable by the rebels, since she would give them access to their white targets while the latter were most vulnerable. Thus, in her very person, Simona represented a passageway to insurgency. Had she been a man, Simona might have been made "lieutenant" or "second captain." But if in fact she was to receive a title, few would have seemed appropriate apart from "queen." In the records I examined, however, it is never clear whether Simona agreed to the plan, or was ever crowned queen.

On the Dos Mercedes sugar plantation not far away, not one, but two women were given queenly titles without attendant kings. A key rebel witness reported that "Rosa, who is a slave of the estate, was to be the Queen, and Dolores the second Queen."[62] Like their counterparts elsewhere in Matanzas, both women knew quite a bit about rebel activities being planned in their district. Dolores, for example, spoke about one of the major organizers who used to come to the plantation to talk to other men there, and she cited five male conspirators by name. She also knew about specific information that passed between these men, the widely rumored support from British allies, and the day the uprising was supposed to take place.

Rosa was to all appearances as deeply entrenched in the insurgency as anyone at Dos Mercedes; in fact, when one rebel participant was asked to name the leaders at Dos Mercedes he included her among them. This is one of the rare occasions when a female queen was cited as one of the primary estate leaders. Like Simona, Rosa also had contact with Mondejar, but it seems that theirs was no ordinary relationship. Rosa claimed the two had had a long-standing romantic connection dating back some years, and she described Mondejar as one "with whom she has had amorous relations since the time she was young," though Mondejar later denied this. Rosa stated that Mondejar was "the first person to speak to her" about the rebellion, noting that others on the estate had also been convinced to join.[63] The extent of their relationship during the insurrectionary movement never came to light, but Rosa testified that she knew about some of Mondejar's attempts to gather money, for example.

So while Rosa was not listed as being married to anyone, she and Simona both maintained significant relationships to a male organizer, in both cases Mondejar. Perhaps one's suitability for queenship *was* predicted on association with a male captain. Put the other way around, those women who had the closest contact with important male leaders emerged most consistently in these testimonies as a choice for queen. In Rosa's case it is not clear if Mondejar ever actually attempted to make her queen. If so, this was never made public. In fact, as with Simona, it is not clear how her naming as queen came about.

On the whole, Rosa's stated knowledge surpassed even that of the male leaders, and one witness's impression of her as one of the estate leaders seemed to be well founded, though this was not corroborated by others. Rosa testified about things that few male rebels could (or would), including frequent exchanges of money, free men coming to the mill to talk about the uprising, plans for obtaining arms and poisons, and organizers and rebel plans on other estates. She also commented on private conversations among free organizers and gave intimate details about where they lived. All in all, she named at least fifteen free and enslaved conspirators, almost all of whom were leaders the authorities were eager to apprehend.[64] She explained that "the devil had gotten into her head and the free men were responsible for everything," hence her intention to confess all she knew.[65]

In addition to her collaborations with Mondejar, Rosa testified about another man, a free woodcutter named Jacobo who worked on the grounds sometime in 1843, whom she accused of trying to collaborate with her to kill the estate overseer. Rosa alleged that Jacobo attempted to furnish her with the means to poison the overseer, giving her "some powders the color of ground-up coffee to throw in the mayoral's coffee." She claimed that "Jacobo was in love with her" and that the mayoral was attempting to fortify the permeable boundaries of Dos Mercedes against black men who in his eyes did not belong there.[66] But Rosa reported that she was unwilling to go through with the assassination: "If the mayoral choked [atoraba; that is, died], she was the one who would pay." It is unclear how much of this actually unfolded, as Jacobo denied most of it. What is significant about Rosa's narrative—in a manner highly reminiscent of Mondejar's solicitation of Simona—is the way in which Jacobo allegedly viewed Rosa's labor, her access to the white overseer, and her bodily movements as important weapons to use against the oppressor.

But as with Simona, it was Rosa's position as a domestic servant that provided the most immediate, vitally important, and exploitable entrée to the overseer. It is intriguing to note that nearly all of the aforementioned women cited as queens worked in some kind of domestic capacity. At the very least, they did not work in the fields. For example, Rosa Lucumí and Petrona Lucumí both were personal cooks for the estate overseer. Luciana Carabalí was similarly described as "a cook and caretaker of chickens," and Merced Criolla was recorded as a house servant and a medical nurse.[67] These positions would have set them apart from other women on their properties. This fact suggests delicate questions: Could field hands be named queens? Did house-servant queens consider themselves superior to women who worked sugar cane and coffee berries? It is certainly possible that women not working in the fields were more likely to be crowned queen because of their stature and privilege within the slave community, or among those who became organizers. But perhaps of greater significance to the rebellion was the exploitability of such privilege. The revolution may have desired stately women as queens, but it needed strategically positioned rebel women even more. Strategic labor, in positions that promised either access to white people or mobility around the estate, and relationships with dynamic male leaders together appear to have made slave women into rebel queens in 1844.

Laying these images side by side should suggest a picture of rebel womanhood that was complex, multilayered, and at times ambivalent. It should highlight the variegated ways in which a wide spectrum of women came to the movement, defining its ideologies, scripting its notions of femininity, and leading and executing its most difficult labors. These images should bring our attention back to where we began with Polonia: to the strange compulsions of insurgency (and intimacy), to the imprecise and in-between places occupied by female and male rebels alike who individually and collectively endorsed rebellion in often contradictory ways. Finally, reconsidering the women of the 1844 movement should open up a larger conversation in slave resistance studies that focuses not (or not solely) on the question of "who led" but on which contributions became central to the movement and why. We will explore the question of leadership in greater detail in the next chapter.

Chapter Six

The Anatomy of a Rural Movement

Between the fall of 1842 and the winter of 1844 mobile slave and free men of color took the news of a coming rebellion to much of western and central Cuba. Women and other men without the privilege and opportunity to be mobile during the day circulated at night and on Sundays, often gathering information more circumspectly. In this way, a broad swath of people shaped the moments they had already ritualized to confront the plantation's violent ethos of containment and unending labor—slipping out when they could to meet with loved ones, enjoying dances and drumming, convening for religious ceremonies—to hear seditious information and outline plans for concerted resistance.

In the course of their daily labor and movements and in purposeful gatherings after dark, groups of slaves ranging from three and four to twenty and thirty met to discuss how and if they would take part in this larger struggle. From sugar mills like Nueva Esperanza and La Victoria to coffee estates like Recompensa and Buena Suerte, from western districts like Sabanilla and Guanábana to more eastern ones like Macuriges and Ceja de Pablo, the radical currents that condemned slavery and colonial rule solidified into defiant plans. By the summer of 1844 authorities reported uncovering conspiratorial factions in districts that spanned nearly the entire expanse of the island's western and central departments, from Havana to Villa Clara.

This chapter will explore the internal anatomy of the rural Matanzas movement. It will focus on the people who emerged as recognized leaders and organizers, their articulated plans for assault and attack, and how they planned to arm themselves. But this chapter will also attempt to understand each of these points through a deeper culture of insurgency that saturated the rural plantation world, and to suggest a different way to appreciate how this movement was coordinated, envisioned, and armed. In particular we will pay close attention to the individuals, many of them women, who were rarely named as insurgent leaders but who nonetheless became central to rebel designs.

To the extent that history has assigned a leader to the 1844 conspiracy, it has largely been Plácido, also known as Gabriel de la Concepción Valdés. As we saw in chapter 4, Plácido was a renowned poet in the late 1830s and early 1840s and a favored guest of creole literary circles. Since the nineteenth century, critics have vigorously debated whether Plácido was a revolutionary poet who plotted an insurgency with other free people of color, or an apolitical bystander who got caught in the clutches of the Spanish Empire.[1]

Regardless of how he emerges as a political figure, in much of the extant literature on La Escalera, Plácido is portrayed as the ideological heart of the movement. For over a century he has remained a martyred icon, even for those who never believed that he organized an insurgent movement. The much-debated diplomatic and military connections beyond Cuba were presumably to be orchestrated by David Turnbull, the abolitionist diplomat said to have facilitated the initial contact between white and colored dissidents. Turnbull, of course, became so notorious for his antislavery activities that he quickly incurred the ire of the Spanish colonial state and the creole planter elite, and he was eventually accused of assisting anticolonial conspirators. Thus, for over a century, this fascination with the enigmatic Plácido and the international controversy sparked by Turnbull have dominated the ways the leadership and organization of the 1844 movement have been discussed.

The witness statements from slaves in the western countryside share one particularly striking feature: when confronted with questions about the leadership of the conspiracy, the witnesses rarely mentioned Plácido, or Turnbull, or any of the men whose names are most familiar to scholars of La Escalera. Some slaves did have reason to know these individuals, or at least they knew enough to mention them in their testimonies, and it is almost certain that a few rural organizers were in touch with men like Marcos Ruiz, Bruno Huerta, Antonio Abad, and even Plácido. But the majority of slaves in the plantation countryside never seem to have heard of any of these people. Most had never traveled to cities like Matanzas or Havana. They had only heard that the British would help their cause, but they received few details about how this would happen.

Yet when they were questioned, again and again, plantation slaves identified the people they understood to be the leaders and organizers of the

1844 movement. Usually they named other slaves with rank and privilege on their own estates or those nearby. Sometimes they identified legally free men of color they knew, or even themselves. In fact, the documents that I examined referred to over 100 people as central leaders on the plantations of the rural region. Such high numbers point to much more than a distinctive mobilization taking place in the rural theater of 1844. They invite us to take a different kind of approach to thinking about insurgency itself, and to use a different set of strategies to narrate how this movement was organized and led. Moreover, these numbers suggest a different set of frameworks for understanding the very category of leadership, in both this and other slave resistance struggles.

This is particularly important because the history of New World slave rebellions has long been fascinated with the figure of the iconic male leader. This history is filled with names whose very utterance conjures up images of seismic rupture. Toussaint Louverture. José Aponte. Nat Turner. Denmark Vesey. Sam Sharpe. These legendary names have become powerful mnemonic devices. They act as a shared invocation that conjures up and magnifies black dissidence. In short, these are individuals who powerfully galvanize the memory of black dissidence, and they also instruct in how to imagine that dissidence.

To narrate these struggles then—to call to mind the ways that enslaved people upended the technologies of slavery from Virginia to Saint-Domingue—is to link those rebellions to their most visible organizers and to craft a story about male icons who loom larger than life. On the one hand, the lives of these individuals and their discursive afterlives have had extremely important political ramifications throughout the African Diaspora. Most important, they remind the descendants of enslaved people that their ancestors resisted, undermined, and systematically organized against some of the most powerful plantation regimes in the region. For these and other reasons, these leaders' legendary status cannot be dismissed as an easy flattening out of enslaved people's struggles.

At the same time, their central position within histories of collective slave struggle must be examined and critiqued for what it obscures and eclipses. Perhaps most important, the focus on these singular charismatic individuals—invariably men who attained stature through their color, mobility, occupation, or literacy—continues to provide an organizing lens through which to study collective resistance.[2] In others, it is *the* analytical framework for understanding black resistant leadership. Moreover, as we saw in the previous chapter, the aggressive forms of masculinity that such histories tend to privilege frequently render many women (as well as other men) marginal or invisible.[3] Thus the activities of highly visible slave men, and other behaviors coded as masculine, become central to the very existence of the slave insurgent narrative in both the colonial archiving practices and in larger historical memories.

These historiographic practices often seduce the researcher, and I admit to having tried to find a Plácido- or Aponte-like figure moving about the Cuban countryside in the early 1840s. But the fact that so many rural slaves were named as "'leaders' and 'captains'" necessarily pointed me in a very different direction. Such a profusion does not mean that there were no "real" leaders of the movement, nor does it fundamentally challenge the fact that those with connections, stature, and mobility—to say nothing of access to white Cuban patriots or British allies—were critical to developing the major plans for that year. It does, however, ask that we think differently—and more expansively—about the ways this and other slave movements were assembled on a local level.

The documents that I consulted for this study have yet to yield one solitary figure or group of figures who stood above all the other actors of the rural countryside. Some of these local captains or "heads" were very well known in their districts. Organizers like the free black José María Mondejar, who traveled miles of rural terrain rallying recruits and support, became vital to the growth of the movement, and I discuss others like him in the pages to come. Yet the task that has emerged for anyone studying the 1844 movement, is not so much to identify the few individuals who organized the rural theater as it is to explore a series of smaller networks that unfolded at the level of the individual plantations. Such a task shifts one's attention from identifying the principal leaders of the insurgent struggle to exploring the many groups of local organizers scattered across the western regions whose proliferation and coordination proved critical to the dissemination of insurgent designs.

Within these organizing cohorts, a few men certainly claimed positions of leadership and authority, and they often retained privileged information for themselves. But shifting the focus from a central body of leaders to a series of organizing clusters requires that the movement *itself* be understood as a series of personalities, geographies, and tactics that had to be constantly negotiated, and whose convergence intimately shaped what "rebellion" meant from one locale to the next. It underlines the fact that each estate, and indeed each person, who came in contact with rebel news had to decide how such news would be interpreted and acted on, which persons would be included in the central planning, how the collective stakes of rebellion would be understood, and what one's personal investment in this new struggle would be. In other words, examining a range of different mobilizations asks for a more complex understanding of how the 1844 movement actually grew and unfolded. It demands attention to the intricate relationships that people across lines of gender and ethnicity developed with the movement's labors and ideologies, as well as the oppositional synergies that all of these people created together.

Within these local leadership collectives, accounts of how slave captains came to assume their positions generally fell into one of three categories. The first includes men like Mariano Lucumí who insisted that "no one induced them." Similar sentiments were echoed by Victor Gangá, who maintained "that the plan to rebel came from his own head, and he had not been counseled by anyone."[4] If this is true, then Mariano and Victor would have likely obtained information about the rebellion through their own personal networks and, on hearing that a movement was afoot, begun to make plans with a few trusted associates. The second group encompasses leaders who were recruited by other slave organizers from nearby plantations. Many stories surfaced of zealous lieutenants such as Casimiro Lucumí, who appointed two acquaintances on a nearby sugar estate to be captains there.[5] These first two types of accounts call attention to rural leadership structures that surfaced more or less organically, as rural slaves received word of (another) massive uprising in the works and made decisions to take part and galvanize others on their estates. The records indicate, however, that these first two types of accounts were in the minority. Most organizers gave a third kind of account, that of being approached by free black men, some merely passing on the news, others urging their contacts to recruit a reliable army. These were men like Manuel Mieres and Pío Romero who worked for varying periods on the rural estates and often traveled through the rural districts and small towns. Such individuals came bearing news of a movement that was uniting efforts in the city with those in the countryside, and promising support from Britain and Haiti.

In most cases, one or two men crowned the rebel hierarchy and worked in concert with a few others who collectively comprised a circle of rebel authority. On the larger plantations, this central organizing contingent was sometimes flanked by a small group of individuals who were not privy to all of the planning but were either assigned to specific tasks or acquired more knowledge of rebel plans than most others on the estate. Most of these men came from the elite strata of plantation workers. A large part of what made these men suitable candidates for leadership lay in the privileges their occupations conferred on them—their opportunities to be mobile, their perceived access to other workers, and their stature and influence with other slaves.[6] If potential estate captains were not already pulled into the resistance momentum by friends, acquaintances, or work associates, these elite attributes must have singled them out, making them more visible to recruiters in search of local organizers.

While continuing to question the very trope of leadership, it is nevertheless useful to examine these groups of laborers to understand what about their access, their labor, and their contact with other slaves enabled them to emerge as conspicuous figures. Slaves who worked in specialized jobs or drove cargo and people were recurrent figures in the movement. But it was the contramayorales or black assistant foremen who were named as leaders with the greatest consistency. Their experiences merit closer investigation.

ⅠⅠⅠⅠⅠⅠ "The Driver Shall Lead Them"[7]

In some ways the contramayorales would seem to be the least likely leaders of a revolutionary movement. As second-in-command to the white overseers, these black drivers were frequently called on to execute the dirtiest and least desirable aspects of policing the slave population. If the brute power of the estate proprietors was made visible through the plantation administrators and the overseers, the power of these overseers was made concrete through their black drivers. To the black foremen fell the unenviable tasks of supervising the labor taking place in the fields and boiling houses, disciplining slaves deemed unruly, and locking in scores of other workers at night. In a manner not unlike their immediate supervisors, the driver's image became soldered to "the badge of their office"—the hide whips they carried—and few depictions of contramayorales failed to include this implement.[8]

This image of naked coercion was heavily tied to an equally powerful image of hypermasculinity. None of the foremen mentioned in the documents were female, and the aggressive forms of discipline that so easily followed the contramayorales seemed inextricable from the presumption of highly masculine displays of force. Alongside this ability to inflict pain, foremen, among the highest-ranking members of the black plantation hierarchy, notoriously received special privileges, including their own separate cabins, small gifts, special clothes, and often the right to demand sexual favors from female slaves.

Yet if the black drivers were often responsible for implementing some of the worst atrocities of the slave regime, they could also act in ways that were protective, supportive, and understanding of other workers. They could function, for example, as protectors and go-betweens, mediating on behalf of other black residents and defending their interests. In addition to threatening their subordinates with violence—which may have been magnified in the eyes of white observers who perceived only burly black men with whips—most drivers would have also had to find nonviolent methods to encourage other slaves to work.

In his article on black drivers in American slave societies, Robert Paquette argues that the authority most drivers held over their work gangs had to be rooted in a certain level of respect, esteem, and validation on the part of the other slaves.[9] White managers and slaveowners both relied on the black driver's acumen and savvy to manage the plantation work gangs efficiently and effectively. Drivers were often selected from newly arrived Africans who seemed to command the respect and admiration of their peers.[10] The contramayorales thus occupied an uneasy netherworld between the power of the white bosses and the subordination of other black workers, a space that Paquette has described as "the conflicted middle ground." This terrain was also a social one, as overseers were often godparents and husbands who attended dances and ancestral rituals and frequently permitted people to exit and enter the estate against regulations.[11]

How then do we reconcile the coercion and intimidation frequently exhibited by these superintendents with their participation and acceptance in families, social networks, and communities? A partial answer to this question might be found in a theme that surfaced repeatedly in antislavery writing of the period. The drivers were not absolved of the pain they inflicted, but the white overseers were unequivocally identified as the source of that violence and the true reason for its existence. In the end, the white power structure is condemned, rather than its black policemen.[12]

It is difficult to know the extent to which enslaved people who worked under the black drivers shared this view. If the contramayorales were complex individuals, the feelings they evoked in other black laborers must have been equally complex. During the course of the trials, black witnesses frequently reported being threatened by contramayoral leaders to take part in the rebellion or to keep the silence. It was probably not uncommon for slave witnesses to use these opportunities to retaliate against their superiors by naming them as rebel captains, accurately or inaccurately. And yet few plans seem to have emerged to overthrow the contramayorales in 1844. Moreover, when enslaved witnesses spoke of those who punished or beat them, they spoke almost invariably of white overseers or masters. If ever there were an ideal moment to seek even greater retaliation against those blacks who had tyrannized them, 1844 would have provided hundreds of slaves with that opportunity. It is entirely possible that such hostilities might have erupted had "the" rebellion come to fruition, as seen on one occasion the previous March. But it is also possible that enslaved people indeed identified the white powerholders as the true culprits of antiblack violence, or that some genuinely admired the drivers, or that slaves' hostilities and antagonisms toward the contramayorales were kept largely within the parameters of black rural communities—as familiar faces were suddenly imprisoned, as torturers failed to discriminate between overseers and overseen, and as the bloody trials reminded all who lived through that time where the racial lines were drawn in Cuba.

Black drivers who emerged as local rebel leaders were not unusual in New World slave revolts. Examples of their participation can be found in revolutionary Saint-Domingue and in numerous other locales.[13] In Cuba, contramayorales figured disproportionately as leaders and participants in many collective uprisings. Gloria García has argued that it would be difficult at best to carry out a substantive rebellion without their participation, complicity, or neutrality. If we take seriously that slaves had a collective memory of resistance that became part of a deeper historical consciousness, it would not be surprising that the contramayorales emerged as local leaders with the greatest consistency.[14]

In the fall of 1843 Román Macúa, a driver on the Nueva Esperanza sugar mill, was contacted by a neighboring boiling house attendant about gathering recruits for a coming insurrection. The attendant convinced Román "that as contramayoral it would be easy and fitting [for him] to prepare the other slaves for the uprising."[15] On the neighboring property of San Vicente, Joaquín Congo claimed that "he would never have gotten involved had he not seen the example of his foreman," and others on the estate offered similar testimonies.[16] Such a report, of course, shift obvious blame away from Joaquín himself. Yet if true, it could hardly have been a small thing for Joaquín to learn that the highest-ranking slave on his plantation was involved in a plot to overthrow the white authority. If Román Macúa and others could command labor and obedience from hundreds of blacks in a setting with few whites, they could also direct those efforts against an out-numbered white hierarchy when the moment of truth arrived.[17]

Other specialized workers besides the foremen also figured prominently in the leadership ranks. Not unlike the contramayorales, masons, carpenters, boiling house workers, tile makers, woodcutters, ox drivers, domestic servants, and of course cart drivers and coachmen had far greater flexibility than the average field laborer and enjoyed varying degrees of independence, and outside contact. The centrality of skilled workers in the rebel leadership was another very familiar theme in Atlantic plantation struggles, especially in the British Caribbean.[18] But the time, access, and mobility these men had to shape a growing movement bespoke not only their social status but also their masculine privilege.

Indeed, the most cursory examination of the rebel captains of 1844 reveals that nearly all of the rural plantation leaders were men. The rebellion of November 1843 foregrounded as central organizers two women whose valiance and bravery have been remembered and celebrated in Cuban history. Yet, as we saw in previous chapters, their centrality in this narrative also resulted from their attunement to highly visible men and to masculine-coded behaviors and bodies. It is difficult to find stories of other women who captained the local struggles of 1843 and 1844, and a surface reading of the testimonies would suggest that women were not included in the leadership ranks. But the example of the women crowned rebel queens illustrates that if we enlarge the definition of what constitutes leadership, surprising numbers of women come into view. Beneath this apparently male surface, then, one can identify more than a few women who were keenly aware of organizational plans, involved in communication networks, and were regular attendees at rebel meetings. And every so often certain women were unexpectedly mentioned as central to the organizing junta. One of the best examples returns us to the story of Eloisa Carabalí on the Buena Suerte mill.

Sometime in either late 1843 or early 1844 a young slave named Dionisio Criollo came to the forefront of the rebel leadership at Buena Suerte. About twenty-five years of age, Dionisio worked as a coachman and domestic servant for the estate owner, Miguel Cárdenas. In the months leading up to the planned Easter uprising, Dionisio recruited an inner circle of organizers made up of slave elites, with one exception. The elite slaves were Candelario Criollo, the estate contramayoral who seemed to act as a kind of second captain; Silvestre Criollo, a much older former contramayoral who now worked as a boiling house attendant and mason; and Ramón Gangá, in his late thirties, who worked as a cart driver and a field laborer. The fourth was Eloisa Carabalí, a widow who worked as a field laborer.[19] She was the only woman in the leadership collective and the only one listed as working solely in the fields.

Nevertheless, Eloisa was depicted as being very much a part of those critical inside conversations about the rebellion, in which she and others "satisfactorily agreed on the plan of uprising that Dionisio expressed to them."[20] Eloisa was also among the central organizers described as "complicit and ready to inform others about the uprising" at Buena Suerte.[21] Alongside Eloisa, three other women, Rita Carabalí, Maquías Criolla, and Isabel Mina, were reportedly told about the plan and were "agreed that the people should rise up," as more than one person testified to their involvement.

It seems that these women, and Eloisa in particular, were particularly vocal in urging other slaves to rise up. One of the other organizers later recalled, for instance, that "the women, especially Eloisa Carabalí, were encouraging [others] for the fight, calling those who did not want to enter cowards."[22] Such an exhortation had explicitly gendered undertones and implied that those who failed to join them were not just cowards but also less than true men. On the nearby mill of Santa Lugarda, Felipe Congo recalled a similar incident with the women on his property. He testified that in December 1843 and January 1844 a Lucumí captain began to spread the word of a rebel movement, "telling them that he did not want to be a slave any longer," and supposedly "everyone" was in agreement. In one of the meetings with many of the Santa Lugarda slaves, Felipe reported that "some of the black women were mocking how their compañeros, the black men, were afraid, because they did not dare to rise up all at one time, distinguishing among themselves these [women], Agustina Lucumí and Constancia Mandinga."[23]

If it is true that Eloisa, Agustina, Constancia, and other women were goading their fellow male plantation residents in this manner, they were deliberately invoking rigid paradigms of manhood to do so, calling on the same tropes of male patriarchal protection that male leaders reportedly used to push other men to join the fight. Corroborating reports of meetings on both estates suggest that significant numbers of slaves on both properties supported the cause of insurrection. In condemning the disinclination to rebel as cowardly, these women may have been caught up in the gusto of the moment. It is intriguing to note that in these descriptions, armed resistance is implicitly coded as male—as much by the men's *failure* to participate in the resistance effort as anything else. The women's exhortations would have thus dexterously performed different functions: on the one hand, shoring up their femininity by calling on their companions to carry out their duties as men and, on the other, casting a shadow on their comrades' manhood by highlighting their own strength and readiness for battle.

Of course, it is also fascinating to consider that Eloisa may have been referring to the cowardice of both her female and male colleagues, which would liken her to Fermina and Carlota Lucumí in their determination that everyone should commit to violent rebel struggle. This would indicate that Eloisa, just as easily as her male counterparts, could be part of a coercive revolutionary ideology that in some ways perpetuated the very violence it sought to undo.

It bears reiterating that among those who organized the 1844 rebellions at Buena Suerte, Eloisa stands out as both the only woman and the only field laborer. Although there were some unusual estates where all the leaders came from the field, fieldworkers—particularly those described *only* as fieldworkers—were outnumbered among the rural Matanzas leadership. But some fieldworkers, like Jacobo Gangá in Yumurí, were among the most widely known and respected commanders in their districts.[24] Though men like Jacobo were not in the majority, calling attention to field laborers who became rebel leaders offers an expanded lens into the rebel leadership structures of 1844. Not only does it allow insight into how "ordinary" plantation slaves helped to shape and spread the 1844 movement, but it also highlights the centrality of women like Eloisa who would not have held positions as contramayorales or carpenters but who were nevertheless seen as central organizers.

In light of all of this, it is intriguing to note that two overseers, Candelario and Silvestre Criollo, shared the inner "knowledge" cohort with Eloisa. It is impossible to know how the dynamics played out at Buena Suerte as a female fieldworker labored alongside two male overseers to advance the coming insurgency. It would be fascinating to know, for example, if Eloisa had more (or less) success in recruiting people than did Candelario, if Silvestre did not feel as compelled to goad people and call them cowards, or if the process of raising a rebellion that encompassed both overseer and overseen was less than seamless. While the records do not tell these kinds of stories, the possible existence of such dynamics hints at the intricacies and complexities of plantation leadership that we must consider when assessing its gendered and classed dimensions.

Across rural Matanzas a general pattern unfolded in which local captains came together from a small cluster of estates to synchronize uprisings in their part of the district. Together these leaders outlined who would send the signals for the rebellion to begin, how the uprisings would be executed on their respective estates, and how the collective force of their four or five plantations would connect with a larger battle. For example in the Yumurí district near the Matanzas Bay, a group of mostly African lieutenants coordinated their efforts across at least six plantations.[25] In the early months of 1844 these estate captains held regular meetings to plan an insurrection that would engulf their respective properties. They frequently slipped out after dark to meet in one another's cabins, gathering repeatedly on the Calderón estate.

The evidence suggests that these small groups of roughly ten to fifteen men—many of whom probably knew each other long before 1844—comprised something of a leadership collective in their part of Yumurí. For the coming rebellion to stand a chance of success, the act of forging alliances across plantation lines would not have been simply advantageous; it would have been compulsory. Leaders like Cleto Gangá from the Calderón estate went to great lengths to galvanize—and strong-arm—people they knew on other estates, designating them as captains on their respective plantations and charging them with enlisting other people.[26]

In many cases, those named as estate captains admitted that they knew the leaders on other nearby properties. Men from the San Lorenzo mill identified leaders from Juan de Dios and Sentmanat, men from Juan de Dios named others from Nazareno and San Lorenzo, leaders from San Lorenzo named leaders from San Francisco, and so forth.[27] One might presume that accusing leaders on other estates would be a convenient way to deflect blame from oneself, but many of those who did so also named themselves as leaders. It is therefore critical to note the frequency with which enslaved people, especially men, testified about their own positions of insurgent leadership. This pattern of slave leaders admitting to their positions of leadership contrasts starkly with the massive denials of involvement by free blacks, and by urban people of color more broadly.

A particularly striking example of this phenomenon can be found in comparing the property of Sentmanat to that of Bolanios, also in Yumurí. When asked "who was supposed to be the principal boss or head on the estate for the day of the uprising," Jacobo Gangá responded, "the principal ones were the declarant [that is, himself] and his companion Marcos Criollo." This same Marcos similarly replied, "They are Jacobo Gangá and the declarant."[28] On the Ingenio Dichoso, Perico Gangá reported that the first and second captains of Dichoso were himself and Dionisio Lucumí, "and their companions recognized them as such."[29] Other leaders gave similar responses, and other slaves agreed with their assessments. This is a distinctive phenomenon that can be easily traced in the testimonies of many rebel leaders. But regardless of whether or not they admitted their roles as leaders, it is clear that certain slave men emerged as the captains of their respective farms and plantations.

One of the most striking features of the 1844 leadership is that its most visible agitators were largely African-born men (and this was even more true of the 1843 rebellions). More to the point, a large number of them were Lucumís. Eleven of the eighteen primary leaders of the Triunvirato rebellion, for example, were Lucumís.[30] Manuel Barcia has demonstrated that this Lucumí prevalence was hardly unique to the 1843 rebellions; on the contrary, most of the organized acts of slave resistance from 1832 to 1843 were crafted or led primarily by Lucumís.[31] But even when the Lucumís were *not* the most numerous participants—as in the 1844 organizing—they were often portrayed as such. The question is, why?

From 1841 to 1845 a surge in Lucumí arrivals made them the largest of the African ethnic groups, but for most of the nineteenth century they were significantly less numerous than the Congos, the Carabalís, and the Gangás. The Lucumís' impact on the west-central slave movements of the 1830s and 1840s therefore cannot be understood solely in terms of their numbers. Rather, it must be understood as part of a broader set of ideas about the Lucumís, and specifically the Yorubas, that circulated throughout the Atlantic world.[32]

While the Lucumís represented a range of ethnolinguistic groups that left from the Bight of Benin, the most recent research indicates that 65 percent of them identified in some way as Yorubas.[33] It is difficult to locate the precise origin of the dominant Atlantic ideas about the Yorubas, but what is clear is that by the 1840s, the Lucumís—from Yorubaland to Cuba—were regarded as fierce warriors and invincible leaders. European observers routinely described Lucumís as "proud," "contentious," "indomitable," "difficult to manage," "lovers of freedom," and "easily excited to violence."[34] Even those who were not Yoruba, but whose departure from ports like Lagos and Ouidah conflated their ethnicities with that of the Yorubas, seem to have identified with and perpetuated the mythology and preeminence of the Yorubas once they were Lucumís in Cuba.

To the extent that the Yorubas believed in their own greatness, this seems to have been evident on both sides of the Atlantic. Years, later the Yoruba ethnographer and historian Samuel Johnson described his people as possessing "[a] love of independence, a feeling of superiority over all others ... [and] never able to admit or consent to a defeat."[35] In the aftermath of the

1843 rebellions and during the 1844 trials, more than a few witnesses—including the Lucumís themselves—portrayed the Lucumís as belligerent and unaccommodating in the milder depictions, and practically unconquerable in the more extreme ones. For example, in March of 1844, a slave named Manuel Mozambique [that is, Macúa] was indicted as a primary rebel organizer in the local region. Manuel was one of several who testified about his conversations with a free Lucumí man named Ramón Vega, who told him that "all the blacks of the other estates were ready to rise up and about fifty thousand men were going to join" for this endeavor. When Manuel answered that "the blacks did not have weapons" and could not overcome the whites, Ramón assured him there were many rifles available in the general stores and other places. Ramón went on to add that "the whites were no match for a thousand lucumies [sic] with rifles," and if Manuel and his companions rose up they "would walk around here like him." Ramón concluded by informing him that "over there in his land . . . the lucumies had no other occupation than to wage war with rifles" and if they had such arms in Cuba they could do "more than all the whites."[36]

These boasts were in many ways borne out in the experiences of 1843. For example, the March organizing was largely attributed to members of the Lucumí nation, and other slaves later spoke of coming out to find "the Lucumís rioting" and "Lucumís in an uproar." The most unforgiving responses of that night were consistently attached to Lucumís like Cristóbal, who was said to have declared of those who refused to join, "Since those inside the cabins did not want to accompany them, we will burn their pigstys."[37] This discourse of Yoruba invincibility was evident across western Cuba long before 1843 but became particularly visible during that year and the following.

The implications here could not be missed: if the Lucumís led, the insurgent army would be feared. On the surface, such audacious claims to bravado and militancy also carried distinctly gendered undertones, implying that to fight like a Lucumí was to fight like a man. There were recorded incidents, for example, in which male Lucumís did not hesitate to compare themselves to other Africans whose wartime manhood seemed open to question. But as we have seen, some of the most vocal and visible rebel organizers of 1843 were Lucumí women. The descriptions of Fermina and Carlota's actions suggest that while the "indomitable Lucumí" persona was taken up differently for men and women, it could also easily be deployed along similar lines for both.

For reasons that are not entirely clear, the Lucumís seem to have clashed most consistently with the Congos of West-Central Africa, both in the organizing of 1844 and in the context of plantation life. This tension is captured in the exchange recorded between the free Lucumí Manuel Mieres and Juan Candela, a Congo slave. Juan's testimony reads as follows: "Manuel asked Juan Candela what nation he was from, and Juan having answered [crossed out word] that he was a Congo, Manuel responded that the Congos are not worth anything, only for playing the drums; that this Congo was going to see what the Lucumís would do out there, that they were going to live or die." Another Lucumí named Santiago also reportedly "asked Juan what nation he was from, and the declarant answered that he was a Congo, to which [Santiago] replied that the Congos were not worth anything . . . the Congos run away and the Lucumís are the only ones who are useful." The account went even further, with Santiago saying "it was a shame that [Juan] was not a Lucumí, that all of the others [non-Lucumís] were weaklings until they died, and that they were only good for drinking liquor." Juan Candela dismissed these taunts as part of the Lucumís' love for stirring up trouble, and their desire to portray themselves as warlike in the face of white people.[38]

As with so many of the other testimonies, it is entirely possible that Juan Candela had underlying motives for embellishing this encounter, but his story accords with several others that show how intricately intertwined the discursive terrain of manhood and African "nation" identity were. During the 1840s both become inextricable from the call to rebellion. In goading Juan Candela to take part in the rebellion, Manuel and Santiago attacked his identity as a Congo, then used *this* tool to chip away at his masculinity. The goal of Manuel and Santiago's taunting was to call Juan Candela to arms, and they deployed the ideal of a proud African masculinity as a powerful instrument of recruitment. Would Juan defend his honor and fight the whites like a man? Santiago had alleged that the Congos were only good for playing the drums, drinking liquor, and turning tail like cowards; what would Juan Candela do to prove him wrong?

The image of "a thousand lucumies with rifles" is inseparable from the events that consumed much of Yorubaland and its environs during the early nineteenth century. Particularly by the 1830s, the southbound jihadic movements and the decline of the powerful Oyo Empire created cycles of warfare that produced thousands of soldiers, political prisoners, refugees, mercenaries, and captives bound for domestic slavery and the slave ships on the coast. The slaves ushered into the Atlantic market therefore included untold numbers of people with extensive exposure to warfare, and sometimes years of military training. While for years the Lucumí slaves shipped to Cuba were mostly men, more and more women were sent across the ocean after 1807 and were also affected by these cycles. Indeed, the region's militarization and widespread conflicts had a significant impact on all those who descended into the slave hold, if only in the fact of their enslavement.[39]

The movement of 1844 would demand a familiar interethnic collaboration and solidarity and require people from throughout the African continent and within Cuba to work closely together. To this end, many others besides the Yorubas came to Cuba with extensive combat experience. As T. J. Desch-Obi has shown, for example, many soldiers in nineteenth-century Angola were well trained in inverted kicks, stick-fighting, and hand-to-hand combat, martial arts that "transformed the human body into a weapon." Some male captives from the Cross River Basin were members of the Ekpe leopard society and other male initiation communities such as those that gave rise to the Abuakúa.[40] These and other examples indicate that many of the African captives bound for Cuba had unusually high levels of personal discipline, physical coordination, and weaponry expertise that became particularly visible during times of rebellion. During moments of rebellion and rebel planning, African Cubans produced a military culture all their own that included drumming, singing, chanting, flag-carrying, and repurposing plantation paraphernalia such as raw hides, iron bars, and machetes.[41] It is also true that many of those sent to the coast had no martial background or combat training, but their experiences of fleeing towns and homes, serving in military camps, living as domestic slaves, and undergoing rape must have also factored into their behavior during rebellions in Cuba. The insurgencies of the 1840s must have triggered many memories.

The combat traditions that converged in Cuba formed in their composite an insurgent culture that was highly masculinized and militarized. Among the most significant representations of this masculine tenor was the repeated statement that among the rewards of the revolution would be the opportunity to "marry white women."[42] One cannot make this claim lightly, for it comes dangerously close to reinforcing the trope of the "savage black brute," that was central to the repression of slave insurgencies across the Americas. An inescapable part of this savagery, so the narrative went, was black male rebels' lust for white women, whom they planned to rape and subdue as soon as the white men were killed. This fantastic product of white anxiety became an important technology in the terrorizing and torturing of black people under the guise of protecting white women and families. That being said, the frequency with which these claims about white women emerge in the testimonies also cannot be ignored. And it is difficult to isolate this aspect of the trial testimonies as a fabrication of the colonial imagination, while giving legitimacy to other parts that speak more of political organizing and sovereignty.

There are a number of different explanations for this oft-reported interest in "marrying the white women" as an intended outcome of the rebellion. The preponderance of black men on the rural estates was frequently noted by foreign visitors, and though a precise study of these numbers has yet to be conducted, the anecdotal reports show that men consistently outnumbered women on the rural plantations, especially the sugar mills. The desire for white female partners may in part be attributable to this demographic imbalance.[43] This expectation for white female partners might also stem from specific military traditions in west and central Africa (and elsewhere) that encouraged military men to take the vanquished women as wives, consorts, and slaves.[44] Although it is difficult to draw definitive conclusions without more research on the subject, the recurrent statements about white-women-as-wives illustrate that for many enslaved men, their vision of racial mastery was closely related to their emotional and sexual desires. In other words, the desire for coupling with white women evinces a very particular vision of freedom, one deeply grounded in patriarchal conquest.

This sentiment certainly did not emerge in all of the male testimonies I reviewed (I have yet to come across this response for female witnesses), and of course the white men of the countryside were licensed to take these liberties with black women all the time. However, this stated connection between white wives and insurgent triumph emerges frequently enough to warrant closer examination. Its presence suggests the importance of considering that for men of African descent, part of the success of their movement was tied up in their conquest of not just white people but specifically white women. It suggests, moreover, that the project of freedom, and with it the attainment of tangible authority, was intricately linked to sexualized forms of power. This was one of many deeply gendered ways that the rebel culture of 1844 expressed itself.[45]

||||||| "Together All of Them Would Proceed":
The Plans for a Rural Insurgency

With varying ideas about what the revolution would look like, estate captains continued to solidify the plans for 1844, carefully spreading the word with trusted colleagues and other contacts. Many slaves were told that a protracted war was imminent and that audacious acts—from which there would be no return—would soon ignite the battle. The vast majority of those questioned stated that the first insurrectionary acts they knew of were to take place on their own soil. On some estates prominent white men, and sometimes women and children, were to be killed. On others, fire was to be set to the plantation grounds. On still others, the enslaved workers were to look for the arrival of a hastily forged liberating (or invading) army of black people from nearby estates. Whatever the inaugural act to signify an insurrection come to life, enslaved people spoke first of consequences on their own plantations, coffee estates, and cattle farms, even if the main rupture would simply be taking their permanent leave. In this respect, the insurgent movement that moved through the western regions was very much like the ones preceding it in Matanzas and elsewhere in the Americas: the sites of enslaved people's humiliation and abuse would be the first to be destroyed or abandoned.

Their intended targets were not abstract, elusive, or mysterious. These undertakings would be personal—in some cases, deeply personal—as the first to die would be their most visible persecutors. They were the men, and less often women, whom most of the slaves knew, saw, and interacted with regularly. For some, this familiarity might have been precisely the reason to shun such plots and reject their implications. For others, obliterating those who had the power—real and perceived—to coerce their labor, torture their bodies, reduce their humanity, and circumscribe their lives may have been precisely what was needed to transform ideas and rumors into a true insurgency. Plans for such lethal action would make the impending battles inescapably real, giving the ensuing struggles shape and form as little else could.

The immediacy, clarity, and personal nature of these planned initial targets is part of what distinguished the rural movement in 1844 from that which unfolded in the urban areas. In the countryside, it was the plantation that set the limits on slave life and enabled systemic torture, and therefore it was the plantation that had to be destroyed. While other dimensions of Cuba's white power structure would eventually be targeted, these targets were often portrayed as farther off in time and space. For most rural black people their anticolonial project consisted of dismantling the plantation and everything it represented. Few other iconic institutions in Cuba would have carried as potent symbolism for rural blacks as the sugar mill or the coffee estate. Particularly for those born in Cuba, the plantation was the original site of antiblack violence.

For rural blacks, the immediate and direct hand of the slaveholding colony was not a faraway captain general who failed to arrest slave ship captains, or a Havana magistrate who accepted bribes. It was a daily, living violence enacted on black people by overseers, managers, and slaveholders. The most meaningful and consequential insurgency would thus be one directed against those immediately responsible for their enslavement. The campaign to "do away with the whites and make the blacks masters of the land" would therefore begin on enslaved people's own territory, and many testified that the slaying of their immediate superiors was to be their first act of liberation.

It is interesting to note that witnesses who spoke of killing white people generally referred to estate owners, managers, overseers, and sometimes accountants. Other white staff members who held more specialized positions, such as the *maestros de azúcar* (boiling-house supervisors) and *maquinistas* (engineers), and even those who did more manual labor, like the *boyeros* (cattle supervisors), were rarely identified as specific targets. If plans were made for their assassination, they were generally swept up in broad references to "the whites of the plantation" who would be killed or pursued. This and other evidence suggests that most of the violence against the region's white people would be aimed at specific individuals, as retribution for specific wrongs. Although it is also true that subjects of interrogation spoke of "killing all the whites," many of the would-be insurgents seem to have been primarily interested in those who directly coerced them to work, handed out paltry food and clothing, restricted their movements, and whipped, humiliated, or otherwise abused them. In other words, those who were constant and tangible reminders that black lives existed for the profit and pleasure of others.

Testimonies of this kind were of course being elicited by a military commission bent on wiping out what its members saw as an expanding contagion of black rebellion. While these statements' recurrence must be read with caution, it is reasonable to conclude that they captured the extent to which the plantation had by 1844 become a deadly conflict zone in which many black people felt permanently under siege. Thus Frantz Fanon's prescient assessment that colonialism is "not a thinking machine, nor a body endowed with reasoning faculties" seems to accurately describe the daily plantation reality for most slaves. The only option, as many organizers saw it, was to "kill all the whites" and "take the land for themselves."

It is critical to note, however, that this vision of insurgent struggle appeared in the testimonies of rural black women only on rare occasions—

a fact that draws renewed attention to the masculinized investments that defined the 1844 movement. The previous chapters show that many rural slaves did not in fact share this destructive vision of liberation, and this was true for both men and women. For others, however, especially for those who became leaders, the violent terms of their resistance had already been determined by the violent terms of their enslavement. This belief was held by women like Eloisa Carabalí and Constancia Mandinga who suggested that part of becoming a leader was using the master's tools more effectively than the master.[46] These women and other insurgents articulated the political imagination of 1844 through a register of bloodshed and upheaval, and many of them would have agreed with Fanon's classic conclusion that colonialism—and in their case, the plantation—constituted "violence in its natural state" and would "only yield when confronted with greater violence."[47]

After eliminating the plantation hierarchy on their own estates, most rural slaves planned to join forces with slaves from a few other plantations or small farms in the area. Those who spoke of such goals said their intentions were either to wait for other rebels to arrive from nearby estates or to march from one plantation to the next. In keeping with previous insurrections in the Matanzas region, one of the army's most effective weapons would be its numbers, and one of its most important battle tactics a continual swelling of its ranks. Usually one plantation was identified as the place where all the insurgents from nearby plantations, potreros, and sitios would meet. For example, according to Dionisio Carabalí—first captain on the San Lorenzo mill—"the signal for the [initial] reunion was going to be the arrival of those of Ingenio Duarte, who would be playing the drums until they arrived at this estate, and together all of them would proceed to Sentmanat, gather people, doing the same as they had done at the Sacramento, until they finally arrived at Camarones, the place appointed [for everyone] to come together."[48]

For many slaves, though certainly not all, this span of four or five neighboring estates encompassed most of the world they knew. This vast acreage would have coincided with an expansive mental geography: the cane fields and coffee patches that many slaves worked for months, the people they saw daily or weekly, the errands that took them to other plantations, and the country roads that took them through this landscape. An attack on their own ingenios and cafetales therefore meant an attack on the landscapes that for some became familiar and recognizable, that for others constituted the only home they knew, and that for all represented a daily map of their comings and goings. All of these reasons should highlight why some slaves had little desire to rebel. For those who joined the insurrectionary movement, success would entail destroying much of the world as they knew it.

While there was a high degree of correspondence among the plans articulated in these local areas, comparatively few slaves explained how a larger battle would play out in the long term. While a handful of country estates would have spanned more than a thousand acres, toppling three, four, or even six ingenios would not have allowed insurgents to spread a revolution throughout the region or around the island. They must have learned that from the rebellions of 1843. It is possible that some witnesses did not want to reveal any more information than necessary about the extent of their plans. But it is much more likely that most simply did not know how the uprising was supposed to play out beyond their individual districts.

On the surface, then, these scattered plans emerging across the western landscape could easily be taken for a random hodgepodge of designs and dismissed as an immature or uncoordinated movement. But closer inspection suggests that this randomness was tethered to something infinitely more important. Bits of information about an anticolonial movement backed by the British had been trickling into the western countryside for over a year, and these rumors catalyzed small groups of people to develop plans with others in easy reach. From about the spring of 1843 to the winter of 1844, these scattered bits of information began to congeal into pockets of rebel clusters. Many, many rebel clusters. If we were to have an aerial view of these clusters, we would see hundreds of little dots positioned in very close proximity. Their closeness and number suggest that from 1843 (at least) to 1844, the western-central regions of Cuba were churning with the energies of black resistance.

The apparent lack of coordination among these dozens of pockets is in some ways less interesting than the simple fact of their existence—so many of them, and with such conspicuously shared goals and ambitions. Marcos Gangá had not spoken with Alejo Criollo, and Domingo Carabalí had had no contact with Limbano Congo, yet they all referenced the same process and the same strategies. The recurrence of this phenomenon is one of the most extraordinary examples of a collective political vision in the history of New World slave rebellions. The slaves in these regions shared the knowledge of their disempowerment, of the racial hierarchies that bound them, of the violence that stifled their lives, and of the opportunity to change these realities. There can be no doubt that groups of military authorities posed the same or similar questions to the slaves they encountered on different estates, and there is every reason to believe that they threatened similar

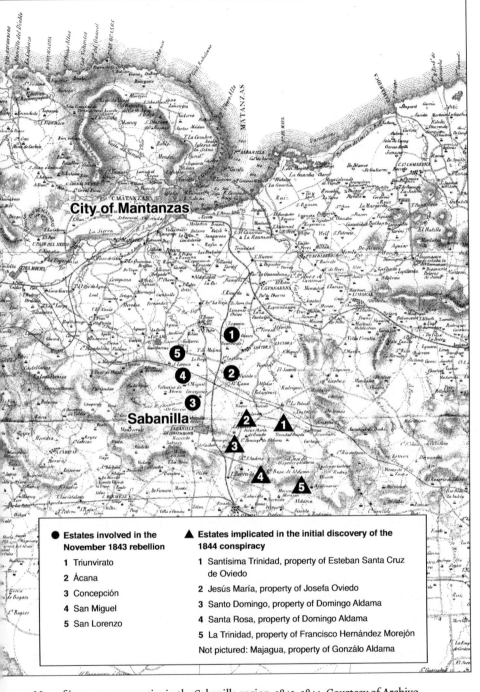

City of Mantanzas

Sabanilla

● Estates involved in the November 1843 rebellion

1 Triunvirato
2 Ácana
3 Concepción
4 San Miguel
5 San Lorenzo

▲ Estates implicated in the initial discovery of the 1844 conspiracy

1 Santísima Trinidad, property of Esteban Santa Cruz de Oviedo

2 Jesús María, property of Josefa Oviedo

3 Santo Domingo, property of Domingo Aldama

4 Santa Rosa, property of Domingo Aldama

5 La Trinidad, property of Francisco Hernández Morejón

Not pictured: Majagua, property of Gonzálo Aldama

Map of insurgent properties in the Sabanilla region, 1843–1844. Courtesy of Archivo Nacional de Cuba.

kinds of punishment wherever they went. But the overlap and connection between the reports in districts as far away as Aguacate and Ceja de Pablo cannot be explained simply by the fact of the trials or the circumstances in which they unfolded.

The rural movement was held together by the cement of a strangely confident knowledge: everyone was going to move at the same time; when the estates in one district rose up, groups of plantations all over western Cuba would be doing the same thing. By the winter of 1844, scores of rebel clusters seemed to be poised for the rebellion to erupt, bolstered by the diffuse but solid consciousness that other groups around them were going to rebel at the same time. If in fact slaves were planning to rise up in nearly every district of Matanzas, they were acting in either the hope or the conviction that they were telling (or had been told) the truth—that indeed "all of the blacks" were rising up with them, and that their cause was receiving powerful help from outside. Partly from their shared experience of enslavement and partly as result of this pervasive rebel momentum, these insurgent visions coalesced across rural Matanzas.

In this decentralized structure, rebel units encompassing as few as three and as many as eight properties formed throughout the region. Given the massive obstacles to covertly organizing hundreds of people whose mobility and access to information were limited by design, the organizing that *did* take place seems all the more remarkable. The appearance of these separate "rebellion clusters," whose plans did not immediately link up but whose aims, intentions, and date of eruption overlapped profoundly, underscores the need to view them as part of a collective movement, even as we acknowledge their distinctiveness. Even in the absence of a centralized authority to seamlessly unify all of these efforts, these mobilizations reveal a striking commonality and coherence across the region.

This shared planning and synergy offer unique insight into the oppositional culture of rural black laborers. The uncoordinated connectedness of these rural clusters calls attention to a collective political consciousness that existed among rural slaves, honed over many years and animated by the exigencies of the 1840s. While the concept of "consciousness" can be slippery and hard to pin down, it is much less difficult to identify the secret gatherings, leadership organs, and pathways of information that dotted the plantation countryside. If a shared critique of plantation violence and injury lived primarily at the level of the mind and the emotion, this critique materialized quite plainly in the rebel cohorts that emerged from one district to the next.

The conditions for such a proliferation were created through the social networks, political strategies, and communication patterns that defined rural black life during the 1830s and 1840s. By 1843 a growing discourse of revolution wove together this tangled web of relationships, movement, and knowledge, solidifying these intangible elements into ever more concrete structures. That no central rural command center ever emerged in 1844 says much about the extent of this political sensibility and the depth of this awareness. Acknowledging this does not flatten a host of opinions, desires, and needs into a monolithic slave community. It does, however, allow us to trace out a series of overlapping goals, strategies, and responses that produced a tactical awareness of the 1844 movement and constituted the movement itself.

The following discussion will turn to one of the most important questions that leaders across the district sought to answer in 1844: how to arm themselves. The exploration of enslaved people's everyday arsenals will further illuminate how rebels envisioned the scope of the 1844 movement. While urban rebels and regional nationalists rarely considered themselves prepared to go to war unless they had firearms, slaves in rural Cuba tended to imagine their tools of war more expansively, out of necessity. Exploring this everyday weaponry will enable an understanding of how an army of enslaved people could effectively envision and coordinate a dynamic and widespread movement.

To Raise the Revolution with Machetes

As rebel captains across the province made plans to join the coming rebellion, one of the most pressing questions they faced was what form their weaponry would take. With almost no access to firearms, how could they coordinate—or even begin to think about—a widespread insurgency? Historians have long posed that same question, and one of the longest-standing arguments against the existence of an 1844 movement is that such a stockpile of weapons was never found.[49] As insurgent leaders and participants were brought to trial, however, most of them referred to at least one weapon they planned on using, and that was their work machetes. Some witnesses responded as did one woman, who did "not know of any other weapons besides the work machetes."[50] It might at first seem odd and short-sighted for so many future rebels to invest their collective hopes in the blades of their machetes, knowing they would certainly face the firearms of the colonial regime.[51] And in fact, most enslaved rebel leaders were searching for weaponry to match that of their colonial adversaries. Yet it will also become clear that while weapons like machetes carried a deceptive veneer of simplicity, they also carried distinct strategic advantages. Perhaps more important, examining the everyday arsenals of enslaved people will push us to think more expansively about the insurgent culture that grew out of rural African Cuban communities, and about slaves' ability to negotiate — and subvert — the broader structures that enslaved them.

It would be a mistake to dismiss the slaves' apparent readiness to go to battle with machetes as a lack of sophistication. First and foremost, machetes and axes represented the one weapon to which most slaves had consistent access, particularly on those estates where canes needed chopping, grasses and bramble needed clearing, and trees and undergrowth needed felling. Implements of this kind were vital to the plantation work arsenal in the early 1840s, as the frontier of Matanzas was pushing south and east, and new mills were constantly under construction. Machetes were among the items that slave witnesses frequently admitted to purchasing for their daily work. Though such a practice was probably not encouraged, it was certainly not unheard of.

In Ceja de Pablo, Juan Criollo stated that he had bought a machete "from a woodsman named Mateo, because [he] the declarant was also working in the fields.[52] In Macuriges, José Criollo spoke of "a knife and some cutting blades that he bought in Bemba." In Sabanilla, Felipe Carabalí recounted that one of the local wagon drivers showed him "two knives that he had bought on a stroke of luck." With the exception of Francisco Gangá, all of those mentioned above were regular field laborers. Here, then, was a weapon that slaves without unusual privileges could buy with seemingly little interference.[53]

Juan Criollo was questioned pointedly about two machete blades found abandoned in the cane fields. While Juan admitted that one belonged to him, he assured the judges that "it did not have any bad purpose." The presiding officers were not convinced, however, possibly because Juan left the knives in the safekeeping of a woman named Mercedes, and because the two instruments were later found hidden in the fields. Although work tools were supposed to be locked up when not in use, at another time there might have been nothing out of the ordinary about finding two abandoned machetes in the cane fields. In April 1844, however, the district officer who discovered the tools handed them over to the senior prosecutor and the mayoral of the estate, declaring that they were "not the kind that are used for work."[54]

When two rebel captains from the Ingenio Dichoso encountered the organizer Casimiro Lucumí, the latter was described as riding "a gold mare, carrying a sack tied down behind him, and in it five midsized machetes bound together."[55] According to these two witnesses, Casimiro made it clear not only that the machetes were intended for an imminent uprising but also that he planned to procure more of them. When Casimiro was later questioned about filing down machetes on his own estate, he responded "that he sharpened . . . twelve machetes so that they would cut cane better, without anyone having ordered him to do so."[56]

Casimiro's sharpening of machetes "without anyone having ordered him to do so" had to have been a routine part of life on a sugar estate. This mundane activity was rendered dubious, however, in a moment of black political unrest. Here the alternate uses of the machete present a striking duality: productive servility on one side and violent resistance on the other. Unlike firearms, the huge blades could be used both as tools to transform sugarcane into profit and backwoods into ordered fields, and as dangerous weapons put to the service of revolution. Capitalism and slavery seem to pursue one another relentlessly on this Janus-faced blade.[57]

It is difficult to believe that slaves like Casimiro, and even the seemingly innocuous Juan, were unaware of this duality. If true, they must have also been aware that a careful narrative of diligence and hard work could hone a machete's dangerous point into a planter's productive fantasy. If the irony of such plans was lost on some of the judges, it could not have been lost on the slaves themselves. The same tools of their labor would now be used to destroy or reappropriate much of what they had built. These elements surely contributed to the machete's power.

John Thornton has pointed out in his study of the Stono rebellion in South Carolina that many of those captured in the slave trade had some military experience, and, as we have seen, taking part in warfare was common for men in kingdoms like Oyo that were rapidly disintegrating and producing many of those who became Lucumís in Cuba. Although by the mid-nineteenth century firearms would have been commonplace on the battlefields of West and Central Africa, most combatants were quite accustomed to hand-to-hand combat using swords, spears, lances, and so forth. Africans in Matanzas with previous combat experience might therefore have been particularly prepared to use the long machete blades for the coming rebellion, especially until other weapons could be procured.[58]

Unlike guns or cannons, machetes could launch a battle quietly, and shed much blood before a single alarm was raised. As seen in the 1843 rebellions, machetes could be formidable weapons when coupled with stealth, surprise, and confusion. Yet another strategic value of the machete was that military officials usually only conducted searches for weapons when they felt there was something special to search for. Unless alerted to things that seemed out of the ordinary—like machetes lying half-hidden in the cane fields and deemed "not the kind used for work"—judicial authorities would have little reason to question the regular implements of slaves' work, much less order searches for them. I have found no indication of machetes being confiscated or their use restricted in the course of the trials, if for no other reason than they were usually needed the next day. It is clear, however, that colonial authorities were very interested in the artillery considered to be the tools of modern warfare—rifles, guns, bullets, and gunpowder. After hearing testimonies that alerted them to the existence of such weapons, officers conducted lengthy and invasive searches, particularly in the homes of free people of color. As weapons, machetes would have been largely invisible precisely because of their ubiquity and necessity. Their strategic value is clear.

And yet, even these compelling arguments cannot completely explain why scores of slaves were willing to enter into armed struggle with only cane-cutting machetes, knowing they would be facing rifles and bullets. To understand their willingness to do so, one must look to other explanations, the strongest of which was the belief that a sacred source of power—in essence a divine arsenal—would protect the new soldiers. To this end, many slave men spoke about leaders who would provide them with ritual amulets to safeguard the new recruits in battle, and shield them from the white people's bullets. I will discuss this at length in chapter 7. Not only does the story of this protection tell us more about what African people brought of themselves and their identities to the making of this movement, but it also sheds light on the culture of insurgency that developed in the rural areas and explains some of the readiness and preparation that may otherwise seem inexplicable.

Fire was another critical weapon that would have eluded those searching for an obvious stockpile. Both 1843 rebellions included the burning of cane fields and sugar buildings. In testimonies that invoked plans to "burn the ingenios, the *bagaceras*, the cane fields, and the *casa de vivienda*," black insurgents revealed unambiguous aims to halt the flow of planting and production, and destroy the machinery of industrial sugar.

As a natural phenomenon, fires constituted no small menace on the rural plantations of Matanzas. Indeed, they counted among the planters' greatest natural enemies. One traveler observed that "during the dry season the sugar planter is in constant dread of his fields catching fire, and his whole crop, and perhaps his buildings, being thus destroyed in a few hours."[59] Everyone was aware of a fire's potential for damage, partly because nearly everyone was called to help put it out once one erupted. Large bells frequently became "an alarm to the neighboring plantations, rung long and loud, in case of fire in the cane fields, or other occasions for calling in aid."[60] Thus, the impact of burning the wealth of Matanzas to the ground could not have been lost on anyone, black or white.

For this reason, the strategic importance of fire for insurgents with few other weapons cannot be overstated. Here was an immensely powerful weapon and, most important, one that could be placed at the disposal of almost any slave, insurgent or no. Like machetes, fires could unleash a battle quietly, consume and destroy almost as pervasively as guns, and spread quickly to other areas. Once set it was often difficult to identify those who ignited them. Even a modest-sized blaze could send an instantaneous signal to potential rebels for miles around. They could also potentially galvanize those previously doubtful or reluctant by signaling that an insurgency had indeed begun, and that on some level the perpetrators would have to be reckoned with. If we accept that machetes and fire were part of a deeper culture of insurgency particular to dispossessed rural rebels, and would therefore make sense as the primary weapons for many combatants, then the weapons cache that others have sought since 1844 might have been there all along, but been so unglamorous as to be invisible.

While machetes and fire formed critical parts of the slave rebel's arsenal, it was clear to most that a battle on the scale they intended could not be fought for long with these implements alone—to remain victorious for months and even years, a range of other weaponry would be needed. Firearms were particularly coveted, but in contrast to machetes they seem to have been fundamentally connected to the office of leadership. In some ways, the solution to how to obtain firearms stood out all around them, as guns of all sorts were kept—sometimes in abundance—in the rooms of overseers and administrators, in local taverns, and in general stores.[61] An army of insurgents would need weapons of many kinds; where better to obtain them than from white creoles and Spaniards? Slaves who had more mobility in their errands to stores, taverns, docks, and warehouses, and those who worked in white people's homes, would have been able to indicate who had guns and where they were kept.

The story of a group of rebels on the Soledad de Jáuregui estate in Havana province illustrates the elaborate circuits that rebels found and created in their search for arms. In late April 1844 a slave named José Antonio Lucumí testified that he went to Soledad every week to take clean clothes to the owner's son. On one of these visits, he came in contact with the contramayoral there, a man from the Arará nation named Leandro. Leandro told him "that he had a keg of Gunpowder . . . which he kept in his cabin in a little room on the left-hand side; saying that said barrel was full, and that he bought it in the nearby town of Jarúco." José Antonio received word that two other Arará slaves had gunpowder stashed away, including another foreman named Mamerto. Leandro and Mamerto would later be reported as the main rebel organizers at Soledad.

The cart driver Chino José proved to be quite an asset; while in Jarúco, he purchased copious amounts of gunpowder and brought it back to Soledad. Chino José and others also obtained gunpowder from the free black men who lived near their home and in town. In this way, a virtual armory was amassed on the grounds of Soledad. Guns and rifles of various kinds, gunpowder, and swords were stowed in the cabins of selected leaders. Chino José himself possessed a special knife with a white handle that was being held by a young woman named Alejandra.[62]

The role of Alejandra—a seemingly harmless observation dropped in among the rest of the testimony—is most intriguing here and allows us to see that the question of weapons reflected a heavily gendered aspect of insurgent ideology. Men were the ones who discussed weapons, men were the ones who obtained them, and men were the ones who planned for their use. In fact, the terrain of weapons becomes even more heavily masculinized the farther one goes from machetes and the closer one gets to firearms. Still, there is a fascinating theme that emerges every so often—where women are designated to store and hide weapons for the coming rebellion. In many ways, this pattern is in keeping with a larger insurgent motif in 1844 of women as keepers of secrets, givers and withholders of information, and, by extension, potential betrayers of the rebellion.

We see that Chino José left his sword in the possession of Alejandra. Juan Criollo, whose knife was found in the cane fields, left his machete in the safekeeping of a woman named Mercedes. The home of the free black woman named Estefanía became a meeting place to exchange weapons. The home of another free black woman named Dolores also became a place to store arms and munitions. Perhaps because they were deemed less likely to come under scrutiny from colonial authorities, these women represented a kind of safe haven for some of the most tangible and incriminating evidence of a rebellion in the making.

If a revolutionary war required firearms in addition to other weapons, it also needed a stable source of funding to buy them. Another intriguing point that the Soledad story makes clear is that slaves were assumed to have access to money, and were expected to supply cash, quickly if necessary. Throughout 1843 and 1844 black people from across the social spectrum were told to gather together whatever funds they could obtain to close the yawning gap in their armed resources. The prevalence of these requests by rural leaders is striking, revealing that most assumed that many slaves would be able to meet them. While nineteenth-century accounts agree that enslaved people could find avenues to acquire money, it is much rarer to find accounts of those slaves taking part in a widespread cash economy. Images of rural Cuban slaves as laborers oppressed by capitalist markets are abundant; depictions of those slaves as earners, consumers, and participants in such markets are exceptional. The idea of slaves in the countryside helping fund a movement to overthrow the colonial plantation regime seems the very antithesis of slavery.

Yet the frequency with which black people, slave and free, spoke about getting together a few doubloons for this or that reveals the regularity with which many had access to some amount of cash, and an apparent intention to contribute this money to the rebel cause. Such a vibrant subterranean economy points to a trail of illicit and semi-illicit materials transacted and circulated throughout the region. If, as Douglas Egerton writes for post-revolutionary Virginia, "the sound of hard money clinking in the pockets of slaves for hire was also the sound of paternal authority being torn asunder," in Cuba, it was the sound of a revolution that black leaders hoped was on the way.[63]

The final point that the Soledad story allows us to see is that the free black communities of Matanzas constituted one of the most important sources of weapons, particularly those not readily available as part of the typical plantation apparatus. In some instances, free people held out the possibility of firearms to entice slaves to join the rebellion. Particularly for reluctant recruits, the promise of arms could turn the tide of their interest, and witnesses spoke frequently about rifles, bullets, or gunpowder that were supposed to be provided by this libre or that libre. And yet, while free people had the independence to buy arms, and the privacy to store them (at least in theory), the slaves often helped to finance their purchase. The above stories suggest that arsenals of weapons, if small, may have very well been moving around Matanzas and other places in western-central Cuba.[64]

The questions of how African insurgents planned to arm themselves, understood themselves ethnically in relation to the project of rebellion, and created dynamic leadership structures shed important light on how enslaved people were imagining and coordinating a larger resistance movement in 1843–44. Such explorations allow deeper insight into the anatomy of the movement itself, and into the broader visions that guided the rural insurgent agenda. By taking seriously the elaborate leadership columns activated on plantations in the countryside, the "humble" everyday weapons that slaves had at their disposal, and the complex networks that enabled a wide swath of insurgents to coordinate their aims and attain weaponry, one can expand the conventional contours of this monumental insurgency.

This chapter has worked to create an alternative knowledge of the 1844 leadership while attempting to push against the trope of "leadership" itself. Partly by exploring the women and nonelite slave men who made critical contributions on their home estates, we can expand the framework of insurgent organizing. In particular, we can loosen the tradition of the iconic leader standing figuratively at the center of most rebel histories by examining those slaves who were critical to local rebel planning, those who helped shape this planning in unacknowledged ways, and those who fell on the periphery of these designs altogether. All of these individuals were critical to the rebel tapestry in rural Matanzas.

Chapter Seven

African Cuban Sacred Traditions and the Making of an Insurgency

One of the most important ways that enslaved men and women entered the 1844 movement was through the realm of the sacred and the spiritual. Facilitating everything from distant sympathy to active endorsement of the project at hand, ritual objects and sacred practices created a powerful and recognizable idiom that intrigued and compelled black people across the western landscape. This cultural infrastructure provided rural black residents with a shared language in which to converse about struggle and deliverance, and a medium in which to conceptualize these possibilities.[1] Sacred rituals, amulets, and protective pouches were among the most visible components of a vast spiritual repertoire that molded the political ethos of rural black Cubans and became critical to a thriving alternative political economy. As such, they stimulated the potential to engage a different vision of collective politics and offered sanction and structure for the growing movement. The terrain of sacred work can therefore offer some new ways to consider how slaves and other dispossessed people articulated their politics, their ideas about emancipation, and their visions of freedom. Against this backdrop, we can begin to investigate João Reis's prudent assertion that "rebellion begins when a religion sides with the oppressed."[2]

As they made their way across the countryside, colonial militias trying to determine the source and inspiration of the movement routinely questioned suspected insurgents about the presence of "witchcraft" and "sorcery." It is not entirely clear why authorities were so interested in the practices they called *brujería,* but I believe these questions suggest a deeper desire to link the ever-present nightmare of slave resistance to "savage" African customs. The recurrent questions about "brujos" and "brujería" illuminate the colonial state's uneasiness about the future of whiteness, as it watched the number of African Cubans grow larger every year. This preoccupation with witchcraft gestures toward a deeper fear that Cuba, the island they "intended to be the brightest star of the American canopy," could easily become "a black-military-republic" if the authorities were not vigilant.[3]

IIIIIII The Traffic in the Sacred

The ritual expertise of the black plantation world was nurtured and maintained through the consciousness and the memories of thousands of Africans who came to Cuba over the course of the nineteenth century. Having survived the Middle Passage, knowledgeable men and women would reconstitute the institutions of priesthood, divination, and ritual healing on the rural plantations as best they could. This black sacred culture had to be maintained by whatever slaves could find in their daily lives — in the cabins, fields, woods, taverns, general stores, and by what lived in their own minds. George Brandon has observed of this consistent innovation that "a shrine existed wherever a collection of appropriate objects could be brought together."[4] In other words, this was a culture that had to be stoked by memory, reinvention, collaboration, and refashioning.

Across the entire social spectrum rural black people — and occasionally white people — knew where to find these ritual priests and experts. And they were often prepared to pay for their work. Particularly in Cuba's plantation countryside, spiritual relics and the people who could make them were in high demand, and some of the more talented spiritualists created a kind of second occupation for themselves. By the nineteenth century religious services and sacred objects counted among the most heavily traded items among African-descended people in Matanzas. Enslaved and free people across the rural landscape bought, sold, and solicited these protections to change the world they could most immediately affect. This traffic traversed the length of western Cuba's black community, encompassing enslaved and free, women and men, Africans and Creoles, city-dwellers and rural residents. The depth of interest in these spiritualists is clear in the many stories about black folks who "came over" to find this or that spiritualist, or about those who came to rely on these ritual skills in order to survive.

When slaves answered questions about "witchcraft practices," they invariably spoke about roots, dirt, bones, herbs, and other items that were religiously incomprehensible to the colonial mind. Not long after the March 1843 insurgency, for example, one of the military officers reported having received "a piece of material filled with dirt . . . [with one witness] declaring them to be witchcraft items."[5] The following year, the authorities arrested a slave named José Lucumí for suspicious items they discovered inside a trunk. These officials were also able to identify "four and a half royal pesos and some pieces of clothing, with a roll of tobacco and some other trifles inside of it, which among them they call witchcraft."[6] Throughout the course of that year, authorities continued to report items such as piles of dirt or pieces of wrapped-up cloth that seemed largely irrelevant to the proceedings at hand. Yet these same officers were also learning to hone a colonial practice of seeing that attuned them to the possibility of something going on beneath the surface. Much of what was found and recorded in 1844 bore a striking resemblance to the material culture of the Congo-Cuban theologies collectively known as Palo.

Scholars of Palo have traced the emergence of these traditions in Cuba to the cabildo culture of the nineteenth century. These cabildos—mainly urban African mutual aid and religious societies—provided Congo-Angolan men and women the safety and autonomy to codify and distill a large corpus of beliefs and practices from West-Central Africa. As the century progressed, these practitioners solidified these practices into a formal, cohesive repertoire of Congo-Cuban thought. This body of knowledge became known as Regla de Congo or, more commonly, Palo. Palo has four different branches—Palo Monte, Palo Mayombe, Palo Briyumba, and Palo Kimbisa— with the first two being the most widely practiced. The genealogy of the cabildos is vital to the story of Palo, but it does not take into account the thousands of rural slaves who helped to shape and forge this religious tradition on the plantations. Although a detailed history of this evolution has yet to be written, scholars who suggest that it emerged from a long process of fusion and recombination are undoubtedly the most accurate.[7]

It is difficult to pinpoint what military authorities envisioned when they inquired about witchcraft during the 1844 trials. "Witchcraft" is an incredibly expansive term that could index a whole range of methodologies and ideas. The kinds of rituals that enslaved people talked about—working herbs, requesting amulets, wearing pouches—were certainly prevalent throughout the African continent. Many of the experiences they detailed, however, can only be described as quintessentially Palo or Palo-inspired.

While most slaves sought the answers most likely to keep them safe, questions about brujos and brujería themselves require that we pay closer attention to the discursive and conceptual terrain of "witchcraft." Such a question (particular from a white military officer) would seem to demand something with magical properties and inexplicable results; something powerful, aggressive, and even frightening. The answers that came most frequently point to a well-established culture of Congo-Cuban ritual and early Palo during the 1840s. On both sides of the Atlantic, Congo-based practices derive their energy from the community of the dead, whose primary purpose is to offer healing, guidance, and protection. It is vital to underscore this redemptive capacity in Congo/Palo work while also recognizing that Palo is best known for an aggressive and more adamant energy. Palo has long had a reputation for being highly effective, immediate, and uncompromising. Historically, people have sought out Palo rituals when no other solution has presented itself. The urgency and resoluteness of early Palo would have been well calibrated to confront the world of the plantation. The kind of power and resources it offered rural people to flout the strictures of race, manipulate one's enemies, and reverse the irreversible would have certainly been legible to the state as dark magic or witchcraft at work.

|||||||| The Congo-Cuban Arsenal

As we have seen in previous chapters, Pedro Domech was a wealthy slaveholder who owned the thriving coffee plantation, Buena Esperanza. In March 1844 Domech learned that a number of slaves on his estate were involved in "witchcraft," were plotting against him, and were planning to join a larger insurgency. Some of this information came to Domech from one of the younger creole slaves named José. José—likely under duress— told Domech about two others on the estate, Manuel and Tomás, who had been pursuing witchcraft. According to Domech, a free black driver named Agustín had "asked José 'to tell my slaves Manuel and Tomás . . . that he had made for them [what they requested].'" The authorities investigated José's story and found it to be true. The item in question was a "witchcraft pot," for which Agustín demanded "half a doubloon to hand over [now] and another half when they experienced favorable results that he promised."[8]

Agustín's "witchcraft pot" is one of the strongest and most recurrent examples of Congo-based ritual work in the course of the 1844 movement. Here the "pot" is a reference to the centerpiece of Congolese spiritual practice, the *nganga* (or the *prenda*, as it is often called in Cuba). Although the term *nganga* can refer to many things, it primarily represents the focal point of Palo practice—an iron cauldron or clay vessel filled with medicines and herbs. *Nganga* can also refer to the central life force in the universe, the essence of a dead ancestor, or the priest himself. In consecrating this cauldron, any number of items might be placed inside, but the most common were earth from a cemetery or crossroads, pieces of wood, herbs, insects, animal bones, and (more rarely) human skulls or bones. The nganga itself is conceived as a microcosm of the universe, and its varied contents likewise mirror the spectrum of what might be found out in the universe.[9] Only a priest or priestess initiated at the highest level could take on the task of assembling a nganga, something always spoken of with reverence and understood as powerful beyond belief. The filled cauldron (now the nganga) would now be the formal home of the spirit/energy in question.

Scholars have differed on how to interpret the many interpretive layers of the nganga, including the physical cauldron, its material contents, the *minkisi* (literally, ritual objects of which the nganga is one), the priest or priestess, the *muerto* (deceased ancestor), and the *mpungu* (deity of the traditional Konglese pantheon). What is most important to understand about Cuban/Palo practice is the difficulty, and perhaps even futility, of separating out these core components into self-contained entities. The fundamental life force of kalunga (literally, the sea, but also the realm of the dead, the line dividing this realm from the world of the living) embodied in the nganga necessarily had to inhabit multiple entities at once, making the nganga itself a living and composite entity.[10]

During the early months of 1843, as widespread sedition took hold of black communities across western Cuba, more and more rebel plans were taking shape in the context of Congolese sacred work. About two weeks after the March 1843 insurgency erupted, authorities questioned a suspected conspirator of the Carabalí nation named Antonio González. Antonio testified that two of his acquaintances, Jacinto Roque and Cristóbal Linares (also written "Linarez," as in the example below), had been working closely with a group of slaves on the Luisa sugar mill. Even before the rebellion broke out, the group had allegedly been planning to eliminate the estate overseer. González recounted that one night, "Cristóbal Linarez went to the Ingenio La Luisa and 'planted the mayoral' under a ceiba tree, and persuaded the slaves 'that with this operation they had nothing to fear from him.'" When asked what he meant by "planted" (*sembró*), González responded, "To plant is a witchcraft operation that they do, and persuade the others that the planted (or buried) person . . . cannot defend himself, and that they will be able to kill him with ease."[11]

Almost exactly a year later, an enslaved man of the Mandinga nation named Antonio stole a handful of gunpowder from his master's armoire, "barely enough to load a pistol." During the course of routine evening chores, he drifted to the edge of the estate to cut grass for the livestock and passed the gunpowder to a Gangá man on a neighboring property. Manuel Gangá returned to his cabin with the gunpowder, and, together with some bits of leaves and straw, he crafted two *muñecos* (dolls or figurines) and buried them in the earth near his cabin. To all appearances, Manuel was "planting" the muñecos in much the same way that Cristóbal Linares had done. The Gangá man intended to unearth the figurines in a year's time, but these plans were thwarted when he was charged with theft and witchcraft in 1844.[12]

These themes of burying or planting emerged on the Industria coffee estate in 1844, according to the testimony of a Mateo Congo. Mateo stated that "he received four pesos from the hand of the chino Antonio, for a witchcraft item that he made with some small saints and mashed-up pumpkin seeds and wrapped up in a piece of paper." Armed with this weaponry, Mateo went to the cabin of another slave named Bonifacio and "buried it in the earth of Bonifacio's cabin, so that [the fetish] might take out the overseer, and replace him with Antonio Perdomo."[13]

Robert Farris Thompson has shown that nineteenth-century Cuban Congos "made *minkisi*-figures to mystically attack slaveholders and other enemies, and for spiritual reconnaissance."[14] The dolls in each of these accounts fit that description well. In the early twentieth century, former slaves still remembered these famous *muñecos de Palo*, also known as Nkuyo, Nkonsi, and Kini-kini, and all were quite feared as spiritual weaponry. During the 1940s and 1950s, Lydia Cabrera conducted interviews with scores of older black Cubans like those who recalled the Palo dolls, nearly all of whom had either been slaves themselves, or were the children of former slaves. One of the monographs that resulted from this extensive fieldwork, *Reglas de Congo*, remains one of the most important volumes about Palo Mayombe and other Congolese spiritual traditions in Cuba. At the time of her research, former slaves and their descendants told Lydia Cabrera it was quite possible to ritually "tie someone up" and in this way to "subdue him, command him." Indeed, ritual tying has been a critical feature of Congo-Cuban practice for two centuries, designed with the aim of binding someone both metaphorically and literally.[15] The burial of items for ritual purposes, including talismans intended for a certain objective, or as part of the initiating *prenda* itself, has also long been a traditional cornerstone of Palo and Congo practice.[16]

In addition to the muñecos and the act of burying, another telling indicator of the ubiquity of Palo at work was the recurrent mention of gunpowder in enslaved people's testimonies. One witness, for example, described a ritual in which the leading spiritualist burned gunpowder to "heighten the witchcraft" and make it take effect faster.[17] These words resonate with contemporary opinions that Palo is known—and distinguished from other practices—for its speed and efficacy.[18] As one of Cabrera's informants explained, "The sorcerer cannot work without gunpowder. All the Reglas de congos use it to summon, to ask, to command, to make their work come out right [dar salida a los trabajos]."[19] For two centuries, then, gunpowder has been a central element of Congo-Cuban sacred practice. The imagery of igniting and detonating contained in the materiality of gunpowder jibes well with the explosiveness so frequently attributed to Congo-inspired work, and also with the sparking of an insurgent movement. The damage that gunpowder can do once loaded into a gun of course, is also obvious.

Historically, gunpowder has also been valued by Paleros because it contains large amounts of sulfur, another ingredient critical to the work of Palo and other Congo-inspired religions. Cabrera describes sulfur as the "sorcerer's incense," and those she spoke with reported that it was indispensable in operations used to do mischief, such as separating lovers or causing accidents or deaths to happen, but was also necessary to bring about justice.[20] That sulfur is also known as "brimstone" in the book of Genesis only further exposes its remarkable association with divine retribution. For example, in its famous discourse on the ends of the earth, the Book of Revelations promises, "The devil who deceived them was thrown into the lake of fire and sulfur, where the beast and the false prophet are also." The Book of Psalms similarly portends of God's wrath: "On the wicked he will rain blazing coals; fire, sulfur, and scorching wind shall be the portion of their cup." Here gunpowder sits in multiple locations at once: it is the container of an element of justice (an "element" in both physics and metaphysics); it is the combustible provocateur that births ritual action; and it is the substance that renders literal guns effective in the coming insurgency. It appeared then for some that the same Sodom and Gomorrah that Yahweh had once destroyed with fire and brimstone had come to Cuba.

Stories analogous to Manuel Gangá's theft of gunpowder (in order to bury two handcrafted muñecos) replicated themselves again and again across the rural plantation landscape in the early 1840s. Sometimes the gunpowder not only reached the hands of local ritual experts but also appeared in Congo-inspired ceremonies and liturgies. One such ceremony took place on the Rosario sugar mill in the district of Tapaste. There a creole man named Alejandro testified to secret meetings that had been taking place in the driver's cabin: "In the meetings that took place in the cabin of

Pablo the driver, [the following measures] always preceded conversations to arrange the insurrection: taking out a board with many statues of different forms that even contained children's skulls with other human bones, this plank was enclosed by a circle of gunpowder, which they set afire as if to pay respect to the aforementioned relics; that afterward they launched into their noisy serenade, and after that came the conversation about the uprising."[21]

The presence of a human bones and most especially a human skull is one of the most classic signs of Congo-Cuban and early Palo at work. Moreover, the plank that was "enclosed by a circle of gunpowder" and subsequently set on fire is another calling card of the Palero. Among the former slaves she interviewed, Cabrera described a ritual expert who used gunpowder in his practice: "He makes a drawing on the floor in front the Nganga, and on top of this [drawing] he places little piles of gunpowder: seven or fourteen, twelve or twenty-one, whatever he is accustomed to. The purpose of this is to determine whether the witchcraft . . . will be effective or not." The Ngangulero places questions before the Nganga to determine if the operation will be successful, basing his or her judgment on whether or not the gunpowder explodes when lit. In effect then, the gunpowder is the one who provides the answers. "When the gunpowder explodes the füiri shoots out to carry out the mission entrusted to it."[22]

In the above ritual, the eruption or silence of gunpowder effectively endows the spirit of the nganga with the power of speech, shaping the living spirit's cognitive thoughts with materiality and substance. "The gunpowder is the one who provides the answers." We see also that the moment of the powder's explosion is the precise moment of the ritual call to action. It is an unleashing, a profound setting in motion—"the füiri shoots out to carry out the mission." Because the theme of exploding gunpowder as a means to extract answers was and is so pervasive in Congo sacred practice, and because the ignited gunpowder in Alejandro's story "always preceded conversations to arrange the insurrection," it seems likely that the resident spiritualist in Pablo's cabin was asking through the gunpowder how to proceed with the planned rebellion.

In the impressive panoply of requests laid at the doors of ritual experts, by far the most recurrent and insistent was that of vengeance and justice. Those who lived through the daily holocausts of the plantation world—its beatings and verbal violence, its sicknesses and sexual assault, its dearth of privacy, sleep, and food—frequently sought redress for these crimes through the mandates of the spirit world. The historical records abound with reports of vengeance sought against overseers and slavemasters. These reports form something of their own narrative, one that carries a discursive power about the arbitrariness of justice, and the delectable irony of the last becoming the first.

While Palo's sometimes vengeful dispensation of justice could take multiple forms, such as grave illness or some other misfortune, it could also manifest itself in the death of the offending party if the motive was particularly grave. Years later, former slaves and their descendants recalled Mayomberos who used the ngangas to attack and free themselves from their enemies, thus acknowledging the nganga's power to take a life, if the situation required it.[23] The former slave Esteban Montejo, for example, spoke of these early Congolese traditions in his recorded memoirs and remembered other slaves' marveling at their ability to exact revenge.

If the testimonies are to be believed, countless slaves arranged to eliminate their masters and overseers in this fashion, though others gave less precise descriptions of their techniques and methods. For example, a rebel captain in the Macuriges district, José María Lucumí, reportedly told one of his lieutenants that "the estate overseer was evil and he was going to look for a *brujo* to kill him, the same as the owner."[24] On the nearby Encanto mill Patricio Gangá, another head captain, allegedly received some "witchcraft" to kill the proprietor and the overseer, Braudilio Piqué and Miguel Hernández, respectively.[25] Throughout the early months of 1844, similar reports continued to emerge of slave leaders who had counseled other slaves "to do witchcraft on the owner so that he would die" or collected money "in order to bring a *brujo* with the aim of placing it on their owner."[26] Still other witnesses spoke of assassination plots linking the slaves of two different owners, such as one man who testified about one estate in which the slaves were "agreed [*ligados*] to throw herbs" on the owner and the mayoral to kill them.[27]

In February of that year, the militias heard testimony about Inés Criolla, a creole woman serving the wealthy sugar planter José María Gálvez in the city of Matanzas. Inés had children on the Gálvez sugar mill, and she managed to obtain her owner's permission to travel into the countryside to visit them. As an emissary from the provincial capital, Inés bore an urgent message from her sister, Josefa. Josefa had solicited the services of a known spiritualist, requesting "that he send her a witchcraft item to place on her owner." It seems, however, that the channels of communication and commerce proved too unwieldy. Because the money did not arrive when it was supposed to, Josefa's request was denied.[28] Indeed, the theme of "doing witchcraft" (*echar brujos*) on the white male plantocracy and their appointed managers was quite possibly the most common articulation of African spiritual practice in the 1844 archives.

|||||||| With the Objective of Preparing the Slaves for an Uprising

When José María Gangá was questioned in 1844 about a planned conspiracy, he testified that a free mulatto "appeared to him one day, stating that all the blacks of the Island were going to rise up against the whites, and handed him a shell [*caracol*], repeating to him several times that he should keep it, that he would talk to him more when he saw him."[29] Robert Farris Thompson argues that shells were sacred objects in Congolese theology and were used throughout the African Atlantic on graves and other sites to "enclose the soul's immortal presence."[30] José María's shell metaphorically reappeared across the plantation landscape as hundreds of slaves were told about an insurgency that would be backed by a sacred source of power. As the resistance movement spread, so too did the distribution of amulets and other forms of ritual protection.

For example, during the winter of 1843 two free black men joined a work crew employed at a local sugar mill known as Calderón. They were Margarito Quintana and Catalino "the mason," both Matanzas residents.[31] Pablo Lucumí, who became a central organizer at Calderón, spoke at length about these two highly wanted conspirators. Pablo implied that by the time the two men broached the subject of the special amulets, he was already familiar with the plans for an insurrection on his home estate. He and others seemed quite amenable to these amulets, which could protect the newly transformed soldiers in battle. Pablo testified that "the free black men Catalino and Margarito Criollo counseled him . . . to buy the witchcraft they had, so that when [the slaves] rose up against the whites, the latter could do them no harm, for the charm would serve them such that even if [the whites] might shoot them with bullet or machete, they would not be able to touch their bodies."[32]

Another slave on the estate similarly testified that Catalino and Margarito "told them to gather seven doubloons to pay them for the talismans they were selling them, with [whose help] they did not need to be afraid of the rifles and machetes of the whites." To seal this promise, the two libres were to "come with rifles and bayonets to take [the Calderón slaves] to Matanzas, where they had many people gathered."[33] This theme of powerful spiritual protection was a familiar one throughout the Atlantic world in the eighteenth and nineteenth centuries, and during this time in Matanzas it was especially so.[34] Scores of others across the countryside maintained that mostly African men in important positions of leadership sold them amulets to ensure their success in a decisive battle. Protective amulets and pouches became one of the most important forms of currency to the 1844 movement, especially in the rural regions.

This power to safeguard with weaponry unknown to the Europeans was highly discussed. In March 1844 military officers arrived at the Encanto sugar mill in Sabanilla. There, they questioned Andrés Mina about a fire on the estate and plans for a coming insurgency. There is little evidence to indicate that Andrés was involved, but that did not stop authorities from arresting and interrogating him. Andrés testified that "he knew the slaves were going to rise up" and named Patricio Gangá and Antonio María Gangá as leaders on his estate who had "incited" him. When questioned about arms and weaponry Andrés stated he knew nothing about the latter, but he did know "that Patricio had witchcraft items [and] was going to give them to the declarant and the other blacks engaged in fighting the whites." Another slave on the Encanto mill similarly testified that Patricio "gave them witchcraft to fight against the whites."[35] When Patricio was questioned, he claimed to know nothing about such items. Even when presented with testimony to the contrary, Patricio continued to deny the allegations.[36]

Over the course of about two years, these conversations regularly crossed lines of geography and legal status. The free black man Narciso Campuzano, for example, spoke of an organizing meeting that brought together several free black men "and one slave he always took for free." Narciso described the group as seated around a table, at whose head sat the libre José Jesús Daniel. José Jesús presumably distributed "witchcraft items" to them all, "with the aim of transmitting them to slaves on the country estates . . . so that they might rise up with the free men and carry out the insurrection."[37] The free black man Miguel Naranjo similarly testified to meetings that he attended in the home of Marcos Ruiz, the famous urban organizer, where they discussed the uprising. According to Miguel, each of the attendees was urged to "work with his acquaintances to win them over" and told to work "in the countryside to incite those of the ingenios, sending them witchcraft so that neither the bullets nor the machetes could pierce them."[38]

These examples highlight the recurring connection between the material culture of early Palo and other African Cuban religions and the organization of the 1844 movement. Slave witnesses consistently reported that movement leaders carried out some form of ritual work — typically making, selling, or procuring amulets — and those responsible for this ritual wisdom and expertise frequently emerged as leading figures in the movement. These amulets and protections became an important lexicon for how rural black people articulated the structural forces that oppressed them and their strategies for resistance and autonomy. They reveal the outlines of a dynamic rural political culture that drew from a range of sources, mundane and spiritual. These ritual objects, and the epistemology that formed them, thus became part of a powerful insurgent agenda to gather awareness, garner support, and encourage solidarity for the bourgeoning movement. Such an intersection allows important insight into how black Cuban laborers envisioned freedom, formulated their critiques of power, and confronted the violence of the plantation world during the 1840s.

What is especially telling about these amulets is not just their ubiquity and pervasiveness in locales across the Americas but the level of *faith* they inspired in black communities, particularly in times of rebellion. In fact, one of the reasons that rebel leaders were able to distribute their amulets so widely was because they were accepted and desired by a wide range of people. In other words, the commerce in sacred items was central to the plantation's social geography. But the amulets traveled a curious arc in this mental universe, and their purpose seemed to evolve from protecting individual black bodies from the tortures of slavery to ensuring the victory of the collective black body in the pursuit of freedom. Hence the amulets seem to mark a distinctive evolution from one state to the next, facilitating passage from daily acts of defense to a permanent utopian freedom. There is a fine line, then, between the idea that the amulets would protect those who enlisted to fight and the idea that the amulets *themselves* would make the fighters free.

The amulet here becomes the focal point of this negotiation, not as a suggestion for divine power at work but rather as the actual site where that work is happening. Not only do the traumas of slavery take on corporeality and "flesh" in the form of these amulets — the amulets themselves embody a tangible, touchable link to a future beyond slavery.[39] In these narratives, the talismans attended to matters of defense to be sure, but recruits were also led to believe that the amulets' purchase, possession, and wearing — to say nothing of their contents — represented (and contained) the very essence of freedom itself. If the quintessential fetish can be understood as "an interstitial negotiating tool," then this definition is useful if we consider Rachel Harding's invocation of "interstitiality" in its most basic sense — the space that intervenes between things. For indeed the amulet was situated between monumental extremes: between bullet and body, torture and wholeness, insurgent and militia, enslavement and freedom.[40]

When authorities interrogated slaves about witchcraft, it was not always clear if they were inquiring about people, objects, or practices. The slaves at least often interpreted "brujos" to mean actual things. The few descriptions that we have of these items indicate that they were usually smaller objects or pouches with medicines and protections inside. Former slaves who spoke to Lydia Cabrera reminded her that sacred work could be carried out with "many types of amulets and talismans, since the soul of a dead person and any spirit . . . might enclose itself in any object: güiros, pots (Mpakas), bags, shells and little statuettes, the kini-kini . . . the famous Palo dolls of the Lucumí."[41] In this way, spiritual fortifications could be easily carried around on one's person, tied up in a skirt or headwrap, or stashed discreetly in the corner of one's cabin.

Telésforo Lucumí, a fifty-five-year-old slave on the sugar mill of La Luisa, was questioned about "witchcraft" items of this kind. Telésforo admitted that "he was the one who brought the fetishes to the [La Luisa] ingenio to sell them; that he makes them with the roots of the yagruma and yaya trees; that these he would place inside a little cow's horn and wrap them in a piece of leather that he sewed." Telésforo also added, perhaps with prompting, "that he would sell them so that they [the slaves, presumably] could fight and do battle." The theme in Telésforo's account that has been handed down to contemporary Cuban traditions is that of wrapping roots and other items—after consecrating them—in a small piece of leather or cloth, tightly sewn into a square or some other shape.[42]

These sewn pouches, animal horns, and herbal packets were common paraphernalia in many African-inspired ritual cultures, and they circulated liberally in communities throughout Cuba and across the Atlantic world.[43] The statement of Ramón Lucumí, on the Matanzas sugar mill of San José, illustrates the proliferation of these amulets. He testified that two Lucumís from a nearby mill "were thinking about rising up to fight against the whites" and requested that Ramón make them an amulet. Ramón gathered the necessary roots and herbs, "ground all these leaves and put them into a leather pouch . . . and took it to the Atrevido mill, where he sold it to the slaves."[44] Joaquín Lucumí similarly charged for his services—four reales for an amulet fashioned from "the horn of a bull three inches long, containing some flesh-colored powders . . . [and] some chicken feathers."[45]

Justo Criollo endured similar questions about witchcraft and sorcery.

African Cuban Sacred Traditions | 211

His account is particularly intriguing because it mentions the slaves on Joaquín Peñalver's Alcancía estate, who rose up in March 1843. According to Justo, "the slaves of Peñalver who survived the revolution in the Vuelta Arriba region were composing witchcraft objects and leather hides smeared with grease and oil, placing them in the sun immediately thereafter. That later, thoroughly dried, they greased them again in the same way, and these would serve for when [the slaves] went to fight, placing them on their chests, against which the bullets would slide off, and fall on the ground." The implication here is that some of the slaves who remained alive at Alcancía in the aftermath of the March rebellion continued to contemplate ways to break their enslavement, using valuable methods to protect themselves if another battle arose.[46] The testimonies include a number of other examples of slaves who used animal horns, herbs, and other materials for the coming rebellion.[47]

These amulets formed one part of a range of warfare preparations—including spiritual consultations, protective ceremonies, and rituals that resonated with those of expansionist states like Oyo and Dahomey—and were reconfigured in the plantation zones of Cuba during times of insurgency.[48] The spiritual cultures that slaves developed in Cuba and elsewhere also relied heavily on military practices from West and Central Africa. In the old kingdom of Kongo and Dahomey, for example, warriors rarely went to battle without ritual preparation, an important step thought to determine "the outcome of battle." T. J. Desch-Obi has explained how these traditions continued in the Americas, enshrined most notably in the Congo and Angolan martial arts that grew up in Brazil and the United States, many of whose practitioners "made use of charms or other forms of conjure to ensure their victory."[49] John Thornton has similarly shown that the tactics employed by Angolan rebels during the Stono Rebellion of 1739 were highly reminiscent of established patterns and traditions of warfare prominent in Central Africa during the seventeenth and eighteenth centuries.[50]

Across western Cuba, gatherings were being convened in 1843 and 1844 to drum up support for the coming rebellion—sometimes literally. The history of New World slave rebellions is replete with these kinds of gatherings, some of which were quite large. In contrast to places like Haiti or Antigua, however, there does not seem to have been one decisive or heavily attended ceremony that acted as a ritual trigger to the rebellion itself. Rather, in a manner mirroring the movement's decentralized political structure, we can identify a series of smaller and more focused rituals on farms, within plantations, and in urban neighborhoods across Matanzas. Among the best examples of these gatherings were those taking place on the Buena Esperanza and Recompensa coffee plantations.

As we have seen in previous chapters, the meetings at Buena Esperanza estate during the early months of 1844 attracted many attendees from miles around, as well as from the city of Matanzas. Although the primary leader at Buena Esperanza was Melchor Mandinga, it was Patricio Mandinga and Blas Lucumí, two organizers from the Owens estate, who emerged as critical at these gatherings. Recall that Patricio and Blas were apprentices in the shoe-making business of Thomas Owens and often traveled to Matanzas, where they connected with a wide spectrum of people. Melchor Mandinga, who was recorded as being near the age of forty, worked as a personal coachman and field laborer. Though we can only guess at the precise homelands of these three individuals, it is plausible that the religious traditions from regions such as Yorubaland, Senegambia, and greater Sierra Leone were represented or combined during these meetings.

A surprising number of men and a few women—at least four slave women were routinely cited as being present—agreed that these meetings were initially held for the purpose of carrying out clandestine religious rituals and encouraging the purchase of protective amulets. The assemblies would open with either sacred ritual ceremonies or with a campaign to sell the amulets. After this was completed, the meetings took a different turn, progressing to talk of the uprising. An outside attendee named Marcelino Criollo confirmed that Patricio and Blas were "dealing with some witchcraft," and Cirila Criolla, a woman attending from Buena Esperanza, similarly asserted, "Patricio and Blas first began by selling their witchcraft." Apparently, the Owens leaders let it be known that with these amulets the slaves "would be free from punishment or reprimand of their owners[,] but if they said anything to the owner, they would be ruined."[51]

Some, like José Gangá, came ready to purchase the protections. The handsome sum of four pesos and twelve reales was money that he did not particularly wish to part with, but José was assured that such a sacrifice was necessary "to help buy weapons, gunpowder, and bullets."[52] Though other participants spoke about the amulets, only a few gave any indication of what they looked like, or explained what leaders did with them. Women like Juana Criolla remembered how the leaders "spread their fetishes out on the floor."[53] José Gangá recalled that the items in question "were composed in a jar used for goats that was filled with reddish brick powders, and several other things of which he is ignorant."[54]

In most accounts, it was only after participants vowed not to speak of the amulets that leaders "began to discuss the uprising to do away with the whites and end up as masters of the land."[55] As Luis Gangá's statement put it, "Later after they were assured that [the others] would keep the silence . . . they proposed to rise up like those in Matanzas, to kill the whites and become masters of the land."[56] The central organizers took pains to convey to all the attendees that their silence was absolutely imperative, and it is possible that precautions were taken to ensure their discretion, such as an oath.[57] At least eleven slaves on two different estates corroborated the core of this story with similar details.

As we saw in the story of Agustín's "witchcraft pot," apparently a number of Domech's slaves were involved in this interstate traffic in sacred items. As seen above, Domech learned from his slave José Ynés that two of his other slaves, Manuel and Tomás, had planned to obtain gunpowder and other items for a ceremony. When Domech learned about the "witchcraft pot," he deemed it and the other incriminating items, perhaps prematurely, to be the same ones "that Thomas the Englishman's slaves used to deceive [my slaves] and get them wrapped up . . . with those of the other estates of this district in the horrific crime."[58]

For his part, Manuel admitted that these charges were true. He spoke of how Patricio would come to the Domech estate every Sunday and steadily gathered recruits for the insurgency. He then went on to name more than twenty-five people who filtered in from the local plantations and the cities to attend the meetings.[59] Tomás similarly confessed to the charges against him. He stated that he and Manuel had both obtained gunpowder from local sources "to use in the witchcraft ceremonies." Yet, while both men identified themselves as conspirators, they insisted that the primary blame for this crime lay with Blas, Patricio, "and the others of Matanzas who incited them."[60]

Those who may not have been attracted to the idea of joining a violent and large-scale rebellion in 1844 may have still been amenable to settling personal scores with those who oppressed them, particularly if such actions were bloodless, largely untraceable, and seemingly unknown to white authorities. One of the richest examples of this comes from the testimonies on the Recompensa coffee estate in the district of Batabanó, situated in Havana's outer rim. The stories at Recompensa centered on Federico, a known Gangá spiritualist, who had apparently been lent by his original owner to help make tiles on a nearby estate.[61] By most accounts, two senior Recompensa slaves, Juan Lucumí and Damián Carabalí, solicited Federico in February 1844 to come to their estate and "work [his] witchcraft, because all of the slaves wanted to get rid of the administrator in any way possible, dead or alive." For three months, Federico hid out at Recompensa; he himself testified that he lived secretly in the cabins of Juan and Damián during that time, though other reports suggest that Federico lived with his lover Hilaria, also known as Adelaida.[62]

To dispose of their estate manager, José González del Valle, Federico gathered various materials to make shrines, powders, and sacred figurines, and kept them in different cabins. Around midnight, long after the bell rang for silence, eight or nine slaves would gather to carry out the necessary rituals near their living quarters.[63] According to different sources, these convocations were held in or near the cabins of Damián, Adelaida, and Petra, or along the paths leading to the slave quarters. All agreed that the rituals were convened with the purpose of "[getting] rid of the estate administrator."[64]

Federico led the group, placing special figurines and other items on the ground. He sprayed them with *aguardiente* (cane liquor), allowing them to "drink," and burned gunpowder.[65] As does the presence of gunpowder, the recurrent mention of a "pot" suggests the Congo-Cuban markings that literally and figuratively adorned the Recompensa gatherings. For example, another attendee named Antonio Carabalí stated "on the same day that he [Federico, presumably] asked for the five pesos . . . [the latter] gave him a pot filled with dirt." In the aftermath of the testimonies, a young Congo boy led authorities to a patch of coffee plants where they found, among other things, "a little pot filled with a dirty mixture," and a bag tied with a cord. Upon searching the cabins of two of the men indicted with Federico, they found "a bag filled with little sacks . . . which the blacks believe contain witchcraft . . . and also a heavily adorned calabash" with some kind of feathers. It is highly possible that Federico used one or all of these items in his work.

Even more intriguing, when Antonio asked for Federico's name, he was told that "he does not have a name, that he had fallen from the sky, and that he was called Siete Rayos."[66] Siete Rayos is the Spanish name given to the Palo *mpungu* (deity) representing lightning and thunder, justice and right deed. Traditionally, Siete Rayos exhibits many of the same characteristics of his famed Yoruba counterpart, Shango.[67] As one of Cabrera's informants observed, "All Paleros worship Siete Rayos, even those dedicated to evil. He is considered the first Palero, the greatest magician, the king of our religion."[68] The implications of Siete Rayos's invocation in this gathering, at least according to this testimony, are therefore highly significant.[69]

While much of the knowledge of Siete Rayos remains in the collective oral histories of Palo practitioners, more has been written about the Yoruba-Fon deity Shango (or "Chango," as it is often written in Cuba). Best known as the god of thunder and lightning, Shango was also the fourth alâfin or ruler of Oyo. As such, he was also a champion of the oppressed and a guardian of high moral principles. Both Shango and Siete Rayos are traditionally seen as aggressive, harsh, and easily antagonized. In contemporary Palo, this energy is generally associated with a dominating, energetic, fervent, and combative masculinity that is linked in many minds with going to war. Further research is needed on the historical veneration of Siete Rayos in order to flesh out the full implications of this testimony.

Though this ritual was clearly directed at eliminating a brutal manager, it hardly seems coincidental that the story surfaced during a time when widespread resistance was being uncovered in districts throughout Matanzas. Federico stated that the Recompensa slaves were indeed involved in the insurgency and had assigned offices such as captain and lieutenant for this purpose, though he was the only one who made this claim.[70] Against this backdrop, the testimony of Petra Bibi Carabalí becomes that much more poignant in her recollection of the rituals with Federico. She stated, "He took out some figurines[,] sprayed rum on them," and then obliged the group to dance and sing "llanllá saraminga qumba há!! branco corá."[71]

Petra continued to describe the ritual: "Federico would throw a little bit of powder on the ground, burn it, and when it started to flame, he would rub his hands together and sing the *llanllá saraminga* and they would respond with the same song." When asked what the words meant, Petra translated, "to take up machetes against the whites."[72] This account strongly suggests that Federico was burning gunpowder and thus utilizing Palo or Palo-inspired rituals to galvanize the other attendees to rebel. Lino Criollo, a cart driver who attended from a nearby estate, reported that he did not sing along as everyone else did "because he did not understand the language."[73] This may or may not have been the case, but given the cultural diversity of the assembly, these words might indeed have been foreign to many of the participants.

Federico's powder was specially obtained for the occasion, and even with the conflicting stories about its source, it is clear that someone had to leave the plantation grounds to get it. According to Federico, the herbs had originated from "carabelas de gente" (a phrase that commonly refers to continental Africans who endured the Middle Passage together) and had a deadly potency: "Even though he has not seen anyone die with those herbs, he does not doubt that they could kill, because the individual who showed them to him said as much."[74] Federico probably also bound the participants with an oath sealed by drinking the rum. This is based on Antonio Carabalí's recollection of the promise "that if anyone who drank that aguardiente later spoke about what they were doing, they would die." Antonio testified that the fear of such consequences initially prevented him from talking about the ritual to authorities, "but now that the others had spoken and no one has died, he would talk about it."[75]

In this way, the slaves at Recompensa prepared a different kind of weapon, invoking spiritual energy to avenge themselves. Moreover, several men from beyond Recompensa's borders attended these ceremonies, some allegedly with their own vendettas in mind. For example, one of the witnesses stated that a Leandro Carabalí "used to come to the dances [that is, the rituals] with others from Juan Granado's coffee plantation . . . and it appeared that he also wanted to get rid of his overseer." Other slaves present from Recompensa included a woman named Emily or Emilia and the aforementioned Adelaida.[76]

The proceedings of the ritual also seem to have been marred by internal strife. Though Emilia Carabalí had recently come out of the infirmary and was still "half sick" by the time of the rituals, Adelaida insisted that Emily attend. During the course of the rituals Emily did something that angered Federico tremendously; Emily says she simply fell asleep. Whatever she did, Federico apparently hit her on the head hard enough to draw blood, telling her, "You are not worth anything, leave here, and do not ever come back." Emily was so furious that she threatened to go to the overseer, but Petra Bibi Carabalí "begged her earnestly not to do so because they would have a hard time, offering instead to dress her wound." Petra washed her wound with alcohol and dressed it with oil, while Adelaida washed the bloody headcloth. Emily refused to attend further rituals.[77]

Nonetheless, the rites continued. Those assembled danced "with the idea of obtaining the expulsion of the Administrator, because he punished them a great deal . . . if they did not achieve this end, they were going to kill him [by poison]." More than one report from May 1844 suggested that the general atmosphere on Recompensa was a rebellious one, that "all the blacks are stirred up," and that "the blacks of Granado . . . wanted to rise up [too]."[78] In these events music, dance, ritual, and rebellion converged explosively, as the assembled slaves attempted to exact their own form of justice. In exchange for these services, Federico was to be compensated handsomely; they gave him "twelve pesos with the promise to give him three reales after the overseer actually left."[79] Perhaps it was fitting that the retribution these slaves sought was reflected in the plantation's actual name, literally "recompense" or "reward."

In numerous other examples, slaves recounted attempts to eliminate the overseers or estate managers in the winter and spring of 1844.[80] While some of these plans did not directly coincide with a larger plan to raise a rebellion in the area, and were undoubtedly singled out by authorities looking for subversion everywhere, they did coincide very closely in time and space with the larger momentum of resistance around the Matanzas-Havana region.

The example at Recompensa invites closer inspection of one additional claim that several participants made in their testimonies. During one of his interrogations, Federico explained that he would "put his figures [*trastes*] on the ground and they would go around them dancing and singing and burning some gunpowder, all this with the idea of obtaining the administrador's expulsion, for he punished them a great deal."[81] Petra Carabalí similarly claimed that "he took out some hoaxes, sprayed them with cane liquor, and let them drink and made them dance and sing, 'llanllá saraminga qumba há!! branco corá.'" These testimonies invite closer scrutiny of the claims "that they danced and sang," as the above episode indicates a close affinity between insurgent dispositions, song, and dance-movement. They suggest the need for future research on how song, drumming, dance, and movement can collectively deepen understanding of the ways in which resistance was taken up in western Cuba during the early 1840s.

|||||||| "The White Men's Bullets"

The proliferation of war amulets in mid-nineteenth century Cuba calls further attention to the masculinized aspects of the impending insurgency in rural Cuba. While oral histories of Regla de Congo and the better-known Regla de Ocha insist that women were central as priestesses and spiritualists in ritual communities, in the records examined for this study, few women spoke in any detail about amulets or other material objects that might be considered "brujerías." Throughout the testimonies, one finds ample explanation for this: fewer women were called to testify and those who appeared were less inclined to provide extensive information. Moreover, for whatever reason, authorities seemed more likely to interrogate men about witchcraft.[82] In addition, many slave witnesses seem to have interpreted questions about "brujerías" to mean early Palo-inspired practices, and in

Cuba these traditions have historically been more patriarchal and male-dominated. That being said, however, they were probably never exclusive to men, and certainly are not so now.

What can be examined with greater certainty is what slave witnesses spoke about in 1844. While several accounts, including those from the Domech estate, indicate that slave women knew about and even embraced the profusion of war amulets in 1844, it is not clear whether they ever purchased amulet protections for themselves, or if male insurgent leaders ever intended that women should use them. By and large, protective war amulets were reported as being fashioned, sold, and purchased by other men. Moreover, the artillery and bullets from which the slave recruits needed protection were typically raced as white and gendered as male—as in "the white men's bullets" or "the white men's guns"—and their targets were similarly raced and gendered as black men. In these and other examples, the visual economy of assault and defense was heavily masculinized, particularly in the symbolic terrain of war amulets.

On rare occasions, slave witnesses did speak of women like Florentina Criolla, a feared local spiritualist who was more than likely a central rebel organizer on her home estate.[83] A number of witnesses testified to Florentina's leading role in the local organizing. A Roberto Gangá, for example, described Florentina as a "witch," stating that "she herself . . . told him that she was going to kill the mayoral in the company of Eusebio the contra-mayoral." Roberto continued that Florentina told him she was going to set fire to the ingenio.[84] When questioned, Florentina denied any part in the uprising and stated that the mayoral took from her the only "witchcraft items" she had, which included a pot.[85] Other witnesses spoke of women like Rufina, the wife of yet another insurgent leader, whose spiritual powers were respected and feared. But the testimonies have yielded very few Florentinas and Rufinas. Usually it was men of various African nations who were reported as selling the necessary amulets and who orchestrated the most visible sacred work of the insurgency. It would, for example, be important to know whether women became more visible in the *making* of the amulets themselves, or in other kinds of spirit work that emerged beyond early Palo practices, such as spiritism or work with orishas or other deities. But the available records suggest that the rebel organizing of 1844 and the increasingly bellicose subculture it spawned helped to militarize African Cuban ritual roles and sacred work, and further entrench a masculine ethos in both.

It is also worth noting that while the Recompensa gathering was defined by many of the hallmarks of early Palo/Congo work, in other African Cuban liturgies women have historically had a much more visible presence as daughters and priestesses of male and female deities, and can be mounted or possessed by a broad pantheon of divinities and ancestors. It is unlikely that rituals such as the one enacted at Recompensa inverted or erased existing ceremonial gender roles and hierarchies; the evidence indicates that they did not. But while the ritual space examined above seems to have been directed by one or two leading men, there is every reason to believe that in other settings women's spiritual expertise was valued and pursued. It is important to note, however, that when witnesses spoke about the Recompensa ceremony they implied that the raw material of movement was essentially open to everyone in the group. In short, the records and contemporary anecdotes suggest that once the work of prayer, song, dance, and possession had begun, all were expected to take part. So in contrast to amulets that were targeted primarily at men and made primarily for a "war" broadly configured as male, collective ritual spaces and sacred dance/song may very well have been predicated on a broader inclusion that encompassed, and even privileged, women. The above examples should lead us to reexamine the complicated position of women at the nexus of a number of different insurrectionary and spiritual labors.

The stories above allow us to see some of the ways that religious cosmologies, especially those that were Congo-inspired, sanctioned and helped to structure enslaved people's political movements. Enslaved insurgents in 1843–44 retraced familiar lines, and drew new ones, calling on the gods, the ancestors, and remembered political templates to guide their impending acts of war. Indeed, this cultural arsenal helped to *translate* this movement into a living reality, providing in the process a compelling—and potentially unexplored—discourse about the possibilities of freedom. Clearly such rituals formed a powerful backdrop, and a resource, for the themes of liberation and sovereignty in enslaved people's insurgencies.

Conclusion

Before the opening of the Ten Years' War (1868–78), which formally began Cuba's struggle for independence, a free mulatta woman named Mariana Grajales told stories to her children. Her son, the renowned general Antonio Maceo, grew up hearing about the horrific moments that black people had lived through in Cuba—among them the trials of La Escalera. Years later, the leaders of Cuba's first black political party, the Partido Independiente de Color, continued to invoke the events of 1844 for their constituents, reminding them of a long history of racial oppression that spilled into the twentieth century. The Partido members called their own struggles with state violence "the epilogue of the trial of La Escalera."[1] These stories illustrate how deeply entrenched the 1844 movement remained in Cuban historical memory for years afterward, particularly among the African-descended.

Mariana Grajales understood something that it took professional historians years to realize. The African Cubans who lived and died a generation before Maceo had a clear vision of their liberation and sovereignty. They understood themselves as political subjects and recognized the importance of creating their own freedom. This consciousness emerged from a surge of daily activities that consistently challenged the cultural hegemony of slaveholders and plantation managers, that is to say, the terrain of their daily existence. For enslaved people on the rural plantations this meant an acute ability to assess the valences of power in the plantation world, establish rival geographies that opposed the fixity of plantation space, forge extensive networks of kin and community, and turn to sacred technologies for defense and protection. It was this consciousness that gave rise to the movements of 1843 and 1844.

The movements of 1843 and 1844 were formed inside, not outside, of a coercive labor regime as enslaved people created sustained structures of resistance that confronted the structures of domination. The licit and illicit movements of black rural laborers through cane fields, boiling houses, cabins, and woodland hinterlands took these spaces from the violent universes that the planter elite imagined and mapped onto them a host of new meanings, political possibilities, and forms of sociality. These contested geographies were spatial, bodily, and psychic ones that helped enslaved Cubans to channel their energy and their mobility into resistant activities such as the organizing of 1844. These rival mobilities and rival geographies shed new light on old realizations: that enslaved people were more than the oppressiveness of their labor, more than the limits of their mobility, and especially in the Cuba of 1844, more than tortures they endured. Through this repurposing and remapping of plantation space, rural black laborers reimagined the variegated possibilities of freedom—both within and beyond the institution of slavery.

Across the western landscape in 1843 and 1844 enslaved people assembled insurgent collectives that frequently crossed lines of gender, ethnicity, plantation borders, and legal freedom. These interwoven conversations, community networks, and the alternative "public spheres" that they created highlight the social and cultural infrastructure that facilitated the emergence of rebel mobilizations in localities across western Cuba. They also draw critical attention to the public and liminal spaces in which the intelligence of 1844 was received and debated. These local cohorts of African and African-descended men and women were also critical to merging the defiant energy swelling in the countryside with the political discussions taking place in the urban centers.

The archival stories of 1843 and 1844 reveal that enslaved women and men truly saw those years as a political movement, one marked by continuous attempts to mobilize, plans to desist and start again, and attempts to plug into wider currents of resistance—currents that circulated throughout the rural regions, between the urban and rural centers, and across the Caribbean Sea and the Atlantic Ocean. Itinerant free men went from plantation to plantation seeking skilled work, traveling merchants stopped by the slave cabins to peddle their wares, rural black people ventured to nearby properties for Sunday dances and drummings, escaped slaves crept into plantations at night to pilfer supplies, other slaves slipped out after dark to visit loved ones and to escape the oppressiveness of the barracks, coachmen and wagon drivers traversed the countryside and spent time in the major cities, and black maritime workers and white seamen arrived in Havana from places like New Orleans, Veracruz, and Kingston.

This contact contributed to an acute awareness by rural black people of what was taking place within their district, across the island, and throughout the Atlantic world. Both male slaves with privilege and nonelite slave men and women helped to forge these connections. In so doing, they redefined the meanings of "urban" and "rural" space and the geographies available to them.

This culture of interaction, exchange, and movement indelibly marked the political awareness of slaves who experienced—and heard about—the Haitian Revolution, its eastward expansion and elimination of slavery in Santo Domingo, the massive slave insurgencies in the British Caribbean, the abolition of slavery in the British territories, the independence wars in Latin America, and the increasing influence of British antislavery forces in Cuba. These political streams that flowed in from the larger Atlantic world picked up (and helped to create) the currents of unrest that emanated from the major cities and the countryside. During the early 1840s, the urban centers of Cuba became crucibles for scores of dissidents—rural and urban slaves, free men of color, and white creole patriots—attempting to organize against slavery and colonialism. Alongside these dissident currents in the urban sphere, armed insurrections and other forms of slave protest broke out repeatedly in the west-central plantation districts during this time, becoming particularly chronic from the mid-1830s to the early 1840s. By 1832 slave rebellions and conspiracies were breaking out at least once a year in Cuba.

Propelled by this momentum, an anticolonial movement began to take shape that initially enjoyed support from a few liberal white creoles and a pair of British abolitionists. Eventually, however, it became a movement composed almost entirely of people of color. By 1843 the recurrent slave agitation beyond the city limits was connecting with the black urban mobilizations in the urban centers. Its participants, organizers, supporters, and even its naysayers found this to be a fruitful moment to discuss new structures of power, citizenship, governance, and productivity.

Thus the conspiracy of La Escalera was at once an intensely local and an intensely transnational affair. It had broad implications for the mobility, labor regimes, and social networks of the plantation countryside, but it had equally strong implications for the maintenance of empire (in Spain and Britain), U.S. annexation, slaveholding, and the political balance of power in the Atlantic world. As such, African Cuban participation in this movement provides alternative ways to think about the larger project of black freedom and how it was constituted transnationally and through deep African sensibilities. In 1844 black Cubans' engagement with the discourse of the Haitian Revolution and the liberal-democratic ideas emanating from

Western metropoles—namely, abolition, constitutionalism, and independence—merged with their own cultural and political infrastructures from the polities of West and Central Africa.

The testimonies that highlight the circulation of spiritual amulets and the broad spectrum of African Cuban ritual practices are among the most provocative in the entire trial record. The centrality of these amulets illustrates some of the ways that Cuban slaves found to express new forms of political subjectivity. Indeed, these sacred objects and rituals became an intimate part of the insurgent lexicon in the 1840s. This suggests the need for a different kind of narrative about 1844 in particular, and about slave resistance in general, that can invite newer and more compelling questions about how black political sensibilities are formed and nurtured.

Extending the theoretical possibilities of what constitutes black freedom additionally suggests the need to rethink who is considered "part" of the insurgency. For this reason, this book is particularly preoccupied with the people who often linger along the peripheries of slave movement histories, and even fall through their cracks. One of its defining questions is what might happen when the small or invisible acts of insurgency are made central to the rebel tapestry. A focus on these comparatively peripheral figures recalibrates the language and the theories for thinking through "legitimate" resistance or "genuine" rebellion.

Expanding the boundaries of this political culture therefore also necessitates reexamining—or perhaps examining for the first time—the roles and the contributions African-descended women during moments of rebellion. The labors of both enslaved and free women of color were central to the production of a broader antislavery literacy, and therefore what Barbadian historian Hilary Beckles has called "an anti-slavery ideology," in movements like that of 1844.[2]

Although they were usually outnumbered by men, women were nevertheless present in this movement as vocal participants, organizers, and highly aware observers whose positionality and voice confound much of what we imagine a "rebel" to be. An important part of this imagining comes from exploring the domestic, emotional, and otherwise immaterial labors of black women. This labor took place in the physical and social spaces they helped to create and became central to the making of the 1844 resistance in ways that have often gone unnoticed. In fact, it was often these women who produced the locales and the opportunities that enabled other more "recognizable" forms of resistance and opposition to emerge.[3] Understanding their often invisible gendered labor is crucial to understanding the formation of a living political culture.

Making a gendered analysis central to reexamination of the 1843 and 1844 movements necessarily produces a new way of thinking about how rebel movements are organized and executed. It creates different ways to understand how women as well as men, especially nonelite men, became involved in these struggles. Privileging the gendered periphery thus sheds important light on the complicated and contradictory ways all slaves responded to and understood the project of insurgency. It redirects attention to the people who seemed to be "doing nothing" or who appeared to be "completely uninvolved" and provides an alternative narrative in which to consider their investment in political movements, connections that are often illegible within the archive. Finally, reframing the center of analysis along a gendered axis continues to trouble and question the ever-fluid boundaries between individual and collective resistance, violent and nonviolent opposition, and personal and political choices. The slaves who were critical to local rebel planning, who helped shape this planning in unacknowledged ways, and who fell on the periphery of these designs altogether were all critical to the rebel tapestry in rural Matanzas.

As we have seen, the events of 1844 emerged during a moment when British antislavery forces were changing the landscape of the Atlantic slave trade and challenging the relationships of colonies and republics to slavery in an unprecedented way. But the nineteenth-century politics that resulted in the 1844 trials are also critical for reframing the history of anticolonial organizing in Cuba, since the best-known and most widely accepted narratives of Cuban anticolonialism rarely include the organized resistance of plantation slaves. The stories in this book necessarily encompass, but also move beyond, an understanding of how black insurgents were incorporated into political projects formulated by white creole patriots, and examine how the autonomous political struggles of rural black people helped to shape anticolonial endeavors on the island. The movement of 1844 can therefore offer some important ways to rethink the temporal, geographic, and ethnic boundaries of Cuban and Latin American independence.

But this anticolonial energy was inextricably connected to and derived from the "antislavery epistemology" that linked the politics of Cuban slaves to a larger black oppositional momentum that reverberated across the Atlantic world from the late eighteenth to the mid-nineteenth centuries. The political soil of 1844 was nourished, so to speak, by a long wave of slave rebellions and protests in Cuba dating back to the 1810s. But the two decades leading up to La Escalera also witnessed some of the largest and most organized slave rebellions and conspiracies in the Atlantic world. This resistance, largely inspired by the Haitian Revolution, included the 1822 Denmark Vesey conspiracy in South Carolina, the 1823 rebellion in Demerara (now Guyana), the Antigua slave rebellion of 1831, the Nat Turner rebellion of 1831 in Virginia, the "Christmas rebellions" of 1831–32 in Jamaica, the 1835 Mâle rebellion in Brazil, and the 1843 slave rebellions in Venezuela and Colombia, among others. As other scholars have argued, the regional wave of antislavery protest and liberatory struggle that Cuban slaves joined in 1844 helped to usher in such events as general emancipation in the British Caribbean.

And indeed, by the 1840s Cuba was one of the few remaining slave societies in the region. It is critical to understand, however, that the actions of rural black Cubans paralleled a number of other regional struggles against white hegemonic power in places where slavery or colonialism had already officially ended. For example, the political organization and state violence that Cuban blacks experienced in the 1840s echoed across the British Caribbean in the years leading up to and following La Escalera. Indeed, the violent protests of newly freed people from Antigua to Jamaica offer valuable insight into the experiences of rural black Cubans, as former slaves exposed the myths of free labor and citizenship in the postemancipation world.[4]

The violent responses of 1844 also found parallels in the revolts taking place on the Latin American mainland as peasants, former slaves, and working people confronted the failed promises of independence. While black laborers in Cuba struggled to dismantle the colonial government and demolish slavery, everyday people in postindependence Latin America confronted local and national elites who had begun to restructure local economies, concentrate land and wealth, and exclude African and indigenous people from the new nation-states. Thus, while the 1844 movement must be studied in its particular social context, situating the movement's struggles as one of a larger set of questions being negotiated by laboring people across the Americas, brings the Cuban strategies, tactics, grievances, and decisions into sharper relief. In turn, studying the resistance of rural black Cubans invites new ways to explore a range of nineteenth-century struggles as freed people, indigenous people, indentured laborers, and others faced newly articulated forms of slavery and empire.

This book has used different methodologies and frameworks to understand the way these movements were formed. It has asked what bodies, political visions, and epistemologies come into focus when we expand the insurgent narrative beyond the most familiar group of protagonists—that is, men of color who were privileged, mobile, literate, skilled, or urban-based, and their white male allies. The stories in this book have demanded that we examine how slaves come to see themselves during moments of political rupture, and the untidy ways they are, and are not, incorporated into organized projects of resistance. They have asked us to redirect our focus and our questions to the ways that heterogeneous groups of people fought for freedom and power.

This fact leads us back to eastern Cuba in the 1860s, and the historical memory that Mariana Grajales passed on to her children. For Grajales and others, the struggles that black people had endured in Cuba were situated between, and constituted by, an acutely honed consciousness and vision of black freedom, and the repressive violence of the colonial state. Such was and is the legacy of 1844: the undoing of this movement was indeed bloody and heinous. The most-cited statistics for the 1844 trials include 78 people executed, 328 sentenced to ten years in prison, 652 to eight years in prison, 312 to six months in prison, 435 banished from Cuba permanently, 27 sentenced to work in public service, 14 who received "light" sentences, and 82 absolved completely.[5] While these numbers appear to be accurate, they only encompass the sentences of those brought to Matanzas to be formally tried.

They do not, for example, include the counts of torture by the lash that were ubiquitous on the rural plantations. With the uprisings of the 1840s, brutal whippings became more and more frequent across the rural landscape, and inflicted on more and more people. From the spring of 1843 to the summer of 1844, they reached perhaps an unprecedented height, as hundreds of estates across the region witnessed punishment after punishment for resistance against the slaveholding regime. During the resistance of 1843 and 1844, it was common for anywhere from five to twenty slaves to be accused of subversion, and sometimes upward of thirty, presumably all of whom needed to be whipped. Custom dictated that rebel slaves should receive at least 100 lashes, that black plantation residents from miles around should be summoned to watch the proceedings, and that lacerated backs should be dressed with contaminants like tobacco leaves, urine, and salt. Those who knew the men and women being beaten could do nothing but watch.

The official numbers also do not include the hundreds who were kept in makeshift plantation jails with little light and ventilation for weeks and months; those who died from whippings and other forms of torture; or those forced to wear iron chains and shackles for months and years afterward. Along with the numerous arrests, the heads severed from black bodies and displayed at conspicuous locations, the oft-ignored declarations of innocence, the general bloodbath that almost literally ran in the streets, and the quiet terror of living in the eerily silent aftermath on those plantations, this must have seemed like much more than a thwarted uprising; indeed, it must have seemed more like the coming of Babylon.

Many of these are not casualties that can be numbered and calculated, and we may never know the true extent of the repression in 1844. We do know that these events have been preserved as part of the collective trauma of enslavement that lived on among black Cubans, and indeed all Cubans, surfacing in the 1860s and 1910s, and even in the 1970s in speeches by Fidel Castro. The 1846 census also revealed that the slave population had declined by 109,736 people. Although the Cuban governor tried to explain this drop by the waning of the slave trade, historians have argued that neither such a decline in the trade nor complications with census taking could account for such a loss.[6]

Numerous accounts have suggested or stated outright that the greatest tragedy of 1844 was the persecution of the free class of color, which is to say the destruction of a thriving black bourgeoisie.[7] What was considered most savage about the trials was the torture of free people of color, many of the methods of which — including being tied down to a ladder and beaten — were common punishments for rural slaves. In other words, poets, painters, landowners, and military sergeants were subjected to the same agonies as rural slaves. The overwhelming number of free people who suffered these and other penalties definitely highlights the colonial government's aim to devastate the free population of color; and the torture, imprisonment, and banishment inflicted on free people have only begun to be fully documented.[8] The point is hardly to diminish or disappear this violence against free people of color, but rather to remember that the punishment of enslaved people was made partly invisible by their "escape" of formal imprisonment and execution by the state (rather than by slaveowners). The horrors of 1844 spread their net to encompass all people of color — free and enslaved; black, mulatto, and African; urban and rural; male and female.

The goal of this book, however, has been to tell a story other than one of slave marginalization and state violence. While we must continue to acknowledge the horror that clings to those years, we also need another story to place alongside, if not supersede, that of the state. The overarching lens of repression obscures from our view the hundreds of afrodescendientes who understood what it meant to conspire against the colonial government, yet took that risk anyway. It silences thousands of people of color until a moment of brutal state retaliation. And it grants many black people visibility only as tortured bodies and casualties of history. While most historians have seen the revelations on Oviedo's property as a beginning (of discovery) that quickly became an ending (of repression), this book has looked over the shoulder of that moment to see what came before it in the slave communities of Matanzas. Doing so brings into view a narrative of organizing, mobilization, and planning that was just as strong as the narrative of repression.

The rebel movement of 1844 cannot be remembered solely as a terrorizing movement of the state that intimidated, subdued, and controlled the black populations of Cuba. It must also be remembered as a complex political movement of enslaved and free Cubans of African descent, who planned judiciously for their freedom. Though this insurgency was discovered before its time, it was one of the most significant and widespread movements ever undertaken against Cuba's colonial regime.

Notes

||||||| Abbreviations

AHN   Archivo Histórico Nacional, Madrid

AHPM   Archivo Histórico Provincial de Matanzas, Matanzas, Cuba

ANC   Archivo Nacional de Cuba

BNJM   Biblioteca Nacional José Martí, Special Manuscript Collections,
        Sala Cubana

CM   Comisión Militar Ejecutiva y Permanente

EC   Escoto Collection

f.   folio

GPM   Gobierno Provincial de Matanzas

GSC   Gobierno Superior Civil

HL   Houghton Library, Harvard University, Cambridge, Massachusetts

v.   vuelta

||||||| Introduction

1. See statement of Merced Criolla, ANC, CM, legajo 33/no. 4, f. 8/6v.

2. See ANC, CM 130/10, *Colección de los fallos pronunciados por una sección de la Comisión Militar establecida en la ciudad de Matanzas para conocer de la causa de conspiración de la gente de color*, no. 1a. As Vincent Brown has demonstrated in the context of Jamaican slavery, this public display of bodily mutilation was carefully calibrated to underscore racial and colonial authority in its most spectacular form. Through this heinous display of black death, the colonial state worked to cement its own political and sacred power. See Brown, "Spiritual Terror and Sacred Authority." Also see Brown, *Reaper's Garden*.

3. Among the more central writers from the late nineteenth and early twentieth centuries who believed the conspiracy was largely engineered by the Spanish colonial government were Morales y Morales, *Iniciadores y primeros martires*, 287–92; González del Valle, *Conspiración de La Escalera*, 57–58; and Sanguily, "Una opinión en contra de Plácido," 425–35. Several contemporary North American scholars have either denied the existence of a movement in 1844 or dismissed its importance. See, for example, Knight, *Slave Society in Cuba*; Klein, *Slavery in the Americas*; Thomas,

Cuba; Foner, *History of Cuba*; and Bergad, *Cuban Rural Society*. For a discussion of the wider trajectory of these debates, see Barcia Zequeira and Barcia Paz, "Conspiración de La Escalera."

4. In this study, Paquette reconstructs the most volatile political debates shaping Cuba's public sphere in the mid-nineteenth century, illustrating how a series of interlocking imperial struggles over the slave trade, colonial rule, and annexation created openings for an anticolonial movement to arise in the 1840s. See Paquette, *Sugar Is Made with Blood*.

5. See, for example, Sarracino, *Inglaterra*; Curry-Machado, "How Cuba Burned with the Ghosts of British Slavery"; and Ortega, "Cuban Sugar Complex in the Age of Revolution." Michele Reid-Vazquez is one of the few historians to have written about the aftermath of La Escalera and the critical efforts of free people to recover property, money, and freedom from the colonial state. See Reid-Vazquez, *Year of the Lash*.

6. Nearly a century passed before academic voices presenting other kinds of perspectives about 1844 gained legitimacy and traction. In addition to the works mentioned above, see de Ximeno, "Pobre histrión"; Castellanos, *Plácido, poeta social y político*; Fernández, *Plácido, el poeta conspirador*; García, "Cuba en la obra de Plácido"; García Rodríguez, "A propósito de la Escalera"; and Barcia Paz, *Seeds of Insurrection*.

7. A number of studies have transformed this historical tradition in recent decades, and the present work is deeply indebted to this literature. See Gaspar, *Bondmen and Rebels*; Bush, *Slave Women in Caribbean Society*; García Rodríguez, "A propósito de La Escalera"; García Rodríguez, *Conspiraciones y revueltas*; Fick, *Making of Haiti*; Reis, *Slave Rebellion in Brazil*; Egerton, *Gabriel's Rebellion*; Sidbury, *Ploughshares into Swords*; Childs, *1812 Aponte Rebellion*; Barcia Paz, *Seeds of Insurrection*; and Barcia Paz, *Great African Slave Revolt*. These and other scholars have highlighted what Michael Craton, in *Testing the Chains*, has called the "internal factors" of slave resistance, that is, the local dynamics of slave communities that enabled a focus on black agency. This book departs from much of the existing historiography, namely through privileging an analysis of gender.

8. For this reading, I take inspiration from the work of several scholars, particularly Jennifer Morgan, whose book *Laboring Women* critically examines the ways gender and reproduction became central organizing tropes for New World slavery. In particular, see her chapter on slave women and resistance. I also turn to the work of historian Robin Kelley, particularly the theory of infrapolitics he elaborates in "'We Are Not What We Seem.'" The work of Dayo Gore, Jeanne Theoharis, and Komozi Woodard offers even more of a theoretical scaffolding to theorize the gendered dimensions of slave insurgency. See Gore, Theoharis, and Woodard, *Want to Start a Revolution?*

9. Michael Gomez insightfully examines this relationship in his introduction to *Exchanging Our Country Marks*. Also see Sweet, *Recreating Africa*; and Young, *Rituals of Resistance*.

10. This is particularly important because previous generations of scholars often did not consider the rebellions of the 1830s and 1840s to be part of the same movement as the conspiracy of La Escalera. See, for example, Llanes Miqueli, *Víctimas del año del Cuero*, 1–4.

11. They include Ferrer, *Insurgent Cuba*, and more recently Sanders, *Black Soldier's Story*. The extensive body of work by Louis Pérez Jr. and Lillian Guerra's *Myth of José Martí* offers similarly insightful analyses of the meanings that intellectuals, politicians, and popular classes have vested in Cuba's national identity and anti-imperial legacy, focusing particular attention on the island's vexed relationship to the United States, and its turbulent mythology of racial exceptionalism. See Pérez, *Cuba between Empires*; and Guerra, *Myth of José Martí*.

12. Spivak's famous article "Can the Subaltern Speak?" is considered by many to be central to the establishment of subaltern studies and postcolonial studies.

13. For colonial archives believing in their own reason and rationality, see Stoler, *Along the Archival Grain*. For other critical work on the archive in cultural studies, see Hartman, "Venus in Two Acts"; Stoler, "Colonial Archives and the Arts of Governance"; Derrida, *Archive Fever*; Mbembe, "Power of the Archive and Its Limits"; Burton, *Archive Stories*; and Arondekar, *For the Record*.

14. See, for example, Trouillot, *Silencing the Past*; Jordan, *Tumult and Silence at Second Creek*; Gaspar, *Bondmen and Rebels*; Pearson, *Designs against Charleston*; Johnson, "Denmark Vesey and His Co-conspirators"; Sidbury, *Ploughshares into Swords*; Fick, *Making of Haiti*; Egerton, *Gabriel's Rebellion*; Viotti da Costa, *Crowns of Glory, Tears of Blood*; Childs, *1812 Aponte Rebellion*; and Ferrer, "Speaking of Haiti."

15. For an elegant probing of how the transatlantic slave trade produced an entire regime of knowledge that turned African people into commodities, see Smallwood, *Saltwater Slavery*.

16. The best-known of these claims was laid out by Michael Johnson in "Denmark Vesey and His Co-conspirators." Johnson's criticism of recent writing on the Denmark Vesey conspiracy of 1822, which he argues has been construed to highlight slaves' resistance, reignited a long-standing controversy on the validity of this and other slave conspiracies. Johnson argues that scholars have long ignored the testimonies of slaves claiming innocence in the proceedings. While Johnson's article offered important methodological critiques in the use of trial records, it ends with the deeply disturbing and the historically defective conclusion that the only conspiracy in 1822 was the one historians created against Vesey. Johnson's argument has since been challenged by a number of different authors, including Paquette and Egerton, "Of Facts and Fables"; and Paquette, "From Rebellion to Revisionism."

17. See statement of Gonzalo Gangá, ANC, CM 33/4, f. 106/64v. Also see statement of Ignacio Congo [possibly Gangá], ibid., f. 105/63v.

18. See testimonies in ibid.

19. See, for example, García Rodríguez, "A propósito de La Escalera"; García, *Conspiraciones y revueltas*; Barcia Paz, *Seeds of Insurrection*, 40–48; Barcia Paz, *Resistencia esclava en las plantaciones cubanas*; and Barcia Zequeira and Barcia Paz, "Conspiración de La Escalera."

20. See Paquette, *Sugar Is Made with Blood*; and Sarracino, *Inglaterra*.

21. Although none of the "giants" in the post-1959 field of slave studies in Cuba produced monographs exclusively on La Escalera, they did produce histories of black Cuban political resistance that became critical to the study of the movement. See, for example, Deschamps Chapeaux, *Negro en la economía habanera*; and Franco,

Gesta heroica del Triunvirato. For other Cuban authors who revisited the conspiracy and its ramifications but did not come down definitively on one side or the other, see Fernández, "Plácido y la conspiración de la Escalera"; Llanes Miqueli, *Víctimas del año del Cuero*; Labarre, "Conspiración de 1844"; and Méndez Capote, *Cuatro conspiraciones.* The Cuban archivist Miguel Sabater has also published a significant article on La Escalera, arguing that it took place, with the critical inclusion of primary sources from the Comisión Militar collection. See Sabater, "Conspiración de La Escalera." Gwendolyn Midlo Hall was among the first North American post-1959 historians to seriously engage the existence of a widespread movement in her comparative study of Cuba and Haiti, *Social Control in Slave Plantation Societies.*

22. For much of the nineteenth century, the island of Cuba was divided into three "departments" for colonial administrative purposes: an Eastern department, a Western department, and a Central department. Each department was subdivided into smaller districts and townships.

23. Nonetheless, I believe it is accurate to employ phrases such as "Francisco stated X," but with the intention of recognizing the historical documentation of what transpired in the cited proceedings rather than of conveying the precise and unadulterated words of any one witness.

24. The most scandalous of these was Pedro Salazar, who was reported to have done everything from taking declarations without the presence of an assisting secretary, to ordering arrests without any visible motive, to removing pages containing crucial evidence from the official report. See Morales y Morales, *Iniciadores y primeros martires*, 315–16.

25. Winthrop Jordan advances a similar argument in his reading of the trial examinations from Second Creek, Mississippi. See Jordan, *Tumult and Silence at Second Creek*, 28.

26. This was true at the time of this writing. However, the Cuban historian Manuel Barcia Paz has conducted ongoing research on La Escalera, and the late Gloria García Rodríguez spent years examining these documents.

27. The use of slave and other subaltern testimonies, particularly those elicited under coercion, has produced intense debates within the literature on slavery and slave rebellions. See, among others, Childs, *1812 Aponte Rebellion*; Gaspar, *Bondmen and Rebels*; Jordan, *Tumult and Silence at Second Creek*; and Johnson, "Denmark Vesey and His Co-conspirators." Also see Scarry, *Body in Pain*; and the articles contained in the 2002 special issue of the *William and Mary Quarterly* on the Denmark Vesey conspiracy of 1822.

28. A perfect example of this is the testimony given by Eleuterio Congo in the aftermath of the November 1843 rebellion. See ANC, CM 30/3, f. 27–29/25v–27.

29. Author's conversation with Gloria García Rodríguez, November 12, 2003.

30. David Barry Gaspar has argued as much for the 1736 slave conspiracy in Antigua. See Gaspar, *Bondmen and Rebels*, 9.

31. See ANC, CM 130/10.

32. It is difficult to know what happened to this rather large group of witnesses who remained on the plantations (i.e., ones never taken to urban prisons), though it can be credibly assumed that those whose names surfaced in particularly incriminat-

ing ways were brutally whipped, and possibly subjected to other tortures. It is can be credibly assumed that many of the others who were *not* taken off the plantation were subjected to private forms of punishment. See, for example ANC, CM 33/4, f. 108/66–66v.

33. Gwendolyn Midlo Hall, for example, has analyzed the 1844 event and characterized it as "a far-reaching conspiracy" in *Social Control in Slave Plantation Societies*, 57–62. For other discussions of this theme, see Márquez, "Plácido y los conspiradores de 1844," 35–51; Ortiz, *Negros esclavos*, 390; García, "Cuba en la obra de Plácido," 47. See as well the discussions throughout García Rodríguez, *Conspiraciones y revueltas*; Paquette, *Sugar Is Made with Blood*; Sabater, "Conspiración de La Escalera"; and Sarracino, *Inglaterra*.

|||||||| Chapter One

1. See Moreno Fraginals, *Ingenio*.

2. See, for example, Alexander, *Transatlantic Sketches*, 363–65. Also see Rawson, *Cuba*, 13; and Barinetti, *Voyage to Mexico and Havanna*, 121.

3. See Barcia Paz, "Sugar, Slavery and Bourgeoisie." Also see Portuondo, "Plantation Factories."

4. Restrictions on slave imports were gradually eased from the 1760s on as part of a general Spanish shift to commercial liberalization and administrative reform. From the 1770s to 1790s, the Bourbon Crown passed a series of legislative reforms, the most famous of which was the 1789 *cédula* or royal decree that removed the Crown's monopoly on slave imports. See Knight, *Slave Society in Cuba*, 10–24.

5. See Allahar, *Class, Politics, and Sugar*, 100–104.

6. This phrase is commonly translated as "Sugar is made with blood."

7. For a discussion of folding the labor exerted by, and the violence enacted against, slaves into the price of slave-produced commodities, see Johnson, *Soul by Soul*, chap. 2.

8. This means that Cuba's slave population had risen by more than 115,000 people in the last decade. See "Estado general de la población de la Isla de Cuba en fin de 1841," ANC, Censo, 1841. Using the Havana port books (1794–1811), Manuel Barcia Paz shows that the actual number of slaves in Cuba at this time was "far greater than previously realized," a fact that has strong implications for the figures in the 1841 census. He shows that the clandestine nature of the slave trade makes determining an exact figure of the number of slaves during that period even more difficult. See Barcia Paz, "Sugar, Slavery and Bourgeoisie," 15–52. Also see Ortega, "From Obscurity to Notoriety."

9. These numbers were reported for the districts of Cimarrones and Sabanilla, respectively. For comparable figures in other districts, see Bergad, *Cuban Rural Society*, 32.

10. Manuel Moreno Fraginals has estimated that from 1791 to 1822 Africans constituted 96.15 percent of the slave population on sugar and coffee plantations in Cuba and from 1823 to 1844, 80.95 percent. Although it is likely that these numbers are a bit high, and particular to the rural estates, they nonetheless capture the soaring African population in Cuba during the nineteenth century. See Moreno Fraginals, "Africa in Cuba," 192.

11. For these figures see Eltis and Richardson, "New Assessment of the Transatlantic Slave Trade," 49.

12. See ibid. Also see Eltis and Richardson, *Atlas of the Transatlantic Slave Trade*, 202. In this study I have used the figures contained in the *Atlas*, a publication based on the figures in the database.

13. See Barcia Paz, "Sugar, Slavery and Bourgeoisie," 145–57. Also see Tomich, *Through the Prism of Slavery*.

14. Eltis, *Economic Growth*, 54–55.

15. In a critical study of the Cuban slave market, these three historians show that although the 1817 antislavery treaty initiated a sharp decline in imports until 1823, at that point, the trade began an overall trend of strong increase. Although the overall trend of slave imports to Cuba had been declining steadily since the 1835 slave trade agreement, from 1842 to 1844 slave imports rose sharply. After that, the numbers continued to increase steadily until 1864. See Bergad, Iglesias García, and del Carmen Barcia, *Cuban Slave Market*, 39, 50, and 70.

16. Because the illegal trade was driven mostly by price and availability of slaves, slave ships pulled their cargo from nearly the entire stretch of Africa's western coast, and some from its eastern coast. For these factors, see ibid., 72–75.

17. For example, prior to 1820, the number of people coming from West-Central Africa far superseded the rest, followed by those coming from the Bight of Biafra, and then Sierra Leone. But from 1821—when the first Anglo-Spanish slave trade treaty was to take effect—to 1840, the largest numbers of ships by far came from the Bight of Biafra. From 1841 to 1845, the numbers of slaves from the Bight of Benin superseded the others, followed by Sierra Leone and West-Central Africa. See Grandío Moráguez, "African Origins of Slaves," 183. Also see Miller, "Central Africa," 66.

18. Significant scholarship on the Cuba slave trade was arguably pioneered by José Luciano Franco's groundbreaking work in the 1960s. Since then, scores of other scholars have built on his research. In addition to Grandío Moráguez and Barcia Paz, other scholars who have made critical contributions to this historiography include Manuel Pérez Beato, Nery Gómez Abreu, Manuel Martínez Casanova, María del Carmen Barcia, Fe Iglesias García, Joseph Dorsey, David Eltis, and Laird Bergad. Grandío Moráguez, "African Origins of Slaves," provides an extremely useful discussion of this historiography.

19. Slave trade historians have engaged in rich and voluminous discussions about the accuracy of the database, much of which is contained in Eltis and Richardson, *Extending the Frontiers*. For example, the database allows scholars to trace a *selected number* of ships from the overall trade, namely, those captured by British Antislavery patrols and prosecuted in the mixed courts of Sierra Leone or Havana. This allows scholars to identify trends from ports throughout the Atlantic world and to make other kinds of comparisons in ways previously unheard of, but because of its specific sampling, it must be used with caution. For a discussion of the features of the database, see Eltis and Richardson, "New Assessment of the Transatlantic Slave Trade," 4–10, and other the articles in *Extending the Frontiers*.

Gwendolyn Midlo Hall has observed that the database is noticeably deficient in voyages to Brazil, and subsequent research has added 7,000 voyages, most of them

Portuguese and Brazilian. See Hall, *Slavery and African Ethnicities*, 28–29. For Cuba in particular, Eltis and Richardson estimate that the second version of the database contains nearly all the Spanish slave ventures from 1808 to 1820, although not including Puerto Rico. They concede that their records may be incomplete for the trade's illegal phase, from 1821 to 1867, but are also confident that they have "some good record of almost all landings" on Cuba during this period, especially after 1830. See Eltis and Richardson, "New Assessment of the Transatlantic Slave Trade," 36–37.

20. This is especially true for the illegal period (i.e., after 1821), because slave ships made every effort to arrive undetected.

21. In recent decades, historians have debated questions such as when Africans came to identify with broad ethnolinguistic groupings often presumed to be clear and secure cultural referents, such as "Yoruba" or "Igbo"; whether this process happened on the continent, in the Americas, or somewhere in between; and how accurately slaves' ethnic names represent their true ethnicity. See Miller, "Central Africa"; Lohse, "Slave Trade Nomenclature"; Hall, *Slavery and African Ethnicities*, 38, 49, 51; and Grandío Moráguez, "African Origins of Slaves," 181. Some of the best discussions on this topic can be found in Falola and Childs, *Yoruba Diaspora*. See, for example, Falola and Childs, "Yoruba Diaspora in the Atlantic World," 5; and Eltis, "Diaspora of Yoruba Speakers."

22. These ethnic names often appear in the historiography with a variety of different spellings. In this book, I spell "Kongo" with a *K* when I am referring specifically to the African geopolitical entity known as the Kingdom of Kongo, because many scholars of the region have identified this as closer to its original spelling. When referring to people or cultural institutions in the *Cuban* context, however, I use the spellings "Congo" (for men) and "Conga" (for women). Although I find "Kongo" to be a legitimate spelling, I refer to slaves from the West-Central African region as "Congo," primarily because this is how their nomenclature appears in the archival documents of 1844. It is also common to see the ethnic name "Mandinga" spelled with a *k*, as in "Mandinka," for both men and women. In this book, I use the spelling "Mandinga," because this is how it appears in the archival documents.

23. For a discussion of the many challenges in identifying the veracity of Africans' ethnic origins in the Americas, see Law, *Oyo Empire*, 282; Law, "Ethnicity and the Slave Trade"; Law, "Ethnicities of Enslaved Africans in the Diaspora"; Northrup, "Igbo and Myth Igbo"; Chambers, "Significance of Igbo in the Bight of Biafra Slave Trade"; Lohse, "Slave Trade Nomenclature"; and Lovejoy, "Ethnic Designations of the Slave Trade." Also see Eltis, "Diaspora of Yoruba Speakers," 17–28; Lovejoy, "Yoruba Factor in the Trans-Atlantic Slave Trade," 42; and Soares, "From Gbe to Yoruba," among others in Falola and Childs, *Yoruba Diaspora*.

24. Spanish and French slave traders generally utilized the term *Congo* to mean anyone from West-Central Africa, unlike the British, who used the term *Angolan*. See Hall, *Slavery and African Ethnicities*, 153. Joseph Miller has also conducted extensive research on the use of the term *Congo* among the Portuguese and Brazilian traders. See Miller, "Central Africa," 41.

25. Thus the captives they sent into the Atlantic trade represented a "more random" assemblage than those sent from other regions farther north. By the nine-

teenth century, the states that would have particular importance for the regional slave trade were Loango, Portuguese Kongo, Angola, and Ndongo. See Miller, *Way of Death*, 258–59.

26. For a discussion of the ethnic groups further south usually designated as "Angolan," such as Umbundu speakers and Kimbundu-language speakers, see Miller, "Central Africa," 41. Oscar Grandío Moráguez argues that over time slaving operations at the mouth of the Congo River (and estuaries like Malebo Pool) sent more slaves to Cuba than any other port in the whole of Africa. Other critical ports were situated along the Loango coast, especially Cabinda, and included Loango and Malembo. See Grandío Moráguez, "African Origins of Slaves," 192. According to Joseph Miller, the Angolan ports further south—namely, Ambriz, Luanda, and Benguela—consistently sent the highest numbers of slaves from the Angola region, albeit to ports throughout the Americas. On the changing ports in the West-Central African trade, see Miller, *Way of Death*, 507–8 and 517–18.

27. These included the islands of São Tomé, Príncipe, Bioko, and Bimbia. Slaves exported from the first two islands in particular counted for a significant portion of the Biafran trade.

28. Because Igboland was situated far from the Calabar coast, Igbos were routinely captured for the trade by predatory groups such as the Aro Confederation. The Aro become a nearly indispensable force to the region's export centers. Interestingly, more Igbo women were captured and sold among the Igbos than among any other ethnicity. The debate over Igbo identity has been particularly important for understanding the ethnic makeup of Carabalí slaves in Cuba. David Northrup argues that Africans brought along a range of different cultural practices, languages, and traditions wherever they were taken in the Americas. Echoing the famous argument made by Sidney Mintz and Richard Price in the 1970s, Northrup emphasizes the importance of shifting and reforming African identities in the Diaspora and rejects the argument that people from the Bight of Biafra came with a comprehensive culture. See Northrup, "Igbo and Myth Igbo"; and Mintz and Price, *Birth of African-American Culture*. The work of Douglas Chambers has critically challenged this belief, advancing a now familiar argument that "the transatlantic slave-trade was much more patterned and much less random (and randomizing) than previously had been simply assumed," underscoring the importance of African cultural continuities in the Americas. See Chambers, "Significance of Igbo in the Bight of Biafra Slave Trade," 101. Also see Gomez, *Exchanging Our Country Marks*; Chambers, "'My Own Nation'"; and Hall, *Slavery and African Ethnicities*, 127–29.

29. Though generally outnumbered by those from West-Central Africa and the Calabar coast, slaves arriving from the Bight of Benin numbered 4,532 between 1841 and 1845. During this four-year period, Bight of Benin captives were more than three times more numerous than those of any other group, but only during this period. See Grandío Moráguez, "African Origins of Slaves," 184. For an additional analysis of the periods with high numbers of Lucumís, see Bergad, Iglesias García, and del Carmen Barcia, *Cuban Slave Market*, 72–75.

30. On Lagos and Ouidah being responsible for 90 percent of all the captives from the Slave Coast, see Eltis, "Diaspora of Yoruba Speakers," 25.

31. In addition to the Fulani-led jihad and the rise of the Sokoto Caliphate, Oyo's disintegration was precipitated by the succession of Ilorin province, a wave of battles over the throne, and the independence wars of Dahomey, all of which contributed mightily to the spike in Bight of Benin slaves. The most definitive studies of the Oyo Empire—by a Western scholar—have been conducted by Robin Law. See esp. Law, *Oyo Empire*. For an excellent discussion of these dynamics, see Ojo, "From 'Constitutional' and 'Northern' Factors."

32. Recent research suggests that approximately 63 percent of those who embarked from Benin ports identified as Yorubas, but there is a significant debate about when and how the multiethnic "Yorubas" came to view themselves as a distinctive group. See López-Valdés, "Notas para el studio etno-histórico de los esclavos lucumí de Cuba"; Grandío Moráguez, "African Origins of Slaves," 20; Eltis, *Economic Growth*, 169; Law, "Ethnicity and the Slave Trade"; Lovejoy, "Yoruba Factor in the Trans-Atlantic Slave Trade," 42; Reid-Vazquez, "Yoruba in Cuba"; Reis and Mamigonian, "Nagô and Mina"; and Eltis, "Diaspora of Yoruba Speakers," 17–28.

33. See Hall, *Slavery and African Ethnicities*, 112–14, 120–21; and Eltis, "Diaspora of Yoruba Speakers," 45. These linguistic/cultural groups are so closely related that they are often described by historians as the Ewe-Fons, the Aja-Fons, or the Ewe-Aja-Fons. Also see Bay, *Wives of the Leopard*.

34. Fernando Ortiz postulated that the Minas were taken from the Gold Coast regions controlled by the Asante Empire, and Hall showed that some were indeed taken from the Volta River region that eventually became part of Asante territory. See Ortíz, *Los Negros Esclavos*, 53; and Hall, *Slavery and African Ethnicities*, 113. However, while the number of Cuban slave arrivals from the Gold Coast counted for 21.8 percent at the turn of the nineteenth century, with few exceptions, the Gold Coast numbers were very low after 1806. If an appreciable number of the Minas were taken from the Windward Coast, this would mean that some of their homelands extended even further west into present-day Côte d'Ivoire and Liberia. For a discussion of Windward Coast versus Gold Coast slaves, see Grandío Moráguez, "African Origins of Slaves," 184.

35. The Arará were taken in large numbers to Saint-Domingue and later in smaller numbers to Cuba. The term *Arará* derives from the name of the town of Allada, believed to be the capital of the Aja people before their lands were incorporated into the Dahomey Empire.

36. In *Slave Traffic*, Dorsey demonstrates that this region remained central to the slave trades in Cuba and Puerto Rico during this period, Anglo-Spanish treaties to the contrary notwithstanding.

37. In fact, Barry contends that the entire region from Senegambia to Sierra Leone should be seen collectively as "Greater Senegambia," and historically the Senegambia region has encompassed a range of different ethnic groups. See Barry, *Sénégambie du XVe au XIXe siècle; and* Rodney, *History of the Upper Guinea Coast*. Also see Gomez, *Exchanging Our Country Marks*, 45–48.

38. See Eltis and Richardson, *Atlas of the Transatlantic Slave Trade*, 194 and 306. An older generation of scholarship pioneered by people like Fernando Ortíz believed the Gangás to have originated from the Kongo-Angola region. See, for example,

Ortiz, *Negros esclavos*, 28. This was in part because Britain's intense patrolling of the Sierra Leonean coast suggested it was unlikely that such high numbers would have been taken from there, and in part because the name *Gangá* is quite similar to the term for one of the sacred implements of Congolese theological practice, the *nganga*. More recently, however, scholars have definitively shown this presumption to be incorrect. See Hall, *Slavery and African Ethnicities*, 35; and Grandío Moráguez, "African Origins of Slaves," 185. My conversations with Joseph Dorsey were most instructive on this subject.

39. Gallinas was one of the three most important ports in the slave trade to Cuba. This was especially the case from 1821 to 1840, when Cuban-based traders established factories there. See Dorsey, *Slave Traffic*, 160–61; and Grandío Moráguez, "African Origins of Slaves," 189.

40. It is difficult, however, to distinguish exactly which regions of the Cuban trade the Mandinga speakers represented. For example, Senegambia as a region counted for approximately 4 percent of the trade from 1790 to 1840, far less than other regions, but these captives must surely have included some of the Mandinga. For discussion of slave trading along the Upper Guinea Coast, see Dorsey, *Slave Traffic*, 157–67.

41. For Philip Misevich's substantial research on this topic, see Misevich, "Origins of Slaves Leaving the Upper Guinea Coast," 165–70. Also see Eltis and Richardson, *Atlas of the Transatlantic Slave Trade*, 194.

42. While the importation of Muslim slaves was forbidden in the early days of the Spanish Empire, by the nineteenth century this ban was rarely if ever respected. At present it is entirely unclear how many Muslims ended up in Cuba. See Lovejoy, "Yoruba Factor in the Trans-Atlantic Slave Trade," 51; and Gomez, *Exchanging Our Country Marks*, 62–65. For a contrasting experience in Brazil, which had a more identifiable Muslim population, see Reis, *Slave Rebellion in Brazil*.

43. From 1836 to 1840, Grandío Moráguez shows that the Macúas were more numerous than any other group brought to Cuba, at 11,054 arrivals. This fact seems astonishing given how little has been written about the Macúas in Cuba, clearly indicating an area for more research. See Grandío Moráguez, "African Origins of Slaves," 193.

44. See Eltis and Richardson, *Atlas of the Transatlantic Slave Trade*, 154–55. A more detailed analysis of Macúa origins and the Mozambique slave trade awaits further research.

45. See O'Hear, "Enslavement of Yoruba," 57–61; and Ojo, "From 'Constitutional' and 'Northern' Factors," 237. Although scholars have challenged the assumption that most conflicts erupted explicitly to obtain captives for sale, there is still a clear and undeniable link between the expansion of African military campaigns during the first half of the nineteenth century and the flourishing of the transatlantic slave trade.

46. See Smallwood's delineation of this phenomenon starting in the seventeenth century and focusing on the Gold Coast, *Saltwater Slavery*, 20–23.

47. See Ojo, "From 'Constitutional' and 'Northern' Factors," 235–37 and 239–41.

48. See Smallwood, *Saltwater Slavery*, 30; Thornton, *Africa and Africans*; and Miller, *Way of Death*, 507–8.

49. For a detailed description of these experiences in seventeenth-century British trading forts, see Smallwood, *Saltwater Slavery*, 36–52.

50. For a discussion of this phenomenon during the early nineteenth century, see Ortega, "From Obscurity to Notoriety," 298.

51. From the forty-seven ships it tracked to the Spanish Caribbean, the database researchers estimate that an average Atlantic crossing took 50.9 days during the period from 1831 to 1864. See Eltis and Richardson, *Atlas of the Transatlantic Slave Trade*, 181.

52. From the same ships documented above, the database shows a 17.9 percent mortality rate for slavers arriving in the Spanish Caribbean between 1831 and 1864. Many of these slaves committed suicide. See ibid. Also see Eltis, *Economic Growth*, 273.

53. For a breakdown of the slave-ship percentages by gender, see Eltis and Richardson, *Atlas*, 162.

54. For a discussion of these experiences in the seventeenth- and eighteenth-century British slave ship, see Smallwood, *Saltwater Slavery*, 120–21. Smallwood describes the intimate way African captives were thrown together with complete strangers as a form of "anomalous intimacy" (101).

55. For more on the *kalunga* in the transatlantic context, see Desch-Obi, "Combat and the Crossing of the *Kalunga*." Also see Desch-Obi, *Fighting for Honor*, 4.

56. See Brown, *Santería Enthroned*.

57. The Slave Trade Database has documented 483 slave-ship voyages that left from the major slaving regions in Africa between 1566 and 1865 that experienced some form of slave resistance. While most of these rebellions took place along the African coast, 22.5 percent of them happened at sea. See Eltis and Richardson, *Atlas of the Transatlantic Slave Trade*, 189–90.

58. See Tinsley, "Black Atlantic, Queer Atlantic," 199.

59. See Barcia Zequeira, *Otra familia*, 56; and Roberts, "Yoruba Family, Gender, and Kinship Roles," 249.

60. For descriptions of this "seasoning" or cultural reorientation process in other parts of the Atlantic world, see Gomez, *Exchanging Our Country Marks*, 155–86; and Eltis, "Diaspora of Yoruba Speakers," 33.

61. This is a line from the poem "The Sugar Estate," by Juan Francisco Manzano; see especially canto II. See Manzano, *Poems by a Slave in the Island of Cuba*.

62. For similar shifts during the British consolidation of Antigua and Demerara (present-day Guyana), see Gaspar, *Bondmen and Rebels*, 188; and Viotta da Costa, *Crowns of Glory, Tears of Blood*, 39–40 and 46–57.

63. In 1841 slaves made up 90 percent of the population of Guamacaro, 70 percent of the population of Macuriges, 76 percent of the population of Sabanilla, and 75 percent of the population of Cimarrones. For these figures, see Bergad, *Cuban Rural Society*, 68.

64. The available figures for the period are conflicting. For the figures cited in the text, see AHPM, GPM: Colonia, Negociado de Estadística, Exp. 13012, 1862. Laird Bergad cites the existence of 344 mills by 1841 in Bergad, *Cuban Rural Society*, 32. Documents in the Cuban National Archive list at least 393 mills throughout the

western department, which includes Havana and Matanzas, by 1841. See "Resumen del Censo de la Población de la Isla de Cuba a fines del año 1841 (impreso) formado de orden del Ex Sr Capn General de la misma . . . Habana 1842" (Donativos: 1842, número de orden. 120, caja: 84, contenido: Censo de Población 1841).

65. See Klein, *African Slavery in Latin America*, 92–102; and Bergad, *Cuban Rural Society*, 169.

66. For this assessment, see Klein, *African Slavery in Latin America*, 92–102 and esp. 93. For the statistical figures of Cuban sugar production, see Moreno Fraginals, *Ingenio*, 2:108 and 3:35–36; esp. appendix 1, "Series estadísticas fundamentales." Also see Ely, *Cuando reinaba su majestad el azúcar*.

67. See Dana, *To Cuba and Back*, 170.

68. Much has been written about the railroad's impact on the expansion of Cuban sugar. The definitive study of the Cuban railroad's history is Zanetti Lecuona and García Álvarez, *Caminos para el azúcar*. Also see Zanetti Lecuona and García Álvarez, *Sugar and Railroads*; Bergad, *Cuban Rural Society*, 108–12; and Allahar, *Class, Politics, and Sugar*, 105–7.

69. There are various theories on the exact period of decline in coffee production in western Cuba, but most assessments concur that this decline began after the 1830s. Moreno Fraginals has estimated that as many as 50,000 slaves on coffee plantations were incorporated into sugar plantation regimes after 1845. See Moreno Fraginals, *Ingenio*, 2:88. Also see Bergad, Iglesias García, and del Carmen Barcia, *Cuban Slave Market*, 29–30. Although coffee was often perceived to be in decline during this period, coffee cultivation actually increased from the 1820s to the 1840s. However, coffee growth was more heavily concentrated in a few districts. For an extensive discussion of this shift, in which sugar's reign was "not inevitable," see Van Norman, *Shade-Grown Slavery*, which constitutes the most detailed English-language study of the plantation coffee economy.

70. See Eltis, *Economic Growth*, 284–85.

71. Chatterjee, *Time for Tea*, 170.

72. See Montejo, *Biography of a Runaway Slave*, 40–41.

73. For a discussion of plantation soundscapes in the U.S. South, see Jordan, *Tumult and Silence at Second Creek*, 20–23.

74. On the passing of the harvest and the coming of the *tiempo muerto*, see Moreno Fraginals, *Ingenio*, 2:37; and Ortiz, *Negros esclavos*, 181.

75. See Bremer, *Homes of the New World*, 323. Daina Ramey Berry elegantly reconsiders the concept of skilled work in Berry, "Swing the Sickle."

76. See Suárez y Romero, *Colección de artículos*, 288 and 280; Dana, *To Cuba and Back*, 112; and Ballou, *History of Cuba*, 146. On more prosperous estates, the mill might only stop for a few hours a week.

77. See Dana, *To Cuba and Back*, 127–28. For detailed accounts of this procedure, see *Cartilla practica del manejo*; and Moreno Fraginals, *Ingenio*.

78. Jonathan Curry-Machado explores the world of these migrant engineers, whose presence reflected Cuba's increasing immersion in the transnational circuits of capital in the nineteenth century. He argues that they became scapegoats in the trials of 1844, and indeed more than a few testimonies accused "English engineers."

However, these references are frequent enough to suggest that some of them may have actually been involved in some way. This is a point that warrants further research. See Curry-Machado, *Cuban Sugar Industry*, 1–22, 49–71, 175–93.

79. See Philalethes, *Yankee Travels*, 27; and Madden, *Island of Cuba*, 132.

80. See Valdés, *Bando de gobernación y policía de la isla de Cuba*.

81. See Madden, *Island of Cuba*, 132.

82. See Van Norman, *Shade-Grown Slavery*, 44–51.

83. For an excellent discussion of Arango's travels and his push for technological change in Cuban sugar mills, see Portuondo, "Plantation Factories." Ada Ferrer argues that the fall of Saint-Domingue and the rise of Cuba's sugar industry were highly interdependent and mutually constitutive processes. Among other things, the Haitian Revolution facilitated a massive transfer of people, knowledge, and equipment from Saint-Domingue to Cuba. See Ferrer, "Cuban Slavery and Atlantic Antislavery," 137–46.

84. See Madden, *Island of Cuba*, 84. For a detailed discussion of the progressive installation of steam engines on Cuban sugar plantations, see Ely, *Cuando reinaba su majestad el azúcar*, 505–24.

85. See Aimes, *History of Slavery in Cuba*, 158; and Moreno Fraginals, *Ingenio*, 2:35.

86. In her pioneering study of slave emancipation in Cuba, Scott countered Moreno Fraginals's long-standing argument about the correlation between the increased mechanization of sugar and the decreased dependence on slave labor. Scott argued that on the contrary, the intensity of slavery on Cuban plantations often *increased* with heightened technological capabilities. See Scott, *Slave Emancipation in Cuba*, 89. Also see Cepero Bonilla, *Azúcar y abolición*; and Bergad, Iglesias García, and del Carmen Barcia, *Cuban Slave Market*, 28 and 58.

87. See Moreno Fraginals, "Africa in Cuba," 194–96.

88. Gwendolyn Midlo Hall demonstrates the enormously escalating mortality level of the period in *Social Control in Slave Plantation Societies*, 15–16. Also see Moreno Fraginals, *Ingenio*, 2:88; and Allahar, *Class, Politics, and Sugar*, 107.

89. See Humboldt, *Island of Cuba*, 227–28.

90. Many documents only mention these women during times of rebellion, when they were targeted with white people on the estate.

91. Thavolia Glymph's recent study of plantation households in the U.S. South powerfully underscores the systematic violence that white plantation mistresses engaged in. See Glymph, *Out of the House of Bondage*.

92. See Ely, *Cuando reinaba su majestad el azúcar*, 461–63.

93. See Madden, *Island of Cuba*, 125.

94. See, for example, Johnson, "'You Should Give Them Blacks to Eat.'"

95. See Montejo, *Biography of a Runaway Slave*, 44.

96. Ibid., 47.

97. See García Rodríguez, *Esclavitud desde la esclavitud*, 157–59.

98. See Bremer, *Homes of the New World*, 325.

99. See, for example, Alexander, *Transatlantic Sketches*, 372. Also see Barcia Zequeira, *Otra familia*, 51–55. These legal provisions were an inheritance of the old *Siete Partidas* legal tradition from thirteenth-century Spain. They included the

ability to bring charges against a harsh master, change owners, issue complaints about inadequate food or clothing, and purchase one's freedom. In the 1940s Frank Tannenbaum argued that the existence of these rights proved that slavery in the Spanish Americas was more benign than that of other regions, such North America. However, this thesis has since been widely critiqued.

100. See Dana, *To Cuba and Back*, 134. Planters like Esteban Santa Cruz de Oviedo became notorious for their routine sexual abuse of black slave women. Marta Rojas discusses this extensively in her book *Harén de Oviedo*.

101. See Finch, "Scandalous Scarcities."

102. Moreover, William Van Norman has argued that the most visible sign of "closer gender parity on cafetales was the construction of family units." See Van Norman, *Shade-Grown Slavery*, 59.

103. See Humboldt, *Island of Cuba*, 212.

104. See ibid., 215.

105. Most studies of the rural Cuban peasantry address rural smallholders as a group but do not treat the particular experience of free black rural communities in any detail. By contrast, studies of the island's free black populations usually focus on the urban areas, especially Havana, Matanzas, and Santiago de Cuba.

106. Tens and arguably hundreds of marriages between African-descended Cuban crossed lines of slavery and freedom in the mid-nineteenth century.

107. It is very likely that free women of color were business and property owners, given the trends in the capital, but it is extremely difficult to get a clear picture of their livelihoods from these records. To date, I have found no study of free black women in the rural plantation zones of Cuba.

108. See Philalethes, *Yankee Travels*, 33.

109. During the first half of the nineteenth century, black residents in the urban centers ran up against ever-increasing social barriers, and racial discrimination became more deeply inscribed in custom and law. See Paquette, *Sugar Is Made with Blood*, 109 and 118–19. Also see Schmidt-Nowara, *Empire and Antislavery*, 23; and Childs, *Aponte Rebellion*, 68–77.

110. This moment in which urban free people of color reached their ascendancy also produced the greatest hardening of racial lines in Cuba. For more on this, see Childs, *Aponte Rebellion*, chap. 2; Paquette, *Sugar Is Made with Blood*, chap. 4; Deschamps Chapeaux, *Negro en la economía habanera*, 1–57; and Llanes Miqueli, *Víctimas del año del Cuero*, 1–4.

111. See statements of José Francisco Matamoros, ANC, CM 39/1, f. 109v–110v; and Cristobal Agramonte, ANC, CM 33/4, f. 277.

112. See statement of Mariano Fuentes Congo, ANC, CM 33/4, f. 97/57.

113. See Reid-Vazquez's insightful discussion of Cuba's free people of color, and free women of color especially, in *Year of the Lash*, 17–41.

114. While white artisans persisted in their crafts throughout the colonial period, people of color nevertheless became *the* skilled labor force of Cuba's cities by the late eighteenth century; white immigrants increasingly distanced themselves from manual labor. See Deschamps Chapeaux, *Negro en la economía habanera*; 15–17; and Klein, *Slavery in the Americas*, 144 and 163.

115. For a detailed discussion of the black militia in colonial Cuba and the path to social ascent that it offered black men, see Deschamps Chapeaux, *Negro en la economía habanera*, 59–86; Childs, *Aponte Rebellion*, 78–94; and Reid-Vazquez, *Year of the Lash*, 117–45.

116. These racial categories were often qualified in church and state documents by such caveats as the shape of the nose, the presence of a beard, and most especially the texture of one's hair. See, for example, Martinez-Alier, *Marriage, Class and Colour*.

117. This is evidenced by the scores of *gente de color* who fought legally and socially to be recognized as white.

118. See Pappademos, *Black Political Activism and the Cuban Republic*, chap. 1.

119. For one of the few English-language studies of urban women of color, see Mena, "Stretching the Limits of Gendered Spaces."

120. The Aponte movement of 1812 only strengthened this conviction and brought visions of Saint-Domingue readily to mind. See Foner, *History of Cuba*, 106 and 177.

121. See, for example, Klein, *Slavery in the Americas*, 219.

122. See Schmidt-Nowara, *Empire and Antislavery*, 15; and Foner, *History of Cuba*, 120–21.

123. See communication from Gerónimo Valdés, August 4, 1843, in HL, EC, MS Span 52/844, no. 2. For an extensive discussion about the importance of the Escoto Collection, see Dorsey and Paquette, "Escoto Papers and Cuban Slave Resistance."

124. Tacón's preference for peninsular Spaniards was well-known, and white (and of course black) creoles were consistently barred from the upper echelons of the colonial bureaucracy.

125. For a discussion of these abuses, see Navarro, *Entre esclavos y constituciones*, 31–39; Martínez-Fernández, *Torn between Empires*, 60–61; Allahar, *Class, Politics, and Sugar*, 97–98; and Wurdemann, *Notes on Cuba*, 251–52.

126. See Martínez-Fernández, *Torn between Empires*, 63; Corwin, *Spain and the Abolition of Slavery*, 55–59; and Navarro, *Entre esclavos y constituciones*, 26–33. Both Saco and del Monte are considered to be among Cuba's earliest prominent nationalists, and both ended up living in exile. See Schmidt-Nowara, *Empire and Antislavery*, 18–21.

127. See Madden, *Island of Cuba*, 55–56.

128. The best and most complete study of the Aponte movement is Childs, *1812 Aponte Rebellion*. Childs skillfully illustrates how enslaved and free people of color utilized the ideological tools and openings provided by the Age of Revolution in the Atlantic world to organize a vast rebel movement in 1812—at precisely the moment that Cuban slavery had begun its most significant phase of expansion. Also see José Luciano Franco's pioneering study, *Conspiración de Aponte*.

129. See García Rodríguez, *Conspiraciones y revueltas*, 76–77, 93. Also see Schmidt-Nowara, *Empire and Antislavery*, 22.

130. See Deschamps Chapeaux, *Negro en la economía habanera*, 21–23; García Rodríguez, *Conspiraciones y revueltas*, 104–8; and Barcia Paz, *Seeds of Insurrection*.

131. See Deschamps Chapeaux, *Negro en la economía habanera*, 19.

132. On the 1825 rebellion, see García Rodríguez, *Conspiraciones y revueltas*, 83–86; García Rodríguez, *Esclavitud desde la esclavitud*; García Rodríguez, *Voices of the En-*

slaved, 171–76; Barcia Paz, *Great African Slave Revolt*. On the 1843 rebellions, see files in the ANC 29/5, 30/3, and 30/4. Also see Franco, *Gesta heroica del Triunvirato*; Franco, "Origen y consecuencias de la sublevación de los esclavos en Matanzas en 1843"; and García Rodríguez, *Conspiraciones y revueltas*, 127–29.

133. See Barcia Paz, *Great African Slave Revolt of 1825*, esp. 120–47. Also see Barcia Paz, *Seeds of Insurrection*, 35; Entralgo, *Liberación étnica cubana*, 19; García Rodríguez, *Conspiraciones y revueltas*, 87–92.

134. For more on the significance of Cuba's slave economy expansion at the height of the British abolitionist movement, see Ferrer, "Cuban Slavery and Atlantic Antislavery," 147–54.

135. The 1817 Treaty of Madrid, officially promulgated in October 1820, constituted the first major attempt to control this trade. The proceedings of cases during the 1820s and 1830s document the high number of illegal traders apprehended off the coasts of Africa and Cuba. See AHN, Estado 8020/23 and 8022/8. Four of the best discussions of these treaties can be found in Aimes, *History of Slavery in Cuba*, 125–28; Murray, *Odious Commerce*, 50–71; Corwin, *Spain and the Abolition of Slavery*, 60–64; and Schmidt-Nowara, *Slavery, Freedom, and Abolition*, 128–37.

136. For locations where slave landings were reported during the early 1840s, see AHN, Estado 8037/39.

137. See, for example, AHN, Estado 8038/4.

138. See Ballou, *History of Cuba*, 189.

139. See documents in AHN, Estado 8038/10, and in ANC, Reales Ordenes y Cédulas. Also see correspondence from the Spanish Minister of State, September 3, 1842, London, AHN, Estado 8038/3.

140. See, for example, the suspicions surrounding the visit of British statesman Lord Morpeth to Cuba in AHN, Estado 8022 and 8057/54. Warnings to maintain close vigilance of Englishmen traveling through the Matanzas countryside continued into 1844. See, for example, O'Donnell's message to the governor of Matanzas in AHPM, GPM, 8/3.

141. Turnbull's previous work investigating illegal slaving with the Mixed Commission and his 1840 publication of *Travels in the West* helped to launch him into the abolitionist limelight. For more details on Turnbull's rise to power, see Paquette, *Sugar Is Made with Blood*, 131–57; Corwin, *Spain and the Abolition of Slavery*, chaps. 2–3; and Schmidt-Nowara, *Empire and Antislavery*, 46.

142. For examples of letters that Turnbull wrote on behalf of Africans who should have been manumitted, see Letter from David Turnbull to Her Majesty's Commissioners, Dahrymple and Kennedy, Havana, April 9, 1842, in AHN, Estado 8038/4. The archives in Madrid contain a wealth of information on Turnbull's other legal actions against slavery. See, for example, his request for the liberation of all slaves born in "English territory," in AHN, Estado 8038/22, and other documents in ibid., 8038/1. Also see Curry-Machado, "How Cuba Burned with the Ghosts of British Slavery." For an excellent study of liberated Africans in the British Caribbean, especially the Bahamas and Trinidad, during the nineteenth century, see Adderley, "New Negroes from Africa."

143. For examples of pleas to remove Turnbull from office, see AHN, Estado

8053/1. Also see Sarracino, *Inglaterra*, 43–44. For additional letters and communiqués documenting Turnbull's scandalous activities, see "Correspondencia acerca de David Turnbull," BNJM, esp. nos. 3, 6, 7, 12, and 14.

144. The Asuntos Políticos and Gobierno Superior Civil collections in Cuba and the Estado collection in Spain are replete with documentation of this deeply entrenched conflict.

||||||| Chapter Two

1. See Camp, *Closer to Freedom*, 12.
2. See ibid., 7.
3. See Glissant, *Caribbean Discourse*, 11; and McKittrick, *Demonic Grounds*, xxi–xxiii.
4. For a discussion of enslaved people's "rival geographies" in the U.S. South, see Camp, *Closer to Freedom*.
5. See ibid., 6–7 and 12.
6. See García Rodríguez, *Esclavitud desde la esclavitud*, 36–37.
7. See statement of José Carabalí, ANC, CM 33/4, f. 89–90/49v–50. Also see statement of Andrés Mina, ibid., f. 23v–24.
8. See statement of Felipe Carabalí, ANC, CM 39/1, f. 182. Also see statement of Ramón Carabalí, who corroborates this claim; ibid., 256 and 265v–266.
9. See, for example, statement of Juan Candela Congo, ANC, CM 32/2, f. 211–13.
10. For a description of the latter see Philalethes, *Yankee Travels*, 56.
11. Frequent references appear in the documentary record to a slave who stayed overnight here, or stopped there, without further explanation. For the reports about José, see ANC, CM, 42/1, f. 5v–8v.
12. See, for example, statement of Ana Carabalí, ANC, CM 33/4.
13. See statements of Antonio Arará, Pío Criollo, José Criollo, and others, ANC, CM 32/2, f. 61–66/59v–64v.
14. See statement of Toribio Criollo, ibid., f. 113v–114/111–112v.
15. For examples, see statement of Tomás Lucumí, slave of Manuel Almagro, ANC, CM 33/4, f. 87/67. Also see ibid., f. 76/36–36v. Also see statement of Luis Gangá, ibid., f. 125 and 141v–142.
16. Egerton uses this term to capture the experiences of Gabriel Prosser, who organized a Virginia slave conspiracy in 1800. See Egerton, *Gabriel's Rebellion*, 25.
17. See, for example, Montejo, *Biography of a Runaway Slave*, 32; Bremer, *Homes of the New World*, 347–49; and Ballou, *History of Cuba*, 194.
18. See, for example, statements of Jacobo Gangá (a) Coba, ANC, CM 31/9, f. v–9v; Marcos Criollo and Desiderio Criollo, ibid., f. 13v–16, among others.
19. See the statement of Julio Criollo, ANC, 31/9, 149v–152v.
20. For more on Miguel's activities, see statement of Diego Lucumí, ibid., f. 103v–104; Pablo Lucumí, ANC, CM 39/1, f. 103–103v.
21. See statement of Pablo Lucumí, ibid. Miguel stated, however, that he had only recruited Pablo and Diego, not any "outside blacks." See ibid., ANC, CM 39/1, f. 104–105v.

22. For these accounts see statement of Catalino Campuzano, ANC, CM 32/3, f. 5/3v–6/4v; Jacinto Lucumí, ibid., f. 56/54–54v.

23. Jacinto went on to say that as a slave, he could not take part in such a plot. For this account, see declaration of Jacinto Lucumí, ibid.

24. For the account of Margarito and Catalino coming to their estates, inciting them to rebel, and selling "witchcraft," see the declarations of Clemencio Criollo, Pablo Lucumí, Camito Gangá, Leon Gangá, Tomás Criollo, and Aniseto Congo, CM 31/9.

25. See, for example, statement of Gonzalo Gangá, ANC, CM 33/4, f. 106/64v.

26. For this account see statement of Marcelino Criollo, ANC, CM 32/3, f. 76–77/74v–75v.

27. See, for example, statement of Silvestre Criollo, ibid., f. 79/77.

28. For frequent attendees from the rural plantations, see the statements taken from Domech's estate, ANC, CM 41/2.

29. Free people of color moving about the countryside were expected to have legal passes signed by the local district captains. Therefore, their presence at Buena Esperanza was presumably just as illegal as that of the slaves.

30. See Cantero, *Ingenios*.

31. One *caballería* equaled roughly three acres.

32. See McKittrick and Woods, *Black Geographies*, 4.

33. See McKittrick, *Demonic Grounds*, xvii–xix.

34. For an important discussion of this phenomenon in the U.S. South, especially the Carolina Lowcountry, see Brown, "'Walk in the Feenda,'" 289–318.

35. See statement of Justo Criollo, ANC, CM, f. 99–101/97v–99v.

36. For the encounters between Dimas and José Santos Criollo, see ANC, CM 34/1; for those involving Patricio Gangá, see CM 33/4.

37. I am grateful to Natasha Lightfoot for helping me think through this point.

38. See, for example, statement of Rafael Gangá, ANC, CM 31/9, f. 40v–41v.

39. See Finch, "Scandalous Scarcities."

40. See statement of Manuel Congo, ANC, CM 33/4, f. 101–2/59v–60; Adán Congo, ibid., f. 102/60v.

41. See, for example, statement of Francisco Criollo, ANC, CM 32/3, f. 133/31v.

42. See Abbot, *Letters Written in the Interior of Cuba*.

43. For this assessment, see Dana, *To Cuba and Back*, 159.

44. This is corroborated by the memories of Esteban Montejo in *Biography of a Runaway Slave*, 25.

45. For other stories describing black estate guards who allowed people to enter the grounds when they were forbidden to do so, see García Rodríguez, *Esclavitud desde la esclavitud*, 158. Also see ibid., 26–27.

46. See Dana, *To Cuba and Back*, 155.

47. See AHPM, Sublevaciones, 7/32, "Comunicación al Gobernador de Matanzas sobre varias acciones cometidas por una cuadrilla de negros cimarrones," Limonar, November 14, 1843.

48. See AHPM, Sublevaciones, 7/33, "Borrador de comunicación al Comandante de Armas de Guamacaro sobre medidas para exterminar la partida de José Dolores, capitán de cimarrones," November 16, 1843.

49. See Sánchez, "José Dolores, capitán de cimarrones."

50. See Barcia Paz, *Seeds of Insurrection*, 70. Also see AHPM, Sublevaciones, 7/31, "Comunicaciones al gobernador de Matanzas sobre captura del negro Pablo (a) Verdugo . . . que pertenece a la cuadrilla de José Dolores," October 21, 1843.

51. See AHPM, Sublevaciones, 7/33, "Borrador de comunicación al Comandante de Armas de Guamacaro."

52. See Benito García to Captain General Gerónimo Valdés, May 12, 1843. Also see Carlos Gheri to Benito García y Santos, Macuriges, June 5, 1843, ANC, GSC, 942/33246.

53. The wealthy landowner José Montalvo y Castillo outright refused to do so. See Montalvo to Captain General Valdés, August 15, 1843, in García Rodríguez, *Esclavitud desde la esclavitud*, 35.

54. For an excellent illustration of this resistance, see García Rodríguez, *Esclavitud desde la esclavitud*, 19.

55. See, for example, ANC, GSC, 942/33246.

56. Herbert Klein has written about this in *Slavery in the Americas*, 155. Also see Egerton, *Gabriel's Rebellion*, 16–17.

57. See ANC, GSC 943/33281.

58. See Pedro de los Peña Julio to the Capitan General of the Island, July 24, 1844, ANC, GSC 943/33274.

59. For instance, Esteban Montejo recalled that he "used to see them [free men] in the woods searching for herbs and guinea pigs." See *Biography of a Runaway Slave*, 48.

60. For examples see statements of Mamerto Arará, ANC, CM 42/1, f. 10v–12v; Marcos Lucumí, ibid., f. 12v–15v.

61. See statement of Vicente Pipa Criollo, ANC, CM 42/1, 5v–8v.

62. Baltasar also denied that any meetings took place at his house. See statement of Baltasar Veytra [Lucumí], ibid., f. 16–17.

63. See statements of Panfilo Criollo, ANC, CM 42/1, f. 18v–19; and Francisco Criollo, ibid., f. 5v–8v.

64. See communication from the Governor of Matanzas, November 18, 1844, in HL, EC, MS Span 52/716, no. 4.

65. Gloria García Rodríguez discusses these fluid boundaries in *Esclavitud desde la esclavitud*, 15. Also see Bremer, *Homes of the New World*, 351; and Philalethes, *Yankee Travels*, 156.

66. See statement of Ignacio Congo, ANC, CM 33/4.

67. See statement of Diego Criollo, ANC, CM 42/1, f. 111v. Other examples abound in the testimony.

68. See Cantero, *Ingenios*.

69. See statement of Antonio Carabalí, ANC, CM 33/4, f. 157–157v.

70. All three men denied being part of a conspiratorial movement, however. See statements of José Gangá, ibid., f. 165; and Domingo Criollo, ibid., f. 165v.

71. See statements of León Mozambique, CM 33/4, f. 178–178v; Eduardo Criollo, ibid., f. 128–128v; and José Criollo, ibid., f. 17v–18.

72. See statements of Calisto Carabalí, ANC, CM 39/1, f. 86–86v; and Perico Gangá, ibid., 87–87v.

73. See statements of Pablo Lucumí, ANC, CM 39/1, f. 103–4; and Diego Lucumí, ibid.

74. See statements of Belén Ramírez, ANC, CM 33/2; and Pío Romero, ANC, CM 48/6.

75. Again, see statement of Belén Ramírez, ANC, CM 33/2.

76. See statement of Jacundo Carabalí, ANC, CM 48/6. For his part, Pío stated that he did not find out about the conspiracy until he was taken prisoner.

77. "Santo Domingo" here refers to the nation of Haiti in the early nineteenth century, but it may be specifically referencing the "Spanish portion."

78. See McKittrick, *Demonic Grounds*, xxi.

|||||||| Chapter Three

1. For a discussion of the series of slave rebellions that erupted during the first half of the nineteenth century, see Barcia Paz, *Seeds of Insurrection*, 33–48.

2. See Finch, "Repeating Rebellion."

3. I am thankful to Barbara Krauthamer and Jennifer Morgan for helping me to think through the points in this paragraph.

4. Cedric Robinson devoted an entire section of his classic study, *Black Marxism*, to examining slave resistance throughout the Americas. He framed these slave rebellions as critical to the making of what he calls "the black radical tradition." My analysis of enslaved people's political consciousness has been influenced by Robinson and others whom he inspired. See *Black Marxism*, 130–66. I am also indebted to Sarah Haley for helping me to think through the ideas in this chapter.

5. See statements of Rafael Aguilar, Vicente Criollo, Mateo Lucumí, and Pedro Lucumí, ANC, CM 29/5. Pedro implies in his statement that he helped to convey this information; however, Aguilar's testimony highlighted Vicente and Mateo.

6. See statement of José Cano, ANC, CM 29/5, f. 60–63.

7. See ibid.

8. See statement of Germán Lucumí, ANC, CM 29/5, f. 54v–55v.

9. See statement of Anacleto Lucumí, ibid., f. 137.

10. See statement of Marcelino Carabalí, ibid., f. 53v–54v.

11. Germán later testified that he ran "to warn the Mayoral and the other [whites]." See statement of Germán Lucumí, ibid., f. 54v–55v.

12. See declaration of José Cano, ibid., f. 60–63.

13. See statement of Rafael Aguilar, ibid., f. 58v–59v. Authorities later confirmed that the main door had indeed suffered significant damage from "many blows, given it appears with a sharp, light-weight instrument."

14. See statement of Vicente Alvero, ibid., f. 84–85v. Also see statement of Francisco María Ychazo, ibid., f. 86–87.

15. See statement of Ignacio Izquiedo, ibid., f. 92–93.

16. See statement of Cayetano Abreu, ibid., f. 93v–95.

17. See statement of José María Fernández, ibid., f. 95v–97v.

18. For a discussion of Peñalver and his distinguished family, see Bergad, *Cuban Rural Society*, 111–12.

19. On the history of the Cuban railroad and the Cardenas-Bemba line in particular, see ibid., 83 and 110–12. Also see Zanetti Lecuona and García Álvarez, *Sugar and Railroads*, 18–30.

20. See statements of María Regla Congo and José Ortega, ANC, CM 30/3.

21. For a discussion of the railroad rebels' arms and place of lodging, see statements of José María Fernández and Antonio José Neyra, ibid., f. 98v–99v.

22. See statements of Tirzo Lucumí, f. 113v–115v; Ángel Lucumí, f. 115v–117v; and Gil Lucumí, f. 119v–120v, all in ibid.

23. See Franco, *Gesta heroica del Triunvirato*, 19; Franco, "Origen y consecuencias de la sublevación de los esclavos en Matanzas en 1843"; García Rodríguez, *Conspiraciones y revueltas*, 127–29; and Paquette, *Sugar Is Made with Blood*, 209–10.

24. See ANC, CM 29/5, f. 151–54.

25. See statement of Vicente Alvero, ibid., f. 84–85v.

26. On the "spatial impulse of enslavement," see Camp, *Closer to Freedom*, 12.

27. See statement of José Cano, ANC, CM 29/5, f. 60–63.

28. See statements of Macario and Zacarías Carabalí, ANC, CM 30/3.

29. See statement of Manuel Gangá, ibid., f. 19–17v/23–21; and Narciso Lucumí, ibid., f. 43–45.

30. See ibid. Also see statements of Narciso Lucumí and Cirilo Lucumí, ibid., f. 23–24/21–22v.

31. See ibid. Also see statement of Agustín Yrazu, ibid.

32. See statement of Benito Manresa, ibid.

33. See statement of Camila Criolla, ibid., f. 105v.

34. See statement of Catalina Gangá, ibid., f. 107v–109v.

35. See statement of Adriano Gangá, ibid., f. 25–27/23–25v.

36. See, for example, statement of Manuel Gangá, ibid., f. 19–23/17v–21.

37. See, for example, statement of Inocencio Carabalí, ibid. For his part, however, Adán testified that no one called to the rebels from inside. See statement of Adán Lucumí, ibid., f. 61–61v.

38. See statement of Juan Miguel Pérez, ibid., f. 88–91.

39. See statements of Catalina Gangá, ibid., f. 107v–109v; Filomena Gangá, ibid., f. 106v–107v.

40. See statement of Juan Miguel Pérez, ibid., f. 88–91.

41. See statement of Gonzalo Lucumí, ibid.

42. See statement of Manuel Gangá, ibid., f. 19–23/17v–21. For a list of the victims, see medical reports included in ibid., f. 76.

43. See statements of Camila Criolla, ibid., f. 104v–106; and Martina Criolla, ibid., f. 110v–112.

44. See statement of María [de] Regla Pérez, ibid., f. 120–22. Also see statement of Adriano Gangá, ibid., f. 25–27/23–25v; Matea Gangá, ibid., f. 125v; and Magdalena Lucumí, ibid., f. 126v. Two other male slaves stated that they later found two of the foreman's daughters as they were escaping: Adriano Gangá, ibid., f. 25–27/23–25v; Eleuterio Congo, ibid., f. 27–29/25v–27. Adán Lucumí denied the charges against him, stating that after being freed from prison, he "went to his cabin and stayed there." However, Adán apparently lied about returning to the prison the next morn-

ing, as he was in fact apprehended on the potrero by the mayoral's son the next day. See statement of Juan Miguel Pérez, mayoral of Ácana, ibid., f. 88–91.

45. Other reports indicate that additional slaves beyond these nine joined the rebel activities, or at least left the estate. See declaration of Mauricio Vrzaimqui, ibid., f. 73.

46. See ibid.

47. See statements of Mauricio Vrzaimqui and Joaquín [Garcilazo] de la Vega, ibid., f. 71–71v.

48. See statement of Juan Berasan, ibid., f. 82.

49. See statement of Manuel Gangá, ibid., f. 21/19v.

50. See statement of Blas Cuesta, ibid., f. 84 and 179. Cuesta testified that fifty-six people had been killed, but other portions of the trial record place the number at fifty.

51. See statements of Mauricio Vrzaimqui, ibid.; and Juan Berasan, ibid. Berasan also reported several slaves missing.

52. See statement of Manuel Gangá, ibid., f. 19–23/17v–21.

53. Inocencio named four other slaves who remained in the forest and did not accompany the rebels. See statement of Inocencio Carabalí, ibid., f. 33v–35v.

54. See statement of Macario Lucumí, ibid., f. 18–19/16v–17.

55. See, for example, statements of Cirilo Lucumí, Gonzalo Lucumí, Narciso Lucumí, and Adán Gangá, ibid.

56. See statement of Inocencio Carabalí, ibid., f. 33v–35v.

57. See statement of Mauricio Vrzaimqui, ibid.

58. For this account, see statement of Anacleto Lucumí, ibid., f. 136v–137v.

59. See statement of Maria del Rosario Lucumí, ibid., f. 150–150v.

60. See ibid.

61. See statement of Pilar Carabalí, ibid., f. 151v–152v. Camila Criolla similarly testified that her companion Juliana was threatened by the latter's husband, and forced to take her child and follow the rebels. However, this contention differs somewhat from Juliana's testimony. Juliana stated that she received (and sought out) multiple orders from her husband, though she did not frame them as particularly coercive. On the same estate, Martina Criolla stated that she was "obliged to follow the rebels." See statements of Camila Criolla, ibid., f. 104v–106; Juliana Criolla, ibid., f. 104; and Martina Criolla, ibid., f. 110v–112.

62. See statements of Filomena Gangá, ibid., f. 107. Also see statements of Catalina Gangá, ibid., f. 109–109v; Matea Gangá, ibid., f. 125v; Martina Criolla, ibid., 111–111v; and Magdalena Lucumí, ibid., f. 126v. Magdalena simply stated that she went as far as Concepción. Also see statement of Martina Criolla, ibid., f. 110v–112.

63. See statement of Juliana Criolla, ibid., f. 103–4.

64. See statement of Catalina Gangá, ibid., f. 108. The slain women included Carlota and the woman who Manuel Gangá stated was shot by a soldier.

65. See the authorities' record of prisoners taken on the morning of November 6, 1843, ibid., f. 189–189v.

66. See statement of Joaquín [Garcilazo] de la Vega, ibid., f. 139–42.

67. See statement of Joaquín [Garcilazo] de la Vega (ibid.), who mentioned two

incapacitated women who were missing. These may have been included in the count of eleven who were missing from the estate in his above statement. Also see statement of Manuel Gangá, ibid., f. 19–23/17v–21.

68. See the list of slaves "to be shot in the back" and the instructions for carrying out this execution, in statement of Joaquín [Garcilazo] de la Vega, ANC, CM 30/3, f. 288v.

69. See ibid., f. 288–292v.

70. Merced Criolla was a nurse on the Encanto sugar estate. See ibid., f. 6–7v.

71. See statement of Juan Lucumí, ANC, CM 29/5, f. 34–35/16–17.

72. Although Aguilar did not list Dionisio Lucumí as one of those who confessed the plot to him, Dionisio nonetheless spoke of the confession as though he had taken part in it, or at least supported it. For this account see statement of Dionisio Lucumí, ibid., f. 80v–82.

73. See statements of Tomás Lucumí, ANC, CM 33/4, f. 83–85v/43–45v; Manuel Mina, ibid., f. 76–77/36–37; and José Carabalí, ibid., f. 90/50v.

74. See statement of Manuel Mina, ibid., f. 76–77/36–37. The military authorities followed up on Manuel Mina's testimony and traveled to the Peñalver estate to ask about the two men he named. See ibid., f. 231–32.

75. For example, Justo Cantero's famous lithograph depicts the properties surrounding the Ingenio La Victoria, most of which were mentioned in the 1844 trial records. See Cantero, *Ingenios*.

76. See statement of José Carabalí, ANC, CM 33/4, f. 89–90/50v–51. For Tomás Lucumí's testimony about the flag, see ibid., f. 86/46.

77. The testimonies of these men provide extensive confirmation that they knew and socialized with one another. See, for example, statement of Mariano Fuentes, ibid., f., 96–97/56–57v and 243v/245, respectively.

78. Antonio González testified against Jacinto Roque and Cristóbal Linares, stating that these two met with slaves from the Cafetal Primavera and the Ingenio Aurora, though both men denied these accusations. See ibid., f. 299–301.

79. See ANC, CM 29/5, f. 159–60. Gherri wrote that he received "a piece of material filled with dirt that was delivered to me by Antonio González and identified by Cristóbal Linares declaring them to be the witchcraft items." It is difficult to know whether these were in fact spiritual items.

80. For these accounts see statements of Vicente Gangá, José Carabalí, and Tomás Lucumí, ibid., f. 87–88/47v–48v and 86/46v. Also see statement of José Carabalí, ibid., f. 89–91/49–51.

81. See statements of Tomás Lucumí, ibid., f. 45v; and Antonio González, ANC, CM 29/5, f. 163–66 and ANC, CM 33/4, f. 299–299v.

82. See statements of Antonio González, ANC, CM 29/5 and 33/4.

83. See statements of Manuel Mina, ANC, CM 33/4, f. 76–77/36–37; and Tomás Lucumí, ibid., f. 45v.

84. See, for example, statements of Jacobo Arará, ANC, CM 32/3, f. 168–171v; and Pedro Carabalí, ibid., f. 175v–178v.

85. Ethnographer Fernando Ortiz has written about at least two sadistic variations on this, including *bocabajo llevando cuenta*—in which the recipient had to count

each lash as he or she received it, and if that person messed up, the whipping would start all over again — and *bocabajo doble*, administered by two overseers, one on each side, who would alternate the lashes. See Ortiz, *Negros esclavos*, 230.

86. For a discussion of these summer rebellions from May to July 1843, see Franco, *Gesta heroica del Triunvirato*, 23–31.

87. See Paquette, *Sugar Is Made with Blood*, 172–73; and Sarracino, *Inglaterra*, 87–88. Miguel Flores and Francis Ross Cocking both agreed in separate communiqués that an unidentified rebel leader preemptively ignited the Bembas rebellion of March 27, 1843.

88. See statement of Jorge Gangá, ANC, CM 33/1, quoted in García Rodríguez, *Voices of the Enslaved*, 191.

89. See statement of Vicente Borrero, ANC, CM 52/1, f. 570v.

90. See statement of José María Mondejar, ANC, CM 39/1, f.197

91. For this account, see statement of José María García, ANC, CM 52/1, f. 578v–79.

92. See, for example, statements of Justo Gangá, ANC, CM 39/1, f. 229v–30; and Bonifacio Berson, ibid., f. 409–10.

||||||| Chapter Four

1. See statements of Patricio Mandinga, ANC, CM, 41/2, f. 55–55v; and Blas Lucumí, ibid., f. 56v.

2. See statement of Jorge López, AHN, Estado 8057/1, f. 1v and 3v.

3. See statements of Pedro Domech, ANC, CM 41/2, f. 2–7.

4. See, for example, statement of Sebastián Peres [Mandinga], ANC, CM 41/2, f. 76. Also see additional testimony ("amplición") of Blas Owens, ibid., f. 80.

5. Sicar has been written in other places as "Sicart."

6. Ivor Miller's analysis of ritual-kinship ties seems particularly important to contextualize this discussion. See Miller, "Formation of African Identities in the Americas."

7. See statement of Sebastián Peres, ANC, CM 41/2, f. 76.

8. See ANC, CM 130/10, no. 11a.

9. Turnbull inherited these contacts from his predecessor Richard Madden, who transferred this list of associates to Turnbull when the latter took office. See Eltis, *Economic Growth*, 118.

10. See Corwin, *Spain and the Abolition of Slavery*, 56–58. Also see Paquette, *Sugar Is Made with Blood*, 160, 170, 176, on Varela.

11. For more on the background of del Monte's salon members, see Paquette, *Sugar Is Made with Blood*, 92, 140, 168, and 250–51. Also see Navarro, *Entre esclavos y constituciones*, 26–27; García, "Cuba en la obra de Plácido," 64 and 67; and Schmidt-Nowara, *Empire and Antislavery*, 32–33.

12. See Méndez Rodenas, *Gender and Nationalism*, 69–103.

13. See Schmidt-Nowara, *Empire and Antislavery*, 18–21.

14. In March 1841 Turnbull's activities were bolstered by the arrival of Gerónimo Valdés as captain general. Even more alarming to the planter class than Valdés's immediate recognition of Turnbull was the new governor's proclamation that all

extant treaties against the slave trade were to be honored and enforced. Valdés's efforts did indeed seem to have a short-term effect, as the number of imported slaves plummeted from 1841 to 1842, dropping by over 9,000 in 1842. However these numbers increased again in 1843, and reached a new height of 10,440 in 1844. On the appointment of General Valdés and its immediate aftermath, see Sarracino, *Inglaterra*, 49; Corwin, *Spain and the Abolition of Slavery*, 79; and Aimes, *History of Slavery in Cuba*, 152.

15. Rodolfo Sarracino and Robert Paquette have scrutinized the original version in the British Foreign Records Office in the greatest detail. See Sarracino, *Inglaterra*, esp. 15–23 and 55–77; and Paquette, *Sugar Is Made with Blood*, 163–67.

16. Both Sarracino and Paquette sought to deduce who the true author of the petition was, as the name was not properly recorded in Cocking's confession. I am following Sarracino's conclusion that Turnbull asked Morilla to write the address. See Sarracino, *Inglaterra*, 57; and Paquette, *Sugar Is Made with Blood*, 163–64 and 175.

17. Paquette, *Sugar Is Made with Blood*, 164.

18. Del Monte's most memorable antislavery act may have been manumitting Juan Francisco Manzano, the only formerly enslaved black Cuban writer to publish his own memoirs, and sending [the latter's] work to England to be printed. Juan Francisco Manzano was arrested during the course of the trials, but he was later exonerated, to "remain under surveillance for one year." See ANC, CM 130/10, case 12a. For an important revisionist reading of Manzano's letters to del Monte that requested his freedom, see Pettway, "Ritual and Reason."

19. See José Luis Alfonso to José Antonio Saco, February 27, 1836; quoted in Schmidt-Nowara, *Empire and Antislavery*, 14.

20. See Schmidt-Nowara, *Empire and Antislavery*, 18–21.

21. See Domingo del Monte to Alexander Hill Everett, Philadelphia, September 7, 1843, in BNJM, Sala Cubana, C.M. Garcia E, no. 1.

22. See García Balañà, "Antislavery before Abolitionism," 229–46.

23. See Domingo del Monte to Alexander Hill Everett, Paris, August 15, 1844, in BNJM, Sala Cubana, C.M. Garcia E, no. 2.

24. The vast majority of these provisions were outlined in the "Address from the Young Creoles." See Paquette, *Sugar Is Made with Blood*, 102 and 163–64; and Sarracino, *Inglaterra*, 58–59.

25. See Sarracino, *Inglaterra*, 61.

26. For several highly suggestive pieces of evidence to this effect, see Paquette, *Sugar Is Made with Blood*, 171–72 and 246–47.

27. Because his parents, the mulatto barber Diego Ferrer Matoso and the Spanish ballerina Concepción Vásquez, were never married, he was alternately known as Gabriel Matoso and Gabriel de la Concepción for most of his life.

28. Since the early 1980s, scholars have relied heavily on two works about Plácido that are part biography and part literary criticism. They are García, "Cuba en la obra de Plácido"; and Castellanos, *Plácido, poeta social y político*. For the biographical information in the text, see García, "Cuba en la obra de Plácido," 2–16.

29. See Nwankwo, *Black Cosmopolitanism*, 110.

30. See, for example, García, "Cuba en la obra de Plácido," 36–39.

31. See, for example, Wurdemann, *Notes on Cuba*, 250.

32. See Pettway, "Braggarts, Charlatans and *Curros.*"

33. See García, "Cuba en la obra de Plácido," 21–26 and 32–33.

34. For example, Plácido met José María Heredia, the distinguished white Cuban poet living in exile in Mexico, who was expelled for his participation in the Soles y Rayos de Bolívar conspiracy. See ibid., 28–29. For a discussion of one of Plácido's boldest and most politically suggestive poems, "La sombra de Padilla," see ibid., 19–20.

35. See, for example, Plácido's final statement before his execution in Fernández, *Plácido, el poeta conspirador*, 297. I am thankful to Matthew Pettway for directing me to this work.

36. See statement of Plácido, Gabriel de la Concepción Valdés, AHN, Estado 8057/1, f. 31.

37. See ANC, CM 130/10, no. 12a.

38. Bernardo Sevillán was charged with having the *diccionario*. He insisted, however, that he did not know how to read and write, and that he had received the book from a now-deceased friend. The other books were found on Jorge López, who admitted to having acquired them in Havana some time ago. See García Rodríguez, *Conspiraciones y revueltas*, 94.

39. See ibid., 95–96. Also see ANC, CM 9/24, ANC, CM 9/25, and ANC, CM 9/27.

40. Santiago Pimienta testified to this effect, though he was careful not to implicate himself. See statement of Santiago Pimienta, AHN, Estado 8057/1, f. 5. Also see statement of Antonio Bernoqui, ibid., f. 7. Some of the testimonies suggest that there was more than one dinner with Jigot at López's home.

41. See statement of Desideria Pimienta, ANC, CM 52/1, f. 464–467v.

42. See statement of Andrea Sotolongo, ibid., f. 469–73.

43. See Mena, "Stretching the Limits of Gendered Spaces," 91–92.

44. See statement of Jorge López, lieutenant of the black battalion of Havana, painter, free, AHN, Estado 8057/1, f. 1v.

45. This and other valuable information provided the judges with a crucial piece that was missing from the early Matanzas planning.

46. See statement of Antonio Bernoqui, ibid., f. 7. The elements that trouble the López and Bernoqui narratives are Plácido's recounting of his recruitment by Domingo del Monte and the fact that Jigot himself had escaped from Cuba by the time of the trials. As such, Jigot could provide no countertestimony to contradict the idea that the Matanzas circle originated with his recruitment. Jigot was therefore an easy target who presumably could no more be hurt by their accusations than defend his position. Santiago Pimienta also testified that "he had heard" similar information to that which Bernoqui provided. See ibid., f. 5–v.

47. For Plácido's explanation of why he was not at the table when such important information was being discussed, see ibid., f. 29.

48. Plácido states that he refused to do so and that the poet Juan Francisco Manzano, whose poems had already been published by Richard Madden, was requested for the task. In Plácido's opinion, "from then on, Delmonte [del Monte] pronounced a silent war against [him]," as seen in the unfavorable publications that emerged in

del Monte's newspaper. See AHN, Estado 8057/1, f. 23v. For his part, Juan Francisco Manzano denied these accusations. See ANC, CM 52/1, f. 616v.

49. See Plácido's statement in AHN, Estado 8057/1, f. 24.

50. For example, the first part of this testimony makes no reference to Plácido's participation in del Monte's salons (and therefore to their acquaintanceship) years before Turnbull arrived. The latter portion, however, is more believable. Plácido stated that del Monte emphasized to him more than once that "many people of his position and influence on the Island were determined to carry out emancipation; and that everyone including the English Government would protect them." See ibid., f. 24–24v.

51. In October 1842, Turnbull attempted to return to eastern Cuba but was summarily arrested, deported, and forbidden to return to the island. See Gerónimo Valdés to the Minister of State, Havana, November 5, 1842, in "Correspondencia acerca de David Turnbull," BNJM, esp. no. 6.

52. For an exhaustive discussion of Alexander Hill Everett, his relationship to del Monte, and his connection to the U.S. president, see Paquette, *Sugar Is Made with Blood*, 189–93; and Sarracino, *Inglaterra*, 73 and 102–3.

53. See Domingo Delmonte [del Monte] to Alexander Hill Everett, Havana, November 20, 1842, in Sala Cubana, BNJM, C.M. García E, no. 1, f. 2–3.

54. See, for example, Alexander Hill Everett to his wife, Boston, January 5 and January 12, 1843, in Sala Cubana, BNJM, C.M. no. 1. For increasing attention to Cuba on the part of U.S. diplomats, congressmen, and presidents during the early 1840s, see Daniel Webster's letter to the U.S. consul in Havana, in Thomas, *Cuba*, 207. For a detailed discussion of the early background to Cuban annexation, see Johnson, *River of Dark Dreams*; Sarracino, *Inglaterra*, chap. 7; and Paquette, *Sugar Is Made with Blood*, chap. 7.

55. During a trip to Jamaica, Cocking sought out Mariño—an illustrious veteran of Venezuela's independence war—to lead the Cuban assault when the time came.

56. See Paquette, *Sugar Is Made with Blood*, 170.

57. See ibid., 167.

58. See Sarracino, *Inglaterra*, 62, 69, and 76.

59. See Paquette, *Sugar Is Made with Blood*, 167; and Sarracino, *Inglaterra*, 81.

60. One of her slaves, Antonio Gangá or Lucumí, worked mostly for himself and on his own. His enslavement thus follows the pattern of some black slaveholders, in which their slaves essentially lived as free people. It was not uncommon for these slaves to be relatives or kin.

61. Many of the people José and Domingo accused later denied these allegations, but parts of their testimonies were eventually corroborated by Rosa and others on the estate.

62. See statement of Rosa Lucumí, ANC, CM 39/1, f. 36.

63. See ibid.

64. See, for example, statements of José Roque and Rosa Lucumí, who alleged that José Marta took money from Roque to buy him "things for the war" but never brought them. José Marta denied this allegation. See ANC, CM 39/1.

65. See statement of José Roque Criollo, ibid., f. 4–v.

66. See ibid., f. 5.

67. See ibid., f. 9.

68. Roque's insistence about Félix Gálvez is one of the more telling examples. After testifying that he saw him at the meeting at Altagracia's house, Roque said that "even though time has passed, he thinks he would remember him." He subsequently picked Félix out of a lineup. Esteban García, Nicolás Torres, and Antonio José Rodríguez all denied the particulars of Roque's accusation but admitted they knew him or were in the habit of seeing him. See their testimonies in CM 39/1.

69. See statement of José Antonio Rodríguez, ibid., f. 559v–561v.

70. See list of accusations against José Roque, ANC, CM 39/1.

71. See statement of Estefanía Goicochea, ANC, CM 52/1, f. 518v.

72. For this account and a list of the others present, see statement of José María Mondejar, ANC, CM 39/1, f. 196–201.

73. See ibid.

74. See, for example, Deschamps Chapeaux, *Negro en la economía habanera*, 89–90; Klein, *Slavery in the Americas*, 140, 146; Alexander; *Transatlantic Sketches*, 375; and Bremer, *Homes of the New World*, 280.

75. See statement of Nicolás González (written as "Gonzales"), and his confrontation with Gregorio la Ceí, ANC, CM 52/1. When confronted with González's accusation, Gregorio denied all of it. The judges were not convinced of his innocence. Gregorio was ultimately sentenced to ten years in prison. See ANC, CM 130/10, Case 12a.

76. These included Pedro Núñez, Bruno Izquierdo, Antonio Abad, and José de la O'García.

77. See confrontation (*careo*) between Bartolo Quintero and Antonio Abad, ANC, CM 52/1, f. 473v–474v; and Julián Gangá, ibid., f. 476–476v. Bartolo denied most of these accusations. Bartolo was frequently accused as an organizer, and the judges were not convinced of his innocence; he was eventually sentenced to ten years in prison overseas.

78. See statement of José de la O'García, AHN, Estado 8057/1, f. 13v. It should be noted that de la O'García himself did not admit to attending meetings at the Núñez house, though he did speak about others who attended.

79. See ibid., f. 14v.

80. See statement of Félix Ponce, AHN, Estado 8057/1, f. 34v. Numerous others testified to having received oaths in the course of pledging their allegiance to the movement. These included the free black men Damaso Ramos, Antonio Márquez, Mariano Pérez, Gavino Montes de Oca, Gregorio la Ceí, Jacobo Fernández, and Secundino Arango. For these and other testimonies, see ANC, CM 57/1.

81. Juan Rodríguez/Miguel Flores was typically referred to as "Flores" or "Miguel Flores" in the documents. He was described by several as a *talabartero*, a saddler or leatherworker, yet he also owned a mahogany furniture store. See statement of Juan Bautista Martínez in AHN, Estado 8057/1, f. 40v.

82. Once again, Antonio Bernoqui gave the most detailed recount of Flores's visit, and once again Jorge López's house became the site of an important meeting. Familiar attendees included Antonio Bernoqui, Jorge López, and Manuel Manzano. See Bernoqui's statement in AHN, Estado 8057/1, f. 8v.

83. The historian Walterio Carbonell has presented evidence that Jigot himself first introduced Flores to Turnbull, and suggests that Flores became the primary source of information about British activities after Turnbull's departure. See Sarracino, *Inglaterra*, 89–90, which cites Carbonnell's work.

84. See Paquette, *Sugar Is Made with Blood*, 172–73; and Sarracino, *Inglaterra*, 87–88. Miguel Flores and Francis Ross Cocking both agreed in separate communiqués that an unidentified rebel leader preemptively ignited the Bembas rebellion of March 27, 1843.

85. Other evidence supports the argument that conspirators were making themselves known to Joseph Crawford in the years leading up to La Escalera. For Crawford's communication with both Flores and the British foreign secretary, see Paquette, *Sugar Is Made with Blood*, 168–70 and 173–74; and Sarracino, *Inglaterra*, 88–89.

86. See Sarracino, *Inglaterra*, 45 and 50–51. Also see Paquette, *Sugar Is Made with Blood*, 152.

87. See statement of Vicente Pipa Criollo, slave of Martin Arostegui, ANC, CM 42/1, f. 115.

88. See statement of José Lucumí, ANC, CM 39/1, f. 106.

89. See statements of Andrés Armas, free bricklayer, ANC, CM 33/4, f. 253v, and Ramón Medrano, silversmith, ANC, CM 52/1, f. 499v.

90. See statement of Isidro Carabalí, slave of José Domínguez Morales, ANC, CM 52/1, f. 402. Also see statement of the celebrated musician and orchestra conductor Claudio Brindis de Salas, ibid., f. 518v–519v.

91. See statement of Félix Ponce, carpenter, ibid., f. 34v.

92. See statement of Marcos Criollo, ANC, CM 31/9, f. 11. Also see statements of Gabriel Garces, free man of color, ANC, CM 52/1, f. 569v, and Ramón Medrano, free silversmith, ibid., f. 499-v.

93. See statements of Blas Lucumí, Joaquín Gangá, Melchor Robaina, Pedro Martir, and Tomás Robaina, ANC, CM 41/2. Several other slaves on the nearby Ruell estate claimed to have been told about "Marcos Ruiz, the coach driver."

94. See statement of Jacobo Fernández, free bricklayer, ANC, CM 57/1. For a list of the estates where Jacobo Fernández worked, see his statement in AHN, Estado 8057/1.

95. For example, the free black man Damaso Ramos stated that the goal was "to liberate the slaves, do away with the Government, and [do away] with all the whites at the same time." ANC, CM 52/1, f. 518–518v.

|||||||| Chapter Five

1. For documentation of Polonia's case and the resulting reward that she was to have received, see ANC, GSC 948/33527 and GSC 943/33287. For a discussion of Polonia's discovery, see Barcia Zequeira and Barcia Paz, "Conspiración de La Escalera."

2. Jenny Sharpe insightfully describes Frederick Douglass's autobiography in this manner. See Sharpe, *Ghosts of Slavery*, xi.

3. Joy James's writing about twentieth-century African American political struggles is particularly instructive here. See James, "Framing the Panther," 138.

4. Historical accounts of eighteenth- and nineteenth-century slave rebellions from a variety of locales have called attention to slave women who revealed rebel plots to their slave owners. See, for example, Rucker, *River Flows On*, 117.

5. See Bush, "Defiance or Submission?"

6. See Dadzie, "Searching for the Invisible Woman."

7. See, for example, ANC, Miscelánea de Expedientes, 629/Af., cited in García Rodríguez, *Esclavitud desde la esclavitud*, 19. Also see Barcia Zequeira, *Otra familia*; Prados-Torreira, *Mambisas*, 27–32; and Castañeda Fuertes, "Female Slave in Cuba."

8. See, for example, Camp, *Closer to Freedom*; and Morgan, *Laboring Women*.

9. See Davis, "Reflections on the Black Woman's Role in the Community of Slaves"; White, *Arn't I a Woman?*; Beckles, *Natural Rebels*; Beckles, *Centering Woman*; Morrissey, *Slave Women in the New World*; Bush, *Slave Women in Caribbean Society*; Stevenson, *Life in Black and White*; Moitt, *Women and Slavery in the French Antilles*; Camp, *Closer to Freedom*; Morgan, *Laboring Women*; Castañeda Fuertes, "Female Slave in Cuba"; Krauthamer, "Particular Kind of Freedom"; and Mena, "Stretching the Limits of Gendered Spaces."

10. For a discussion of the significant roles that Fermina and Carlota played in the November insurgency, see Franco, *Gesta heroica del Triunvirato*. Also see ANC, CM 30/3.

11. The authorities ordered that eight ringleaders—the ones who had not been killed in battle or who had not managed to escape—be parceled out and shot on the four major estates involved in the uprising: Triunvirato, Ácana, Concepción, and San Miguel. See ANC, CM 30/3, f. 288v–289.

12. See Beckles, *Natural Rebels* and *Centering Woman*; and Bush, *Slave Women in Caribbean Society*.

13. See declaration of Fermina Lucumí, see ANC, CM 30/3, f. 257–257v.

14. See Franco, *Gesta heroica del Triunvirato*, 23–31.

15. See declaration of Filomena Gangá, ibid., f. 107.

16. See declaration of Catalina Gangá, ibid., f. 107v–109v.

17. Ibid.

18. See declaration of Camila Criolla, ibid., f. 105.

19. See declaration of Martina Criolla, ibid., f. 110v–112.

20. See declarations of Matea Gangá, ibid., f. 125v; and Magdalena Lucumí, ibid., f. 126v.

21. See communication dated November 19, 1843, ibid., f. 127v–129.

22. See declaration of María [de] Regla [Pérez], f. 120–22. Also see declaration of Adriano Gangá, ibid., f. 25–27/23–25v.

23. During the postrevolutionary years, these two women—especially Carlota—were consistently portrayed as audacious, unrepentant, and full of rage. Carlota's image has been circulated through memorial statues, drawings, and pervasively on the Internet. See, for example, http://www.afrocubaweb.com/carlota.htm.

24. This may in part be thanks to the scholarship of José Luciano Franco, who highlighted the roles of these two women in his analysis of the rebellion. See Franco, *Gesta heroica del Triunvirato*.

25. See declaration of Fermina Lucumí, ibid., f. 64v–65v, ibid. Also see her subsequent statement, f. 256–257v.

26. See declaration of Filomena Gangá, ibid., f. 106v–107v. However, Filomena was also described as a cook for the *mayoral* (estate foreman) and may have therefore found it prudent to emphasize her shock at these "repugnant" actions.

27. See declaration of Fermina Lucumí, ANC, CM 30/3, f. 256v.

28. See statements of Alejo Criollo and Antonio Lucumí, ANC, CM 34/1.

29. See, for example, statement of Francisco Criollo, ANC, CM 32/3, f. 133–131v.

30. See declaration of Nestor Lucumí, ANC, CM 33/4, f. 69/29.

31. For further discussion of this phenomenon, see Johnson, *Soul by Soul*; Morgan, *Laboring Women*; and Smallwood, *Saltwater Slavery*.

32. See declaration of Eusebia Criolla, ANC, CM 31/9, f. 117v–118. Also see statements of Pedro Gangá, ibid., f. 118v–119v; and Bienvenido Gangá, ibid., f. 119v–121.

33. "Bienbenido" is a phonetic spelling of Bienvenido. "Purisima Concepcion de Echeverria" was written as such in the text, without the tonic accents. Here is the original Spanish for the quotation: "que habia como un año que estando en la casa de bibienda de su señor, oyó á su companero Pedro Ganga, que noticiaba á los de su clase Antonio y Bienbenido en lengua que en el Ingenio Purisima [smudge] Concepcion de Echeverria, intentaba levantarse contra los blancos, asegurando que absolutamente sabe mas, que lo que lleva declarado."

34. See declaration of Eusebia Criolla, ibid., f. 117v–118.

35. See declaration of Ramón Criollo, ANC, CM 32/3, f. 174/172v.

36. See declarations of Jacobo Arará, ibid., f. 170/168 v; Francisco Mina, ibid., f. 110/108v; Manuel Congo, ibid., f. 108/106.

37. See declaration of Cecilia Criolla, ibid., f. 66/64–64v.

38. See declaration of Teresa Mina, ANC, CM 33/4, f. 26/22v.

39. It is not clear from this description if Antonia was working—that is, tending the plants—or deliberately concealing herself. See declaration of Antonia Robaina, ANC, CM 41/2, f. 12v–13v.

40. See, for example, declarations of Felipe Congo, ibid., f. 86/84; Tranquilino Gangá, f. 87/85; Justo Criollo, f. 100/98; and Justo Mina, f. 83/81.

41. For an additional example of this, see declarations of Victoriano Mandinga, ANC, CM 39/1, f. 177; and Dolores Criolla, ibid., f. 53.

42. See statement of Merced Criolla, ANC, CM 33/4, f. 6–7v.

43. In his discussion of the black urban landscape in Bahia, for example, João Reis notes that "captains of the [street] corners" were elected in a manner similar to the ceremonial crowning of kings. Such a street environment calls important attention to the *flexibility* of the kingship, and the adaptability of such an institution to various settings, needs, and purposes. See Reis, *Slave Rebellion in Brazil*, 164. Other experiences of this kind have been documented in Haiti, Antigua, and the United States. Also see David Barry Gaspar's interpretation of the *ikem* dance in Antigua during the 1730s, in *Bondmen and Rebels*, 249–52.

44. See Kiddy, "Who Is the King of Congo?," 153.

45. A discussion of the Asantehemaa's role is contained in Wilks, *Asante in the Nineteenth Century*. The "stool" mentioned in the text is the Golden Stool, the literal and figurative seat of Asante power and the symbolic unity of the Asante nation.

46. The role of the Kpojito, and the reigns of several particularly powerful Kpojitos, is detailed in Bay, *Wives of the Leopard*, chap. 3.

47. See Smith, *Kingdoms of the Yoruba*, 93–95. Throughout Africa, most royal women exercised their greatest power through their sons and frequently attempted to win the throne for them. In fact, more than a few such women were involved in volatile successions and coups.

48. For two excellent studies of Afro-Cuban cabildos, see Rushing, "Cabildos de Nación"; and Howard, *Changing History*.

49. For scholars who have written about the institution of African kingship in other parts of the Americas, there has been an ongoing question as to whether the kings held political relevance and stature in the larger black community, or whether their positions were more symbolic. Elizabeth Kiddy convincingly argues for the former position in "Who Is the King of Congo?," 153–55.

50. See, for example, statements of Alejo Criollo, Dimas Criollo, Luciana Carabalí, and José Santos Criollo, among others, ANC, CM 34/1.

51. See statement of Santiago Gangá, ANC, CM 33/4, f. 21/17v.

52. See statement of Merced Criolla, ibid., f. 8/6v.

53. See ibid., f. 9/7. It was certainly in Merced's interest to deny taking such a position before the authorities, but others agreed that she had declined.

54. See statement of Teresa Mina, ibid., f. 136v.

55. For the naming of these positions, see statements of Alejo Criollo, Antonio Lucumí, Luciana Carabalí, and Dimas Criollo, ANC, CM 34/1.

56. See David Barry Gaspar's description of a royal coronation modeled after Akan heads of state that preceded slaves' planning of rebellions in Antigua; Gaspar, *Bondmen and Rebels*, 249–52.

57. See statement of Merced Criolla, ibid., f. 6–7v.

58. See statement of Patricio Gangá, ANC, CM 33/4, f. 7v–9.

59. See statement of Simona Criolla, ANC, CM 39/1, f. 401–401v. For corroboration of her testimony, see statements of Juan de Dios Gangá, ibid., f. 401; Domingo Roque, ibid.

60. See statement of Domingo Gangá, ibid., f. 34.

61. See statement of Domingo Gangá, ibid., f. 122v.

62. See statement of Victoriano Mandingo, ibid., f. 35v. This constitutes the only reference I have seen to two queens.

63. See statements of Rosa Lucumí, ibid., f. 12, and Domingo Gangá, ibid., f. 32.

64. See statement of Rosa Lucumí, ibid., f. 36–36v.

65. See ibid., f. 36.

66. For the mayoral's warning "that he did not want any blacks from outside [the premises]," see ibid., f. 12v.

67. For Luciana Carabalí's position, see statement of Alejo Criollo, ANC, CM 34/1.

|||||||| Chapter Six

1. In *Sugar Is Made with Blood*, Robert Paquette suggests that as a figure of colonial Cuban history, only José Martí has received more attention than Plácido the poet,

4–5. Some of the best-known work on the 1844 movement has focused on Plácido's life and work. See, for example, the critical work of Walterio Carbonnell ("¿Plácido, conspirado") and Enildo García ("Cuba en la obra de Plácido"). Also see Castellanos, *Plácido, poeta social y político*; and Bueno, *Acerca de Plácido*, which also contains Fernández, "Plácido y la conspiración de La Escalera." Ifeoma Kiddoe Nwankwo's recent study of racial and political identities in the Black Atlantic, *Black Cosmopolitanism*, contains an excellent chapter on Plácido.

2. See Edwards, *Charisma and the Fictions of Black Leadership*.

3. Though of course not exclusively, as we saw in chapter 5.

4. See statement of Mariano Lucumí, Ingenio Achury, ANC, CM 33/4, f. 170v–171v.

5. See, for example, statements of Perico Gangá, ANC, CM 39/1, f. 87–87v; and Patricio Gangá, ANC, CM 33/4, f. 7v–9.

6. Elite status appears to have been a salient factor in the selection of estate leaders, but it was not the only factor. Many accounts suggest that gender, individual charisma, age, and cultural background also determined who became a part of the central leadership cohort.

7. This is taken from the title of Robert Paquette's article "The Drivers Shall Lead Them."

8. See Robert Paquette's extensive historiographic discussion of black agricultural foremen across the America, in ibid. For a discussion of the contramayoral in nineteenth-century Cuba, see Barcia Paz, "Contramayorales."

9. See Paquette, "Drivers Shall Lead Them."

10. See García Rodríguez, *Esclavitud desde la esclavitud*, 26–27.

11. See ibid. For the seriousness of this infraction, see Midlo Hall, *Social Control in Slave Plantation Societies*, 75–77.

12. See, for example, Ortiz, *Negros esclavos*, 204–8 and 229–35. See also Cirilo Villaverde, *Cecilia Valdés*, 414–16; Madden, *Island of Cuba*, 126–27 and 151; Bremer, *Homes of the New World*, 338–39; and Alexander, *Transatlantic Sketches*, 373.

13. These included Haiti, Berbice, Demerara, Barbados, Jamaica, Louisiana, Georgia, and the Virgin Islands. On colonial Saint-Domingue, see Fick, *Making of Haiti*. On the proliferation of drivers in other slave revolts in the Americas, see Paquette, "Drivers Shall Lead Them," 44–49.

14. See García Rodríguez, *Esclavitud desde la esclavitud*, 26–27.

15. See statement of Justo Criollo, ANC, CM 32/3, f. 99–101/97v–99v.

16. See statement of Joaquín Congo, ibid., f. 112–13/110–111v.

17. See, for example, Michael Craton's contention that black drivers in Jamaica used the influence they already possessed as leaders on the estate to incite slaves to rebel in 1831. See Craton, *Testing the Chains*, 251–52.

18. In other Caribbean contexts, see Gaspar, *Bondmen and Rebels*, 227–36; and Craton, *Testing the Chains*, 245 and 299.

19. See statements of Silvestre Criollo, ANC, CM 32/3, f. 79/77; and Ramón Gangá, ibid., f. 74/72–72v.

20. See statement of Eloisa Carabalí, ibid., f. 75/73–73v.

21. See statement of Pedro Criollo, slave of Leonardo Izquierdo, ibid., f. 59–60.

22. See statement of Ramón Gangá, ibid., f. 74/72–72v. Also see statement of Isidro Alfaro y Castillo, free black, servant of Miguel Cárdenas, ibid., f. 21/19–19v.

23. See statement of Felipe Congo, ibid., f. 86/84.

24. See statement of Jacobo Gangá, ANC, CM 31/9, f. 6v–9v.

25. The central leaders on these estates were as follows: León and Cleto Gangá from the Juan de Dios Ingenio (also known as Calderón), Marcos Criollo and Jacobo Gangá from the Sentmanat Ingenio, Rafael Gangá from the San Francisco *potrero*, Dionisio Carabalí and Felipe Mandinga from the San Lorenzo Ingenio, and Cleto Carabalí from the Nazareno Ingenio. At least four others were also cited as in some kind of leadership capacity. See ANC, CM 31/9.

26. See, for example, statements of Dionisio Carabalí, ibid., f. 94v–95v; and Perico Gangá, ANC, CM 39/1, f. 87–87v.

27. See statements of slave witnesses from the properties Marqués and Juan de Dios, ANC, CM 31/9, f. 64v–72.

28. See the statements of Jacobo Gangá (a) Coba, ibid., f. 6v–9v; Marcos Criollo, ibid., f. 9v–13; Camito Mina, ibid., f. 24–26; and Manuel Mina, ibid., f. 30–32v.

29. See statements of Antonio Congo, ANC, CM 33/2; and Perico Gangá, ANC, CM 39/1, f. 87–87v. However, both Perico and Dionisio implied that they had only accepted the leadership roles because they felt coerced to do so.

30. For a list of these leaders condemned in the Triunvirato rebellion and their respective ethnicities, see ANC, CM 30/3, f. 292v.

31. Manuel Barcia Paz has documented no fewer than thirteen major rebellions and small-scale opposition movements from 1832 to 1843 that were organized or enacted overwhelmingly by Lucumí slaves. For an account of these activities, see Barcia Paz, *Seeds of Insurrection*, 34–41.

32. See Falola and Childs, *Yoruba Diaspora*.

33. See Grandío Moráguez, "African Origins of Slaves."

34. See de la Torre, *Spanish West Indies*, 51. Also see Bremer, *Homes of the New World*, 332 and 314.

35. See Samuel Johnson, *History of the Yoruba*, xxii and 19–20.

36. See statement of Manuel Mozambique, ANC, CM 39/1, f. 193–94. Also see the statements of Serafin Lucumí, Felipe Carabalí, Luis Gangá, Basilio Lucumí, Emilio Gangá, and Silverio Carabalí in 39/1. Ramón consistently denied the accusations against him, even on the occasions when he was brought face to face with several of his accusers who gave specific details.

37. See statement of Manuel Gangá, ANC, CM 29/5, f. 19–23/17v–21.

38. See statement of Juan Candela Congo, ANC, CM 32/2, f. 30–32/28–30.

39. For a discussion of the African influence on Cuban slave rebellions of the 1840s, see Barcia Paz, *Seeds of Insurrection*, 41–46.

40. See Desch-Obi, *Fighting for Honor*, 30; and Miller, *Voice of the Leopard*, 6–7.

41. On the military experience African slaves used in American rebellions, see Thornton, "African Dimensions of the Stono Rebellion"; Lovejoy, "Yoruba Factor in the Trans-Atlantic Slave Trade," 46–47; Miller, *Voice of the Leopard*; and Barcia Paz, *Seeds of Insurrection*, 41.

42. As one of many examples, see statement of Ángel Criollo, ANC, CM 31/9, f. 136–37.

43. See Finch, "Scandalous Scarcities." It would be fascinating to know if fewer of these claims surfaced on coffee plantations, where the demographic balance was noticeably different.

44. See O'Hear, "Enslavement of Yoruba."

45. I am grateful to Jessica Johnson for helping me to think through this point.

46. This phrasing is a reference to black feminist critic Audre Lorde's famous declaration that "the master's tools will never dismantle the master's house," and her essay by the same name. See Lorde, "The Master's Tools," 110–13.

47. See Fanon, *Wretched of the Earth*, 60.

48. See statements of Dionisio Carabalí, ANC, CM 31/9, f. 95; and Dionisio Gangá, ibid., f. 93v.

49. See, for example, writings of General José de la Concha, cited in Morales y Morales, *Iniciadores y primeros martires*, 287; and Bretos, *Matanzas*, 82.

50. I have counted at least forty-eight witnesses from eight *legajos* who spoke of relying primarily or solely on machetes and other work tools. The woman in question was Cecilia Criolla, who also spoke of using homemade arrows. See ANC, CM 32/3, f. 66/64–64v.

51. When women slaves testified about machetes being used for a possible uprising, it was generally with the suggestion or outright statement that someone *else* would be using them.

52. See statements of Juan Criollo, ANC, CM 33/5, f. 12v–15.

53. See statement of Felipe Carabalí, ANC, CM 39/1, f. 182 and José Criollo, ANC, CM 33/4, f. 21/17v–22/18. See statement of Juan Criollo, ANC, CM 33/5, 12v–15.

54. See ibid. Capitan de Partido, José Velasco, turned over to the presiding judge the machetes, which apparently the estate mayoral had deemed "not the kind that are used for work."

55. See statements of Calisto Carabalí, ANC, CM 39/1, f. 86–86v; and Perico Gangá, ibid., f. 87–87v.

56. See statement of Casimiro Lucumí, slave of Don Manuel Pérez, ibid., f. 92–94.

57. This is of course a reference to Eric Williams's famous book *Capitalism and Slavery*.

58. See, for example, Thornton, "African Dimensions of the Stono Rebellion," 1109–11. For further discussion of firearms and other weaponry in Yorubaland and Dahomey, see Smith, *Kingdoms of the Yoruba*, 101.

59. See Rawson, *Cuba*, 57.

60. See Dana, *To Cuba and Back*, 148–49.

61. See statement of Tomás Lucumí, ibid., f. 86–46. Also see statements of Matías Mina and León Congo, ANC, CM 39/1, f. 403v–404; and José Lucumí, ibid., f. 106–7.

62. Throughout the testimony, witnesses mentioned knives—usually in the possession of alleged leaders—that seemed distinctive in some way. I suggest this is because they were not readily recognizable as machetes or other work instruments, or because they were being carried outside of normal work hours.

63. See Egerton, *Gabriel's Rebellion*.

64. See, for example, statement of José María Bayona, ibid., f. 502v–504.

|||||||| Chapter Seven

1. For comparative perspectives on religion as a "language" of slave rebellion, see Bellegarde-Smith, "Spirit of the Thing," 53. Also see Carolyn Fick's analysis of Vodou in the Haitian Revolution, in *Making of Haiti*, 94. The following authors explore the importance of African religious practices and radical black Christianity for slave rebellion in other Atlantic contexts: Gaspar, *Bondmen and Rebels*, 249–54; Gomez, *Exchanging Our Country Marks*, 1–4; Rucker, *River Flows On*, chaps. 3–6; Thornton, "African Dimensions of the Stono Rebellion"; and Dayan, *Haiti, History, and the Gods*.

2. See Reis, *Slave Rebellion in Brazil*, 113.

3. See letter from Domingo Delmonte [del Monte] to Alexander Everett Hill, Havana, November 20, 1842, in Sala Cubana, BNJM, C.M. García E, no. 1, f. 2–3.

4. See Brandon, *Santería from Africa to the New World*, 74–75.

5. See Carlos Gherri to Apolinar de la Gala, ANC, CM 29/5, f. 159–60.

6. See statement of José Ricardo Lucumí, a slave of twenty-two years, ANC, CM 34/2, cited in Sabater, "Conspiración de La Escalera," 35.

7. For further discussion on the origins of Regla de Congo, see Ochoa, *Society of the Dead*, 9, 217; Martínez, *Kongo Graphic Writing*, 122. For the dynamic evolution of Kongo practices in the United States and elsewhere in the African Atlantic, see Young, *Rituals of Resistance*, 118–22.

8. José Ynés's age would make this testimony more dubious, were it not for the fact that authorities found the materials in question. See ANC, CM 42/2, f. 133–34.

9. See Cabrera, *Reglas de Congo*, 126–27; and Martínez, *Kongo Graphic Writing*, 152. Wyatt MacGaffey offers a thorough discussion of similar (if not the same) religious concepts among the Bakongo of Lower Kongo in *Kongo Political Culture*, 80. It is interesting to note that in the Kongo, the use of a pot has historically been much more connected to *ndoki*, or the dark side of *nkisi*. For MacGaffey's complete discussion of *nkisi*, see chap. 5, esp. 79–88.

10. See Ochoa, *Society of the Dead*, 11–12 and 31–39; and Martínez, *Kongo Graphic Writing*, 158–59.

11. Other parts of the trial record refer to an estate overseer who was indeed assassinated at La Luisa, but it is not clear whether he died of unknown causes (i.e., allegedly as a result of this endeavor), or whether he was killed during the rebellion that broke out at La Luisa that same month.

12. See statement of Manuel Gangá, ANC, CM, Fondo: Religiones africanas, 1/96, f. 5v–6v. Also see testimonies of Matias Caballero, Felipe Ferrer, María Mandinga, and Antonio Mandinga, ibid., f. 7–8.

13. See statement of Mateo Congo, quoted in Sabater, "Conspiración de La Escalera," 14–38.

14. See Thompson, *Flash of the Spirit*, 125.

15. See Cabrera, *Reglas de Congo*, 126. Also see Thompson, *Flash of the Spirit*, 128.

16. See Cabrera, *Reglas de Congo*, 169. For a discussion of comparable burial practices in the U.S. southern Lowcountry, see Young, *Rituals of Resistance*, 115.

17. See statement of Antonio Carabalí, ANC, CM 32/1, f. 27.

18. Again for a discussion of the Kongolese concept and use of *ndoki*, see MacGaffey, *Kongo Political Culture*, chap. 6.

19. See Cabrera, *Reglas de Congo*, 145. For more on the use of gunpowder, see Martínez, *Kongo Graphic Writing*, 129–30.

20. See ibid., 145. On the use of sulfur in contemporary Palo practice, see Martínez, *Kongo Graphic Writing*, 129.

21. See statement of Alejandro Criollo, cited in Sabater, "Conspiración de La Escalera," 36.

22. See Cabrera, *Reglas de Congo*, 146.

23. Ibid., 145–46.

24. See statement of Nestor Lucumí, slave of Simón Pérez, ANC, CM 33/4, f. 69/29–29v and 186. For his part, José María refused to testify either way.

25. See statement of Santiago of the Gangá nation, ANC, CM 33/4, f. 16v.

26. See, for example, statement of Isidro Carabalí, ANC, CM 39/1, f. 401–2. Also see statement of Domingo Gangá, ibid., f. 31v.

27. See statement of Domingo Gangá, ibid., f. 31v.

28. See statement of José Roque, ANC, CM 39/1, f. 4 and 8–9v.

29. See statement of José María Gangá Longoba, ANC, CM 32/3, f. 160v.

30. See Thompson, *Flash of the Spirit*, 135.

31. See statement of Clemencio Criollo, ANC, CM 31/9, f. 62–63.

32. See statement Pablo Lucumí, ibid., f. 65v.

33. See statements of Cleto Gangá and Pablo Lucumí, ibid., f. 65v–66.

34. For an important discussion of the use of Kongolese amulets in the South Carolina Lowcountry, see Young, *Rituals of Resistance*. For comparable examples in other slave societies, see Gomez, *Exchanging Our Country Marks*, 43–45; Rucker, *River Flows On*, 35–37 and 164–67; Fick, *Making of Haiti*, 111; and Reis, *Slave Rebellion in Brazil*, 93.

35. See statement of Pablo Lucumí, ANC, CM 33/4, f. 27/23–23v.

36. See statement of Patricio Gangá, ibid., f. 129.

37. See statement of Narciso Campusano, ANC, CM 32/3, f. 154v–156.

38. See statement of Miguel Naranjo, ANC, CM 39/1, f. 418. These were critical gatherings where Miguel claimed to have seen well-known organizers such as Plácido and Jorge López.

39. See Harding, *Refuge in Thunder*, 27–28.

40. See ibid., 28.

41. See Cabrera, *Reglas de Congo*, 127.

42. See statement of Telésforo Lucumí, ANC, CM 33/1, quoted in García Rodríguez, *Voices of the Enslaved*, 189.

43. The Cuban amulets, for example, recall the passages from the Koran that Muslim leaders in Bahia used to safeguard slave combatants during the 1835 rebellion. See Reis, *Slave Rebellion in Brazil*, 93; and Harding, *Refuge in Thunder*, 22–27. For a

compelling discussion of conjure bags in the U.S. South, see Young, *Rituals of Resistance*, 118–34. Similar examples of this kind abounded from Haiti to South Carolina. See, for example, Fick, *Making of Haiti*; and Gomez, *Exchanging Our Country Marks*.

44. See statement of Ramón Lucumí, ANC, CM 33/1, quoted in García Rodríguez, *Voices of the Enslaved*, 189.

45. See statement of Ramón Congo, ANC, CM 32/2, esp. f. 218v.

46. See statement of Justo Criollo, ANC, CM 34/2, quoted in Sabater, "Conspiración de La Escalera."

47. See, for example, García Rodríguez, *Voices of the Enslaved*, 189.

48. Several authors have argued convincingly that prewarfare canons predicated on spiritual consultations, protective ceremonies, and ritual preparations, which became central to precolonial expansionist states like Kongo-Angola and Dahomey, were reconfigured in the plantation zones of Haiti and Cuba during times of insurgency. See, for example, Desch-Obi, "Deadly Dances"; Desch-Obi, "Combat and the Crossing of the *Kalunga*," 356–61; and Thornton, "African Dimensions of the Stono Rebellion," 1101–13.

49. See Desch-Obi, "Deadly Dances."

50. See Thornton, "African Dimensions of the Stono Rebellion," 1112–13.

51. It is not clear if they meant that the proposed rebellion would be ruined or that those who betrayed them would be ruined. See statements of Marcelino Criollo and Luis Gangá, ANC, CM 41/2, f. 25v–26v.

52. See declarations of José Gangá, ibid., f. 67v–71v; also Luis Gangá, ibid., f. 26v–27v; and Clara Criolla, ibid., f. 37v–38.

53. For Juana Criolla's statement, see ibid., f. 36–36v. Also see that of Domingo Carabalí, ibid., f. 36–36v.

54. See statement of José Gangá, ibid., f. 67v–71v.

55. See, for example, statement of Cirila Criolla, ibid., f. 22–23.

56. See statement of Luis Gangá, ibid., f. 26v–27v.

57. For the assertion that Patricio and Blas "were dealing with some witchcraft [*trataron de unos brugerias*]," see statement of Marcelino Criollo, ibid., f. 25v–26v. In other instances, rebel leaders allegedly promised similar protection. See, for example, statements of Andrés Mina, ANC, CM 33/4, f. 23v–24; and Pablo Lucumí, ibid., f. 27/23–23v.

58. See statement of Pedro Domech, ANC, CM 41/2, f. 133–34.

59. See statement of Manuel Robaina, ibid., f. 157–61.

60. See statement of Tomás Rabaina, ibid., f. 154v–157.

61. See statement of Federico Gangá, ANC, CM 32/1, f. 5–6v.

62. In addition to Federico's testimony above, see statements of Juan Lucumí, f. 17; Petra Carabalí, f. 19–20; Damián Carabalí, f. 17v–18; and Adelaida Gangá, f. 20; all in 32/1.

63. These included, according to various reports, Damián Carabalí, Juan Lucumí, Adelaida Gangá, Emily Carabalí, Lino Criollo, Leandro Carabalí, Antonio Carabalí, Domingo Congo, and Federico Gangá. See ibid.

64. For these accounts of dancing at night with muñecos (which I have translated as "figurines"), see above testimonies of Federico, Juan, and Damián, respectively.

65. Usually to "drink" in a ceremonial context meant to allow deities or sacred objects to ritually consume animal blood. However, in this context, the act of drinking appears to refer to consuming the cane liquor.

66. For this statement, see statement of Antonio Carabalí, ANC, CM 32/1, f. 27.

67. For more information on Siete Rayos, see Cabrera, *Reglas de Congo*, 129.

68. See ibid., 63.

69. See ibid., 129.

70. See statement of Federico Gangá, CM 32/1, f. 30.

71. See statement of Petra Carabalí Bibi, ibid., f. 19–20. Her original testimony reads: "[Federico] los reunia sacaba unas camelitas le hechaba aguardiente y les daba á vever les hacia bailar y cantar llanllá saraminga qumba há!! branco corá." I have translated *camelitas* as figurines, although a *camelo* is literally defined as a hoax. It makes sense, though, that Federico would have been spraying liquor on an actual figurine, or some concrete representation of one of the deities.

72. See ibid. Antonio Carabalí gave similar testimony; see ibid., f. 27.

73. See statement of Lino Criollo, ibid., f. 22v.

74. See statement of Federico Gangá, ibid., f. 16v–17.

75. See statement of Antonio Carabalí, ibid., f. 27.

76. Several other witnesses named persons from outside the estate grounds who attended the rituals. See testimonies of Damián Carabalí, Juan Lucumí, and Petra Carabalí, ANC, CM 32/1. For the involvement of Emilia and Adelaida, see testimony of Juan Lucumí, ibid.

77. See statement of Emily Carabalí, ibid., f. 21. She was the only one who mentioned this violent incident.

78. See statement of Petra Carabalí, ibid., f. 19–20.

79. See statement of Juan Lucumí, ibid., f. 17. Federico corroborated that he had been paid for these services. These depositions sometimes refer to the targeted individual as the mayoral and other times as the administrador.

80. See, for example, testimonies of Isidro Carabalí, ANC, CM 39/1, f. 401; Francisco Gangá, ibid., f. 401; Antonio Congo, ibid., f. 402v–403.

81. See testimonies of Petra Carabalí and of Federico Gangá, ANC, CM, 32/2, f. 19–20 and 16v–17, respectively.

82. Future study of additional portions of the trial record may bring other trends to light.

83. See declarations of Julián Lucumí, Julio Criollo, and Roberto Gangá, ANC, CM 31/9, folios 144v–152v and 184–85. It is important to note however, that Florentina denied most of the accusations against her. When questioned about herbs and other items associated with "witchcraft operations," Florentina stated that the mayoral had taken them from her.

84. See statement of Roberto Gangá, ANC, CM 31/9. The testimonies differ on who was actually supposed to start the fire. Some said it was Florentina; others said it was Eusebio. Roberto's statement suggests that Florentina was to carry out the act itself with Eusebio present, but this is not entirely clear.

85. See statement of Florentina Criollo, ANC, CM 31/9.

IIIIIIII Conclusion

1. For the best discussion to date of Mariana Grajales, see Prados-Torreira, *Mambisas*, esp. 64. On the Partido Independiente de Color, see Helg, *Our Rightful Share*, 153–55 and 180.

2. See Beckles, *Natural Rebels*, 172. Jennifer Morgan has similarly shown that women in the early colonies of Barbados and South Carolina "were careful observers of the colonial landscape and responded to moments of unrest as did enslaved men." See Morgan, *Laboring Women*, 189.

3. See Barcia Zequeira, *Otra familia*. For descriptions of the domestic labor of enslaved women in Cuba, see statement of Emily Carabalí, ANC, CM 32/1; Suárez y Romero, *Colección de artículos*; and Montejo, *Biography of a Runaway Slave*.

4. For an excellent discussion of the violent protests against black poverty and disenfranchisement that erupted in Antigua and other parts of the British Caribbean after general emancipation in 1834, see Lightfoot, *Troubling Freedom*.

5. For these figures, see Morales y Morales, *Iniciadores y primeros martires*.

6. The number of recorded slaves in Cuba declined from 436,495 in 1841 to 326,759 in 1846. In my research, this is the only recorded slave population decline in the entire nineteenth or eighteenth century. For these figures, see Ortiz, *Negros esclavos*, 321–22. Also see Midlo Hall, *Social Control in Slave Plantation Societies*, 60–61.

7. Some authors have also lamented the forestalling of a multiracial independence movement in Cuba as a result of the trials of La Escalera. For these two discussions, see Llanes Miqueli, *Víctimas del año del Cuero*, 1–4; Thomas, *Cuba*, 205; Rauch, *American Interest in Cuba*, 42–43; and Deschamps Chapeaux, *Negro en la economía habanera*, chap. 1.

8. The most important study of this impact on the free population of color is Reid-Vazquez, *Year of the Lash*. See esp. chaps. 2–4.

Bibliography

||||||| Archival Collections

Archivo Nacional de Cuba, Havana, Cuba
    Asuntos Políticos
    Comisión Militar Ejecutiva y Permanente
    Gobierno Superior Civil
Archivo Histórico Nacional, Madrid, Spain
    Estado
    Ultramar
Archivo Histórico Provincial de Matanzas, Matanzas, Cuba
    Gobierno Provincial de Matanzas (Sublevaciones)

||||||| Libraries

Biblioteca de Literatura y Linguística, Havana, Cuba
Biblioteca Nacional José Martí, Havana, Cuba
    Special Manuscript Collections, Sala Cubana
Houghton Library, Harvard University, Cambridge, Massachusetts
    The José Augusto Escoto Collection
The Library of Congress, Washington, D.C.
The New York Public Library, New York, New York
The Schomburg Center for Research in Black Culture, New York, New York

||||||| Newspapers

Diario de La Habana　　　　　　　*Morning Journal* (Jamaica)
El Faro Industrial　　　　　　　　*Royal Gazette & Jamaican Standard*
Jamaica Despatch, Chronicle, & Gazette

||||||| Published Primary Documents and Travel Narratives

Abbot, Abiel. *Letters Written in the Interior of Cuba, between the Mountains of Arcana, to the East, and of Cusco, to the West, in the Months of February, March, April, and May, 1828.* Boston: Bowles and Dearborn, 1829.

Alexander, James E. *Transatlantic Sketches, Comprising Visits to the Most Interesting Scenes in North and South America, and the West Indies. With Notes on Negro Slavery and Canadian Emigration.* London: R. Bentley, 1833.

Ballou, Maturin Murray. *History of Cuba; or, Notes of a Traveller in the Tropics; Being a Political, Historical, and Statistical Account of the Island, from Its First Discovery to the Present Time.* New York: J. C. Derby, 1854.

Barinetti, Carlos. *A Voyage to Mexico and Havanna: Including Some General Observations on the United States. By an Italian.* New York: C. Vinton, 1841.

Bremer, Fredrika. *The Homes of the New World: Impressions of America.* Translated by Mary Howitt. New York: Harper & Bros., 1853.

Cantero, Justo Germán. *Los ingenios; Colección de vistas de los principales ingenious de azúcar de la isla de Cuba.* Havana: L. Marquier, 1857.

Cartilla practica del manejo de ingenios ó fincas destinadas á producir azúcar. Irún, Spain: La Elegancia, 1862.

Chateausalins, Honorato Bernard. *El vademecum de los hacendados cubanos o guía práctica para curar la mayor parte de las enfermedades.* Havana: Manuel Soler, 1854.

Dana, Richard Henry. *To Cuba and Back: A Vacation Voyage.* Boston: Ticknor and Fields, 1859.

de la Torre, José María. *The Spanish West Indies: Cuba and Porto Rico: Geographical, Political, and Industrial.* Translated by J. T. O'Neil. New York: J. H. Colton, 1858.

Humboldt, Alexander von. *The Island of Cuba.* Translated by J. S. Thrasher. New York: Derby & Jackson, 1856.

Jimeno, Francisco. "Cartas de Francisco Jimeno a Manuel Sanguily, 1886." General Collection, Schomburg Center for Black Research and Culture, New York.

Johnson, Samuel. *The History of the Yorubas from the Earliest Times to the Beginning of the British Protectorate.* London: G. Routledge & Sons, Ltd., 1921.

Kimball, Richard Burleigh. "Letters from Cuba." *Knickerbocker* 21 (May 1845): 41–47.

Madden, Richard Robert. *The Island of Cuba: Its Resources, Progress, and Prospects, Considered in Relation Especially to the Influence of Its Prosperity on the Interests of the British West India Colonies.* London: Partridge & Oakey, 1853.

Mann, Mary Peabody. *Juanita: A Romance of Real Life in Cuba Fifty Years Ago.* Boston: D. Lothrop, 1887. Reprint, Charlottesville: University Press of Virginia, 2000.

Manzano, Juan Francisco. *The Autobiography of a Slave.* Translated by Evelyn Picon Garfield. Detroit: Wayne State University Press, 1996.

———. *Poems by a Slave in the Island of Cuba, Recently Liberated.* Translated by R. R. Madden. London: T. Ward, 1840.

Marquéz, José de Jesús. "Plácido y los conspiradores de 1844." *Revista Cubana* 20 (1894): 35–51.

Montgomery, Cora. *The Queen of Islands, and the King of Rivers.* New York: Adam, 1850.

Philalethes, Demoticus. *Yankee Travels through the Island of Cuba; or, The Men and Government, the Laws and Customs of Cuba, as Seen by American Eyes.* New York: D. Appleton, 1856.

Rawson, James. *Cuba*. New York: Lane & Tippett, 1847.

Sanguily, Manuel. "Una opinión en contra de Plácido (notas críticas)." *Hojas Literarias* 4 (August 1894): 425–35.

Súarez y Romero, Anselmo. *Colección de artículos*. Havana: Establecimiento tip. La Antilla, 1859.

Valdés Gerónimo. *Bando de gobernación y policía de la isla de Cuba, espedido por Gerónimo Valdés, Presidente, Gobernador y Capitán General*. Havana: Printed by the Government and Captaincy General of Her Majesty, 1842.

Villaverde, Cirilo. *Cecilia Valdés or El Angel Hill*. Translated by Helen Lane. New York: Oxford University Press, 2005.

Wurdemann, John G. F. *Notes on Cuba, Containing an Account of Its Discovery and Early History; A Description of the Face of the Country, Its Population, Resources, and Wealth; Its Institutions, and the Manners and Customs of Its Inhabitants. With Directions to Travellers Visiting the Island*. Boston: J. Munroe, 1844.

|||||||| Secondary Sources

Adderley, Rosanne. *"New Negroes from Africa": Slave Trade Abolition and Free African Settlement in the Nineteenth-Century Caribbean*. Bloomington: Indiana University Press, 2006.

Afolayan, Funso, and John Pemberton. *Yoruba Sacred Kingship: "A Power Like That of the Gods."* Washington, D.C.: Smithsonian Institution Press, 1996.

Aimes, Hubert. *A History of Slavery in Cuba, 1511 to 1868*. New York: G. P. Putnam's Sons, 1907.

Allahar, Anton. *Class, Politics, and Sugar in Colonial Cuba*. Lewiston, N.Y.: Edwin Mellon, 1990.

Arondekar, Anjali. *For the Record: On Sexuality and the Colonial Archive in India*. Durham, N.C.: Duke University Press, 2009.

Barcia Paz, Manuel. *Con el látigo de la ira: Legislación, represión y control en las plantaciones cubanas, 1790–1870*. Havana: Ciencias Sociales, 2000.

———. "Los contramayorales negros y mulatos en la Cuba decimonónica." *Gabinete de Arqueología* 2 (2002): 88–93.

———. *The Great African Slave Revolt of 1825: Cuba and the Fight for Freedom in Matanzas*. Baton Rouge: Louisiana State University Press, 2012.

———. *La resistencia esclava en las plantaciones cubanas, 1790–1870*. Pinar del Río: Vitral, 1998.

———. *Seeds of Insurrection: Domination and Resistance on Western Cuban Plantations, 1808–1848*. Baton Rouge: Louisiana State University Press, 2008.

———. "Sugar, Slavery and Bourgeoisie: The Emergence of the Cuban Sugar Industry." In *Sugarlandia Revisited: Sugar and Colonialism in Asia and the Americas, 1800 to 1940*, edited by Ulbe Bosma, Juan Giusti-Cordero, and G. Roger Knight, 147–60. New York: Berghahn, 2007.

Barcia Zequeira, María del Carmen. *La otra familia: Parientes, redes y descendencia de los esclavos en Cuba*. Havana: Casa de las Américas, 2003.

Barcia Zequeira, María del Carmen, and Manuel Barcia Paz. "La conspiración de La Escalera: El precio de una traición." *Catauro* 2, no. 3 (2001): 199–204.

Barnes, Sandra, ed. *Africa's Ogun: Old World and New*. Bloomington: Indiana University Press, 1989.

Barry, Boubacar. *La Sénégambie du XVe au XIXe siècle: Traite négrière, Islam et conquête coloniale*. Paris: L'Harmattan, 1988.

Bascom, William. *Shango in the New World*. Austin: Afro and Afro-American Research Institute, University of Texas at Austin, 1972.

Bay, Edna. *Wives of the Leopard: Gender, Politics, and Culture in the Kingdom of Dahomey*. Charlottesville: University of Virginia Press, 1998.

Beckles, Hilary McD. *Black Rebellion in Barbados: The Struggle against Slavery, 1627–1838*. Bridgetown, Barbados: Antilles, 1984.

———. *Centering Woman: Gender Discourses in Caribbean Slave Society*. Princeton, N.J.: Markus Wiener, 1999.

———. *Centering Woman: Gender Discourses in Caribbean Slave Society*. Kingston: I. Randle, 1999.

———. *Natural Rebels: A Social History of Enslaved Black Women in Barbados*. New Brunswick, N.J.: Rutgers University Press, 1989.

Behrendt, Stephen, David Eltis, Herbert Klein, and David Richardson, eds. *The Trans-Atlantic Slave Trade: A Database on CD-ROM*. Cambridge: Cambridge University Press, 1999.

Bellegarde-Smith, Patrick. "The Spirit of the Thing: Religious Thought and Social/Historical Memory." In *Fragments of Bone: Neo-African Religions in a New World*, edited by Patrick Bellegarde-Smith, 52–69. Urbana: University of Illinois Press, 2005.

———, ed. *Fragments of Bone: Neo-African Religions in a New World*. Urbana: University of Illinois Press, 2005.

Benítez-Rojo, Antonio. *The Repeating Island: The Caribbean and the Postmodern Perspective*. Translated by James Maraniss. Durham, N.C.: Duke University Press, 1996.

Bergad, Laird. *Cuban Rural Society in the Nineteenth Century: The Social and Economic History of Monoculture in Matanzas*. Princeton, N.J.: Princeton University Press, 1990.

Bergad, Laird, Fe Iglesias García, and María del Carmen Barcia. *The Cuban Slave Market, 1790–1880*. New York: Cambridge University Press, 1995.

Berry, Daina Ramey. *"Swing the Sickle for the Harvest Is Ripe": Gender and Slavery in Antebellum Georgia*. Urbana: University of Illinois Press, 2007.

Brandon, George. *Santeria from Africa to the New World: The Dead Sell Memories*. Bloomington: Indiana University Press, 1993.

Bretos, Miguel. *Matanzas: The Cuba Nobody Knows*. Miami: University Press of Florida, 2010.

Brown, David. *Santería Enthroned: Art, Ritual, and Innovation in an Afro-Cuban Religion*. Chicago: University of Chicago Press, 2003.

Brown, Ras Michael. "'Walk in the Feenda': West-Central Africans and the Forest in the South Carolina–Georgia Lowcountry." In *Central Africans and*

Cultural Transformations in the American Diaspora, edited by Linda M. Heywood, 289–318. New York: Cambridge University Press, 2002.

Brown, Vincent. *The Reaper's Garden: Death and Power in the World of Atlantic Slavery* Cambridge, Mass.: Harvard University Press, 2008.

———. "Spiritual Terror and Sacred Authority in Jamaican Slave Society." *Slavery & Abolition* 24, no. 1 (2003): 24–53.

Bueno, Salvador. *Acerca de Plácido.* Havana: Letras Cubanas, 1985.

Burton, Antoinette, ed. *Archive Stories: Facts, Fictions, and the Writing of History.* Durham, N.C.: Duke University Press, 2005.

Bush, Barbara. "Defiance or Submission? The Role of the Slave Woman in Slave Resistance in the British Caribbean." *Immigrants and Minorities* 1 (1982): 16–38.

———. *Slave Women in Caribbean Society, 1650–1838.* Bloomington: Indiana University Press, 1990.

Cabrera, Lydia. *El monte: Igbo, finda, ewe orisha, vititi nfinda: Notas sobre las religiones, la magia, las supersticiones y el folklore de los negros criollos y el pueblo de Cuba.* Miami: Universal, 1975.

———. *Reglas de Congo: Palo monte mayombe.* Miami: Universal, 1986.

Camp, Stephanie. *Closer to Freedom: Enslaved Women and Everyday Resistance in the Plantation South.* Chapel Hill: University of North Carolina Press, 2004.

Canizares, Raul. *Walking with the Night: The Afro-Cuban World of Santeria.* Rochester, N.Y.: Destiny, 1993.

Carbonnell, Walterio. "¿Plácido, conspirado?" *Revolución y cultura* 2 (February 1987): 57.

Castellanos, Jorge. *Plácido, poeta social y político.* Miami: Universal, 1984.

Castañeda, Humbert. "El caso de Mr. David Turnbull, el consul inglés." *Revista de la Universidad de La Habana* 168–69 (July–October 1964): 127–53.

Castañeda Fuertes, Digna. "The Female Slave in Cuba during the First Half of the Nineteenth Century." In *Engendering History: Caribbean Women in Historical Perspective*, edited by Verene Shepherd, Bridget Brereton, and Barbara Bailey, 141–54. London: J. Currey, 1995.

Cepero Bonilla, Raúl. *Azúcar y abolición: Apuntes para una historia crítica del abolicionismo.* Havana: Cenit, 1948.

Chambers, Douglas B. "'My Own Nation': Igbo Exiles in the Diaspora." *Slavery and Abolition* 18, no. 1 (1997): 72–97.

———. "The Significance of Igbo in the Bight of Biafra Slave Trade: A Rejoinder to Northrup's 'Myth Igbo.'" *Slavery and Abolition* 23, no. 1 (2002): 101–20.

Chatterjee, Piya. *A Time for Tea: Women, Labor and Post/Colonial Politics on an Indian Plantation.* Durham, N.C.: Duke University Press, 2001.

Childs, Matt D. *The 1812 Aponte Rebellion in Cuba and the Struggle against Atlantic Slavery.* Chapel Hill: University of North Carolina Press, 2006.

Clark, Vévé. "Developing Diaspora and Literacy and Marasa Consciousness." *Theatre Survey* 50, no. 1 (May 2009): 9–18.

Conrad, Robert Edgar. *Children of God's Fire: A Documentary History of Black Slavery in Brazil*. Princeton, N.J.: Princeton University Press, 1983.

Corwin, Arthur. *Spain and the Abolition of Slavery in Cuba, 1817–1886*. Austin: Institute of Latin American Studies, University of Texas, 1967.

Craton, Michael. *Testing the Chains: Resistance to Slavery in the British West Indies*. Ithaca, N.Y.: Cornell University Press, 1982.

Curry-Machado, Jonathan. *Cuban Sugar Industry: Transnational Networks and Engineering Migrants in Mid-Nineteenth Century Cuba*. New York: Palgrave Macmillan, 2011.

———. "How Cuba Burned with the Ghosts of British Slavery: Race, Abolition and the Escalera." *Slavery and Abolition* 25, no. 1 (2004): 71–93.

Dadzie, Stella. "Searching for the Invisible Woman: Slavery and Resistance in Jamaica." *Race and Class* 32 (1990): 21–38.

Daniel, Yvonne. *Dancing Wisdom: Embodied Knowledge in Haitian Vodou, Cuban Yoruba, and Bahian Candomblé*. Urbana: University of Illinois Press, 2005.

Davis, Angela. "Reflections on the Black Woman's Role in the Community of Slaves." In *Words of Fire: An Anthology of African-American Feminist Thought*, edited by Beverly Guy-Sheftall, 200–218. New York: New Press, 1995.

Dayan, Joan. *Haiti, History, and the Gods*. Berkeley: University of California Press, 1995.

Derrida, Jacques. *Archive Fever: A Freudian Impression*. Translated by Eric Prenowitz. Chicago: University of Chicago Press, 1996.

Desch-Obi, T. J. "Combat and the Crossing of the *Kalunga*." In *Central Africans and Cultural Transformations in the American Diaspora*, edited by Linda M. Heywood, 353–70. New York: Cambridge University Press, 2002.

———. "Deadly Dances: The Spiritual Dimensions of Kongo-Angolan Martial Art Traditions in the New World." In *Fragments of Bone: Neo-African Religions in a New World*, edited by Patrick Bellegarde-Smith, 70–89. Urbana: University of Illinois Press, 2005.

———. *Fighting for Honor: The History of African Martial Art Traditions in the Atlantic World*. Columbia: University of South Carolina Press, 2008.

Deschamps Chapeaux, Pedro. *El negro en la economía habanera del siglo XIX*. Havana: Unión de Escritores y Artistas de Cuba, 1971.

de Ximeno, José Manuel. "Un pobre histrión (Plácido)." In *Primer Congreso Nacional de Historia*, 371–77. Havana: Instituto Cívico Militar, 1943.

Dorsey, Joseph. *Slave Traffic in the Age of Abolition: Puerto Rico, West Africa, and the Non-Hispanic Caribbean, 1815–1859*. Gainesville: University Press of Florida, 2003.

———. "It Hurt Very Much at the Time: Patriarchy, Rape Culture, and the Slave Body–Semiotic." In *The Culture of Gender and Sexuality in the Caribbean*, edited by Lewis Linden, 294–322. Gainesville: University Press of Florida, 2003.

Dorsey, Joseph, and Robert Paquette. "The Escoto Papers and Cuban Slave Resistance." *Slavery and Abolition* 15, no. 3 (1994): 88–95.

———. "Women without History: Slavery, Jurisprudence, and the International Politics of Partus Sequitur Ventrem in the Spanish Caribbean." *Journal of*

Caribbean History 28, no. 2 (1995): 165–208. Reprinted in *Caribbean Slavery in the Atlantic World*, ed. Hilary Beckles and Verene Shepard. Princeton, N.J.: Markus Wiener, 2000.

Dubois, Laurent. *Avengers of the New World: The Story of the Haitian Revolution.* Cambridge, Mass.: Harvard University Press, 2004.

Edwards, Erica. *Charisma and the Fictions of Black Leadership.* Minneapolis: University of Minnesota Press, 2012.

Egerton, Douglas. *Gabriel's Rebellion: The Virginia Slave Conspiracies of 1800 and 1802.* Chapel Hill: University of North Carolina Press, 1993.

Eltis, David. "The Diaspora of Yoruba Speakers, 1650–1865: Dimensions and Implications." In *The Yoruba Diaspora in the Atlantic World*, edited by Toyin Falola and Matt D. Childs, 17–39. Bloomington: Indiana University Press, 2004.

———. *Economic Growth and the Ending of the Transatlantic Slave Trade.* New York: Oxford University Press, 1987.

Eltis, David, and David Richardson. "A New Assessment of the Transatlantic Slave Trade." In *Extending the Frontiers: Essays on the New Transatlantic Slave Trade Database*, edited by David Eltis and David Richardson. New Haven, Conn.: Yale University Press, 2008.

———. *Atlas of the Transatlantic Slave Trade.* New Haven, Conn.: Yale University Press, 2010.

———, eds. *"Extending the Frontiers: Essays on the New Transatlantic Slave Trade Database.* New Haven, Conn.: Yale University Press, 2008.

Ely, Ronald. *Cuando reinaba su majestad el azúcar: Estudio histórico-sociológico de una tragedia latinoamericana: El monocultivo en Cuba, origen y evolución del proceso.* Buenos Aires: Sudamericana, 1963.

Entralgo, Elías José. *La liberación étnica cubana.* Havana: University of Havana, 1953.

Falola, Toyin, and Matt D. Childs. "The Yoruba Diaspora in the Atlantic World: Methodology and Research." In *The Yoruba Diaspora in the Atlantic World*, edited by Toyin Falola and Matt D. Childs, 1–16. Bloomington: Indiana University Press, 2004.

———, eds. *The Changing Worlds of Atlantic Africa: Essays in Honor of Robin Law.* Durham, N.C.: Carolina Academic, 2009.

———, eds. *The Yoruba Diaspora in the Atlantic World.* Bloomington: Indiana University Press, 2004.

Fanon, Frantz. *The Wretched of the Earth.* New York: Grove, 1963.

Fernández, Daisy Cué. *Plácido, el poeta conspirador.* Santiago de Cuba: Oriente, 2007.

———. "Plácido y la conspiración de La Escalera." *Santiago* 42 (1981): 145–206.

Ferrer, Ada. "Cuban Slavery and Atlantic Antislavery." In *Slavery and Antislavery in Spain's Atlantic Empire*, edited by Josep Fradera and Christopher Schmidt-Nowara, 134–57. New York: Berghahn, 2013.

———. *Insurgent Cuba: Race, Nation, and Revolution, 1868–1898.* Chapel Hill: University of North Carolina Press, 1999.

————."Speaking of Haiti: Slavery, Revolution, and Freedom in Cuban Slave Testimony." In *The World of the Haitian Revolution*, edited by David Geggus and Norman Fiering, 223–47. Bloomington: Indiana University Press, 2009.

Fick, Carolyn. *The Making of Haiti: The Saint Domingue Revolution from Below*. Knoxville: University of Tennessee Press, 1990.

Finch, Aisha. "The Repeating Rebellion: Slave Resistance and Political Consciousness in Nineteenth-Century Cuba, 1812–1844." Paper presented at the Cubanist Book Project Seminar, John L. Warfield Center for African and African American Studies, University of Texas, Austin, February 19, 2013.

————. "Scandalous Scarcities: Black Slave Women, Plantation Domesticity, and Travel Writing in Nineteenth-Century Cuba." *Journal of Historical Sociology* 23 (Winter 2010): 101–43.

Fischer, Sibylle. *Modernity Disavowed: Haiti and the Cultures of Slavery in the Age of Revolution*. Durham, N.C.: Duke University Press, 2004.

Foner, Philip Sheldon. *A History of Cuba and Its Relations with the United States*. New York: International Publishers, 1963.

Fradera, Josep M., and Christopher Schmidt-Nowara. *Slavery and Antislavery in Spain's Atlantic Empire*. New York: Berghahn, 2013.

Franco, José Luciano. *La conspiractión de Aponte*. Havana: Publicaciones del Archivo Nacional, 1963.

————. *La gesta heroica del Triunvirato*. Havana: Ciencias Sociales, 1978.

————. "Introducción al proceso de La Escalera." *Boletín del Archivo Nacional* 67 (January–December 1974): 54–63.

————. "Origen y consecuencias de la sublevación de los esclavos en Matanzas en 1843." *Granma*, September 12, 1973.

García, Daniel Martínez. "La sublevación de La Alcancía: Su rehabilitación histórico en el proceso conspirativo que concluye en La Escalera (1844)." *Rábida* 19 (2000): 41–48.

García, Enildo. "Cuba en la obra de Plácido, 1809–1844: Análisis y bibliografía comentada." Ph.D. diss., New York University, 1982.

García Balañà, Albert. "Antislavery before Abolitionism: Networks and Motives in Early Liberal Barcelona, 1833–1844." In *Slavery and Antislavery in Spain's Atlantic Empire*, edited by Josep Fradera and Christopher Schmidt-Nowara, 229–55. New York: Berghahn, 2013.

García Rodríguez, Gloria. "A propósito de La Escalera: El esclavo como sujeto político." *Boletín del Archivo Nacional* 12 (2000): 1–13.

————. *Conspiraciones y revueltas: La actividad política de los negros en Cuba (1790–1845)*. Santiago de Cuba: Oriente, 2003.

————. *La esclavitud desde la esclavitud*. Havana: Ciencias Sociales, 2003.

————. *Voices of the Enslaved in Nineteenth-Century Cuba: A Documentary History*. Translated by Nancy Westrate. Chapel Hill: University of North Carolina Press, 2011.

Gaspar, David Barry. *Bondmen and Rebels: A Study of Master-Slave Relations in Antigua*. Baltimore: Johns Hopkins University Press, 1985.

Gaspar, David Barry, and David Patrick Geggus, eds. *A Turbulent Time: The French Revolution and the Greater Caribbean*. Bloomington: Indiana University Press, 1997.

Geggus, David P., ed. *The Impact of the Haitian Revolution in the Atlantic World*. Columbia: University of South Carolina Press, 2001.

Genovese, Eugene. *From Rebellion to Revolution: Afro-American Slave Revolts in the Making of the Modern World*. Baton Rouge: Louisiana State University Press, 1979.

Glissant, Edouard. *Caribbean Discourse: Selected Essays*. Translated by Michael Dash. Charlottesville: University Press of Virginia, 1989.

Glymph, Thavolia. *Out of the House of Bondage: The Transformation of the Plantation Household*. Cambridge. New York: Cambridge University Press, 2008.

Gomez, Michael A. *Black Crescent: The Experience and Legacy of African Muslims in the Americas*. New York: Cambridge University Press, 2005.

———. *Exchanging Our Country Marks: The Transformation of African Identities in the Colonial and Antebellum South*. Chapel Hill: University of North Carolina Press, 1998.

Gómez-Barris, Macarena. *Where Memory Dwells: Culture and State Violence in Chile*. Berkeley: University of California Press, 2009.

González del Valle, Francisco. *La conspiración de La Escalera*. Havana: Siglo XX, 1925.

Gore, Dayo F. *Radicalism at the Crossroads: African American Women Activists in the Cold War*. New York: New York University Press, 2011.

Gore, Dayo F., Jeanne Theoharis, and Komozi Woodard. *Want to Start a Revolution? Radical Women in the Black Freedom Struggle*. New York: New York University Press, 2009.

Grandío Moráguez, Oscar. "The African Origins of Slaves Arriving in Cuba, 1789–1865." In *Extending the Frontiers: Essays on the New Transatlantic Slave Trade Database*, edited by David Eltis and David Richardson, 176–202. New Haven, Conn.: Yale University Press, 2008.

Guerra, Lillian. *The Myth of José Martí: Conflicting Nationalisms in Early Twentieth-Century Cuba*. Chapel Hill: University of North Carolina Press, 2005.

Guha, Ranjit. *Elementary Aspects of Peasant Insurgency*. Durham, N.C.: Duke University Press, 1983.

Guterl, Matthew Pratt. *American Mediterranean: Southern Slaveholders in the Age of Emancipation*. Cambridge, Mass.: Harvard University Press, 2008.

Harding, Rachel E. *A Refuge in Thunder: Candomblé and Alternative Spaces of Blackness*. Bloomington: Indiana University Press, 2000.

Hartman, Saidiya. *Scenes of Subjection: Terror, Slavery, and Self-Making in Nineteenth-Century America*. New York: Oxford University Press, 1997.

———. "Venus in Two Acts." *Small Axe* 12 (2008): 1–14.

Helg, Aline. *Our Rightful Share: The Afro-Cuban Struggle for Equality*. Chapel Hill: University of North Carolina Press, 1995.

Hernández y Sánchez-Barba, Mario. "David Turnbull y el problema de la esclavitud en Cuba." *Anuario de Estudios Americanos* 14 (1957): 292.

Herskovits, Melville J. *Dahomey: An Ancient West African Kingdom*. New York: J. J. Augustin, 1938.

————. *The Myth of the Negro Past*. New York: Harper & Brothers, 1941.

Heywood, Linda, ed. *Central Africans and Cultural Transformations in the American Diaspora*. New York: Cambridge University Press, 2002.

Howard, Philip. *Changing History: Afro-Cuban Cabildos and Societies of Color in the Nineteenth Century*. Baton Rouge: Louisiana State University Press, 1998.

James, C. L. R. *The Black Jacobins: Toussaint Louverture and the San Domingo Revolution*. New York: Dial, 1938.

James, Joy. "Framing the Panther: Assata Shakur and Black Female Agency." In *Want to Start a Revolution? Radical Women in the Black Freedom Struggle*, edited by Dayo Gore, 138. New York: New York University Press, 2009.

Johnson, Elizabeth. "The Historiography of Slave Rebellion: Cuba in Hemispheric Perspective." *Journal of Caribbean History* 31, no. 1–2 (1997): 103–18.

Johnson, Michael. "Denmark Vesey and His Co-conspirators." *William and Mary Quarterly* 58, no. 4 (October 2001): 915–76.

Johnson, Samuel. *The History of the Yorubas: From the Earliest Times to the Beginning of the British Protectorate*. London: Routledge & Kegan Paul, 1921.

Johnson, Sara. "'You Should Give Them Blacks to Eat': Cuban Bloodhounds and the Waging of an Inter-American War of Torture and Terror." *American Quarterly* 61, no. 1 (March 2009): 65–92.

Johnson, Walter. *River of Dark Dreams: Slavery and Empire in the Cotton Kingdom*, Cambridge, Mass.: Harvard University Press, 2013.

————. *Soul by Soul: Life inside the Antebellum Slave Market*. Cambridge, Mass.: Harvard University Press, 1999.

Jordan, Winthrop D. *Tumult and Silence at Second Creek: An Inquiry into a Civil War Slave Conspiracy*. Baton Rouge: Louisiana State University Press, 1993.

Kelley, Robin. "'We Are Not What We Seem': Rethinking Black Working-Class Opposition in the Jim Crow South." *Journal of American History* 80, no. 1 (1993): 75–112.

Kiddy, Elizabeth. "Who Is the King of Congo? A New Look at African and Afro-Brazilian Kings in Brazil." In *Central Africans and Cultural Transformations in the American Diaspora*, edited by Linda M. Heywood, 153–82. New York: Cambridge University Press, 2002.

Kiple, Kenneth. *Blacks in Colonial Cuba, 1774–1899*. Gainesville: University Presses of Florida, 1976.

Klein, Herbert S. *African Slavery in Latin America and the Caribbean*. New York: Oxford University Press, 1986.

————. *Slavery in the Americas: A Comparative Study of Virginia and Cuba*. Chicago: University of Chicago Press, 1967.

Knight, Franklin W. *Slave Society in Cuba during the Nineteenth Century*. Madison: University of Wisconsin Press, 1970.

Krauthamer, Barbara. "A Particular Kind of Freedom: Black Women, Slavery, Kinship, and Freedom in the American Southeast." In *Women and Slavery*, vol. 2, edited by Gwyn Campbell, 100–127. Athens: Ohio University Press, 2008.

Labarre, Roland. "La conspiración de 1844: Un 'complot por lo menos dudoso' y una 'atroz maquinación.'" *Anuario de Estudios Americanos* 43 (1986): 127–41.

Law, Robin. "Ethnicities of Enslaved Africans in the Diaspora: On the Meanings of 'Mina' (Again)." *History of Africa* 32 (2005): 247–67.

———. "Ethnicity and the Slave Trade: 'Lucumí' and 'Nagô' as Ethnonyms in West Africa." *History in Africa* 24 (1997): 205–19.

———. *The Oyo Empire, 1600–1836: A West African Imperialism in the Era of the Atlantic Slave Trade.* Oxford: Clarendon, 1977.

Lightfoot, Natasha. *Troubling Freedom: Antigua and the Aftermath of British Emancipation, 1831–1858.* Durham, N.C.: Duke University Press, forthcoming.

Llanes Miqueli, Rita. *Víctimas del año del Cuero.* Havana: Ciencias Sociales, 1984.

Llevarías y Martínez, Joaquín. *La Comisión Militar Ejecutiva y Permanente de la Isla de Cuba.* Havana: Siglo XX, A. Muñiz, 1929.

Lohse, Russell. "Slave Trade Nomenclature and African Ethnicities in the Americas: Evidence from Early Eighteenth-Century Costa Rica." *Slavery and Abolition* 23, no. 3 (2002): 73–92.

López-Valdes, Rafael. "Notas para el estudio etno-histórico de los esclavos lucumí de Cuba." *Anales del Caribe* 6 (1986): 54–74.

Lorde, Audre. "The Master's Tools Will Never Dismantle the Master's House." In *Sister Outsider: Essays and Speeches*, 110–13. 1984. Reprinted with forward by Cheryl Clarke. Berkeley: Crossing Press, 2007.

Lovejoy, Paul. "The Yoruba Factor in the Trans-Atlantic Slave Trade." In *The Yoruba Diaspora in the Atlantic World*, edited by Toyin Falola and Matt D. Childs, 40–55. Bloomington: Indiana University Press, 2004.

———. "Ethnic Designations of the Slave Trade and the Reconstruction of the History of Trans-Atlantic Slavery." In *Trans-Atlantic Dimensions of Ethnicity in the African Diaspora*, edited by Paul Lovejoy and David Trotman, 9–42. New York: Continuum, 2003.

Lovejoy, Paul, and David Trotman, eds. *Trans-Atlantic Dimensions of Ethnicity in the African Diaspora.* New York: Continuum, 2003.

Lowe, Lisa. "The Intimacies of Four Continents." In *Haunted by Empire: Geographies of Intimacy in North American History*, edited by Ann Laura Stoler, 191–212. Durham, N.C.: Duke University Press, 2006.

MacGaffey, Wyatt. *Kongo Political Culture: The Conceptual Challenge of the Particular.* Bloomington: Indiana University Press, 2000.

———. *Religion and Society in Central Africa: The BaKongo of Lower Zaire.* Chicago: University of Chicago Press, 1986.

Martínez-Fernández, Luís. *Torn between Empires: Economy, Society, and Patterns of Political Thought in the Hispanic Caribbean, 1840–1878.* Athens: University of Georgia Press, 1994.

Martínez-Ruiz, Bárbaro. *Kongo Graphic Writing and Other Narratives of the Sign.* Philadelphia: Temple University Press, 2013.

Matory, James L. *Sex and the Empire That Is No More: Gender and the Politics of Metaphor in Oyo Yoruba Religion.* Minneapolis: University of Minnesota Press, 1994.

Matthews, Gelien. *Caribbean Slave Revolts and the British Abolitionist Movement.* Baton Rouge: Louisiana State University Press, 2006.

Mbembe, Achille. "The Power of the Archive and Its Limits." In *Refiguring the Archive,* edited by Carolyn Hamilton et al., 19–27. Cape Town: David Phillip, 2002.

McKittrick, Katherine. *Demonic Grounds: Black Women and the Cartographies of Struggle.* Minneapolis: University of Minnesota Press, 2006.

McKittrick, Katherine, and Clyde Woods, eds. *Black Geographies and the Politics of Place.* Cambridge, Mass.: South End, 2007.

Mena, Luz. "Stretching the Limits of Gendered Spaces: Black and Mulatto Women in 1830s Havana." *Cuban Studies* 36, no. 1 (2005): 87–104.

Méndez Capote, Renée. *Cuatro conspiraciones.* Havana: Instituto Cubano del Libro, 1975.

Méndez Rodenas, Adriana. *Gender and Nationalism in Colonial Cuba: The Travels of Santa Cruz y Montalvo, Condesa de Merlin.* Nashville, Tenn.: Vanderbilt University Press, 1998.

Midlo Hall, Gwendolyn. *Slavery and African Ethnicities in the Americas: Restoring the Links.* Chapel Hill: University of North Carolina Press, 2005.

———. *Social Control in Slave Plantation Societies: A Comparison of St. Domingue and Cuba.* Baltimore: Johns Hopkins University Press, 1971.

Miller, Ivor L. "The Formation of African Identities in the Americas: Spiritual 'Ethnicity.'" *Contours: A Journal of the African Diaspora* 2, no. 2 (Fall 2004): 193–222.

———. *Voice of the Leopard: African Secret Societies and Cuba.* Jackson: University Press of Mississippi, 2009.

Miller, Joseph. "Central Africa during the Era of the Slave Trade, c. 1490s–1850s." In *Central Africans and Cultural Transformations in the American Diaspora,* edited by Linda Heywood, 21–70. New York: Cambridge University Press, 2002.

———. *Way of Death: Merchant Capitalism and the Angolan Slave Trade, 1730–1830.* Madison: University of Wisconsin Press, 1988.

Mintz, Sidney, and Richard Price. *The Birth of African-American Culture: An Anthropological Perspective.* Boston: Beacon, 1992.

Misevich, Philip. "The Origins of Slaves Leaving the Upper Guinea Coast in the Nineteenth Century." In *Extending the Frontiers: Essays on the New Transatlantic Slave Trade Database,* edited by David Eltis and David Richardson, 155–75. New Haven, Conn.: Yale University Press, 2008.

Moitt, Bernard. *Women and Slavery in the French Antilles, 1635–1848.* Bloomington: Indiana University Press, 2001.

Montejo, Esteban. *Biography of a Runaway Slave.* Translated by W. Nick Hill. East Haven, Conn.: Curbstone, 1994.

Morales y Morales, Vidal. *Iniciadores y primeros martires de la revolución cubana.* Havana: Moderna Poesía, 1931.

Morena Vega, Marta. *The Altar of My Soul: The Living Traditions of Santería.* New York: One World, 2000.

Moreno Fraginals, Manuel. "Africa in Cuba: A Quantitative Analysis of the African Population in the Island of Cuba." In *Comparative Perspectives on Slavery in New World Plantation Societies*, edited by Vera Rubin and Arthur Tuden, 187–201. New York: New York Academy of Sciences, 1977.

———. *El ingenio: Complejo económico social cubano del azúcar.* 3 vols. Havana: Ciencias Sociales, 1978.

Morgan, Jennifer. *Laboring Women: Reproduction and Gender in New World Slavery.* Philadelphia: University of Pennsylvania Press, 2004.

Morrissey, Marietta. *Slave Women in the New World: Gender Stratification in the Caribbean.* Lawrence: University Press of Kansas, 1989.

Murray, David. *Odious Commerce: Britain, Spain, and the Abolition of the Cuban Slave Trade.* Cambridge: Cambridge University Press, 1985.

Navarro García, Jesús Raúl. *Entre esclavos y constituciones: El colonialismo liberal de 1837 en Cuba.* Sevilla: Escuela de Estudios Hispano-Americanos, 1991.

Northrup, David. "Igbo and Myth Igbo: Culture and Ethnicity in the Atlantic World." *Slavery and Abolition* 21, no. 3 (2000): 1–20.

Nwankwo, Ifeoma Kiddoe. *Black Cosmopolitanism: Racial Consciousness and Transnational Identity in the Nineteenth-Century Americas.* Philadelphia: University of Pennsylvania Press, 2005.

Ochoa, Todd Ramón. *Society of the Dead: Quita Manaquita and Palo Praise in Cuba.* Berkeley: University of California Press, 2010.

O'Hear, Ann. "The Enslavement of Yoruba." In *The Yoruba Diaspora in the Atlantic World*, edited by Toyin Falola and Matt D. Childs, 56–76. Bloomington: Indiana University Press, 2004.

Ojo, Olatunji. "From 'Constitutional' and 'Northern' Factors to Ethnic/Slave Uprising: Ile-Ife, 1800–1854." In *The Changing Worlds of Atlantic Africa: Essays in Honor of Robin Law*, edited by Toyin Falola and Matt D. Childs, 233–52. Durham, N.C.: Carolina Academic, 2009.

Ortega, José Guadalupe. "The Cuban Sugar Complex in the Age of Revolution, 1789–1844." Ph.D. diss., University of California, Los Angeles, 2007.

———. "From Obscurity to Notoriety: Cuban Slave Merchants, and the Atlantic World." In *The Changing Worlds of Atlantic Africa: Essays in Honor of Robin Law*, edited by Toyin Falola and Matt D. Childs, 287–306. Durham, N.C.: Carolina Academic, 2009.

Ortiz, Fernándo. *Hampa-afrocubana: Los negros brujos (apuntes para un estudio de etnología criminal).* Madrid: Librería de Fé, 1906.

———. *Los negros esclavos.* Havana: Ciencias Sociales, 1975.

Pappademos, Melina. *Black Political Activism and the Cuban Republic.* Chapel Hill: University of North Carolina Press, 2011.

Paquette, Robert. "The Drivers Shall Lead Them: Images and Reality in Slave Resistance." In *Slavery, Secession, and Southern History*, edited by Robert Paquette and Louis A. Ferleger, 31–58. Charlottesville: University Press of Virginia, 2000.

———. "From Rebellion to Revisionism: The Continuing Debate about the Denmark Vesey Affair." *Journal of the Historical Society* 4, no. 3 (Fall 2004): 291–334.

———. *Sugar Is Made with Blood: The Conspiracy of La Escalera and the Conflict between Empires over Slavery in Cuba*. Middletown, Conn.: Wesleyan University Press, 1988.

Paquette, Robert, and Doug Egerton. "Of Facts and Fables: New Light on the Denmark Vesey Affair." *South Carolina Historical Magazine* 105, no. 1 (January 2004): 8–48.

Pearson, Edward, ed. *Designs against Charleston: The Trial Record of the Denmark Vesey Slave Conspiracy*. Chapel Hill: University of North Carolina Press, 1999.

Pérez, Louis, Jr. *Cuba and the United States: Ties of Singular Intimacy*. Athens: University of Georgia Press, 2003.

———. *Cuba between Empires, 1878–1902*. Pittsburgh: University of Pittsburgh Press, 1983.

———. *Cuba in the American Imagination: Metaphor and the Imperial Ethos*. Chapel Hill: University of North Carolina Press, 2008.

———. *The War of 1898: The United States and Cuba in History and Historiography*. Chapel Hill: University of North Carolina Press, 1998.

Pérez de la Riva, Juan. *El Barracón y otros ensayos*. Havana: Ciencias Sociales, 1975.

Pettway, Matthew. "Braggarts, Charlatans and Curros: Black Masculinity and Humor in the Poetry of Gabriel de la Concepción Valdés." Paper presented at the Cubanist Book Project Seminar, John L. Warfield Center for African and African American Studies, University of Texas, Austin, February 19, 2013.

———. "Ritual and Reason: Negotiating Freedom in the Literature of Juan Francisco Manzano." *PALARA* no. 16 (2012): 64–77.

Portuondo, Maria. "Plantation Factories: Science and Technology in Late-Eighteenth-Century Cuba." *Technology and Culture* 44, no. 2 (2003): 231–57.

Portuondo Zúñiga, Olga. *Entre esclavos y libres de Cuba colonial*. Santiago de Cuba: Oriente, 2003.

Prados-Torreira, Teresa. *Mambisas: Rebel Women in Nineteenth-Century Cuba*. Gainesville: University Press of Florida, 2005.

Rauch, Basil. *American Interest in Cuba: 1848–1855*. New York: Columbia University Press, 1948.

Reid-Vasquez, Michele *The Year of the Lash: Free People of Color in Cuba and the Nineteenth-Century Atlantic World*. Athens: University of Georgia Press, 2011.

———. "The Yoruba in Cuba: Origins, Identities and Transformations." In *The Yoruba Diaspora in the Atlantic World*, edited by Toyin Falola and Matt D. Childs, 111–29. Bloomington: Indiana University Press, 2004.

Reis, João José. *Slave Rebellion in Brazil: The Muslim Uprising of 1835 in Bahia*. Baltimore: Johns Hopkins University Press, 1993.

Reis, João José, and Beatriz Gallotti Mamigonian. "Nagô and Mina: The Yoruba Diaspora in Brazil." In *The Yoruba Diaspora in the Atlantic World*, edited by Toyin Falola and Matt D. Childs, 77–110. Bloomington: Indiana University Press, 2004.

Roberts, Kevin. "Yoruba Family, Gender, and Kinship Roles in New World Slavery." In *The Yoruba Diaspora in the Atlantic World*, edited by Toyin Falola and Matt D. Childs, 248–59. Bloomington: Indiana University Press, 2004.

Robinson, Cedric. *Black Marxism: The Making of the Black Radical Tradition.* Chapel Hill: University of North Carolina Press, 1983.

Rodney, Walter. *A History of the Upper Guinea Coast, 1545–1800.* Oxford: Clarendon Press, 1970.

Rojas, Marta. *El harén de Oviedo.* Havana: Letras Cubanas, 2003.

Rucker, Walter C. *The River Flows On: Black Resistance, Culture, and Identity Formation in Early America.* Baton Rouge: Louisiana State University Press, 2006.

Rushing, Fannie Theresa. "Cabildos de Nación, Sociedades de la Raza de Color: Afro Cuban Participation in Slave Emancipation and Cuban Independence, 1865–1895." Ph.D. diss., University of Chicago, 1992.

Sabater, Miguel. "La conspiración de La Escalera: Otra vuelta de la tuerca." *Boletín del Archivo Nacional* 12 (2000): 14–38.

Sánchez, Juan. "José Dolores, capitán de cimarrones: Un capítulo inédito de las rebeldías de esclavos en Matanzas." *Bohemia* 66 (November 1974): 50–53.

Sanders, Mark, ed. *A Black Soldier's Story: The Narrative of Ricardo Batrell and the Cuban War of Independence.* Minneapolis: University of Minnesota Press, 2010.

Sarracino, Rodolfo. *Inglaterra: Sus dos caras en la lucha cubana por la abolición.* Havana: Letras Cubanas, 1989.

———. "Inglaterra y las rebeliones esclavas cubanas: 1841–51." *Revista de la Biblioteca Nacional José Martí* 28, no. 2 (Mayo 1986): 37–82.

Scarry, Elaine. *The Body in Pain: The Making and Unmaking of the World.* New York: Oxford University Press, 1985.

Schmidt-Nowara, Christopher. *Empire and Antislavery: Spain, Cuba, and Puerto Rico, 1833–1874.* Pittsburgh: University of Pittsburgh Press, 1999.

———. *Slavery, Freedom, and Abolition in Latin America and the Atlantic World.* Albuquerque: University of New Mexico Press, 2011.

Scott, Rebecca. *Slave Emancipation in Cuba: The Transition to Free Labor, 1860–1899.* Pittsburgh: University of Pittsburgh Press, 1985.

Sharpe, Jenny. *Ghosts of Slavery: A Literary Archaeology of Black Women's Lives.* Minneapolis: University of Minnesota Press, 2003.

Sidbury, James. *Ploughshares into Swords: Race, Rebellion, and Identity in Gabriel's Virginia, 1730–1810.* New York: Cambridge University Press, 1997.

Skidmore-Hess, Cathy. "Queen Njinga, 1582–1663: Ritual, Power, and Gender in the Life of a Precolonial African Ruler." Ph.D. diss., University of Wisconsin–Madison, 1995.

Smallwood, Stephanie. *Saltwater Slavery: A Middle Passage from Africa to American Diaspora.* Cambridge, Mass.: Harvard University Press, 2007.

Smith, Robert. *Kingdoms of the Yoruba.* London: Currey, 1988.

Soares, Mariza. "From Gbe to Yoruba: Ethnic Change and the Mina Nation in Rio de Janeiro." In *The Yoruba Diaspora in the Atlantic World*, edited by Toyin Falola and Matt D. Childs, 231–47. Bloomington: Indiana University Press, 2004.

Spivak, Gayatri Chakravorty. "Can the Subaltern Speak?" In *Marxism and the Interpretation of Culture*, edited by Cary Nelson and Lawrence Grossberg, 271–316. Urbana: University of Illinois Press, 1988.

Stern, Steve. "New Approaches to the Study of Peasant Rebellion and Consciousness: Implications of the Andean Experience." In *Resistance, Rebellion, and Consciousness in the Andean World, 18th to 20th Centuries*, edited by Steve Stern, 3–28. Madison: University of Wisconsin Press, 1987.

Stevenson, Brenda D. *Life in Black and White: Family and Community in the Slave South*. New York: Oxford University Press, 1996.

Stolcke, Verena. *Marriage, Class, and Colour in Nineteenth-Century Cuba: A Study of Racial Attitudes and Sexual Values in a Slave Society*. New York: Cambridge University Press, 1974.

Stoler, Ann Laura. *Along the Archival Grain: Epistemic Anxieties and Colonial Common Sense*. Princeton, N.J.: Princeton University Press, 2009.

———. "Colonial Archives and the Arts of Governance: On the Content in the Form." In *Refiguring the Archive*, edited by Carolyn Hamilton et al., 83–102. Cape Town: David Philip, 2002.

Stuckey, Sterling. *Slave Culture: Nationalist Theory and the Foundations of Black America*. New York: Oxford University Press, 1987.

Suárez y Romero, Anselmo. *Colección de artículos*. Havana: La Antilla, 1859.

Sweet, James. *Recreating Africa: Culture, Kinship, and Religion in the African-Portuguese World, 1441–1770*. Chapel Hill: University of North Carolina Press, 2003.

Thomas, Hugh. *Cuba; or, The Pursuit of Freedom*. New York: Da Capo, 1998.

Thomson, Sinclair. *We Alone Will Rule: Native Andean Politics in the Age of Insurgency*. Madison: University of Wisconsin Press, 2002.

Thompson, Robert Farris. *Flash of the Spirit: African and Afro-American Art and Philosophy*. New York: Random House, 1983.

Thornton, John. *Africa and Africans in the Making of the Atlantic World, 1400–1800*. New York: Cambridge University Press, 1998.

———. "African Dimensions of the Stono Rebellion." *American Historical Review* 96, no. 4 (1991): 1101–13.

Tinsley, Omise'eke. "Black Atlantic, Queer Atlantic: Queer Imaginings of the Middle Passage." *GLQ: A Journal of Lesbian and Gay Studies* 14, no. 2–3 (2008): 191–215.

———. *Thiefing Sugar: Eroticism between Women in Caribbean Literature*. Durham, N.C.: Duke University Press, 2010.

Tomich, Dale. *Through the Prism of Slavery: Labor, Capital, and World Economy*. Lanham, Md.: Rowman & Littlefield, 2004.

Trouillot, Michel-Rolph. *Silencing the Past: Power and the Production of History*. Boston: Beacon, 1995.

Van Norman, William. *Shade-Grown Slavery: The Lives of Slaves on Coffee Plantations in Cuba*. Nashville, Tenn.: Vanderbilt University Press, 2013.

Van Young, Eric. *The Other Rebellion: Popular Violence, Ideology, and the Mexican Struggle for Independence, 1810–1821*. Stanford, Calif.: Stanford University Press, 2001.

Viotti da Costa, Emilia. *Crowns of Glory, Tears of Blood: The Demerara Slave Rebellion of 1823*. New York: Oxford University Press, 1997.

Walker, Daniel. *No More, No More: Slavery and Cultural Resistance in Havana and New Orleans.* Minneapolis: University of Minnesota Press, 2004.

White, Deborah G. *Ar'nt I a Woman? Female Slaves in the Plantation South.* New York: Norton, 1985.

Wilks, Ivor. *Asante in the Nineteenth Century: The Structure and Evolution of a Political Order.* New York: Cambridge University Press, 1975.

Williams, Eric. *Capitalism and Slavery.* Chapel Hill: University of North Carolina Press, 1994.

Williams, Raymond. *Marxism and Literature.* Oxford: Oxford University Press, 1977.

Young, Jason. *Rituals of Resistance: African Atlantic Religion in Kongo and the Lowcountry South in the Era of Slavery.* Baton Rouge: Louisiana State University Press, 2007.

Zanetti Lecuona, Oscar, and Alejandro García Álvarez. *Caminos para el azúcar.* Havana: Ciencias Sociales, 1987.

———. *Sugar and Railroads: A Cuban History, 1837–1959.* Translated by Franklin Knight and Mary Todd. Chapel Hill: University of North Carolina Press, 1998.

Index

Italicized page numbers refer to illustrations.

industry of, 242 (n. 69); Moscón, 84; Recompensa, 213–20; significance of, 33–34

Collective politics and consciousness, 188, 190, 199, 221

Colored committee, 116–17, 119

Combat experience of rebels, 182–83, 193

Comisión Militar Ejecutiva y Permanente, 14, 48–49

La Concepción estate, 91, 92, *189*

Congo, Antonio, 78

Congo, Eleuterio, 234 (n. 28)

Congo, Felipe, 177

Congo, Joaquín, 175

Congo, Mateo, 204

Congo-Cuban theologies. *See* Palo practices

Congo ethnicity, 25

Congo nomenclature, 237 (nn. 22, 24)

Constancia Mandinga, 187

Containment and policing, 39–40, 51, 69–71

Contramayorales, 56, 173–74, 175–76

Crawford, Joseph, 137

Creoles, black. *See* Criollo people

Creoles, white liberal, 115–16, 117, 118, 127

Criollo people: Andrés, 78; Camila, 147; Candelario, 176, 178; Catalino, 59; Ciriaco, 56; ; Dimas, 63–64; Dionisio, 60–61; Eusebia, 153–54, *155*; Inés, 207; Juan, 192; Juliana, 99; Julio, 58; Justo, 211–12; Lino, 216; Merced, 1, 2, 103, 157, 162–63; Perico, 56; Rafael, 76; Ramón, 156; Silvestre, 74, 176, 178; Simona, 163–64, *165*; Vicente Pipa, 137

Cuba: in early nineteenth century, 18; enslaved population, 22–23, 241 (n. 63); government departments, 234 (n. 22); government repression, 2, 5; growth of, 21–22; Havana map of, *52*; literature of, 118; Mantanzas, *189*; militarization of, 46–47;

nationalism, 115; Tacón administration, 46–47, 115, 245 (n. 124); U.S. relations with, 128

Dahomey Kingdom, 26–27, 159–60, 239 (n. 31)

Dance and drumming, Sunday, 43–45

Dance and resistance, 218, 268 (n. 64)

de Campo Flórida, Marqués, 70

Deceased ancestors, 203

de la Concepción Valdés, Gabriel. *See* Plácido

del Monte y Aponte, Domingo: relations with Everett, 127–28; relations with Plácido, 126–27, 256 (n. 48); salons of, 118; significance of, 5, 115; on slavery, 117

Desch-Obi, T. J., 183

Dichoso leaders, 179

Dimas Criollo, 63–64

Dionisio Carabalí, 1–2

Dionisio Criollo, 60–61

Dionisio Lucumí, 103–4

Dios estate leaders, 264 (n. 25)

Dolls and figurines in sacred practices, 204

Dolores, José, 68–69

Domech, Pedro, 112–13, 202, 214

Domestic and curative labors, 36–37, 166

Dorsey, Joseph, 27

Dos Felices estate (Mesa property), 76

Dos Mercedes estate, 129–30, 131, 164–66

Drinking in sacred practices, 269 (n. 65)

Drivers, black, 173–76

Drivers and muleteers, 54–55, 67, 134–35

Echeverría estate, 153–54

Egerton, Douglas, 57, 197

1825 rebellion, 48

1843 rebellions: Bemba, 79–88, 95, 98; causes, 222–23; conditions for,

79–80; 1844 movement linked to, 9–10, 101–2; gendered aspects, 80–81, 146–50; impact of, 109; origin of, 108; rebels in, 96–101; significance of, 80; Triunvirato, 88–92, 93–94, 146–47, 189

1844 movement: Bemba linked to, 102–7; causes, 222–23; deniers, 191, 231 (n. 3); insurgent properties, 189; legacy of, 229; origin of, 50; prime suspects, 121; reach of, 126–33; rural movement, 184–91; spread of, 133–40; targets of, 185–86; Triunvirato linked to, 107–10. *See also* Bemba rebellion; La Escalera, trials of; Triunvirato rebellion

Elem Kalabar, 25

Eleuterio Congo, 234 (n. 24)

Eloisa Carabalí, 21, 176–78, 187

Employment of free blacks, 36–37, 43–44, 71–72

Encanto estate: leaders, 163; Palo on, 207, 209; rebels, 103, 161

Engineers, 37

La Escalera, trials of: accused conspirators, 3; aftermath of, 227–28; archives of, 10–11; conspiracy deniers, 5–6; goals of, 9; historical background, 4–8; impact of, 17, 270 (n. 7); legacy of, 2, 221; name origin, 1; records of, 13–16, 150–51, 233 (n. 16); scholarship on, 13, 233 (n. 21). *See also* 1843 rebellions; 1844 movement

Ethnicities of enslaved Africans, 23–28, 237 (n. 21)

Eusebia Criolla, 153–54, 155

Everett, Alexander Hill, 127–28

Ewe-Fons, 239 (n. 33)

Fanon, Frantz, 187

Federico Gangá, 214–18

Felipe Carabalí, 55, 192

Felipe Congo, 177

Ferdinand, King, 46

Fermina Lucumí. *See* Lucumí, Fermina

Fieldworkers as leaders, 178

Figurines in sacred practices, 204, 268 (n. 64)

Filomena Gangá, 99–100

Firearms, 193, 195–98

Fire as weaponry, 194–95

Flores, Miguel, 136–37, 258 (n. 81), 258 (n. 83)

Forests, 62–64

Francisco Matamoros, José, 43

Free rural population, 41–42

Free urban population. *See* Urban population, free

Free women. *See* Homes, women's

Fuentes Congo, Mariano, 106

Gallinas port, 240 (n. 39)

Gálvez, Féliz, 131

Gálvez, José María, 207

Gangá ethnicity, 24, 27, 239 (n. 38)

Gangá people: Adán, 94; Catalina, 89, 100, 147; Federico, 214–18; Filomena, 99–100; Gonzalo, 12–13; Jacob, 179; José, 213; Luis, 214; Patricio, 64, 207, 209; Pedro, 153–54, 155; Perico, 76; Polonia, 1, 141, 142, 143; Roberto, 219

Garcia Rodriguez, Gloria, 13, 175, 234 (n. 26)

García y Santos, Benito, 69

Gender. *See* Women and gender

Geographies: contested, 222–23; insurgent, 53, 62–64, 65–66, 189; rival, 51–52, 53, 78, 79

Gheri, Carlos, 69–70

Gigaut, Luis. *See* Jigot, Luis

Giles Romana Morales, María, 120

Glissant, Edouard, 53

Goicochea, Estefanía, 132

González, Antonio, 203

Gonzalo Gangá, 12–13

Gonzalo Lucumí, 90

Govin, José, 164

Grajales, Mariana, 221, 227

Veytra, Baltasar and Maria, 74
Vicente Pipa Criollo, 137
Villa, Altagracia, 129–30, 131–32, 133
Violence: of archive, 11–12; as form of control, 39–40; gendered aspects, 40–41, 186–87; in sentencing, 227–28; against women, 244 (n. 100)
Vives, Dionisio, 46
von Humboldt, Alexander, 38

Wagon drivers and muleteers, 54–55, 56
Walcott, Derek, 29, 34, 51
Warfare in Africa, 28–29, 182–83, 193
Weaponry: arrows, 265 (n. 50); fire, 194–95; firearms, 193, 195–98; free blacks and, 197; knives, 192, 265 (n. 62); machetes, 191, 192, 195–98; Palo, 217–18; spiritual, 204; women and, 196–97
Webster, Daniel, 128
West and Central African slave trade, 25, 238 (n. 26)
Whippings and torture, 227–28
White people: artisans, 244 (n. 114); Committee of 1841, 115–19; creoles, 115–19; in 1844 movement, 127; killing, 186–87; overseers, 173, 174, 175; shortages of, 67; as targets, 186, 206–7, 217–18; women, 39, 147, 148, 150, 183–84; workers, 38–39, 242 (n. 78)

Witchcraft. *See* Palo practices
Women and gender: abuse of, 244 (n. 100); and archives, 144–45, 150–51; betrayal and, 142–43; domestic and curative labors of, 36–37; 1843 rebellions and, 80–81, 146–50; as enablers, 152, 224–25; free, 43, 44, 129; homes of, 112–14, 122–24, 129–33; leaders and leadership, 146–50, 170–71, 176; Lucumí, 181; at margins, 152–57; mobility and, 64, 73; motivations of, 143–44; Palo and, 218–20; ratios of, on estates, 184; rebel narrative in relation to, 98–100; in sacred practices, 218–20; trial records and, 150–51; urban, 122–24; violence and, 40–41, 186–87; weapons and, 196–97, 265 (n. 51); white, 39, 47, 148, 150, 183–84; as witnesses, 149. *See also* Homes, women's; Masculinity; Queens of the rebellion
Writers, Cuban, 115, 117, 118, 255 (n. 18)
Wurdermann, John, 84

Ynés, José, 266 (n. 8)
Yoruba ethnicity, 26, 180–81, 239 (n. 32)
Yumurí district, 179

Zacarías Carabalí, 88

Envisioning Cuba

MICHELLE CHASE, *Revolution within the Revolution: Women and Gender Politics in Cuba, 1952–1962* (2015).

AISHA K. FINCH, *Rethinking Slave Rebellion in Cuba: La Escalera and the Insurgencies of 1841–1844* (2015).

CHRISTINA D. ABREU, *Rhythms of Race: Cuban Musicians and the Making of Latino New York City and Miami, 1940–1960* (2015).

ANITA CASAVANTES BRADFORD, *The Revolution Is for the Children: The Politics of Childhood in Havana and Miami, 1959–1962* (2014).

TIFFANY A. SIPPIAL, *Prostitution, Modernity, and the Making of the Cuban Republic, 1840–1920* (2013).

KATHLEEN LÓPEZ, *Chinese Cubans: A Transnational History* (2013).

LILLIAN GUERRA, *Visions of Power in Cuba: Revolution, Redemption, and Resistance, 1959–1971* (2012).

CARRIE HAMILTON, *Sexual Revolutions in Cuba: Passion, Politics, and Memory* (2012).

SHERRY JOHNSON, *Climate and Catastrophe in Cuba and the Atlantic World during the Age of Revolution* (2011).

MELINA PAPPADEMOS, *Black Political Activism and the Cuban Republic* (2011).

FRANK ANDRE GURIDY, *Forging Diaspora: Afro-Cubans and African Americans in a World of Empire and Jim Crow* (2010).

ANN MARIE STOCK, *On Location in Cuba: Street Filmmaking during Times of Transition* (2009).

ALEJANDRO DE LA FUENTE, *Havana and the Atlantic in the Sixteenth Century* (2008).

REINALDO FUNES MONZOTE, *From Rainforest to Cane Field in Cuba: An Environmental History since 1492* (2008).

MATT D. CHILDS, *The 1812 Aponte Rebellion in Cuba and the Struggle against Atlantic Slavery* (2006).

EDUARDO GONZÁLEZ, *Cuba and the Tempest: Literature and Cinema in the Time of Diaspora* (2006).

JOHN LAWRENCE TONE, *War and Genocide in Cuba, 1895–1898* (2006).

SAMUEL FARBER, *The Origins of the Cuban Revolution Reconsidered* (2006).

LILLIAN GUERRA, *The Myth of José Martí: Conflicting Nationalisms in Early Twentieth-Century Cuba* (2005).

RODRIGO LAZO, *Writing to Cuba: Filibustering and Cuban Exiles in the United States* (2005).

ALEJANDRA BRONFMAN, *Measures of Equality: Social Science, Citizenship, and Race in Cuba, 1902–1940* (2004).

EDNA M. RODRÍGUEZ-MANGUAL, *Lydia Cabrera and the Construction of an Afro-Cuban Cultural Identity* (2004).

GABINO LA ROSA CORZO, *Runaway Slave Settlements in Cuba: Resistance and Repression* (2003).

PIERO GLEIJESES, *Conflicting Missions: Havana, Washington, and Africa, 1959–1976* (2002).

ROBERT WHITNEY, *State and Revolution in Cuba: Mass Mobilization and Political Change, 1920–1940* (2001).

ALEJANDRO DE LA FUENTE, *A Nation for All: Race, Inequality, and Politics in Twentieth-Century Cuba* (2001).